FROMMER'S

COMPREHENSIVE TRAVEL GUIDE

Atlanta '95

by Rena Bulkin

MACMILLAN • USA

ABOUT THE AUTHOR

Rena Bulkin began her travel writing career in 1964 when she set out for Europe in search of adventure. She found it writing about hotels and restaurants for the *New York Times* International Edition. She has since authored dozens of magazine articles and 15 travel guides to far-flung destinations.

MACMILLAN TRAVEL

A Prentice Hall Macmillan company
15 Columbus Circle
New York, NY 10023

ISBN 0-02-860044-4

ISSN 1047-7888

Design by Michele Laseau
Maps by Geografix Inc.

Special Sales

Bulk purchases (10+ copies) of Frommer's Travel Guides are available to corporations at special discounts. The Special Sales Department can produce custom editions to be used as premiums and/or for sales promotion to suit individual needs. Existing editions can be produced with custom cover imprints such as corporate logos. For more information write to: Special Sales, Prentice Hall, 15 Columbus Circle, New York, NY 10023

Manufactured in the United States of America

Contents

1 Introducing Atlanta   1

1. History   4
2. Famous Atlantans   12
3. Recommended Books & Films   13

SPECIAL FEATURES
- What's Special About Atlanta *3*
- Dateline *4*

2 Planning a Trip to Atlanta   15

1. Information & Money   16
2. When to Go   16
3. What to Pack   29
4. Tips for the Disabled, Seniors, Singles, Gay Men & Lesbians, Students & Families   29
5. Getting There   33

SPECIAL FEATURES
- What Things Cost in Atlanta *16*
- Atlanta Calendar of Events *17*
- Frommer's Smart Traveler: Airfares *34*

3 For Foreign Visitors   36

1. Preparing for Your Trip   37
2. Getting To and Around the U.S.   40

SPECIAL FEATURE
- Fast Facts: For the Foreign Traveler *41*

4 Getting to Know Atlanta   49

1. Orientation   50
2. Getting Around   54

SPECIAL FEATURES
- Fast Facts: Atlanta *56*

5 Atlanta Accommodations   59

1. Downtown   61
2. Midtown   73
3. Buckhead   86
4. Georgia's Stone Mountain   97
5. Druid Hills/Emory University/ Brookhaven   99
6. Off I-20   101

SPECIAL FEATURES
- Frommer's Smart Traveler: Hotels *69*
- Frommer's Cool for Kids: Hotels *73*

6 Atlanta Dining   102

1. Downtown   103
2. Midtown   112

3. Buckhead   125
4. Virginia-Highland   140
5. Sweet Auburn   145
6. Decatur   146
7. Chamblee   147
8. Specialty Dining   148

SPECIAL FEATURES

• Frommer's Smart
  Traveler: Restaurants
  110
• Frommer's Cool for
  Kids: Restaurants
  112

7 What to See & Do in Atlanta   153

1. The Top Attractions   155
2. More Attractions   183
3. Cool for Kids   193
4. Organized Tours   201
5. Sports & Recreation   202

SPECIAL FEATURES

• Suggested Itineraries
  154
• Did You Know? *154,
  157*
• Frommer's Favorite
  Atlanta Experiences
  162

8 A Walking Tour of Sweet Auburn   207

9 Atlanta Shopping   213

1. Shopping Areas   214
2. Department Stores & Malls   219
3. Shopping around Town   221

10 Atlanta Nights   224

1. The Performing Arts   225
2. The Nightclub Scene   231
3. More Entertainment   238
4. Film & Video   238

11 About the Olympics   239

1. Information Sources   240
2. Obtaining Tickets   240
3. The Events   242
4. Accommodations & Dining   242
5. Transportation   243

Index   244

List of Maps

Metropolitan
   Atlanta   30–31
City Layout   53
Downtown
   Accommodations   63
Midtown
   Accommodations   76–77
Buckhead
   Accommodations   89
Downtown Dining   109
Midtown/Virginia-Highland
   Dining   118–19

Buckhead Dining   131
Central Atlanta Sights   163
Downtown Area
   Sights   165
Georgia's Stone Mountain
   Park   171
Metropolitan Atlanta
   Sights   186–87
Walking Tour—Sweet
   Auburn   210-11

What the Symbols Mean

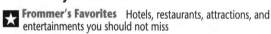 **Frommer's Favorites**   Hotels, restaurants, attractions, and entertainments you should not miss

 **Super-Special Values**   Really exceptional values

In Hotel and Other Listings

The following symbols refer to the standard amenities available in all rooms:

   A/C   air conditioning
   MINIBAR   refrigerator stocked with beverages and snacks
   TEL   telephone
   TV   television

The following abbreviations are used for credit cards:

   AE   American Express
   CB   Carte Blanche
   DC   Diners Club
   DISC   Discover
   ER   EnRoute
   EURO   Eurocard
   JCB   Japanese Credit Bureau
   MC   MasterCard
   V   Visa

Invitation to the Reader

In researching this book, I have come across many wonderful establishments, the best of which I have included here. I'm sure that many of you will also come across appealing hotels, inns, restaurants, guesthouses, shops, and attractions. Please don't keep them to yourself. Share your experiences, especially if you want to comment on places I have covered in this edition which have changed for the worse. You can address your letters to me:

Rena Bulkin
Frommer's Atlanta '95
c/o Macmillan Travel
15 Columbus Circle
New York, NY 10023

A Disclaimer

Readers are advised that prices fluctuate in the course of time and travel information changes under the impact of the varied and volatile factors that affect the travel industry. The author and publisher cannot be held responsible for the experiences of readers while traveling. Readers are invited to write to the publisher with ideas, comments, and suggestions for future editions.

Safety Advisory

Whenever you're traveling in an unfamiliar city or country, stay alert. Be aware of your immediate surroundings. Wear a moneybelt and keep a close eye on your possessions. Be particularly careful with cameras, purses, and wallets, all favorite targets of thieves and pickpockets.

1

Introducing Atlanta

•	What's Special about Atlanta	3
1	History	4
•	Dateline	4
2	Famous Atlantans	12
3	Recommended Books & Films	13

THEY CALL IT THE BIG A, THE CAPITAL OF THE NEW SOUTH, AND THE International Gateway City—all names evocative of Atlanta's dynamism, dash, and spirit. This ever-expanding city—the 13th largest metropolitan area in the United States—teems with energy. Its architecturally innovative downtown area is a sleek showplace of glittering glass skyscrapers, a setting worthy of the city's role as the South's major marketplace and its hub of finance, communications, and transportation.

This is the home of the world's largest airport. It's one of the nation's top meeting and convention cities—headquarters for hundreds of businesses, including Delta Air Lines, Lockheed, Days Inns, Ritz-Carlton, Holiday Inn, Georgia-Pacific, Coca-Cola (never ask for a Pepsi here), Turner Broadcasting System, and Scientific Atlanta. It is the major shopping center of the Southeast region; home to 29 colleges and universities; and a southern crossroads where three interstate highways converge. The city hosted the Democratic National Convention in 1988 and Super Bowl XXVIII in 1994. And at this writing it is gearing up for the Summer Olympics in 1996.

Atlanta is also called the Dogwood City, and this name evokes another of its alluring aspects. Coexisting with the bustling metropolis is a very southern city of magnolias and colonnaded white mansions. Every spring (and spring here can begin in February), the city blossoms with delicate pink dogwood buds, fragrant honeysuckle and yellow jasmine, and beautiful pink, white, and red azaleas. Drive a few miles out of the metropolitan area and you'll find yourself in verdant countryside.

Big-city Atlanta celebrates holidays with small-town exuberance. Annual events include chili and barbecue cookoffs, traditional Fourth of July picnics and parades, and Christmas chestnut roasts. The city's patron saint is *Gone With the Wind* author Margaret Mitchell (the book comes up almost on a daily basis), and history—especially Civil War history—is venerated. And while it's extremely dynamic, this is also a leisurely city where people are never in so much of a rush that they dispense with southern graciousness and hospitality. Atlanta is consistently ranked as one of the best places in the country to live— a sentiment that any resident will enthusiastically confirm.

To this appealing mix of urban sophistication and southern gentility add a vibrant cultural scene, with a growing theater community; major art and science museums; prestigious symphony, ballet, and opera companies; big-league sports; a culinary spectrum that ranges from fried chicken 'n' biscuits to beluga caviar; hot nightlife; and a delightfully temperate climate.

Add further a clean and safe state-of-the-art urban masstransportation system and visitor attractions that run the gamut from legacies of the Confederacy to black heritage sites (Martin Luther King, Jr., was born and is buried here), from historic homes to the futuristic SciTrek Museum, and from a newly refurbished zoo to tours of the high-tech CNN Center studios. And that's not to mention theme parks, a presidential library (Jimmy Carter's, of course), a

What's Special about Atlanta

Architectural Highlights
- Peachtree Center, a downtown "urban village" comprising 14 city blocks.
- Swan House, designed in the manner of a 16th-century Palladian villa.
- The fabulous Fox Theatre, a lavish 1920s movie palace featuring replicas of art and furnishings from King Tut's tomb.

Parks and Gardens
- Piedmont Park, designed by noted landscape artist Frederick Law Olmsted, and the adjacent Atlanta Botanical Garden.
- Grant Park, a Civil War battle site which now houses the zoo (see below) and Cyclorama, a 360-degree cylindrical painting of the Battle of Atlanta.
- Georgia's Stone Mountain Park, with 3,200 acres of lakes and wooded parkland, is the site of vast Mount Rushmore–like sculpture wide.

For Kids
- Zoo Atlanta, a 40-acre facility with animals housed in large open enclosures which simulate natural habitats.
- Birth Home of Martin Luther King, Jr.—along with the nearby Center for Nonviolent Social Change, an opportunity for kids to learn about America's foremost black leader and the history of the civil rights movement.
- Center for Puppetry Arts, a puppetry museum that offers first-rate productions.
- Yellow River Wildlife Game Ranch, an idyllic 24-acre animal preserve where kids can feed, pet, and mingle with friendly animals along a tree-shaded forest trail.
- Six Flags Over Georgia, a major theme park with over 100 rides, shows, and attractions.
- Fernbank Museum of Natural History, Atlanta's largest museum, with an IMAX Theater, children's discovery rooms, and many fascinating exhibits.

After Dark
- Coca-Cola Lakewood Amphitheatre, used for headliner entertainment, with most seating on a sloping lawn.
- Alliance Theatre, the largest resident professional theater in the Southeast.
- Atlanta Symphony Orchestra, one of America's most highly acclaimed orchestras.
- Kenny's Alley in Underground Atlanta—a nightlife complex perfect for an evening of clubhopping.

magnificent botanical garden and conservatory, a winery that's a replica of a 16th-century French château, and Georgia's Stone Mountain Park, one of the nation's most gorgeous parks and the third most-visited paid tourist attraction in the United States (after Disneyworld and Disneyland).

1 History

Dateline

- **1782** Explorers discover Cherokee village of Standing Peachtree.
- **1820s** Cherokee and Creek leaders cede millions of acres to white settlers in hopes of keeping peace.
- **1833** Atlanta's first permanent settler, Hardy Ivy, builds log cabin near present-day intersection of Courtland and Ellis streets.
- **1837** The town, newly named Terminus, is selected as site of railroad terminus connecting Georgia with the Tennessee River. The same year, 17,000 Native Americans are forced to march westward on a "Trail of Tears."
- **1843** Terminus is renamed Marthasville.
- **1845** The first locomotive chugs into town; the city is renamed Atlanta.
- **1851** Georgia secedes from the Union, Civil War begins, and Atlanta

➤

It is most fitting that Atlanta in the 1990s is an international gateway/transportation hub. The city was conceived as a rail crossroads for travel north, south, east, and west, and its role as a strategic junction has always figured largely in its destiny. It all began with a peach tree.

The Standing Peachtree

Today, just about everything in Atlanta is called "Peachtree" something, but the first Peachtree reference was in 1782 when explorers discovered a Cherokee village on the Chattahoochee River called Standing Peachtree. Since peach trees are not native to the region, some historians maintain the village was actually named for a towering "pitch" tree (a resinous pine). Nevertheless, the Indian village became the location of Fort Peachtree, a tiny frontier outpost, during the War of 1812; a Peachtree Road connecting Fort Peachtree to Fort Daniel (in Gwinett County) was completed by 1813.

In 1826, surveyors Wilson Lumpkin and Hamilton Fulton first suggested this area of Georgia as a practical spot for a railroad connecting the state with northern markets. This was not yet the heyday of railroads (canals were still the most popular mode of transport), and the report was more or less ignored for a decade. But in 1837, the state legislature approved an act establishing the Western & Atlantic Railroad here. Today a marker known as Zero Milepost in Underground Atlanta marks the W & A Railroad site around which a city grew. The new town was unimaginatively dubbed "Terminus." But future governor Alexander H. Stephens, visiting what was still dense forest in 1839, predicted that "a magnificent inland city will at no distant date be built here."

The Trail of Tears

One aspect of the city's inception, however, was far from "magnificent." In the early 1800s, most of Georgia was still Native American territory. White settlers coveted the Cherokee and Creek lands they needed to expedite the railroad and further expand their settlements. To keep the peace, native leaders throughout the 1820s signed numerous treaties ceding millions of acres. They adopted a democratic form of government similar to the white man's, complete with a constitution and supreme court; erected schools and shops; built farms; and accepted Christianity. But the white frontierspeople cared little whether the Native Americans adapted—they wanted them to leave.

With Pres. Andrew Jackson's support, Congress passed a bill in 1830 forcing all southern tribes to move to lands hundreds of miles away on the other side of the Mississippi River. When the U.S. Supreme Court ruled against the order, Jackson ignored their ruling and backed the Georgia settlers. In 1832, the state gave away Cherokee farms in a land lottery; the white settlers assumed control over the land at gunpoint. The issue culminated in 1837, when 17,000 Native Americans were rounded up by federal soldiers, herded into camps, and forced on a cruel westward march called the "Trail of Tears." Some 4,000 died on the 800-mile journey to Oklahoma, and even those who survived suffered bitterly from cold, hunger, and disease.

Terminus and its surroundings were now firmly in the hands of the white settlers.

A City Grows

Terminus soon began its evolution from a sleepy rural hamlet to a thriving city, a

Dateline

becomes a major Confederate supply depot and medical center.

■ **1864** Union forces under General William Tecumseh Sherman burn Atlanta.

■ **1865** Civil War ends.

■ **1877** Atlanta becomes the permanent capital of Georgia.

■ **1886** Newspaper editor Henry Grady inspires readers with vision of a "New South." John S. Pemberton introduces Coca-Cola.

■ **1888** Atlanta adopts the symbol of a phoenix rising from the ashes for its official seal.

■ **1900** Atlanta University professor W. E. B. Du Bois founds the NAACP.

■ **1904** Piedmont Park, designed by Frederick Law Olmsted as site of the Cotton States and International Exposition, becomes Atlanta's central park.

■ **1917** Fire destroys 73 square blocks of the city.

■ **1929** Atlanta's first airport opens; Delta Air Lines takes to the skies and becomes Atlanta's home carrier.

➤

Dateline

- **1936** Margaret Mitchell's blockbuster novel, *Gone With the Wind,* is published.
- **1939** The movie version of *Gone With the Wind* premiers in Atlanta.
- **1952** The city of Atlanta incorporates surrounding areas, increasing its population by 100,000 and its size from 37 to 118 square miles.
- **1960** Sit-ins and boycotts protesting segregation begin. The million-square-foot Merchandise Mart is erected, the first of many downtown buildings designed and developed by John Portman.
- **1961** Ivan Allen, Jr., defeats segregationist Lester Maddox in mayoral election. Atlanta's public schools and the Georgia Institute of Technology are peacefully desegregated.
- **1964** Atlanta native Martin Luther King, Jr., wins Nobel Peace Prize. The Beatles perform at Atlanta Stadium.
- **1965** 106 civic and cultural leaders die in plane crash at Orly Airport in Paris; the $18

➤

meeting point of major rail lines. In 1843, the town was renamed Marthasville, for ex-governor Wilson Lumpkin's daughter Martha. No one in Marthasville took note in 1844 when a 23-year-old army lieutenant, William Tecumseh Sherman, was stationed for two months in their area, but the knowledge he gained of local geography would vitally affect the city's history two decades later. The first locomotive, the Kentucky, chugged into town in 1845, and shortly thereafter the name Marthasville was deemed too provincial for a burgeoning metropolis. J. Edgar Thomson, the railroad's chief engineer, suggested Atlanta (a feminized form of Atlantic).

In 1848, the newly incorporated city held its first mayoral election, an event marked by dozens of street brawls. Moses W. Formwalt, a maker of stills and member of the Free and Rowdy party, was elected over temperance candidate John Norcross. But if Atlanta was a bit of a wild frontier town, it also had civic pride. An 1849 newspaper overstated things poetically:
Atlanta, the greatest spot in all the nation,
The greatest place for legislation,
Or any other occupation—
The very center of creation.

Storm Clouds Gather: Antebellum Atlanta

By the middle of the 19th century, the 31-state nation was in the throes of a westward expansion and the institution of slavery was a major issue of the day. In his 1858 debate with Stephen Douglas, Abraham Lincoln declared, "This government cannot endure permanently half slave and half free." A year later it was obvious that only a war would resolve the issue. In 1861 (a year that began dramatically in Atlanta—with an earthquake), Georgia legislators voted for secession and joined the Confederacy. In peacetime, the railroads had fashioned Atlanta into a center of commerce, known as the Gate City. In wartime, this transportation hub would emerge into perilous relief as a major Confederate military post and supply center—the vital link between Confederate forces in Tennessee and Virginia. Federal forces early on saw the city's destruction as essential to Northern victory.

On a lighter note, Atlanta made the following ridiculous bid to become the capital of the Confederacy: "The city has good railroad connections, is free from yellow fever, and can supply the most wholesome foods and, as for 'goobers,' an indispensable article for a Southern legislator, we have them all the time." The lure of plentiful peanuts notwithstanding, the Confederacy chose Richmond, Virginia, as its capital.

A City Burns

Atlanta was not only a major Southern supply depot, it was also the medical center of the Confederacy. Throughout the city, buildings were hastily converted into makeshift hospitals and clinics, and trains pulled into town daily to disgorge sick and wounded soldiers. By 1862, close to 4,000 soldiers were convalescing here, and the medical crisis was further aggravated by a smallpox epidemic. That same year, Union spy James J. Andrews and a group of Northern soldiers disguised as civilians seized a locomotive called the General, with the aim of blocking supply lines by destroying tracks and bridges behind them. A wild train chase ensued, and the raiders were caught and punished (most, including Andrews, were executed). The episode came to be known as "the Great Locomotive Chase," one of the stirring stories of the Civil War and the subject of two subsequent movies. The General is today on view at the Big Shanty Museum in Kennesaw (details in Chapter 7).

The locomotive chase was an Atlanta victory, but the Northern desire to destroy the Confederacy's supply link remained intact. In 1864, Gen. Ulysses S. Grant ordered Maj. Gen. William T. Sherman to "move against Johnston's army to break it up, and get into the interior of the enemy's country as far as you can, inflicting all the

Dateline

million Atlanta-Fulton County Stadium is built.

- **1966** Baseball's Braves move from Milwaukee and the Falcons become a new NFL expansion team.

- **1968** Martin Luther King, Jr., is assassinated in Memphis.

- **1974** Atlanta's first black mayor, Maynard Jackson, is inaugurated. Atlanta Brave Hank Aaron hits his record-breaking 715th home run.

- **1976** Georgian Jimmy Carter elected president. Georgia World Congress Center, the nation's largest single-floor exhibit space, is completed.

- **1979** MARTA rapid-transit train system opens.

- **1980** New Hartsfield International Airport dedicated.

- **1983** Martin Luther King, Jr.'s birthday becomes national holiday.

- **1988** Atlanta hosts Democratic National Convention.

- **1989** Underground Atlanta, a major retail/restaurant/entertainment complex, opens with great fanfare.

➤

Dateline

■ 1992 Atlanta gears
up for Super Bowl
XXVIII in 1994
and the 1996
Olympics with the
opening of the
70,500-seat Georgia
Dome.

damage you can against their resources." Georgians had great faith that the able and experienced Gen. Joseph E. Johnston, whom they called "Old Joe," would repel the Yankees. As Sherman's Georgia campaign got under way, an overly optimistic editorial in the *Intelligencer* scoffed at the notion of Federal conquest, claiming "we have no fear of the results, for General Johnston and his great and invincible satellites are working out the problem of battle and victory at the great chess board at the front." Johnston himself was not as sanguine. Sherman had 100,000 men to his 60,000, and the Union troops were better armed. By July, Sherman was forcing the Confederate troops back, and Atlanta's fall seemed a foregone conclusion, Johnston informed Confederate Pres. Jefferson Davis that he was outnumbered almost two to one and was in a defensive position. His candid assessment was not appreciated, and Davis removed him from command, replacing him with the pugnacious 32-year-old Gen. John Bell Hood. The change of leadership only further demoralized the ranks, and Sherman openly rejoiced when he heard the news.

Some disgruntled Confederate soldiers deserted. Hood abandoned the defensive tactics of Johnston, aggressively assaulting his opponent. His policy cost thousands of troops and gained nothing. In the Battle of Peachtree Creek on July 20, 1864, Union casualties totaled 1,710, Confederate, 4,796. Throughout the summer, the city suffered a full-scale artillery assault. Over 8,000 Confederates perished in the Battle of Atlanta on July 22, while Union deaths totaled just 3,722. And after hours of fierce fighting on July 28, the Confederates had lost another 5,000 men, the Federals, 600. The Yankees further paralyzed the city by ripping up train rails, heating them over huge bonfires, and twisting them around trees into useless spirals of mangled iron that came to be known as "Sherman's neckties." The most devastating bombardment came on August 9—"that red day ... when all the fires of hell, and all the thunders of the universe seemed to be blazing and roaring over Atlanta."

By September 1, when Hood's troops pulled out of the area, first setting fire to vast stores of ammunition (and anything else that might benefit the Yankees), the town was in turmoil. Its roads were crowded with evacuees, its hospitals, hotels, and private residences flooded with wounded men. Crime and looting were rife, and food was almost unavailable; the price of a ham-and-eggs breakfast with coffee soared to $25! Rooftops were ripped off houses and buildings, there were huge craters in the streets, and many civilians were dead. The railroads were in Sherman's hands. On September 2, Mayor James M. Calhoun, carrying a white flag to the nearest Federal unit, officially surrendered the city. The U.S. Army entered and occupied Atlanta, raising the Stars and Stripes at city hall for the first time in four years.

Claiming he needed the city for military purposes, Sherman ordered all residents to evacuate. Atlantans piled their household goods on wagons and, abandoning their homes and businesses, became refugees. Before departing Atlanta in November, Union troops leveled railroad facilities and burned the city, leaving it a wasteland—defunct as a military center and practically uninhabitable. The Yankees marched out of the city to the music of "The Battle Hymn of the Republic."

In January 1865, there was $1.64 in the treasury, the railroad system was destroyed, and most of the city was burned to the ground.

A City Rebuilds

Slowly, exiled citizens began to trickle back into Atlanta. Confederate money was worthless. At the inauguration of his second term in 1865, Lincoln pledged "malice toward none, charity for all"—but after his assassination later that year, this policy was replaced with one of harsh Republican vengeance. It wasn't until 1876 that Federal troops were withdrawn and Atlanta was freed from military occupation. Still, the city was making a remarkable recovery. Like the ever-resilient Scarlett O'Hara ("It takes more than Yankees or a burning to keep me down"), Atlanta rolled up its sleeves and began rebuilding. A Northern newspaper reported, "From all this ruin and devastation a new city is springing up . . . the streets are alive from morning till night with drays and carts and hand-barrows and wagons . . . with loads of lumber and loads of brick. . . . "

In postwar years, Atlanta was filled with carpetbaggers and adventurers hoping to turn a quick buck, and with them came gambling houses, brothels, and saloons. But the city also boasted hundreds of new stores and businesses, churches, schools, banks, hotels, theaters, and a new newspaper, the *Atlanta Constitution*. Blacks chartered Atlanta University in 1867, today the world's largest predominantly black institution of higher learning. Moreover, the railroads were operative once again. Newspaper editor Henry Grady inspired readers with his vision of an industrialized and culturally advanced "New South." He was Atlanta's biggest civic booster. A new constitution in 1877 made Atlanta the permanent capital of the state

IMPRESSIONS

The terminus of that railroad will never be anything more than an eating house.

—James M. Calhoun, 1836 (Calhoun later became mayor of Atlanta)

Atlanta lies . . . diamond like, in the very center of Georgia, yea, of the South, rough and unpolished . . . in the eyes of jealousy and prejudice, but destined . . . to becoming a bright and glittering jewel in the diadem of Southern cities.

—Luther J. Glenn, Atlanta Mayor, 1858 inaugural address

of Georgia. Two years later, General Sherman visited the city he had destroyed and was welcomed with a ball and, lest he get any funny ideas, a grand military review.

In 1886 a new headache cure was introduced–a syrup made from the cocoa leaf and the kola nut which would eventually become the world's most renowned beverage, Coca-Cola. Atlanta adopted the symbol of a phoenix rising from the ashes for its official seal in 1888 and, the following year, dedicated the gold-domed state capitol and opened a zoo in Grant Park. Piedmont Park was built in 1904 as the site of the Cotton States and International Exposition—a $2.5 million world's fair–like extravaganza with entertainments ranging from Buffalo Bill and His Wild West Show to international villages. Former slave Booker T. Washington gave a landmark address, and John Philip Sousa composed the "King Cotton March" to mark the event.

The Twentieth Century

At the turn of the century, Atlanta's population was 90,000, a figure that more than doubled two decades later. Though a massive fire swept through the city and destroyed almost 2,000 buildings in 1917, the city was on a course of rapid growth. In 1929, Atlanta opened its first airport on the site of today's Hartsfield International, presaging the growth of a major air-travel industry. The same year, Delta Air Lines took to the skies and became Atlanta's home carrier. Margaret Mitchell's blockbuster Civil War epic *Gone With the Wind,* which went on to become the world's second-best-selling book (after the Bible) and the basis for the biggest-grossing picture of all time, was published in 1936. Louis B. Mayer turned down a chance to make the film version for MGM, because "no Civil War picture ever made a nickel."

A more dire legacy of the Civil War and the institution of slavery was racial strife, and the early years of the 20th century were marked by violent race riots. Atlanta University professor W. E. B. Du Bois founded the NAACP in 1900. In 1939, black cast members were unable to attend the glamorous premiere of *Gone With the Wind* because the theater was segregated. And as late as 1960, segregation in Atlanta (as everywhere in the South) was still firmly entrenched

IMPRESSIONS

No one goes anywhere without passing through Atlanta.
—Francis C. Lawley, *London Times* reporter, 1861

I want to say to General Sherman, who is an able man . . . though some people think he is kind of careless about fire, that from the ashes he left us in 1864 we have raised a brave and beautiful city; that we have caught the sunshine in our homes and built therein not one ignoble prejudice or memory.
—Henry Grady, *Atlanta Constitution* editor, 1886

and backed by state law. Unlike much of the South, though, the city has, for the most part, adopted a progressive attitude regarding race relations. Even before the civil rights movement there were black advancements—the hiring of black police officers, the election of a black to the Atlanta Board of Education, the desegregation of a public golf course in 1955, and, in 1959, the desegregation of public transit. Mayor Bill Hartsfield (who held office for almost three decades) called Atlanta "a city too busy to hate." And his successor, Mayor Ivan Allen, Jr., called on Atlantans to face race problems "and seek the answers in an atmosphere of decency and dignity."

Without screaming mobs, Atlanta peacefully desegregated its public schools and the Georgia Institute of Technology in 1961. Atlanta native Dr. Martin Luther King, Jr., headquartered his Southern Christian Leadership Conference here and made Ebenezer Baptist Church, which he co-pastored with his father, a hub of the movement. In 1974 Atlanta inaugurated its first black mayor, Maynard Jackson, and, following a term by another black mayor, Andrew Young, Jackson is once again in office.

In 1966 Atlanta went major league when the Braves and the Falcons came to town. Atlantans went wild in 1974 when Hank Aaron broke Babe Ruth's home-run record here.

The 1960s also saw the beginning of downtown development with the rise of the million-square-foot Merchandise Mart, designed by an innovative young Atlanta architect named John Portman. It became the nucleus for the nationally renowned Peachtree Center complex. Portman's futuristic design for the downtown Hyatt Regency (1967) introduced a towering atrium-lobby concept that revolutionized hotel architecture in America. Today Peachtree Center—a 13-city-block "pedestrian village"—comprises three Portman-designed megahotels, the 5.9-million-square-foot Atlanta Market Center (including the Apparel Mart and the high-tech-oriented INFORUM), 200,000 square feet of retail space, a restaurant row, and six massive office towers, its various elements connected by covered walkways and bridges. This is an open-ended project, still very much in a process of expansion.

MARTA rapid-transit trains began running in 1979. Today just about every part of Atlanta is accessible by bus or subway.

In 1980, a revitalized black neighborhood called Sweet Auburn became a National Historic District, its 10 blocks of notable sites including Martin Luther King, Jr.'s boyhood home, his crypt, the church where he preached, a museum, and the Center for Nonviolent Social Change. It is probably *the* major black history attraction in the country.

Media mogul Ted Turner inaugurated CNN here in 1980, following with Superstation TBS, Headline News, and TNT. The High Museum of Art opened its doors in 1983. And in 1989, Underground Atlanta, a retail/restaurant/entertainment complex with a historical theme, garnered national attention.

In the 1990s, when other big cities are struggling to survive, Atlanta continues to soar. The city is very busy gearing up for the 1996 Olympics (expected to generate $3.5 billion) with new hotels, tour packages, and megastadiums. Of the last, most notable are the $214 million, 70,500-seat Georgia Dome and the 10,000-seat open-air Olympic Velodrome at Stone Mountain Park. An Olympic Village is also being erected on the campus of the Georgia Institute of Technology.

Atlanta in the nineties remains a forward-looking city that is constantly renewing itself—a dynamic metropolis where the past is honored and the present enthusiastically embraced. The city's motto is "Resurgens." The phoenix has risen from the ashes and taken wing.

2 Famous Atlantans

Henry Louis "Hank" Aaron (b. 1934) An outfielder with the Milwaukee (later Atlanta) Braves, Aaron broke Babe Ruth's record in 1974 with his 715th home run. He retired in 1976 with 755 homers.

Henry Woodlin Grady (1850–1889) Managing editor of the *Atlanta Constitution,* Grady preached post–Civil War reconciliation, and worked passionately to draw Northern capital and diversified industry to the agrarian South. His name is synonymous with the phrase "The New South."

Joel Chandler Harris (1848–1908) Called "Georgia's Aesop," he created Uncle Remus, the wise black raconteur of children's fables. His tales of Br'er Rabbit and Br'er Fox were the basis for Disney's delightful animated feature *Song of the South.*

Robert Tyre "Bobby" Jones (1902–1971) Golf's only Grand Slam winner, he was the founder of the Masters Tournament. Jones has been called the world's greatest golfer; he retired from the game in 1930 but his record remains unsurpassed. He also held academic degrees in engineering, law, and English literature.

Martin Luther King, Jr. (1929–1968) Civil rights leader, minister, orator, and Nobel Peace Prize winner, King preached Mohandas Gandhi's doctrine of passive resistance.

IMPRESSIONS

It stinks, I don't know why I bother with it, but I've got to have something to do with my time.
—Margaret Mitchell, author of *Gone With the Wind*

Gone With the Wind *is very possibly the greatest American novel.*
—Publishers Weekly

We're going to ride these buses desegregated in Atlanta, Georgia, or we're going to ride a chariot in heaven or push a wheelbarrow in hell.
—Rev. William Holmes Borders, civil rights leader, 1957.

Margaret Mitchell (1900–1949) Author of the definitive southern blockbuster novel, *Gone With the Wind*. Originally a journalist, Mitchell began writing "the book" in 1926 when a severe ankle injury forced her to give up reporting. *GWTW* is, next to the Bible, the world's best-selling book.

John C. Portman (b. 1924) Architect/developer who revolutionized hotel design in America with his lofty atrium-lobby concept and almost singlehandedly designed Atlanta's skyline. He has been called "Atlanta's one-man urban-renewal program."

Robert Edward "Ted" Turner III (b. 1938) Dubbed "the mouth from the South," America's most dynamic media mogul, Ted Turner, owns 24-hour cable news networks CNN and Headline News, along with entertainment networks Superstation TBS and TNT, not to mention a portion of MGM and the Atlanta Braves and Atlanta Hawks.

Robert W. Woodruff (1889–1985) Coca-Cola Company president, philanthropist, and leading Atlanta citizen for over half a century. He put Coca-Cola on the map worldwide; promoted civil rights; and gave over $400 million to Atlanta educational, artistic, civil, and medical projects such as Emory University, the Woodruff Arts Center, and the High Museum.

3 Recommended Books & Films

Books

Bridges, Herb, *Frankly My Dear . . . Gone With the wind Memorabilia* (Mercer University Press, 1986).

Bryan, T. Conn, *Confederate Georgia* (UGA Press, 1953).

Coleman, Kenneth, *Georgia History in Outline* (UGA Press, 1960).

Gardner, Gerald and Harriette, *Pictorial History of Gone With the Wind* (Bonanza Books, 1980).

Garrison, Webb, *The Legacy of Atlanta: A Short History* (Peachtree Publishers, Ltd., 1987).

Jackson, Maynard, Jane Sobel, and Art Klonsky, *Atlanta* (Bolton Pub. Services, Inc., 1985).

Kahn, Clifford, Harlan Joye, and Bernard West, *Living Atlanta: An Oral History of the City 1914–1918* (UGA Press, 1990).

Key, William, *The Battle of Atlanta and the Georgia Campaign* (Peachtree Publishers, Ltd., 1981).

Martin, Harold H., *Atlanta & Environs: A Chronicle of Its People and Events* (UGA Press, 1987).

McCarley, J. Britt, *The Atlanta Campaign/CW Driving Tour of Atlanta Battlefields* (Cherokee Pub. Co., 1989).

McKenzie, Barbara, *Flannery O'Connor's Georgia* (UGA Press, 1980).

Miles, Jim, *Fields of Glory: A History and Tour of the Atlanta Campaign* (Rutledge Hill Press, 1989).

Shavin, Norman, and Bruce Galphin, *Atlanta: Triumph of a People* (Capricorn Corporation, 1985).

Sibley, Celestine, *Atlanta: A Brave and Beautiful City* (Peachtree Publishers, Ltd., 1986).

—*Peachtree Street USA* (Peachtree Pub-lishers, Ltd., 1986).

Films

Many films focus on Atlanta. The two most famous are *Gone With the Wind* (1939) and *Driving Miss Daisy* (1989). Films made in Georgia (not necessarily Atlanta) include *Conrack* (1973), *Smokey and the Bandit* (1976), *Little Darlings* (1979), *Smokey and the Bandit II* (1980), *Cannonball Run* (1980), *Four Seasons* (1980), *Sharkey's Machine* (1981), *The Big Chill* (1982), *Friday 13th: Jason Lives* (1986), *Mosquito Coast* (1986), *School Daze* (1987), *Glory* (1989), *My Cousin Vinnie* (1991), *Fried Green Tomatoes* (1991), and *Pet Sematary II* (1992).

2

Planning a Trip to Atlanta

1	Information & Money	16
•	What Things Cost in Atlanta	16
2	When to Go	16
•	Atlanta Calendar of Events	17
3	What to Pack	29
4	Tips for the Disabled, Seniors, Singles, Gay Men & Lesbians, Students & Familes	29
5	Getting There	33
•	Frommer's Smart Traveler: Airfares	34

IF YOU'RE GOING TO A BEACH RESORT, THERE'S LITTLE NEED TO PLAN YOUR vacation—you can wing it. But when visiting a city where dozens of sightseeing attractions and activities vie for your time, planning is the key to optimum enjoyment.

1 Information & Money

As soon as you know you're going to Atlanta, write to or call the **Atlanta Convention & Visitors Bureau (ACVB),** 233 Peachtree St. NE, Suite 2000, Atlanta 30303 (☎ **404/222-6688**). They'll send you a copy of *Atlanta Now* (a visitor's guide), a book of discount coupons, a *Metro Atlanta Attractions Guide,* a map, and a 2-month calendar of events; they can also advise you on anything from Atlanta's hotel and restaurant scene to the best tour packages available, not to mention Olympics information. You can call weekdays between 8:30am and 5:30pm. May 1 through December 25 you can also call a toll free 24-hour number (**800/ATLANTA**) for an informational recording.

2 When to Go

The Climate

Atlanta's temperate climate is a delight year round. The city enjoys four distinct seasons, but the variations are less extreme than else-

What Things Cost in Atlanta	U.S. $
Taxi from airport to downtown, for one person	15
Bus from airport to downtown	8
Double at the Ritz-Carlton Atlanta (very expensive)	160–295
Double at Marriott Suites (expensive)	174
Double at the Comfort Inn downtown (moderate)	69–149
Double at Travelodge Atlanta Downtown (inexpensive)	76–86
Double at Cheshire Motor Inn (budget)	41–48
Three-course dinner at the Hedgerose Heights Inn, including wine, tax, and tip (very expensive)	45 and up
Three-course dinner at Partners, including wine, tax, and tip (expensive)	35 and up
Three-course dinner at Kudzu Café, including wine, tax, and tip (moderate)	25 and up
Three-course Dinner at Rocky's Brick Oven Pizza, including wine, tax and tip (inexpensive)	17 and up
Three-course dinner at The Varsity (budget)	5
Theater ticket at the Alliance	14–34

where. It seldom snows much in winter, and sweltering summer hot spells are short-lived, with few days reaching, let alone surpassing, the 90°F mark. Spring and autumn are long seasons, and, in terms of natural beauty and heavenly climate, they're optimum times to visit. Annual rainfall is about 48 inches, and the wettest months are December through April and July.

Atlanta's Average Daytime Temperature and Rainfall

	Jan	Feb	Mar	Apr	May	June	July	Aug	Sept	Oct	Nov	Dec
Temp. °F	45	46	52	60	69	77	79	79	73	63	52	43
Rainfall"	4.4	4.5	5.3	4.4	3.1	3.8	4.7	3.6	3.2	2.4	2.9	4.3

Atlanta Calendar of Events

Note: Some events, such as the Georgia Renaissance Festival, begin in one month and continue for several months thereafter. These are listed in the month of inception. So do look back a few months prior to your visit for ongoing events. **Also:** To get to the Old Courthouse in Decatur, site of several below-listed events, take MARTA to the Decatur station.

January

- **Martin Luther King Week,** the second week of the month, is a major happening, comprising more than 30 events attended by over 300,000 people. It begins with an interfaith service and includes plays, musical tributes, seminars, films, a parade down Peachtree Street to Auburn Avenue, and speeches by notables (including Mrs. Coretta Scott King). There are also concerts by major performers (in past years Kris Kristofferson, Stevie Wonder, and the Neville Brothers, among others). For details, contact the King Center (☎ **404/524-1956**).
- **Atlanta Boat Show.** The Miami-based National Marine Manufacturer's Association produces this 5-day event at the Georgia World Congress Center. One of the largest inland marine shows in the United States, it features houseboats, yachts, cabin cruisers, saltwater craft, pleasure craft, rowboats, and canoes, not to mention displays of fishing gear, waterskiing equipment, and other water-related items. Admission is $6 for adults, $3 for children 12 and under. For details, call **305/531-8410.**

February

- **Ringling Brothers Barnum & Bailey Circus** comes to the Omni Coliseum for about 20 performances each year in early February. For information call **404/681-2100,** for tickets call Ticketmaster at **404/249-6400.**
- **Cathedral Antiques Show.** For four days in mid-February, 30 to 35 dealers of high-quality antiques display their wares at the Cathedral of St. Philip. The merchandise ranges from

18th- and 19th-century furnishings to Oriental rugs. A sit-down lunch, served in a genteel setting, is available each day. Admission is $6 per day, or you can attend the preview party for $25 and come back all four days for free. For details, call **404/365-1000.**

- **Southeastern Flower Show.** One of the South's premier gardening events, it takes place at 650 Ponce de Leon Avenue for five days, usually including Valentine's Day but sometimes as late as early March. It offers 100,000 square feet of stunning landscapes and gardens displaying both flowers and vegetables. Other displays might include anything from a bamboo forest to a wildlife refuge. Garden-related products and patio furniture are sold, and there are demonstrations of gardening techniques, photography exhibitions, and events for children. Admission is $10 for adults, with discounts for seniors and children. Proceeds benefit the Atlanta Botanical Garden. For information, call **404/888-5638.**

March

- **Atlanta Home and Garden Show.** Sponsored by the Southern Exposition Management Company (SEMCO), this four-day mid-month event takes place at the Georgia World Congress Center. The emphasis is on display gardens and landscaping ideas, and there are seminars on subjects ranging from southern gardens to antique restoration. Admission is $7 for adults, $6 for seniors, $4 for children 7–12, under 7 free. Call **404/998-9800** for details.

★ St. Patrick's Day Parade

A major production here, with some 7,000 marchers each year and 150,000 viewers. The mayor and other local politicians attend, and there are sports celebrities, high school bands, majorettes, clowns, cloggers, drill teams, and bagpipers. The parade culminates near Underground Atlanta with concerts of Irish music, dance, and other festivities. If you want to continue celebrating, head over to Limerick-Junction, 822 N. Highland Ave. (☎ **874-7147**), a cozy pub that provides the requisite green beer, bagpipe players, and Irish fare. **Where:** The parade begins at Peachtree Street and Ralph McGill Boulevard. **When:** March 17. **How:** Just show up. Check the local paper for details.

- **The High Museum Atlanta Wine Auction.** Events begin with a gala wine reception and formal dinner on Friday night. On Saturday, you can discuss wines with prominent winemakers, sample premium wines and gourmet fare prepared by Atlanta's finest chefs, and participate in a silent auction. There are displays of wine-related art. The event culminates with the auctioning off of great wines, fabulous trips, wine dinners, and artworks. It all takes place the last weekend of the month under a tent at a location determined annually. Proceeds benefit the museum. Admission to the gala is $225. Tickets for the auction are $75 per couple, $50 per person. Call **404/898-1144** for details.

April

★ The Atlanta Dogwood Festival

Culminating in Piedmont Park on a weekend in mid-April, this environmentally themed spring celebration is a biggie, with several related events taking place the week prior. Activities include concerts, house and garden tours, and bicycle tours of Buckhead to view azaleas and dogwoods in bloom. On the final weekend, there are musical performances, food booths, hot-air balloon races, kite-flying contests, children's activities, a juried arts and crafts show, canine frisbee championships, and Earth Day celebrations featuring presentations by environmental groups—all in Piedmont Park.

Where: Several locations around town and Piedmont Park. **When:** Nine days in mid-April. **How:** Admission is free to Piedmont Park events; there are charges for other activities. For details, call **404/952-9151** or check the local papers for a full listing of events.

- **Antebellum Jubilee.** Demonstrations of early American/Southern arts and crafts, a re-created Civil War encampment, string bands, and concerts on the dulcimer, harp, and zither, are all part of this annual celebration at Georgia's Stone Mountain Park the first two weekends in early April. All festival activities are included in the price of regular admission to the plantation. For details, call **404/498-5702.**
- **The Easter Egg Hunt** is another early April happening, held on the south lawn of the Old Courthouse in Decatur. There are prizes for those who collect the most eggs. Admission is free. For details, call **404/371-8386.**
- **Stone Mountain Village Easter Egg Hunt.** On Saturday morning of Easter weekend, a hunt for painted eggs and candy departs from The Children's Hour, a toy store at 5377 Manor Drive. Prizes include gift certificates for toys. There are separate areas for children ages 2 to 4 and 5 to 7. Admission is free. Call **404/408-1351** or **404/879-4971** for details.
- **Easter Sunrise Services** are held at the top and the base of Georgia's Stone Mountain at 6:30am. Park gates open at

4am and the skylift begins operation at 4:30am (though it seems more appropriate to walk up if you're in good shape). For details, call **404/498-5702.**

- **Lasershow,** also at Stone Mountain Park, is a sight-and-sound spectacular of laser lights and fireworks choreographed to popular, patriotic, country, and classical music. It begins on April weekends (Friday, Saturday, and Sunday nights at 9pm). Don't miss it. Admission is free. Beginning in early May through Labor Day, Lasershow can be seen nightly at 9:30pm. For details, call **404/498-5702.**
- **The Sweet Auburn Festival,** a 4-day event in mid-April, features a parade, historical and cultural activities, children's activities, and music. For details, call **404/577-0625.**
- **The Inman Park Festival** takes place the last weekend in April in an Atlanta suburb noted for its gorgeous turn-of-the-century Victorian mansions. Activities include a tour of homes, music (jazz bands, cloggers), an arts-and-crafts festival/flea market, a parade, a Saturday-night street dance, and food vendors. Tickets are about $10, good for all events both days. For more information, call **404/242-4895.**

★ The Georgia Renaissance Festival Spring Celebration

This re-creation of a 16th-century English county fair in a 30-acre "village" called Willy Nilly features a juried crafts show with over 100 craftspeople (many of them demonstrating 16th-century skills); continuous entertain-ment on 10 stages (there are over 100 shows each day); period foods; a birds of prey show; and a cast of costumed characters including jousters, jugglers, storytellers, giant stilt walkers, minstrels, magicians, choral groups, and knights in shining armor. King Henry VIII and one of his wives oversee the festivities.
Where: In Fairburn—10 miles south of the airport on I-85, exit 12. **When:** On eight weekends, from the last Saturday in April through the second Sunday in June (plus Memorial Day). **How:** You can purchase tickets at the door or via Ticketmaster (☎ 249-6400). Admission is $10 for adults, $5 for ages 5 to 12, under 5 free. For details, call **404/964-8575.**

May

- **Blue Sky Concerts** are free performances of jazz, classical, bluegrass, and rock music, held at noon every Wednesday in May on the south lawn of the Old Decatur Courthouse. Bring a blanket and a picnic lunch. For more information, call **404/371-8386**.
- **Concerts on the Square,** a similar series at the courthouse, takes place every Saturday night in May at 7:30pm. It

traditionally opens with a performance by the Dekalb Symphony Orchestra. For details, call **404/371-8386.**

- **The Gardens for Connoisseurs Tour,** proceeds of which go to the Atlanta Botanical Garden, visits outstanding private gardens the weekend of Mother's Day. Tickets are $20 for the entire tour, $5 per garden. For details, call **404/876-5859.**

- **Springfest.** There's good food to eat at this event, which includes the annual BBQ Pork Cookoff. It takes place on a weekend early in May at Georgia's Stone Mountain Park. Continuous live entertainment on three stages (emphasizing folk and country music and featuring some big names, like John Michael Montgomery and Waylon Jennings), a vast arts and crafts show, children's activities, and southern food booths round out the events. All activities are free. For information, call **404/498-5702.**

- **Kingfest.** This free outdoor internationally themed festival takes place during a weekend in mid-May at the Martin Luther King, Jr. Center (details in Chapter 7). Events include international dance performances, arts and crafts exhibits, foods, concerts, theater, an art market, and more. Admission is free. For details, call **404/524-1956.**

- **Midtown Music Festival.** Sponsored by the Midtown Alliance, an Atlanta civic association, this terrific festival takes place on a weekend in mid-May at a lot on 10th and Peachtree Streets. Events—beginning Friday night—include dozens of concerts on five stages (many of them big-name performers such as Billy Dean, James Brown, Al Green, Eddie Money, and Joan Baez), a Southeastern artist's market, and ethnic food booths from regional restaurants. Kids' activities, too: face painting, special performances, arts and crafts, circus workshops, and more. Admission is $11 for one day, $17 for all three days; free for children under 12. Call **404/798-7785.**

- **Decatur Arts Festival,** a 3-day event on the south lawn of the Old Decatur Courthouse, takes place Memorial Day weekend. It features an art show on the lawn, various juried shows nearby, a garden tour, storytellers, mimes, jugglers, puppet shows, clowns, children's art activities, great food, and performances by music, dance, and theater groups. A great family outing. For details, call **404/371-8386.**

- **A Taste of the South.** Part of Stone Mountain Park's Memorial Day weekend celebrations, this happening has music, dance, regional foods (everything from collard greens to grits), art, crafts demonstrations, and more. For details, call **404/498-5702.**

- **The Atlanta Jazz Festival,** during Memorial Day weekend, features free ongoing concerts in Grant Park (at the main stage next to Cyclorama). The afternoon begins with local performers and goes on to major stars by evening—for example, Wynton Marsalis, Sun Ra, Nancy Wilson, Dizzy Gillespie, Max Roach, and Sonny Rollins. Arrive early to get a good space, and bring a blanket and a picnic lunch. Some years, there's also a concert (admission is charged) featuring major jazz artists at the Chastain Park Amphitheatre at Powers Ferry Road and Stella Drive. For details on any of the above, call **404/817-6815.**

June

- **The Atlanta Film & Video Festival,** which takes place for two weeks in mid-June at the Image Film/Video Center, 75 Bennett St. NW, Suite M1 (and other Atlanta theaters), features about 70 films and videos by some of the country's most important independent media artists. Admission is $6 per film, with discounts available for students and seniors. Call **404/352-4225** for details.

- **Kingfest.** This free outdoor festival takes place during a weekend in mid-June at the Martin Luther King, Jr. Center (details in Chapter 7). Events begin on a Friday evening with a concert by a major artist such as Ahmad Jamal. Saturday is "kids' day," filled with children's activities— puppet making, pony rides, face painting—and performances by young people. And Sunday is "gospel day," presenting premier gospel singers. During the festival, Freedom Plaza will be transformed into an artist's market. Admission is free. For details, call **404/524-1956.**

- **The Annual Shakespeare Festival** offers three or four productions between mid-June and mid-August, performed in a 400-seat theater tent at Oglethorpe University, 4484 Peachtree Road. Preceding the performances, there's entertainment on the lawn (music and farcical vignettes). Everyone brings a pre-performance picnic or arranges in advance to purchase it on the premises. The company, made up of Actors Equity pros for the most part, offers both traditional and innovative Shakespearean productions as well as other classics. A recent season included *SHREW: The Musical* (set in 1940s Palm Beach), *The Merchant of Venice, A Midsummer Night's Dream*, and Molière's *The Imaginary Invalid.* Picnic grounds open at 6:30pm, the pre-show begins at 7pm, the actual show at 8pm. Admission is $16 to $20 for adults, $3 less for seniors, $10 to $15 for students. Call for tickets as far in advance as possible, especially for weekend performances (☎ **404/264-0020**). To order a picnic, call **404/396-5361.**

⭐ A Taste of Atlanta

The Southeast's largest outdoor food festival lets you sample fare from over 60 noted Atlanta restaurants. While strolling about tasting everything from bratwurst to fajitas, and Caribbean softshell crab to chicken cordon bleu (not to mention luscious desserts), guests enjoy continuous live entertainment, an arts and crafts fair, and cooking demonstrations. There's a children's area featuring kids' favorite foods, magicians, clowns, crafts, and games. Proceeds from the event benefit the National Kidney Foundation of Georgia.

Where: In a lot at 10th and Peachtree Sts. **When:** Three days in mid-June. **How:** Admission is $5 (free for children under 12), and food tastings are 50¢ to $2. For details, call **404/248-1315.**

- **The Stone Mountain Village Annual Arts & Crafts Festival** (see Chapter 9, "Atlanta Shopping") is held on Father's Day weekend. Over 200 Southeast craftspeople and antique dealers display their wares, local community groups set up fabulous food booths, and entertainment (cloggers, clowns, country music, and more) is offered continually in the Village Gazebo. For details, call **404/871-4971.** Admission of $1 is rebated with a purchase of $5 or more; under 12 free.

- **Beach Party.** Decatur's not on the ocean, but that doesn't stop its residents from throwing this bash every year on the Friday closest to June 21 on the south lawn of the Old Decatur Courthouse. The lawn is covered with sand, plastic palms and volleyball courts are erected, a disc jockey provides music, food and drink are sold, and there are sandcastle-building, hula hoop, and dance contests. For details, call **404/371-8386.**

- **NationsBank Summer Film Festival.** Don't miss this event at the fabulous Fox Theatre (see Chapter 7). About a dozen films are shown from June through August, mostly on Monday and Thursday nights, and the shows include vintage cartoons, a sing-along organ concert (follow the bouncing ball), and a feature film at just $5.50 per ticket. Coupon books are available at a discount, a good bet for families. For details, call **404/881-2100.**

- **The Gay Pride Parade,** usually the last Sunday in June, proceeds from a downtown site (selected annually) to Piedmont Park. The whole month is event-filled (June is National Gay Pride Month), including performances by the Gay Men's Chorus and musical entertainment/art market in Piedmont Park. For details, call **404/662-4533.**

July

- **The Asian Cultural Experience.** The Atlanta Botanical Garden (details in Chapter 7) celebrates Asian culture during a weekend in early July with demonstrations of crafts such as Chinese calligraphy, ikebana, Japanese embroidery, Chinese opera make-up, and origami. Saturday evening features music, dancing, fireworks, and a dragon

parade on the great lawn. Other events might include
musical performances, games, children's activities, tai chi
demonstrations, Asian art shows, and bonsai exhibits.
Admission is included with Garden admission price. For
details, call **404/876-5858.**

• **Independence Day** is celebrated at Georgia's Stone
Mountain Park's 3-day **Fantastic Fourth Celebration**—a
star-spangled festival of free concerts, sports competitions,
patriotic music, clogging, choreographed fireworks displays,
and Lasershows. For details, call **404/498-5702.**

You can also celebrate **the Fourth in Decatur.**
Festivities begin with a Pied Piper Parade departing at
6pm from the Decatur Baptist Church on Courthouse
Square. Decorate yourself, your bicycle, or your car and
join in. The parade is followed by a concert at 7:30pm
(bring a picnic and blanket) and a great fireworks display.
Everything is free. For details, call **404/371-8386.**

An old-fashioned **Fourth of July Parade** takes place
in Stone Mountain Village, from Mountain Street at the
foot of the west gate of Stone Mountain Park along Main
Street through the Village shop area. There are bands,
floats, cloggers, baton twirlers, and more. The parade
begins at 10am. For details, call **404/879-4971.**

• **The National Black Arts Festival** is a 7- to 10-day affair
(even-numbered years only) in late July and early August,
with more than 150 events (most of them free) taking place
throughout the city. Billed as "a celebration of the works
of artists of African descent," it features dozens of events—
concerts (including big names like Nancy Wilson and Cecil
Taylor), theater, film, dance, storytelling, poetry readings,
performance art, art and folk-art exhibitions, children's
activities, African puppet shows, and that's not the half of
it. For details, call **404/730-7315.**

September

• **The Montreux Atlanta International Music Festival**
(patterned after the Montreux jazz festival in Switzerland),
is a 4- to 6-day affair (including Labor Day) featuring
jazz, blues, gospel, reggae, and zydeco (Cajun) music in
Piedmont Park and local theaters. Both regional and
internationally known artists perform, and the fun usually
includes late-night jam sessions at local hotels. Most events
are free. Call **404/817-6815** for details.

• **Blue Sky Concerts and Concerts on the Square.** The
fall schedules of these concert series (see May) begin in
Decatur. Concert times are the same as above. The final
Saturday night concert is all "golden oldies." For details,
call **404/371-8386.**

• **The Yellow Daisy Festival** at Georgia's Stone Mountain
Park is a vast outdoor arts-and-crafts show (over 400

exhibitors) with musical entertainment, a flower show, great food, storytellers, and puppetry. Taking place in early September, it has been rated the nation's number one arts and crafts festival. About 300,000 people attend each year. For details, call **404/498-5702.**

- **Sesame Street Live.** Early to midmonth this show comes to the Omni Coliseum. Call **404/681-2000** for information, **404/249-6400** for tickets.

- **Georgia Music Festival.** This statewide celebration of music takes place for a week to 10 days midmonth. Events (many of them free) include jazz, gospel, bluegrass, country, and rock concerts, as well as dancing, seminars, and contests at varied locations. Call **404/656-3596** for details.

★ Arts Festival of Atlanta

One of the nation's oldest and largest outdoor art events, this contemporary visual and performing arts festival features regional, national, and international artists. Indoor art exhibits are supplemented by a 280-booth outdoor Artist Market. Stages are set up for music, dance, and theater performances. Children's activities are numerous. And food concessions throughout the park offer everything from funnel cakes to fajitas.

Where: Piedmont Park (plus performances and special exhibits at sites selected annually). **When:** Nine days, beginning the second or third week of September. **How:** All events are free. For details, call **404/885-1125.**

October

- **The Heritage Festival** takes place in early October on the south lawn of Courthouse Square in Decatur. It celebrates the old days with candlemaking, blacksmithing, and other crafts demonstrations; bluegrass music and other entertainment; and food booths. Admission is free. For details, call **404/371-8386.**

- **The American Association of University Women's Annual Book Fair** is a 4-day event in Lenox Square Mall around the first week in October. AAUW collects and categorizes over 75,000 used books each year for the fair. All are in good condition, some are valuable, and prices are low. Proceeds go to scholarship for women. Admission is free. Hours are 10am to 9:30pm. Call **404/355-1861** to find out the fair's location in the mall and exact dates.

- **The Miller Lite Chili Cookoff** is held at Georgia's Stone Mountain Park on a weekend day early in the month. You can sample thousands of varieties of chili, Brunswick stew, and chili dogs. Entertainment varies each year but will likely include cloggers, country music, jalapeño-eating contests, and other folksy fun. For details, call **404/498-5702.**

- **The Annual Scottish Festival and Highland Games,** held midmonth at Stone Mountain, is a gathering of the clans comprising three days of military tattoos, Highland dancers, pipe and drum concerts, Scottish harping and fiddling, sword dancing, reels, lilts, and athletic events such as the hammer throw and caber toss. For details and admission charges, call **404/634-7402** or **404/396-5728**.

★ **The Georgia Renaissance Fall Festival**

This 16th-century fair is the autumn complement to the spring celebration described above (see April listing for details). All of its offerings are the same, but since it's in October, a haunted house is added to the attractions and shops are geared up for holiday shopping.
Where: In Fairburn—10 miles south of the airport on I-85, exit 12. **When:** Four weekends in October. **How:** You can purchase tickets at the door or via Ticketmaster (☎ **404/249-6400**). Admission is $10 for adults, $5 for ages 5 to 12, under 5 free. For details, call **404/964-8575**.

- **Fall Gardening Festival.** Designed to teach people about fall gardening, this one-day mid-month event at the Atlanta Botanical Garden (details in Chapter 7) features about 50 nonprofit exhibitors, display gardens, produce competitions, a plant and flower expo, food, music, door prizes, and children's activities. Admission is free, but a $1 donation is suggested. For details, call **404/876-5858**.
- **Sunday in the Park at Oakland Cemetery.** On a Sunday midmonth, this graveyard party features storytellers, historians, guided tours, a hat contest, a turn-of-the-century concert, and Victorian boutiques. Details on Oakland Cemetery in Chapter 7. Admission is free. You can reserve a $5 picnic supper. Call **404/688-2107** for details.

November

- **Walt Disney's World on Ice** comes to the Omni Coliseum early to mid-November. Call **404/681-2100** for information, **404/249-6400** to charge tickets.
- **Veteran's Day Parade.** Atlanta mounts an impressive version of this parade each year, on the 11th, with floats, drill teams, marching bands, clowns, color guards, and more. The parade begins at 11am from Lenox Square (in front of the Ritz Carlton) and proceeds south. For details, call **404/416-0377**.
- **The High Museum Antique Show & Sale,** at Phipps Plaza on a weekend in mid-November, features about 50 exhibitors—outstanding international antique dealers all. In addition, it usually offers lectures (some of them at luncheons), a tour of homes rich in decorative arts, daily high teas, and a Sunday brunch. Admission to the show

and high tea is $8 per day at the door, $7 with advance purchase. For details, call **404/898-1152.**

- **Holiday Celebrations** in Atlanta Kick off with a dazzling array of events at Stone Mountain Park from late November through December 30. A "tree of lights" atop the mountain is visible from miles away; the park's roads offer a stunning display of lights, animated scenes, music, and traditional decorations; and activities include visits with Santa, candlelight plantation tours, carriage rides, holiday sing-along train rides, a special Lasershow, and lots of entertainment. For details, call **404/498-5702.**
- **Stone Mountain Village Candlelight Shopping.** From the day after Thanksgiving through Christmas, this charming shopping village is candlelit, and visitors are lured into decorated shops by the aroma of mulling cider. A jolly St. Nick, gaily lighted trees, and carriage rides are part of the fun. It's a delightful way to do your holiday shopping. No admission. Call **404/879-4971** for details.

Christmas is heralded in Atlanta by the **Lighting of the Great Tree** (a traditionally decorated 80-foot pine topped by an 8-foot star) on Thanksgiving night. There are choirs singing Christmas carols. It all takes place at Underground Atlanta at Peachtree Fountains, across from Five Points MARTA station. Arrive early via MARTA; traffic comes to a standstill as hundreds of thousands converge to view the spectacle. For details, call **404/523-2311.**

The last Friday in November, the **Fidelity Tree Lighting** takes place in front of the Fidelity Bank at Commerce Drive and Clairmont Avenue in Decatur. In addition to lighting a 60-foot tree, festivities include caroling, choruses, and food vendors. The fun begins at 7:30pm. Decatur's seasonal events also feature a **Candlelight Tour of Homes,** a **Bonfire and Christmas Carol Sing-Along** (with a marshmallow roast around a blazing fire), a **Breakfast with Santa** at a local Holiday Inn, and strolling carolers. For details, call **404/371-8386.**

December

- **Christmas at Callanwolde,** at Callanwolde Fine Arts Center, 980 Briarcliff Road NE, is usually held during the first two weeks in December (some years it begins in late November). Noted interior and floral designers decorate the Gothic-Tudor mansion, and shops (sweets, toys, pottery, garden, etc.) are set up in different rooms. Activities also include concerts on 3,752-pipe Aeolian organ, children's breakfasts with Santa, caroling and hymn singing, and other entertainment. Admission: $8 adults, $6 seniors, $5 children 12 and under. For details, call **404/872-5338.**

• **Country Christmas.** The Atlanta Botanical Garden throws this fete on the first Sunday in December. The garden house is beautifully decorated, and highlights of the afternoon include carolers, bell ringers, children's theater, entertainers, chestnuts roasting on an open fire, horse-drawn carriage rides, cranberry and popcorn stringing, and strolling mimes, musicians, and magicians. Christmas crafts like wreath making are demonstrated, and you can shop for handcrafted gifts and homemade baked goods. Refreshments include mulled wine and cider. Of course there's a giant tree. And throughout December, there's a vast poinsettia display here. Admission is free the day of the fete. For details, call **404/876-5858.**

★ **Egleston Children's Christmas Parade and Festival of Trees**

Both of these events raise money for Egleston Children's Hospital. The parade is a major to-do with award-winning bands, lavish holiday-themed floats, helium-balloon comic characters, Santa Claus, carolers, costumed storybook characters, clowns, and celebrity guest appearances (for example, Mary Lou Retton or Marie Osmond). The parade kicks off the 9-day Festival of Trees for which Atlanta artists, interior designers, florists, and corporations innovatively decorate and donate trees, wreaths, and Christmas vignettes which are exhibited and auctioned off. The festival also features national entertainers (like Shari Lewis and Lambchop and Sesame Street actors), musical performances, children's activities, an antique carousel, the "pink pig" monorail ride, ice-skating demonstrations, and an international area of heritage displays from 28 countries. **Where:** The parade proceeds from Marietta and Spring streets to West Peachtree Street and Ralph McGill Boulevard. The Festival of Trees takes place at the Georgia World Congress Center, 285 International Blvd. **When:** The parade begins at 10:30am the first Saturday in December; the 9-day festival follows. **How:** For details on the parade, call **404/264-9348** or check the local papers. Admission to the Festival of Trees is $8 for adults, $5 for seniors and children 2 to 12, under 2 free. For details, call **404/325-NOEL.**

• **The Peach Bowl Game.** The final event of the year, some time between Christmas and New Year's (occasionally in early January) at the Georgia Dome. It's one of 18 post-season college football games played around the country. Call **404/223-9200** for information, **404/249-6400** to charge tickets.

• **New Year's Eve.** The Big Peach that rings in Atlanta's New Year is dropped at the stroke of midnight from the

138-foot light tower at Underground Atlanta. But festivities begin earlier (about 8pm) with music for dancing in the streets (it progresses from '60s tunes through the '90s), a pyrotechnic display and laser show, balloons, and a marching band. Some 250,000 revelers converge on the complex for this event. Several on-premises nightclubs offer dinner/party packages. Call **404/523-2311** for details.

3 What to Pack

The most important aspect of a traveler's wardrobe is comfort. It can get very unpleasant trekking around even the most fascinating attractions when your shoes hurt or your clothing is too warm. In summer especially, the ideal ensemble is sneakers, shorts, and a T-shirt—in other words, the least amount of clothing you can wear in public without causing a commotion. You might, however, wish to carry a light jacket or shawl in hot weather, since interior spaces are always frigidly air-conditioned.

In winter, pack a coat, hat, and boots, but don't get carried away—this isn't Wisconsin. A fold-up umbrella is always a good idea, and if you don't use it, so much the better. People definitely dress up for dinner and evening entertainments (theater, concerts), so be sure to bring along one or two elegant outfits for nighttime wear. Jackets and ties for men are essential. This is no hick town—Atlanta is the fashion capital of the South.

One thing I like to pack is a 75- or 100-watt light bulb, especially if I'm staying at a moderately priced or budget hotel where bedside lamps seldom provide adequate wattage for reading. You don't need to pack a travel iron. Almost all hotels these days provide irons at the front desk. Find out if your hotel offers hairdryers before you pack one.

One final note: If you are taking along any vital medication—or anything else that would be devastating to lose—carry it in your hand luggage. Better safe than sorry.

4 Tips for the Disabled, Seniors, Singles, Gay Men & Lesbians, Students & Families

A free newspaper called *Creative Loafing,* available at over 3,000 locations around town (hotels, restaurants, shops, MARTA stations, etc.), lists numerous events each issue and has special sections for "Gay and Lesbian Activities" and "Singles." For a free copy prior to your visit call **800/950-5623.**

FOR THE DISABLED Mobility International USA (☎ **503/343-1284**) offers accessibility information, has many interesting travel programs for the disabled, and publishes a quarterly newspaper called *Over the Rainbow* ($10 per year to subscribe). Help is also available from **MossRehab Hospital** (☎ **215/456-9603**).

Metropolitan Atlanta

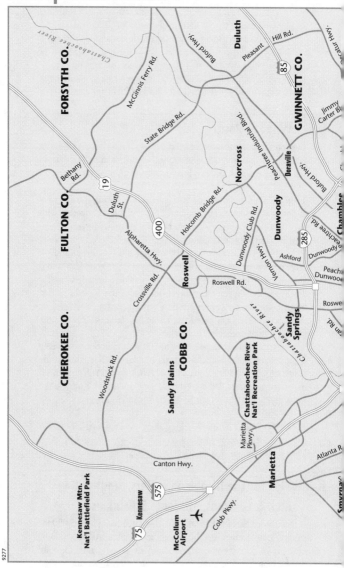

Tour packager **Evergreen Travel Service,** 4114 198th Ave. SW, Suite 13, Lynnwood, WA 98036 (☎ **206/776-1184** or **800/435-2288**), offers tours designed for the blind, the visually impaired, the hearing impaired, the elderly, and the physically or mentally disabled.

And a publisher called **Twin Peaks Press,** Box 129, Vancouver, WA 98666 (☎ **206/694-2462** or **800/637-2256** for orders only),

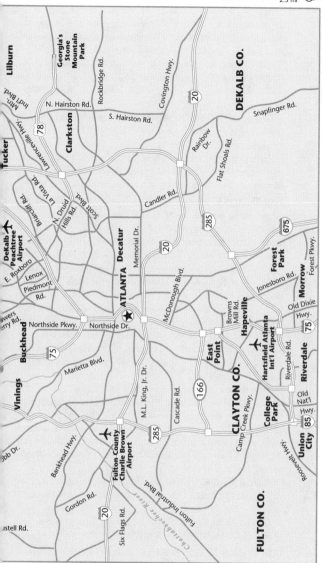

0 — 4.0 km
— 2.5 mi

specializes in books for the disabled. Write for their *Disability Bookshop Catalog*, enclosing $3.

Amtrak (☎ 800/USA-RAIL) provides redcap service, wheelchair assistance, and special seats with 72 hours' notice. The disabled are also entitled to a 25% discount on one-way regular coach fares. Documentation from a doctor or an ID card proving your disability is required. Amtrak also provides wheelchair-accessible sleeping accommodations on long-distance trains, and guide dogs are permissible and travel free of charge. Write for a free booklet called *Amtrak's America* from Amtrak Distribution Center, P.O. Box 7717, Itasca, IL 60143, which has a chapter detailing services for passengers with disabilities. **Note:** If you will need help with bags on arrival, arrange it with Amtrak when you reserve. The Atlanta station has no redcap service unless you request it.

Greyhound (☎ 800/752-4841) allows a disabled person to travel with a companion for a single fare. Call at least 48 hours in advance to discuss special needs.

Airlines don't offer special fares to the disabled. When making your flight reservations, ask where your wheelchair will be stowed on the plane and if a guide dog may accompany you.

FOR SENIORS If you haven't already done so, consider joining the **American Association of Retired Persons (AARP),** 601 E St. NW, Washington, DC 20049 (☎ 202/434-2277). Annual membership costs $8 per person or per couple. You must be 50 to join. Membership entitles you to many discounts. Write to Purchase Privilege Program, AARP Fulfillment at the above address to receive AARP's *Purchase Privilege* brochure—a free list of hotels, motels, and car-rental firms nationwide that offer discounts to AARP members. AARP Travel Experience from American Express arranges a wide array of discounted group tours and cruises for members (☎ 800/927-0111 for tours, **800/745-4567** for cruises).

Another good source of reduced-price information is a book called *The Discount Guide for Travelers Over 55* by Caroline and Walter Weinz (E. P. Dutton).

Elderhostel is a national organization that offers low-priced educational programs for people over 60 (your spouse or companion must be at least 50). Programs are generally a week long, and prices average about $335 per person, including room, board, and classes. For information on programs in Atlanta call or write Elderhostel headquarters, 75 Federal St., Boston, MA 02110 (☎ **617/426-8056**) and ask for a free catalog.

Amtrak (☎ **800/USA-RAIL**) offers a 15% discount off the lowest available coach fare (with certain travel restrictions) to people 62 or older.

Greyhound also offers discounted fares for senior citizens. Call your local Greyhound office for details.

FOR SINGLE TRAVELERS The main problem for single travelers is meeting up with other people. There is, of course, the bar scene (see Chapter 10). Another good way to meet people is to go on a hike, river-rafting trip, or other such excursion, many of which are listed in the *Atlanta Journal-Constitution* "Weekend" section. You'll find other people-meeting activities listed there as well.

Another tip: choose a bed-and-breakfast facility; it's easy to meet people over coffee and muffins in the communal dining room.

FOR GAY MEN & LESBIANS   Atlanta has a large gay community and you can access it via a free magazine called *Etcetera Magazine*, like *Creative Loafing* (see above) available in front of MARTA stops and in some shops, bars, and restaurants. If you'd like a copy in advance of your trip, send $2 for a current issue to P.O. Box 8916, Atlanta, GA 30306. Or, when you arrive call **404/525-3821** to find out where you can pick up an issue near your hotel. You can also call that number for information on gay resources in town ("we call ourselves the gay 411," an *Etcetera* representative assured me).

Another free gay publication is *Southern Voice.* Call **404/876-1819** for a free issue, a distribution point near your hotel, or, once again, information on gay resources in Atlanta.

FOR STUDENTS   The key to securing discounts is valid student ID. Be sure to carry one and keep your eyes open for special student prices at attractions, theaters, transportation facilities, etc.

FOR FAMILIES   Careful planning makes all the difference between a successful, enjoyable vacation and one that ends with exhausted, irritable parents and cranky kids. Here are just a few hints to help:

Get the Kids Involved   Let them, if they're old enough, write to tourist offices for information and color brochures. If you're driving, give them a map on which they can outline the route. Let them help decide your sightseeing itinerary.

Packing   Although your home may be toddler-proof, hotel accommodations are not. Bring blank plugs to cover outlets and whatever else is necessary.

En Route   Carry a few simple games to relieve the tedium of traveling. A few snacks will also help and save money. If you're using public transportation (Amtrak, airlines, bus), always inquire about discounted fares for children.

Accommodations   Children under 12, and in many cases even older, stay free in their parents' rooms in most hotels. Look for establishments that have pools and other recreational facilities. Reserve equipment such as cribs and playpens in advance.

5   Getting There

By Air

Hartsfield Atlanta International Airport, 10 miles south of downtown, is the world's largest and second-busiest airport and transfer hub. The airport is bordered by I-75 and I-85, which converge going toward downtown. I-285, known as the Perimeter because it rings the city, is also accessible from the airport.

Delta Air Lines, which is based at Hartsfield, is the major carrier to Atlanta ("We call home over 500 times a day" is their motto), connecting it to pretty much the entire country as well as 34 countries internationally. Other major carriers include American,

Atlantic Southeast, Continental, Northwest, TWA, United, USAir, and ValuJet.

BEST-FOR-THE-BUDGET-FARES   Generally, the least expensive fares (except for specially promoted discount fares announced in newspaper travel sections) are advance-purchase fares that involve certain restrictions. For example, in addition to paying for your ticket 3 to 21 days in advance of your trip, you may have to leave or return on certain days, stay a maximum or minimum number of days, and so on. Also, advance-purchase fares are often nonrefundable. Nonetheless, the restrictions are usually within the framework of one's vacation plans. The further in advance you reserve, the better your options, since sometimes there are a limited number of seats sold at discounted rates.

Just what kind of savings are we talking about with advance-purchase fares? At this writing, if you flew on Delta, regular round-trip coach fares and lowest advance-purchase fares are as follows between Hartsfield Atlanta International Airport and these cities:

	Regular Fare	**Advance Purchase**
Boston-Atlanta	$872	$239
Chicago-Atlanta	$682	$169
Los Angeles-Atlanta	$1,302	$448
Miami-Atlanta	$724	$198
New Orleans-Atlanta	$576	$198
New York-Atlanta	$872	$209

By the time you read this, fares will no doubt have changed, but the vast savings accrued from buying advance-purchase tickets will remain the same.

Frommer's Smart Traveler: Airfares

1. Call *all* the airlines that serve your destination to find the best fare.

2. Try to make your reservation 30 days in advance to take advantage of the lowest fares.

3. Keep checking fares as your departure date nears; airlines would rather fill a seat than have it fly empty, so they may cut fares dramatically in the days just before a flight leaves.

4. Investigate the cost of charter flights.

5. Avoid high-season travel, especially holidays. You can often get lower fares if you're willing to take midweek flights.

6. Always ask for the lowest fare, not just a discount fare.

7. Ask your airline about package deals that include accommodations and rental cars as well as airfare. Many of the major carriers have such deals and most of them are excellent values.

A final note: when you reserve, be sure to inquire about money-saving packages that include hotel accommodations, car rentals, tours, and other like expenses, with your airfare. Delta, especially, will be offering some very attractive packages for the Olympics. For Delta reservations and flight information, call toll free **800/221-1212.**

By Train

Amtrak operates the *Crescent* daily between Atlanta and New York, with stops in Washington, D.C., Philadelphia, and other intermediate points. The *Crescent* also goes beyond Atlanta to many points south. And other Amtrak trains connect with most of the country. To find out if your city connects via rail with Atlanta, call toll free **800/USA-RAIL.** The Amtrak station is at 1688 Peachtree Street, just off I-85.

Like the airlines, **Amtrak** offers several discount fares, and though not all are based on advance purchase, you may increase your options by reserving early. At this writing, regular round-trip coach fares and discount fares are as follows between Atlanta and these cities.

	Full Fare	Discount Fare
Boston-Atlanta	$318	$166
Chicago-Atlanta	$342	$178
Los Angeles-Atlanta	$494	$254
Miami-Atlanta	$506	$178
New Orleans-Atlanta	$190	$102
New York-Atlanta	$294	$154

Once again, inquire (via the above toll-free number) about money-saving packages that include hotel accommodations with your train fare.

By Bus

Greyhound buses (☎ **404-384-9651** or **800/231-2222** for reservations and information) connect the entire country with Atlanta. The bus terminal is in the heart of downtown Atlanta at 81 International Blvd., at Williams Street.

The fare structure on buses is complex and not always based on distance traveled. The good news is that when you call Greyhound, they'll always give you the lowest-fare options. Once again, advance-purchase fares booked 3 to 21 days prior to travel represent big savings—up to 50%.

By Car

Three major interstate highways (I-20, I-75, and I-85) converge close to the center of downtown Atlanta. For car-rental information, see "Getting Around" in Chapter 4.

3

For Foreign Visitors

1   Preparing for Your Trip   37

2   Getting To and Around the U.S.   40

•   Fast Facts: For the Foreign Traveler   41

Aᴌᴛʜᴏᴜɢʜ Aᴍᴇʀɪᴄᴀɴ ꜰᴀᴅs ᴀɴᴅ ꜰᴀsʜɪᴏɴs ʜᴀᴠᴇ sᴘʀᴇᴀᴅ ᴀᴄʀᴏss Eᴜʀᴏᴘᴇ and other parts of the world so that America may seem like familiar territory before your arrival, there are still many peculiarities and uniquely American situations that any foreign visitor will encounter.

1   Preparing for Your Trip

Entry Requirements

DOCUMENT REGULATIONS   Canadian citizens may enter the U.S. without visas; they need only proof of residence.

Citizens of the U.K., New Zealand, Japan, and most western European countries traveling on valid passports may not need a visa for fewer than 90 days of holiday or business travel to the U.S., providing that they hold a round-trip or return ticket and enter the U.S. on an airline or cruise line participating in the visa waiver program.

(Note that citizens of these visa-exempt countries who first enter the U.S. may then visit Mexico, Canada, Bermuda, and/or the Caribbean islands and then reenter the U.S., by any mode of transportation, without needing a visa. Further information is available from any U.S. embassy or consulate.)

Citizens of countries other than those stipulated above, including citizens of Australia, must have two documents:

- a valid **passport,** with an expiration date at least six months later than the scheduled end of the visit to the U.S.; and
- a **tourist visa,** available without charge from the nearest U.S. consulate. To obtain a visa, the traveler must submit a completed application form (either in person or by mail) with a $1^1/_2$-inch square photo and demonstrate binding ties to a residence abroad.

Usually you can obtain a visa at once or within 24 hours, but it may take longer during the summer rush from June to August. If you cannot go in person, contact the nearest U.S. embassy or consulate for directions on applying by mail. Your travel agent or airline office may also be able to provide you with visa applications and instructions. The U.S. consulate or embassy that issues your visa will determine whether you will be issued a multiple- or single-entry visa and any restrictions regarding the length of your stay.

MEDICAL REQUIREMENTS   No inoculations are needed to enter the United States unless you are coming from, or have stopped over in, areas known to be suffering from epidemics, particularly cholera or yellow fever.

If you have a disease requiring treatment with medications containing narcotics or drugs requiring a syringe, carry a valid signed prescription from your physician to allay any suspicions that you are smuggling drugs.

CUSTOMS REQUIREMENTS   Every adult visitor may bring in free of duty: one liter of wine or hard liquor; 200 cigarettes or 100 cigars (but no cigars from Cuba) or three pounds of smoking tobacco; $100 worth of gifts. These exemptions are offered to travelers who spend at least 72 hours in the United States and who have not claimed them within the preceding six months. It is altogether forbidden to bring into the country foodstuffs (particularly cheese, fruit, cooked meats, and canned goods) and plants (vegetables, seeds, tropical plants, and so on). Foreign tourists may bring in or take out up to $10,000 in U.S. or foreign currency with no formalities; larger sums must be declared to Customs on entering or leaving.

Insurance

There is no national health system in the United States. Because the cost of medical care is extremely high, we strongly advise every traveler to secure health coverage before setting out.

You may want to take out a comprehensive travel policy that covers (for a relatively low premium) sickness or injury costs (medical, surgical, and hospital); loss or theft of your baggage; trip-cancellation costs; guarantee of bail in case you are arrested; costs of accident, repatriation, or death. Such packages (for example, "Europe Assistance" in Europe) are sold by automobile clubs at attractive rates, as well as by insurance companies and travel agencies.

Money

CURRENCY & EXCHANGE   The U.S. monetary system has a decimal base: one American **dollar ($1)** = 100 **cents** (100¢).

Dollar bills commonly come in $1 ("a buck"), $5, $10, $20, $50, and $100 denominations (the last two are not welcome when paying for small purchases and are not accepted in taxis or at subway ticket booths). There are also $2 bills (seldom encountered).

There are six denominations of coins: 1¢ (one cent or "penny"), 5¢ (five cents or "a nickel"), 10¢ (ten cents or "a dime"), 25¢ (twenty-five cents or "a quarter"), 50¢ (fifty cents or "a half dollar"), and the rare $1 piece.

TRAVELER'S CHECKS   Traveler's checks denominated in U.S. dollars are readily accepted at most hotels, motels, restaurants, and large stores. But the best place to change traveler's checks is at a bank. Do not bring traveler's checks denominated in other currencies.

CREDIT CARDS   The method of payment most widely used is the credit card: VISA (BarclayCard in Britain), Mastercard (EuroCard in Europe, Access in Britain, Chargex in Canada), American Express, Diners Club, Discover, and Carte Blanche. You can save yourself trouble by using "plastic money" rather than cash or traveler's checks in most hotels, motels, restaurants, and retail stores (a growing number of food and liquor stores now accept credit cards). You must have a credit card to rent a car. It can also be used as proof of identity (often carrying more weight than a passport), or as a "cash card," enabling you to draw money from banks that accept them.

Note: The "foreign-exchange bureaus" so common in Europe are rare even at airports in the United States, and nonexistent outside major cities. Try to avoid having to change foreign money, or traveler's checks denominated other than in U.S. dollars, at a small-town bank, or even a branch in a big city; in fact, leave any currency other than U.S. dollars at home—it may prove more nuisance to you than it's worth.

Safety

GENERAL While tourist areas are generally safe, crime is on the increase everywhere, and U.S. urban areas tend to be less safe than those in Europe or Japan. Visitors should always stay alert. This is particularly true of large U.S. cities. It is wise to ask the city's or area's tourist office if you're in doubt about which neighborhoods are safe. Avoid deserted areas, especially at night. Don't go into any city park at night unless there is an event that attracts crowds—for example, New York City's concerts in the parks. Generally speaking, you can feel safe in areas where there are many people, and many open establishments.

Avoid carrying valuables with you on the street, and don't display expensive cameras or electronic equipment. Hold on to your pocketbook, and place your billfold in an inside pocket. In theaters, restaurants, and other public places, keep your possessions in sight.

Remember also that hotels are open to the public, and in a large hotel, security may not be able to screen everyone entering. Always lock your room door—don't assume that once inside your hotel you are automatically safe and no longer need be aware of your surroundings.

DRIVING Safety while driving is particularly important. Question your rental agency about personal safety, or ask for a brochure of traveler safety tips when you pick up your car. Obtain written directions, or a map with the route marked in red, from the agency showing how to get to your destination. And, if possible, arrive and depart during daylight hours.

Recently more and more crime has involved cars and drivers. If you drive off a highway into a doubtful neighborhood, leave the area as quickly as possible. If you have an accident, even on the highway, stay in your car with the doors locked until you assess the situation or until the police arrive. If you are bumped from behind on the street or are involved in a minor accident with no injuries and the situation appears to be suspicious, motion to the other driver to follow you. *Never* get out of your car in such situations. You can also keep a pre-made sign in your car which reads: PLEASE FOLLOW THIS VEHICLE TO REPORT THE ACCIDENT. Show the sign to the other driver and go directly to the nearest police precinct, well-lighted service station, or all-night store.

If you see someone on the road who indicates a need for help, do *not* stop. Take note of the location, drive on to a well-lighted area, and telephone the police by dialing **911.**

Park in well-lighted, well-traveled areas if possible. Always keep your car doors locked, whether attended or unattended. Look around you before you get out of your car, and never leave any packages or valuables in sight. If someone attempts to rob you or steal your car, do *not* try to resist the thief/carjacker—report the incident to the police department immediately.

You may wish to contact the local tourist information bureau in your destination before you arrive. They may be able to provide you with a safety brochure.

2 Getting To and Around the U.S.

Travelers from overseas can take advantage of the **APEX (Advance Purchase Excursion) fares** offered by all the major U.S. and European carriers. Aside from these, attractive values are offered by **Icelandair** on flights from Luxembourg to New York and by **Virgin Atlantic Airways** from London to New York/Newark.

Some large American airlines (for example, TWA, American Airlines, Northwest, United, and Delta) offer travelers on their transatlantic or transpacific flights special discount tickets under the name **Visit USA,** allowing travel between any U.S. destinations at minimum rates. They are not on sale in the United States, and must, therefore, be purchased before you leave your foreign point of departure. This system is the best, easiest, and fastest way to see the United States at low cost. You should obtain information well in advance from your travel agent or the office of the airline concerned, since the conditions attached to these discount tickets can be changed without advance notice.

The visitor arriving by air, no matter what the port of entry, should cultivate patience and resignation before setting foot on U.S. soil. Getting through Immigration control may take as long as two hours on some days, especially summer weekends. Add the time it takes to clear Customs and you'll see that you should make very generous allowance for delay in planning connections between international and domestic flights—an average of two to three hours at least.

In contrast, travelers arriving by car or by rail from Canada will find border-crossing formalities streamlined to the vanishing point. And air travelers from Canada, Bermuda, and some places in the Caribbean can sometimes go through Customs and Immigration at the point of departure, which is much quicker and less painful.

For further information about travel to Atlanta, see "Getting There" in Chapter 2, and "Arriving" in Chapter 4, Section 1.

International visitors can also buy a **USA Railpass,** good for 15 or 30 days of unlimited travel on Amtrak. The pass is available through many foreign travel agents. Prices in 1994 for a 15-day pass are $208 off-peak, $308 peak; a 30-day pass costs $309 off-peak, $389 peak. (With a foreign passport, you can also buy passes at some Amtrak offices in the U.S., including locations in San Francisco, Los Angeles, Chicago, New York, Miami, Boston, and Washington, D.C.) Reservations are generally required and should be made for each part of your trip as early as possible.

Visitors should also be aware of the limitations of long-distance rail travel in the U.S. With a few notable exceptions (for instance, the Northeast Corridor line between Boston and Washington, D.C.), service is rarely up to European standards: delays are common, routes are limited and often infrequently served, and fares are rarely significantly lower than discount airfares. Thus, cross-country train travel should be approached with caution.

The cheapest way to travel the U.S. is by **bus.** Greyhound, the nation's nationwide bus line, offers an **Ameripass** for unlimited travel for 7 days (for $250), 15 days (for $350), and 30 days (for $450). Bus travel in the U.S. can be both slow and uncomfortable, so this option is not for everyone.

Fast Facts: For the Foreign Traveler

Automobile Organizations   Auto clubs will supply maps, suggested routes, guidebooks, accident and bail-bond insurance, and emergency road service. The major auto club in the United States, with 955 offices nationwide, is the American Automobile Association (AAA). Members of some foreign auto clubs have reciprocal arrangements with the AAA and enjoy its services at no charge. If you belong to an auto club, inquire about AAA reciprocity before you leave. The AAA can provide you with an International Driving Permit validating your foreign license. You may be able to join the AAA even if you are not a member of a reciprocal club. To inquire, call toll free **800/336-4357**. In addition, some automobile rental agencies now provide these services, so you should inquire about their availability when you rent your car.

Automobile Rentals   To rent a car you need a major credit card. A valid driver's license is required, and you usually need to be at least 25. Some companies do rent to younger people but add a daily surcharge. Be sure to return your car with the same amount of gas you started out with; rental companies charge excessive prices for gasoline. All of the major car rental companies are represented in Atlanta. Atlanta Rent-A-Car (☎ **404/763-1160**) offers particularly low prices (see Chapter 4, Section 2 for details).

Business Hours   Offices are usually open Monday through Friday from 9am to 5pm. Banks are open Monday through Friday from 9am to 3pm and sometimes on Saturday mornings. The post office is open Monday through Friday from 8:30am to 5pm and on Saturday from 8:30am to noon. Shops are generally open from 10am to 5 or 6pm. Those in malls tend to stay open late, to about 9pm Monday through Saturday and until 5 or 6pm on Sunday. Museum days and hours of operation vary (see individual listings in Chapter 7, "What to See and Do in Atlanta").

Climate   See "When to Go" in Chapter 2.

Currency   See "Money" in "Preparing for Your Trip," above.

Currency Exchange You will find currency exchange services in major airports with international service. Elsewhere, they may be quite difficult to come by. In New York, a very reliable choice is Thomas Cook Currency Services, Inc.,which has been in business since 1841 and offers a wide range of services. They also sell commission-free foreign and U.S. traveler's checks, drafts, and wire transfers; they also do check collections (including Eurochecks). Their rates are competitive and service excellent. They maintain several offices in New York City (☎ for the Fifth Avenue office is **212/757-6915**), at the JFK Airport International Arrivals Terminal (☎ **718/656-8444**), and at La Guardia Airport in the Delta terminal (☎ **718/533-0784**).

Drinking Laws See "Liquor Laws" in "Fast Facts: Atlanta," Chapter 4.

Electricity The United States uses 110-120 volts, 60 cycles, compared to 220-240 volts, 50 cycles, as in most of Europe. In addition to a 100-volt converter, small appliances of non-American manufacture, such as hairdryers or shavers, will require a plug adapter, with two flat, parallel pins.

Embassies & Consulates All embassies are located in the national capital, Washington, D.C.; some consulates are located in major cities, and most nations have a mission to the United Nations in New York City. Foreign visitors can obtain telephone numbers for their embassies and consulates by calling "Information" in Washington, D.C. (☎ **202/555-1212**).

Nations with official consulates in Atlanta include: Canadian Consulate General, Suite 400, South Tower, One CNN Center, Atlanta, GA 30303 (☎ **404/577-1512**); Consulate of France, 285 Peachtree Center Avenue, Suite 2800, Atlanta, GA 30303 (☎ **404/522-4226**); Consulate General of the Federal Republic of Germany, 229 Peachtree Street NE, Suite 1000, Atlanta, GA 30303-1618 (☎ **404/659-4760**); British Consulate General, 245 Peachtree Center Avenue, Marquis One Tower, Suite 2700, Atlanta, GA 30303 (☎ **404/527-5762**); Consulate General of Japan, 400 Colony Square, Suite 2000, Atlanta, GA 30361 (☎ **404/892-2700**), and the Consulate of Mexico, One CNN Center, 410 South Omni International, Atlanta, GA 30303 (☎ **404/688-3258**). For complete information, contact the Atlanta Chamber of Commerce, International Dept., P.O. Box 1740, Atlanta, GA 30301 (☎ **404/586-8470**).

Emergencies In all major cities (including Atlanta), you can call the police, an ambulance, or the fire department through the single emergency telephone number **911.** Another useful way of reporting an emergency is to call the telephone-company operator by dialing **0.**

See also listing for the Travelers Aid Society in Chapter 4 under "Tourist Information."

Gasoline [Petrol]   One U.S. gallon equals 3.75 liters, while 1.2 U.S. gallons equals one Imperial gallon. You'll notice there are several grades (and price levels) of gasoline available at most gas stations. And you'll also notice that their names change from company to company. The unleaded ones with the highest octane are the most expensive (most rental cars take the least expensive "regular" unleaded) and leaded gas is the least expensive, but only older cars can take this any more, so check if you're not sure.

Holidays   On the following legal national holidays, banks, government offices, post offices, and many stores, restaurants, and museums are closed:

January 1 (New Year's Day)
Third Monday in January (Martin Luther King Day)
Third Monday in February (Presidents Day, Washington's Birthday)
Last Monday in May (Memorial Day)
July 4 (Independence Day)
First Monday in September (Labor Day)
Second Monday in October (Columbus Day)
November 11 (Veteran's Day/Armistice Day)
Last Thursday in November (Thanksgiving Day)
December 25 (Christmas)
Finally, the Tuesday following the first Monday in November is Election Day, and is a legal holiday in presidential-election years.

Languages   Major hotels may have multilingual employees. Unless your language is very obscure, they can usually supply a translator on request.

Legal Aid   The foreign tourist, unless positively identified as a member of the Mafia or of a drug ring, will probably never become involved with the American legal system. If you are pulled up for a minor infraction (for example, of the highway code, such as speeding), never attempt to pay the fine directly to a police officer; you may wind up arrested on the much more serious charge of attempted bribery. Pay fines by mail, or directly into the hands of the clerk of the court. If accused of a more serious offense, it's wise to say and do nothing before consulting a lawyer. Under U.S. law, an arrested person is allowed one telephone call to a party of his or her choice. Call your embassy or consulate.

Mail   If you want your mail to follow you on your vacation and you aren't sure of your address, your mail can be sent to you, in your name, c/o General Delivery at the main post office of the city or region where you expect to be. The addressee must pick it up in person and produce proof of identity (driver's license, credit card, passport, etc.).

Generally to be found at intersections, mailboxes are blue with a red-and-white stripe and carry the inscription U.S. MAIL. If your mail is addressed to a U.S. destination, don't forget to add the five-figure postal code, or ZIP (Zone Improvement Plan) Code, after the two-letter abbreviation of the state to which the mail is addressed (CA for California, FL for Florida, NY for New York, and so on).

Multilingual Visitor Assistance   Under the auspices of the Georgia Council for International Visitors is a language bank of about 45 languages. If you need a translator, interpreter, or tour guide who speaks your language, call **404/873-6170.** The office is open Monday to Friday from 9am to 5pm.

Newspapers and Magazines   With a few exceptions, such as the *New York Times, USA Today,* the *Wall Street Journal,* and the *Christian Science Monitor,* daily newspapers in the United States are local, not national.

There are also innumerable newsweeklies like *Newsweek, Time,* and *U.S. News & World Report,* as well as specialized periodicals, such as the monthly magazines devoted to a single city. In Atlanta, the major daily is the *Atlanta Journal-Constitution.* The city magazine is called *Atlanta.*

The airmail editions of foreign newspapers and magazines are on sale only belatedly, and only at airports and international bookstores in the largest cities.

Radio and Television   Audiovisual media, with three coast-to-coast networks—ABC, CBS, and NBC—joined in recent years by the Public Broadcasting System (PBS) and the cable network CNN, play a major part in American life. In the big cities, televiewers have a choice of about a dozen channels (including the UHF channels), most of them transmitting 24 hours a day, without counting the pay-TV channels showing recent movies or sports events. In smaller communities, the choice may be limited to four TV channels (there are 1,200 in the entire country), and a half dozen local radio stations (there are 6,500 in all), each broadcasting a particular kind of music—classical, country, jazz, pop, or gospel—punctuated by news broadcasts and frequent commercials.

Safety   See "Safety" in "Preparing for Your Trip," above.

Taxes   In the United States there is no VAT (Value-Added Tax) or other indirect tax at a national level. Every state, and each city in it, has the right to levy its own local tax on all purchases, including hotel and restaurant checks, airline tickets, and so on. In Atlanta hotel tax is 13%. That includes room tax (7%) and sales tax (6%).

Telephone, Telegraph, Telex   The telephone system in the U.S. is run by private corporations, so rates, especially for long distance service, can vary widely—even on calls made from public telephones. Local calls in the U.S. usually cost 25¢.

Generally, hotel surcharges on long-distance and local calls are astronomical. You are usually better off using a public pay telephone, which you will find clearly marked in most public buildings and private establishments as well as on the street. Outside metropolitan areas, public telephones are more difficult to find. Stores and gas stations are your best bet.

Most long-distance and international calls can be dialed directly from any phone. For calls to Canada and other parts of the U.S., dial 1 followed by the area code and the seven-digit number. For international calls, dial 011 followed by the country code, city code, and the telephone number of the person you wish to call.

For reversed-charge or collect calls, and for person-to-person calls, dial 0 (zero, *not* the letter "O") followed by the area code and number you want; an operator will then come on the line, and you should specify that you are calling collect, or person-to-person, or both. If your operator-assisted call is international, ask for the overseas operator.

For local directory assistance ("information"), dial **411;** for long-distance information, dial 1, then the appropriate area code and **555-1212.**

Like the telephone system, telegraph and telex services are provided by private corporations like ITT, MCI, and above all, Western Union, the most important. You can bring your telegram in to the nearest Western Union office (there are hundreds across the country), or dictate it over the phone (a toll-free call, **800/325-6000**). You can also telegraph money, or have it telegraphed to you, very quickly over the Western Union system.

Telephone Directory   There are two kinds of telephone directories available to you. The general directory is the so-called White Pages, in which private and business subscribers are listed in alphabetical order. The inside front cover lists the emergency number for police, fire, and ambulance, and other vital numbers (like the Coast Guard, poison-control center, crime-victims hotline, and so on). The first few pages are devoted to community-service numbers, including a guide to long-distance and international calling, complete with country codes and area codes.

The second directory, printed on yellow paper (hence its name, Yellow Pages), lists all local services, businesses, and industries by type of activity, with an index at the back. The listings cover not only such obvious items as automobile repairs by make of car, or drugstores (pharmacies), often by geographical location, but also restaurants by type of cuisine and geographical location, bookstores by special subject and/or language, places of worship by religious denomination, and other information that the tourist might otherwise not readily find. The Yellow Pages also include city plans or detailed area maps, often showing postal ZIP Codes and public transportation routes.

Time   The United States is divided into four time zones (six, if Alaska and Hawaii are included). From east to west, these are: eastern standard time (EST), central standard time (CST), mountain standard time (MST), Pacific standard time (PST), Alaska standard time (AST), and Hawaii standard time (HST). Always keep changing time zones in mind if you are traveling (or even telephoning) long distances in the United States. For example, noon in New York City (EST) is 11am in Chicago (CST), 10am in Denver (MST), 9am in Los Angeles (PST), 8am in Anchorage (AST), and 7am in Honolulu (HST).

"Daylight saving time" is in effect from the last Sunday in April through the last Saturday in October (actually, the change is made at 2am on Sunday) except in Arizona, Hawaii, part of Indiana, and Puerto Rico. Daylight saving time moves the clock one hour ahead of standard time.

Tipping   This is part of the American way of life, on the principle that you must expect to pay for any service you get. Here are some rules of thumb:

> Bartenders: 10%–15%.
> Bellhops: at least 50¢ per piece; $2–$3 for a lot of baggage.
> Cab drivers: 15% of the fare.
> Cafeterias, fast-food restaurants: no tip.
> Chambermaids: $1 a day.
> Checkroom attendants (restaurants, theaters): $1 per garment.
> Cinemas, movies, theaters: no tip.
> Doormen (hotels or restaurants): not obligatory.
> Gas-station attendants: no tip.
> Hairdressers: 15%–20%.
> Redcaps (airport and railroad station): at least 50¢ per piece, $2–$3 for a lot of baggage.
> Restaurants, nightclubs: 15%–20% of the check.
> Sleeping-car porters: $2–$3 per night to your attendant.
> Valet parking attendants: $1.

Toilets   Foreign visitors often complain that public toilets are hard to find in most U.S. cities. True, there are none on the streets, but the visitor can usually find one in a bar, restaurant, hotel, museum, department store, or service station—and it will probably be clean (although the last-mentioned sometimes leaves much to be desired). Note, however, a growing practice in some restaurants and bars of displaying a notice that "toilets are for the use of patrons only." You can ignore this sign, or better yet, avoid arguments by paying for a cup of coffee or soft drink, which will qualify you as a patron. The cleanliness of toilets at railroad stations and bus depots may be more open to question, and some public places are equipped with pay toilets, which require you to insert one or more coins into a slot on the door before it will open.

The American System of Measurements ——————

Length

1 inch (in.)	=	2.54cm					
1 foot (ft.)	=	12 in.	=	30.48cm	=	.305m	
1 yard	=	3 ft.			=	.915m	
1 mile (mi.)	=	5,280 ft.					= 1.609km

To convert miles to kilometers, multiply the number of miles by 1.61 (for example, 50 mi. × 1.61 = 80.5km). Note that this conversion can be used to convert speeds from miles per hour (m.p.h.) to kilometers per hour (km/h).

To convert kilometers to miles, multiply the number of kilometers by .62 (for example, 25km × .62 = 15.5 mi.). Note that this same conversion can be used to convert speeds from kilometers per hour to miles per hour.

Capacity

1 fluid ounce (fl. oz.)			=	.03 liters	
1 pint	=	16 fl. oz.	=	.47 liters	
1 quart	=	2 pints	=	.94 liters	
1 gallon (gal.)	=	4 quarts	=	3.79 liters	= .83 Imperial gal.

To convert U.S. gallons to liters, multiply the number of gallons by 3.79 (example, 12 gal. × 3.79 = 45.58 liters.)

To convert U.S. gallons to Imperial gallons, multiply the number of U.S. gallons by .83 (example, 12 U.S. gal. × .83 = 9.95 Imperial gal.).

To convert liters to U.S. gallons, multiply the number of liters by .26 (example, 50 liters × .26 = 13 U.S. gal.).

To convert Imperial gallons to U.S. gallons, multiply the number of Imperial gallons by 1.2 (example, 8 Imperial gal. × 1.2 = 9.6 U.S. gal.).

Weight

1 ounce (oz.)			= 28.35 g		
1 pound (lb.)	= 16 oz.		= 453.6 g	= .45 kg	
1 ton			= 2,000 lb.	= 907 kg	= .91 metric tons

To convert pounds to kilograms, multiply the number of pounds by .45 (example, 90 lb. × .45 = 40.5kg).

To convert kilograms to pounds, multiply the number of kilos by 2.2 (example, 75kg × 2.2 = 165 lb.).

Area

1 acre			=	.41 ha		
1 square mile (sq. mi.)	=	640 acres	=	2.59 ha	=	2.6km²

To convert acres to hectares, multiply the number of acres by .41 (example, 40 acres × .41 = 16.4ha).

To convert square miles to square kilometers, multiply the number of square miles by 2.6 (example, 80 sq. mi. × 26 = 208km²).

To convert hectares to acres, multiply the number of hectares by 2.47 (example, 20ha × 2.47 = 49.4 acres).

To convert square kilometers to square miles, multiply the number of square kilometers by .39 (example, 150km² × .39 = 58.5 sq. mi.).

Temperature

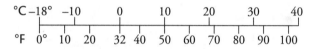

To convert degrees Fahrenheit to degrees Celsius, subtract 32 from °F, multiply by 5, then divide by 9 (example, 85°F – 32 × 5/9 = 29.4°C).

To convert degrees Celsius to degrees Fahrenheit, multiply °C by 9, divide by 5, and add 32 (example, 20°C × 9/5 + 32 = 68°F).

4

Getting to Know Atlanta

1	Orientation	50
2	Getting Around	54
•	Fast Facts: Atlanta	56

ATLANTA IS A FAIRLY COMPACT CITY RATHER THAN A SPRAWLING METROPOLIS. After a few days in town, you'll know your way around.

1 Orientation

Arriving

In the International Gateway City, transportation is state-of-the-art and getting to your hotel from plane, train, or bus is a cinch.

BY AIR Hartsfield Atlanta International Airport is just 10 miles south of downtown. It's a beautiful and well-planned airport, with ample parking space (and low parking charges), retail shops, facilities for the handicapped, and banking and currency-exchange facilities.

There are several options for getting from the airport to your hotel. The cheapest, if your luggage is manageable, is to take Atlanta's subway (MARTA), which has a stop right in the airport. The fare is just $1.25. Almost all hotels are very close to MARTA rail stations.

A taxi from the airport to a downtown hotel costs $15 for one passenger, $8 each for two or more. To midtown and Buckhead hotels, the fare is $25 for one passenger, $26 for two, $9 each for three or more.

Atlanta Airport Shuttle Vans (☎ **524-3400** or toll free ☎ **800/842-2770**) operate between the airport and most downtown and midtown hotels. They depart from the Delta baggage claim/ground transportation area in the South Terminal. You can catch one about every 30 minutes in either direction from 7am to 11pm seven days a week. Cost is $8 one way, $14 round trip; children under 5 ride free. It's a very well organized system, with destinations clearly marked and helpful attendants on hand. Vans also ply the route between the airport and Buckhead hotels. Cost is $12 one way, $20 round trip, free for children under 5. Some properties further afield are also served. Call **768-7600** or toll free **800/277-1165** for information about transport to suburban locations. When you leave Atlanta, check with your hotel desk about departure times; for some hotels, reservations are required a day in advance.

BY TRAIN **Amtrak** trains arrive in Atlanta at 1688 Peachtree Street, just off I-85. From this very central location, you can take a taxi to your hotel or to the nearest MARTA station (Arts Center). For information, call **800/USA-RAIL.**

BY BUS The **Greyhound** bus terminal, 81 International Blvd. at Williams Street, is in the heart of downtown. The Peachtree Center MARTA station is about two blocks away, and taxis are available. For information, call **404/384-9651** or **800/231-2222.**

Tourist Information

For information about hotels, restaurants, and attractions, contact the **Atlanta Convention & Visitors Bureau (ACVB),** 233 Peachtree St. NE, Suite 2000, Atlanta 30303 (☎ **404/222-6688**). Call or write in advance to obtain a copy of *Atlanta Now* (the official visitor's guide), a *Metro Atlanta Attractions Guide,* a map, a book of discounts, and a 2-month calendar of events. You can call weekdays between 8:30am and 5:30pm. May 1 through December 25 you can also call a toll free 24-hour number (**800/ATLANTA**) for an informational recording.

In town, you can visit ACVB information centers at:

Peachtree Center Mall, 231 Peachtree St. Open Monday to Friday 10am to 5pm. No phone.

Lenox Square, 3393 Peachtree Rd. Open Monday to Friday 10am to 5pm. No phone.

Underground Atlanta, 65 Upper Alabama St. (☎ **404/577-2148**). Open Monday to Saturday 10am to 9:30pm, Sunday noon to 6pm.

Hartsfield Atlanta International Airport, near the car rental booths between the north and south baggage claim areas. Open Monday to Saturday 9am to 9pm, Sunday noon to 6pm. No phone.

FOR TROUBLED TRAVELERS   The **Travelers Aid Society** is a nationwide network of voluntary nonprofit social-service agencies providing help to travelers in difficulty. This might include anything from crisis counseling to straightening out ticket mix-ups, not to mention illness, car breakdowns, reuniting families accidentally separated while traveling, or locating missing relatives (sometimes just at the wrong airport).

In Atlanta, Travelers Aid has offices at the airport (☎ **766-4511**) open daily 10am to 6pm; at the Greyhound Bus Terminal, 81 International Blvd. at Williams St. (☎ **404/527-7411**) open Monday to Friday noon to 8pm, Saturday 10am to 6pm; and at 40 Pryor St. SW, at Marietta St. (☎ **527-7400**, a 24-hour number) open Monday to Friday 8am to 5pm.

City Layout

Atlanta is girded by a beltway called I-285, always referred to as the Perimeter. As a tourist, you'll be spending most of your time within the confines of the Perimeter. Two interstate highways (I-75 and I-85) converge just above the airport and proceed north, forking off just northwest of Piedmont Park: I-75 goes west, I-85 east. A fourth interstate highway just below the downtown area, I-20, is an east-west artery that cuts all the way through Georgia (and Atlanta), connecting South Carolina with Alabama.

As for the major streets, there's a joke that all directions here begin with "Go to Peachtree...." That's because there are a few dozen Peachtrees—Peachtree Street, Lane, Road, Avenue, Circle, Drive, Plaza, and Way, not to mention West Peachtree Street, Peachtree Industrial Boulevard, Peachtree Memorial Drive, Peachtree Battle Avenue, Peachtree Valley Road, etc., etc., etc. So be sure to emphasize which Peachtree you're looking for when you ask for directions. That being said, Peachtree Street (which becomes Peachtree Road above midtown) and Piedmont Avenue are Atlanta's two major north-south arteries. Peachtree is a two-way thoroughfare, while Piedmont has two-way traffic above 14th Street, but south-to-north only below

14th Street. Major east-west streets include Memorial Drive, North Avenue, Ponce de Leon Avenue, 14th Street, and, in Buckhead, East and West Paces Ferry drives. With map in hand, you'll find getting around Atlanta very easily.

ATLANTA NEIGHBORHOODS IN BRIEF You can't really get the feel of a city until you understand the characteristics of its neighborhoods. Herewith, a brief rundown of Atlanta's diverse districts.

Downtown Atlanta's financial and business hub, this beautifully planned area of sleek skyscrapers includes the futuristic Peachtree Center hotel/convention center/trade mart/office-tower complex. Here, too: Underground Atlanta, an exciting mix of shops, restaurants, and nightclubs fronted by a 138-foot light tower; Omni Coliseum, featuring sports action and big-name entertainment; the mammoth Georgia World Congress Center, one of the largest meeting and exhibition halls in the nation; the 71,500-seat Georgia Dome, built for Olympic events and Super Bowl XXVIII; CNN Center, Ted Turner's media HQ; Georgia-Pacific Center, housing the downtown branch of the High Museum of Art; the golden-domed, century-old State Capitol, a major landmark; the downtown branch of the Atlanta Historical Society; and the SciTrek Museum. In the general area are Oakland Cemetery (it's mentioned in *Gone With the Wind,* and Margaret Mitchell is one of the many notables buried here) and Grant Park (the zoo and Cyclorama). This is a downtown that pulsates with big-city excitement, but its scale is human—and you can still find a place to park.

Sweet Auburn This famous black neighborhood, also called the Martin Luther King, Jr., Historic District, is just below downtown's central area. Under the auspices of the National Park Service, it was designated a park in 1980 to honor King, whose boyhood home, crypt, and church are located here. In spite of the yoke of segregation, affluent black businesspeople and professionals flourished here from the early part of the 20th century through the 1950s. Today it's one of Atlanta's major sightseeing draws.

Midtown Though its boundaries have never been definitively decided, midtown basically encompasses the area north of downtown from about Ponce de Leon Avenue to 26th Street. It includes Piedmont Park, Atlanta's major recreation area; the Woodruff Arts Center, home of the Atlanta Symphony Orchestra, the Alliance Theatre, and the High Museum of Art; the famed Fox Theatre, a 1920s Moorish-motif movie palace; Ansley Park, a 230-acre residential greenbelt area, designed at the turn of the century by Frederick Law Olmsted; and Colony Square, an office/hotel/retail complex. AT&T, IBM, and Southern Bell maintain corporate offices in midtown.

Buckhead Named for an 1838 tavern called the Buck's Head, this is Atlanta's silk-stocking district—one of America's most beautiful and affluent communities. It begins about 6 miles north of

City Layout

0 ━━━━ 1 km
  ━━━━ .6 mi
N

Northside Dr.

Piedmont Rd.

Roswell Rd.

Peachtree Rd.

W. Paces Ferry Rd.

BUCKHEAD

E. Paces Ferry Rd.

Peachtree Rd.

E. Paces Ferry Rd.

Piedmont Rd.

Lenox Rd.

Buckhead

↓ 3 miles to Atlanta

3 miles to Buckhead ↑

Atlanta

75 85

Northside Dr.

Spring St.

Piedmont Ave.

MIDTOWN

Piedmont Park

VIRGINIA-HIGHLAND

Monroe Dr.

Georgia Institute of Technology

W. Peachtree St.

Peachtree St.

Ponce de Leon Ave.

North Ave.

North Ave.

Marietta St.

Piedmont Ave.

Boulevard

LITTLE FIVE POINTS

Highland Ave.

DeKalb Ave.

Spring St.

DOWNTOWN

SWEET AUBURN

To Decatur →

Decatur St.

Georgia State University

M. L. King, Jr., Dr.

Decatur St.

Peachtree

Oakland Cemetery

20

20

Capitol Ave.

Grant St.

Georgia Ave.

75 85

Grant Park

Boulevard

Atlanta Ave.

Atlanta Ave.

9278

downtown. Here you'll find tree-shaded residential areas of magnificent mansions surrounded by verdant acreage, elite shops and boutiques (including Lenox Square and Phipps Plaza malls, two exclusive shopping enclaves), superb restaurants, and first-class hotels. Buckhead is also a burgeoning business area. Its major sightseeing attraction is the Atlanta Historical Society, centered on a Palladian villa designed by noted architect Phillip Schutze and surrounded by 32 woodland acres. The Greek Revival Governor's Mansion is also in Buckhead.

Virginia-Highland   Every major American city has a district that claims kinship with New York's Greenwich Village. In Atlanta it's the Virginia-Highland section, so named for its central avenues, northeast of downtown. Here you'll find ethnic eateries, dozens of antique shops, bookstores, sidewalk cafés, art galleries, lively bars and bistros, and browsable shops selling everything from healing crystals to recycled clothing. Virginia-Highland is colorful, casual, and unpretentious.

Little Five Points   Just below Virginia-Highland, Little Five Points offers similar offbeat ambience and emporia. It is also the location of the Jimmy Carter Library/Carter Presidential Center, which opened in 1986 to house the correspondence and memorabilia of this Georgia-born president. Many Victorian homes make for an architecturally interesting stroll. The neighborhood is centered at the junction of Euclid and Moreland avenues.

Decatur   Founded in 1823 by Commodore Stephen Decatur, a dashing naval hero of the War of 1812 who died in a duel, this quaintly charming village centers on an old courthouse square. About a 15-minute drive east from downtown, Decatur is the scene of numerous annual events, festivals, and concerts, and it houses the sprawling Dekalb Farmer's Market, an international food market that must be seen to be believed. Like Virginia-Highland and Little Five Points, Decatur weaves color and texture into Atlanta's tapestry of neighborhoods.

2   Getting Around

If you're here for a few days, you'll get a pretty good feel for the layout of the city. It's not complicated. And getting around the city is easy and affordable.

By Public Transportation

The Metropolitan Atlanta Rapid Transit Authority (MARTA) operates an extensive and efficient subway and bus network, making it possible to reach just about any part of town by public transportation.

MARTA RAPID RAIL   MARTA's subway or rapid-rail service began in 1979. The stations are clean and safe, and it's a pleasure to use. Eventually, this will be a 61-mile, 45-station system. At press time, the rail system extends 38.6 miles and includes 33 stations. There are two lines: south-north Orange Line trains travel between the airport and Doraville; east-west Blue Line trains travel between Indian Creek (east of Decatur) and Hightower. The lines intersect at Five Points Station in downtown Atlanta. Fare is just $1.25 for any ride, payable in exact change, tokens, or TransCards. Tokens, available at the stations, cost $12 for ten. A weekly TransCard, available at the RideStore in the Five Points Station, good for unlimited bus and rail travel for one week, is $11.

MARTA trains generally arrive and depart every 8 to 10 minutes during operating hours: Monday to Saturday from 5am to 1am, Sunday and holidays from 6am to 12:30am. Free transfers are available between bus and rail when you board a bus or enter a rail station. Parking is free at all rail stations.

For MARTA schedule and route information, call **848-4711** Monday to Friday from 6am to 10pm, Saturday and Sunday from 8am to 4pm. For information regarding the elderly and the disabled, call **848-3340.**

BUSES   Basically, you can get anywhere in Atlanta by bus. MARTA buses operate on a 1,550-mile network of 150 routes. The fare system is the same as described above for rail service. To find out what bus to take, call **848-4711** for route information (same hours as above). Drivers do not carry change; you must have exact change, a token, a transfer, or a TransCard. Special shuttle buses operate from downtown in conjunction with major stadium sports events and conventions; call the above number for details.

By Taxi

Taxi fares are a bit complicated in Atlanta. In the so-called Downtown Zone (roughly east to west between Piedmont Avenue and Northside Drive, north to south from 14th Street to Ralph Abernathy Boulevard), you pay a flat rate of $4 for one or two passengers, $2 for each additional rider. That's fine if you're going from one end of this extensive zone to the other; unfortunately, though, you pay the same if you only go one block.

There's also a flat rate for rides between downtown and the airport: $15 for one passenger, $8 each for two or more. Between the airport and midtown or Buckhead, the rate is $25 for one passenger, $26 for two, $9 each for three or more.

Outside these specified zones, Atlanta cabs charge a $1.50 drop when you get in and 20¢ for each additional $\frac{1}{6}$ mile for the first passenger and a flat rate of $1 for each additional passenger, adult or child.

There are many taxi companies in town. If you need to call for a taxi, try Yellow Cabs (☎ **521-0200**) or Checker Cabs (☎ **351-1111**).

If you have a complaint about taxi service, call **658-7600.**

By Car

Atlanta's transit system (MARTA) is very good. However, a car is certainly a convenience, and, in most places you'll visit, parking isn't a problem. Given my druthers, I prefer to have one. All of the major car-rental companies are, of course, represented here and reachable via toll-free numbers.

I always rent from *Atlanta Rent-A-Car* (☎ **404/763-1160**), a local independently owned company that has been serving Atlanta for over 15 years. This company's rates are very low (I've yet to find lower), they stock a full range of compact and midsize cars and vans, and they offer friendly, competent service. They have 18 locations—including one close to the airport—and provide free courtesy pick-up anywhere in the city. At press time, Atlanta Rent-A-Car's compacts begin at just $19.95 a day with 100 free miles, $10 a day and 19¢ a mile with no free miles. The same car costs $99.95 a week with 500 free miles. It's always best to reserve in advance.

Fast Facts: Atlanta

Area Code   404.

Airport   Atlanta is served by the Hartsfield Atlanta International Airport, 10 miles south of downtown. It is the world's third-busiest airport and transfer hub. (Flights to just about everywhere are routed through the city; in fact, there's a saying, "Even if you fly to hell, you still have to go through Atlanta.")

Babysitters   Most hotels will arrange babysitters for you. If yours doesn't, a highly recommended service is A Friend of the Family (☎ **255-2848**). All of their sitters are carefully screened, bonded, and at least 21 years of age. On request, they can send someone who is also trained in CPR and first aid and/or who speaks a foreign language. You can interview the sitter in advance on the phone or in person. Rate is $6 to $8 per hour, with a 4-hour minimum, plus a $15 agency fee. Advance notice of 24 hours is appreciated but not required. A Friend of the Family also provides pet care and companions for adults.

Buses   See "Getting Around," above.

Car Rentals   See "Getting Around," above.

Climate   See "When to Go," in Chapter 2.

Dentists   The Georgia Dental Association of Atlanta (☎ **636-7553**), offers a free referral service. They'll refer you to a dentist close to your hotel, or if need be, one who can accommodate special needs (for example, a dentist who does cosmetic work, offers home visits or senior-citizen discounts, keeps emergency hours, or otherwise specializes). The service operates weekdays from 8:30am to 5pm. At other times, inquire at your hotel desk.

Doctors   The Medical Association of Atlanta (☎ 881-1714), with over 2,000 member physicians in town, runs a free referral service for every kind of medical specialty and subspecialty. Hours are Monday to Friday from 9am to 4pm. At other times, inquire at your hotel desk. (See also "Hospitals," below.)

Drinking Age   You must be at least 21 to consume liquor in Georgia. (See also, "Liquor Laws," below.)

Drugstores   Big B Drugs, 1061 Ponce de Leon Ave. at Highland Avenue (☎ 876-0381), is open 24 hours and offers full pharmaceutical services.

Emergencies   To report a fire, summon the police, or procure an ambulance, simply dial **911.** See also listing for the Travelers Aid Society in "Tourist Information," above.

Eyeglasses   Head over to Opti-World, in the Around Lenox Shopping Center (enter the Lenox Square Mall on Peachtree Road, just below Lenox Road, look for Neiman-Marcus, and veer to the right; ☎ 262-2020). This eyeglass department store offers 1-hour service on contacts and eyeglasses (including bifocals and trifocals), stocks the largest selection of frames in Atlanta (from designer to economy), provides on-premises eye examinations by independent doctors of optometry, maintains a complete contact-lens center, and gives 15% discounts to senior citizens and college students.

Hairdressers   To some of us, a gifted hairdresser can be the most essential of services. Stan Milton, 721 Miami Circle NE, off Piedmont Road (☎ 233-6241), is one of Atlanta's most talented and celebrated stylists. He's done dozens of makeovers for local TV personalities, and his devoted clientele comes from all over the South. He's wonderful at finding your optimum look. The salon also does a beautiful job on perms and hair coloring, and an excellent staff proffers every salon service—facials, manicures/pedicures, waxing, massage, video imaging (letting you see yourself in different styles before you take the plunge), and full days of beauty services. The salon is elegant but very relaxed and friendly. I appreciate Milton's commitment to the environment; he uses only products that are natural, chemical free, and biodegradable. While you're here, ask for a complimentary makeup application. Haircuts are $20 to $55 for women, $15 to $25 for men, and $10 to $15 for children. Perms are $45 to $65. Reserve as far in advance as possible.

Hospitals/Emergency Rooms   Piedmont Hospital, 1968 Peachtree Road, just above Collier Road (☎ 605-3297), offers 24-hour full emergency-room service. It also offers a free physician-referral service for all medical problems (☎ 605-3556) weekdays between 9am and 5pm.

Libraries   The Atlanta Fulton Public Library, 1 Margaret Mitchell Sq., at Forsyth Street and Carnegie Way (☎ 730-1700), is the city's central branch. In addition to the usual well-stocked library inventory, it has African-American records, books, and photographs; many books in Spanish; and city newspapers from all over the world. Two only-in-Atlanta library features are an extensive collection of first and rare editions of *Gone With the Wind* and a permanent exhibit on Margaret Mitchell. In addition, the library features frequent art exhibits, classes, films, lectures, and storytelling; inquire when you visit. Open Monday to Thursday from 9am to 9pm, Friday and Saturday from 9am to 6pm, and Sunday from 2 to 6pm.

Liquor Laws   No alcohol is served at bars, restaurants, or nightclubs between 2:55am Saturday and 12:30pm Sunday. The drinking age is 21.

Newspapers/Magazines   The major newspaper in town is the *Atlanta Journal-Constitution.* You'll also find it helpful to pick up a current issue of *Atlanta* magazine when you're in town; it has all the current theater, movie, club, gallery, and museum listings, among other informative data. And keep an eye out for *Creative Loafing,* an offbeat free publication available in shops, restaurants, and on the street; it offers much interesting info.

Police   See "Emergencies," above.

Population   2.8 million.

Road Conditions   Call 656-5267, a 24-hour number.

Taxis   Call Yellow Cabs (☎ 521-0200) or Checker Cabs (☎ 351-1111).

Tickets   For tickets to almost all sports and performing arts events, call Ticketmaster (☎ 249-6400).

Time   Call 603-3333. Atlanta is on Eastern Standard Time.

Transit Information   To find out how to get from point A to point B via MARTA (bus and rail), dial **848-4711.**

Weather   Call **603-3333.**

5

Atlanta Accommodations

1	Downtown	61
•	Frommer's Smart Traveler: Hotels	69
2	Midtown	73
•	Frommer's Cool for Kids: Hotels	73
3	Buckhead	86
4	Georgia's Stone Mountain	97
5	Druid Hills/Emory University/Brookhaven	99
6	Off I-20	101

As a major convention city, Atlanta is capable of accommodating vast numbers of visitors. It has 55,337 rooms at 340 properties (up from 29,000 rooms only 12 years ago). These accommodations exist at all levels; there are budget digs (though not as many as I'd like to see), bed-and-breakfast lodgings, and bastions of luxury. Presented below are my choices in all price brackets, each one offering excellent value in its category.

Note: Although 100% occupancy is a rarity in Atlanta, booking well in advance assures you a room in the hotel of your choice.

Savvy travelers can save considerably on hotel rates. Be sure to take advantage of weekend rates. Even top-of-the-line hotels often slash prices 30% to 50% on weekends—and at some properties "weekends" include Friday, Saturday, and Sunday nights. Always inquire about the availability of these rates when you reserve. That doesn't mean you can only travel on weekends; rather, you can usually get the lower rate for that segment of your stay. Be sure to verify that your reservation has been made at the weekend rate before hanging up the phone (if possible, request written confirmation), and check on it again when you register at the hotel. At many properties, you can't just show up at the desk for checkout Monday morning and expect to pay weekend rates; you have to be so registered in advance. In addition, weekend rates are often subject to availability, so reserving considerably in advance is advisable.

Also inquire about reduced-price packages (they may include extras such as meals, parking, theater tickets, and golf fees) and reduced rates for senior citizens, families, and active-duty military personnel.

Many preferential rates are available only when you reserve via toll-free reservation numbers. These numbers are supplied in all applicable listings below. Days Inns offer drastically reduced Super Saver rates if you reserve 30 days or more in advance (subject to availability).

Weekend and special rates aren't the whole picture. Keep in mind the perspective of the hotelier. A hotel makes zero dollars per night on an empty room. Hence, though they don't bruit it about (for obvious reasons), most hotels are willing to bargain on rates rather than leave a room unoccupied. Haggling won't work when hotels are running close to 100% occupancy, but whenever a rate is quoted it's a good idea to ask, "Can I get a better deal?" If the reservations clerk can't help you, ask to speak to the desk captain. I'm not saying you won't risk a snub or two, but those who persevere can nurse wounded feelings all the way to the bank. An especially advantageous time to secure lower rates is late afternoon or early evening on the day of your arrival, when a hotel's likelihood of filling up with full-price bookings is remote.

How to Read the Listings

The hotels listed below are divided first by location, then alphabetically by price category within a given district. Since most Atlanta attractions are within the downtown/midtown/Buckhead areas, almost all of the hotels here are in, or close to, those sections of town.

(See Stone Mountain listings for camping.) When within walking distance, the nearest MARTA subway stop is listed.

Hotels listed in the **budget** category are those charging $60 or less for a double room. Those with rates ranging from $60 to $85 are rated **inexpensive** (don't blame me, I didn't create inflation), $85 to $130 rooms make up the **moderate** grouping, $130 to $175 I've listed as **expensive,** and anything above that ranks as **very expensive.** Any extras included in the rates (for example, breakfast or other meals) are listed for each property. Add 13% hotel tax to the rates listed, and keep in mind that the prices quoted are subject to change. If you have a car, be sure to consider the price of parking in your hotel garage.

Bed & Breakfast

Bed & Breakfast Atlanta, 1801 Piedmont Ave. NE, Suite 208 (☎ **404/875-0525** or toll free **800/967-3224**), is a professional reservation service that carefully screens facilities in the Atlanta area. Their list comprises close to 100 homes and inns, all accommodations offering private bath. They include a turreted Queen Anne–style Victorian home with nine fireplaces near the Carter Library; a delightful honeymoon cottage with a Jacuzzi in "Miss Daisy's" Druid Hills; a 1930s bungalow near Piedmont Park; an elegant 1920s Tudor-style home in Buckhead, a fully furnished garden cottage in Ansley Park; and a sunny contemporary home with pool and sauna in the Emory University area. They even have kosher homes on their roster. And many additional B&B accommodations in all price ranges will be available to serve visitors during the 1996 Summer Olympics. Owners Madalyne Eplan and Paula Gris have been running B&B Atlanta since 1979. All rates include continental breakfast, in many cases extended considerably beyond the usual roll and coffee. Reserve as far in advance as possible for the greatest possible selection. Call during office hours, which are Monday to Friday from 9am to noon and 2 to 5pm.

The rates run the gamut from $52 to $240 (the latter for a luxurious Buckhead guest cottage on a four-acre estate that accommodates four people). Weekly and monthly rates are available (in guesthouses and apartments) for long-term visitors. There's no fee. American Express, MasterCard, and VISA are accepted.

Accommodations for the Olympics

See Chapter 11 (**About the Olympics**) for details on how to obtain accommodations during the games.

1 Downtown

Downtown hotels primarily cater to the business/convention traveler, but a tourist will also enjoy the services and facilities of these properties.

Very Expensive

Atlanta Hilton & Towers, 255 Courtland St., between Baker and
Harris Sts., Atlanta, GA 30303. ☎ **404/659–2000** or toll free
800/HILTONS. Fax 404/222–2868. 1,224 rms, 41 suites. A/C TV
TEL **MARTA:** Peachtree Center.

Rates: Sun–Thurs, $165–$185 single; $185–$205 double. Fri–Sat, $99
per room for up to four people (sometimes extended to include
additional nights in low season). Tower rooms $205 single; $225 double;
business-class rooms $125 single; $145 double. Extra person $20.
Children of any age free in parents' room. AE, CB, DC, MC, DISC, ER, V.
Parking: $9 valet, $8 self.

One of Atlanta's top convention hotels, with 104,000 square feet of
meeting and exhibit space, the Hilton is a glamorous downtown
enclave, with a plushly furnished lobby, paneled in rich mahogany.
A bank of glass elevators provides a futuristic note. Cheerfully
decorated rooms, in a variety of color schemes, offer AM/FM alarm-
clock radios, bedside and desk phones with two lines and computer
jacks, and remote-control cable TVs with free HBO, On-Command
Video pay-movie options, plus video checkout and account-review
functions. Many rooms have minibars.

A special floor of the Hilton is geared to business travelers, offering
speedy private registration, concierge services, nightly bed turndown,
in-room bars/refreshment centers, and complimentary continental
breakfast in a private lounge.

The above services are also featured in the Tower section of the
hotel. Here the lounge is even more luxurious and provides panoramic
downtown views. In addition to continental breakfast, Tower guests
enjoy complimentary cocktail-hour hors d'oeuvres in the lounge and
superior in-room amenities.

Dining/Entertainment: The Hilton's premier restaurant is the
very highly acclaimed Nikolai's Roof, a 30th-floor dining room offering spectacular skyline vistas. It evokes the opulent reign of Tsar
Nicholas II, who employed the most brilliant chefs of France. Only
multicourse prix-fixe dinners are offered. Trader Vic's, a South Seas–
Polynesian restaurant found at numerous Hiltons, here offers its
exotic signature setting of tapa-bark walls, thatched roofing, and
primitive carvings. Potent rum drinks are a specialty. It's open for
dinner nightly and weekday dim sum lunches. The Garden Terrace,
a very pretty lobby-level eatery centered around a vast fountain, serves
buffet meals at breakfast and lunch and Sunday champagne brunch.
Adjoining it are the Cafe Express Deli (a 24-hour facility) and Le
Café, the Hilton's casual dining facility, open daily from 6am to 2am.
There's live music nightly at the Bogart-and-Bergman-themed
Casablanca Bar. It offers billiards, happy-hour hors d'oeuvres, and a
large-screen TV on which sports events are aired. Finally, there's
Another World, a plush disco adjoining Nikolai's.

Services: Room service from 6am to 2am, nightly bed turndown
on request, babysitting, lobby information desk, valet parking.

Downtown Accommodations

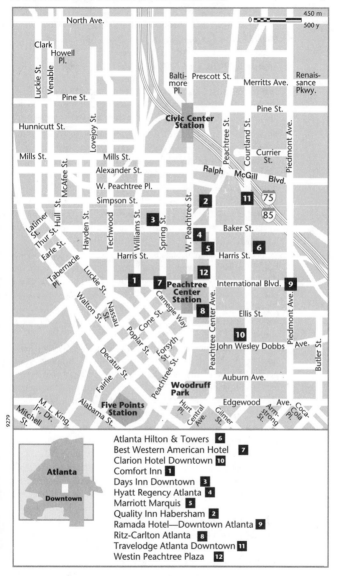

Atlanta Hilton & Towers **6**
Best Western American Hotel **7**
Clarion Hotel Downtown **10**
Comfort Inn **1**
Days Inn Downtown **3**
Hyatt Regency Atlanta **4**
Marriott Marquis **5**
Quality Inn Habersham **2**
Ramada Hotel—Downtown Atlanta **9**
Ritz-Carlton Atlanta **8**
Travelodge Atlanta Downtown **11**
Westin Peachtree Plaza **12**

Facilities: Four outdoor tennis courts, a 1/10-mile outdoor jogging track, outdoor pool/sundeck, exercise room (Lifecycles, treadmills, stair machines, free weights), sauna, whirlpool, business center, shops (gifts, toys, jewelry, women's clothing), shoeshine stand, airport shuttle.

Hyatt Regency Atlanta, 265 Peachtree St. NE, between Baker and Harris Sts., Atlanta, GA 30303. ☎ **404/577-1234** or toll free **800/233-1234.** Fax 404/588-4137. 1,279 rms, 58 suites. A/C MINIBAR TV TEL **MARTA:** Peachtree Center.

Rates: Mon–Thurs, $165–$205 single; $180–$245 double. Fri–Sun, $89 per room. Regency Club $200–$265 single or double, Business Plan $15 over regular rates. Extra person $20. Children under 18 free in parents' room. Packages and promotional rates often available via the toll-free number. AE, CB, DC, DISC, MC, V. **Parking:** $15 (self or valet).

Designed in 1967 by famed Atlanta architect John Portman, this hotel was the prototype not only for future downtown hotels in the city, but for hotel architectural design throughout America. It features a 23-story open-air atrium lobby filled with lush greenery which thrives in the sunlight streaming through a lofty skylight. The indoor-garden motif is further enhanced by balconies draped with vine-covered trellises. Another Portman innovation is the central bank of bubble-glass elevators lit by marquee lights which glide silently up and down the atrium.

The Hyatt accommodates guests not only in this original building, but in two later additions—the 24-story International Tower and the 22-story Ivy Tower. Rooms in all three Hyatt buildings feature plush modern furnishings and are equipped with remote-control cable TVs offering free HBO and Spectravision pay movies (video checkout and account review are further options), AM/FM alarm-clock radios, and safes.

The 22nd floor of the main building houses the Regency Club, a hotel within the hotel providing a comfortable private lounge where guests enjoy complimentary buffet breakfasts and hors d'oeuvres with wine and beer from 5 to 8pm. Concierges are on duty throughout the day, and Club floor guests enjoy upgraded amenities and services. On the 21st floor are Business Plan rooms equipped with personal work stations, in-room faxes, desk phones with computer jacks, and coffeemakers. Business Plan guests get free local calls and other perks.

Dining/Entertainment: The blue dome capping Polaris, the Hyatt's revolving rooftop restaurant, is a landmark on the city's skyline. It's a lovely setting, with each mauve velvet upholstered chair and banquette providing full window views. Open for dinner and Sunday buffet brunches, Polaris offers a classic menu featuring steak, seafood, and prime rib. You can enjoy the same spectacular views over cocktails in the adjoining lounge. Overlooking the hustle and bustle of the lobby is the Kafe Köbenhavn, designed for informal dining. Open from 6am to midnight, it features buffets at all meals (a low-fat section is a plus) as well as an à la carte coffee shop menu. One level below the lobby is Avanzare, a charming Italian restaurant with an 1,800-gallon saltwater aquarium along one wall. Fresh pizzas and pastas, tempting antipastas, seafood dishes, and premium wines by the glass are featured. Open for lunch weekdays, dinner nightly. A coffee cart in the lobby purveys cappuccino, espresso, and pastries for quick breakfasts and desserts evenings. And the Ampersand Lounge airs sporting events on a large-screen TV.

Services: Room service from 6am to 12:30am, lobby concierge, airport shuttle, automated check-in via credit card.

Facilities: Health club (with rowing machines, Lifecycles, stair machines, treadmills, free weights, and multi-station Universal machine); tennis/golf nearby by arrangement, barber shop and beauty salon, gift shop, Delta Air Lines desk, large outdoor pool with sun deck and whirlpool, business center. The Hyatt connects to the vast Peachtree Center shopping mall via a covered walkway.

 Ritz-Carlton Atlanta, 181 Peachtree St. NE, at Ellis St. (main entrance on Ellis), Atlanta, GA 30303. ☎ **404/659-0400** or toll free **800/241-3333.** Fax 404/688-0400. 447 rms, 24 suites. A/C MINIBAR TV TEL **MARTA:** Peachtree Center.

Rates: Sun–Thurs, $169–$295 single or double; Fri–Sat, $119 per room. Club Level $265 single or double; suites $450–$985. Extra person $15. Children 18 and under free in parents' room. AE, CB, DC, DISC, ER, MC, V. **Parking:** $12 (valet only).

It's hard to believe that this very traditional-looking hostelry—with Persian rugs strewn on marble floors, silk-tapestried and African mahogany-paneled walls hung with a collection of museum-quality 18th- and 19th-century paintings, and valuable antiques throughout its public areas—was built as late as 1984. The impeccable service also harks back to another, more gracious, era; you'll be cosseted as never before. Elegantly residential rooms, many with bay windows, are furnished with beautiful mahogany pieces (some have four-poster beds) and equipped with every amenity. Your remote-control cable TV (with movie channels) is concealed in a handsome armoire. Other in-room amenities include an AM/FM alarm-clock radio, terry robe, scale, fresh flowers, and an extra phone in the bath; additional phone lines are available if needed. The telephone service offers call waiting, conference calling, and a do-not-disturb feature wherein calls are routed to the hotel operator.

The two top floors of the Ritz-Carlton (24 and 25) constitute the Club Level, a hotel within a hotel featuring upgraded room amenities, a private elevator, and a plush concierge-staffed lounge where guests enjoy a lavish complimentary continental breakfast, afternoon tea, cocktails with hors d'oeuvres, and late-night cordials. Of course, the rooms and lounge on these high floors offer great city views.

Dining/Entertainment: The hotel's premier dining room is The Restaurant, an equestrian-themed setting with 19th-century, gilt-framed hunt paintings on pine-green walls. Highly acclaimed, it offers traditional haute-cuisine items such as roasted quail, braised pheasant, and grilled salmon medallions. It's open for dinner only; a pianist entertains. After dinner, you might retreat to the adjoining Bar where a jazz trio plays Tuesday to Saturday night till 1am. A very reasonably priced lunch buffet is served in The Bar weekdays. The warmly intimate peach and earth-toned Café, on the lobby level, open daily from 6:30am to midnight, is the hotel's informal dining room.

It's a gem, with glittering crystal chandeliers overhead, lavish floral arrangements, and shaded table lamps and wall sconces enhancing the cozy ambience. A pianist entertains here during Sunday brunch. An afternoon tea, complete with fresh-baked scones and watercress sandwiches, is served in the lobby lounge daily; a pianist entertains here from 11:30am to 4:30pm.

Services: 24-hour room service, twice-daily maid service, nightly turndown with a chocolate, complimentary shoeshine, your regional paper delivered to your door on request, evening pressing service, babysitting, car rental, limousine, multilingual concierge staff.

Facilities: Gift shop, business center, airport shuttle, on-premises fitness center (Stairmasters, treadmills, exercise bikes, sauna, steam, free weights), use of the nearby state-of-the-art Peachtree Center Athletic Club for $12 per visit. Facilities at the latter include a lap pool, indoor track, over 60 pieces of cardiovascular equipment (including stair and rowing machines, exercise bikes, and treadmills), sauna, steam, and racquetball/squash/basketball/volleyball courts.

★ **The Westin Peachtree Plaza,** 210 Peachtree St., at International Blvd., Atlanta, GA 30303. ☎ **404/659-1400** or toll free **800/228-3000.** Fax 404/589-7586. 1,020 rms, 48 suites. A/C TV TEL **MARTA:** Peachtree Center.

Rates: Mon–Thurs, $165–$185 single; $190–$210 double. Fri–Sat, 50% off regular rates. Club level $210 single; $235 double. Extra person $25. Children under 18 free. Inquire about packages. AE, CB, DC, DISC, ER, JCB, MC, V. **Parking:** $12.50 self, $13 valet.

Though the John Portman–designed Westin is a 73-story megahotel with over 1,000 rooms, it is invitingly residential within. The atrium lobby—under a 5-story skylight and utilizing acres of pink-hued Portuguese marble—divides into softly lit alcoves wherein plush sofas, fine artworks, rich mahogany paneling, and Persian rugs combine to create warmly intimate seating areas. Numerous trees and plants add an indoor garden look, and glittering marquee-lit facades evoke Copenhagen's Tivoli Gardens.

Rooms, decorated in soft hues (mauve, peach, beige) with sage and teal accents, have walnut furnishings. Handsome armoires house remote-control cable TVs offering Spectravision pay movies and a gratis step-training exercise video (the step is provided). And in-room amenities include TV speakers in the bath, two phones (desk and bedside) with voice-man messaging, wall safes, irons and full-size ironing boards, hair dryers, and AM/FM alarm-clock radios. Medium and deluxe rooms are on higher floors, and the latter have minibars. Club Level (floors 43–47) guests enjoy a stunning concierge-staffed lounge offering fax and copy machines plus complimentary continental breakfast, cocktail-hour hors d'oeuvres, and evening desserts. In-room amenities and services are also upgraded.

Dining/Entertainment: The revolving Sun Dial Restaurant, on the 71st and 72nd floors, offers a breathtaking 360-degree city-skyline panorama. Plushly furnished with horseshoe booths, and designed so that every table provides optimum views, it features sophisticated

American cuisine. The revolving Sun Dial Lounge, on the 73rd floor, is a romantic setting for exotic cocktails and light appetizer fare. Several other facilities are on the lobby level. The highly acclaimed Savannah Fish Company, with seating overlooking a splashing 100-foot horizontal waterfall, specializes in fresh seafood and sushi. A jazz trio entertains nightly in the lobby, near the Café—a delightful restaurant serving both buffet and à la carte American meals plus an award-winning Japanese breakfast. The Oak Bar, a plush venue of warm woods and rich leathers, specializes in liqueurs and coffee drinks. The International Bar features an array of beers and wines by the glass. And the adjoining Sidewalk Café serves specialty coffees, light fare, and pastries.

Services: Concierge, 24-hour room service, airport shuttle.

Facilities: Health club (with stair machines, Lifecycles, treadmills, and free weights), beautiful large pool (under a retractable skylight for year-round indoor/outdoor use), and tropically planted sundeck, comprehensive business center, car rental, 17,000-square-foot shopping gallery which connects with Macy's Peachtree Center Mall (see Chapter 9) is a block away. The Westin Kid's Club offers many free perks for families (call the hotel for details).

Expensive

 Marriott Marquis, 265 Peachtree Center Ave., between Baker and Harris Sts., Atlanta, GA 30383. ☎ **404/521-0000** or toll free **800/228-9290.** Fax 404/521-6870. 1,674 rms, 80 suites. A/C TV TEL **MARTA:** Peachtree Center.

Rates: Sun–Thurs, $165 single or double, Fri–Sat, $109 per room (including free parking and continental breakfast). Concierge level $210 single or double. Extra person $20. Children under 12 free. AE, CB, DC, DISC, MC, V. **Parking:** $15 (self or valet).

A dramatic downtown landmark, the Marriott Marquis, with its towering tapered-glass exterior, is my personal favorite of Atlanta's Portman-designed megahotels. Fronted by a vast fountain that looks like a flying saucer, it focuses within on a soaring 50-story atrium in which a massive plum-colored fiber sculpture cascades through space from the skylight ceiling to a point just above the lobby. Another vertical design element is a central bank of illuminated bullet-shaped glass elevators, intended as a form of functional kinetic sculpture. Vines draped over interior balcony railings create a hanging-garden effect. And light classical piano music played in all public areas combines with these natural elements to further humanize a modern environment that might otherwise overwhelm.

In the very attractive rooms, contemporary artwork hangs on pale-peach walls; custom-designed bedspreads and drapes, of imported Belgian fabrics are amber and peach, with lavender and plum accents; carpets are a muted aubergine hue; and furnishings are handsome walnut pieces. Amenities include digital bedside clocks, AM/FM radios, phones with voice-mail messaging, remote-control cable TVs with free HBO and Spectravision pay movies (you can also pick up messages, review your account, or pay your bill via video), and hair dryers in the bath. Closets have folding-mirror doors; inside, you'll find an iron and ironing board.

Floors 42 and 43 comprise the Concierge Level, with its own plushly furnished private lounge (a wall of windows affords stunning views). Your rate here includes an extensive continental breakfast, snacks and juices throughout the day, a lavish hors d'oeuvres spread at cocktail hour, and late-night desserts and coffee. Rooms offer special amenities, as well as services such as nightly bed turndown.

Dining/Entertainment: The Garden Level, above the lobby, is a vast, marble-floored expanse. Here you'll find all the hotel's restaurants and lounges as well as the entrance to the Peachtree Center. The Atrium Café, open for all meals, is an indoor sidewalk café, bordered by a large marble planter; it features light fare. Pompano's, an elegant steak and seafood restaurant entered via a glass-walled arcade with gorgeous aquariums of variegated tropical fish at either end, seats diners amid a forest of ficus trees. The Arbors, a plant-filled restaurant with a lovely garden ambience and windows overlooking fountains, is the hotel's casual restaurant, offering steak, seafood, and sandwiches. La Fuente features traditional Mexican fare in an adobe-walled, south-of-the-border setting. In nice weather, you can enjoy fajitas al fresco at umbrella tables on the adjoining patio. The Garden Lounge on this floor is an elegant piano bar. And up a brass-railed stairway, seemingly suspended in space, is the Grandstand Bar. Champions, the Marquis's major nightclub and an exciting sports-themed bar, is covered more extensively in Chapter 10.

Services: 24-hour room service, limousine, *USA Today* delivered daily to your room, airport shuttle, lobby concierge.

Facilities: Full health club (with Lifecycles, stair machines, treadmills, a rowing machine, an array of Universal workout machines, and free weights), large swimming pool under a retractable skylight roof with an adjoining whirlpool, business center, video game room, florist, drugstore, Delta Air Lines desk, travel agent, clothing boutiques, magic shop, gift shop, unisex hair stylist, shoeshine stand. The Marquis connects, via a covered walkway, to dozens of shops at the Peachtree Center Mall.

Moderate

Best Western American Hotel, 160 Spring St. NW, at Carnegie Way, Atlanta, GA 30303. ☎ **404/688-8600** or toll free **800/621-7885.** Fax 404/658-9458. 300 rms, 21 suites. A/C TV TEL **MARTA:** Peachtree Center.

Rates: $119–$139 single; $139–$159 double. Executive Club level $20 additional per night. Parlor suites $225–265. Extra person $20. Children under 18 stay free in parents' room. Inquire about weekend packages. AE, CB, DC, DISC, MC, V. **Parking:** $6 (valets only).

When it was first built in 1962 as an Americana Hotel, this was downtown's most glamorous property, attracting guests like Mary

Martin, Carol Channing, Doris Day, and Pearl Bailey. Today, in the shadow of downtown's modern megahotels, the American seems decidedly retro, its public areas, though refurbished, reflecting late-fifties/early-sixties interior-decorating ideas such as mirrored columns and blond wood paneling. However, everything's in tip-top shape after a recent $2 million renovation.

Rooms are newly decorated in a variety of styles and color schemes. They're all equipped with cable TVs offering Spectravision movies, AM/FM alarm-clock radios, and phones with computer jacks and credit card slots. Some rooms have sofas and loveseats. Windows that open are a nice feature. Floors 8 and 9 comprise an Executive Club Level with a private concierge-staffed lounge; guests on these floors enjoy a complimentary continental breakfast and cocktail-hour hors d'oeuvres here daily, free newspapers, express checkout, and nightly bed turndown with chocolate mints.

Dining/Entertainment: The pubby, wood-paneled Gatsby's Restaurant, vaguely evoking the 1920s (walls are covered with news headlines heralding Lindbergh's flight, ads for Pierce Arrow cars, vintage photographs, and *Saturday Evening Post* covers) is open nightly for reasonably priced steak and seafood dinners. In the adjoining lounge, open to 2am nightly, sporting events are aired on a large-screen TV. There's also a poolside coffee shop called the Outside Inn. It's open 6:30am to 5pm.

Services: Airport shuttle, concierge, valet parking, room service 7am to 10pm.

Facilities: Medium-size outdoor pool/sundeck, guest privileges (for a $10 fee) at the very comprehensive Peachtree Center Athletic Club (see Ritz-Carlton facilities above for details), small on-premises workout room (with some Universal and Nautilus equipment, exercise bikes, and a Stairmaster), gift shop, barber, full range of audiovisual equipment available.

The Clarion Hotel Downtown, 70 John Wesley Dobbs Ave., at Courtland St., Atlanta, GA 30303. ☎ **404/659-2660** or toll free

---

Frommer's Smart Traveler: Hotels

Value-Conscious Travelers Should Take Advantage of the Following:

1. Weekend rates. Even top-of-the-line hotels slash prices 30% to 50% on weekends—and at some properties weekends include Friday, Saturday, and Sunday nights.

2. Reduced-price packages and reduced rates for senior citizens, families, and active-duty military personnel.

3. Preferential rates, available only when you reserve via toll-free reservation numbers.

4. Bargaining for lower rates.

800/426-2121. Fax 404/524-5390. 213 rms, 6 suites. A/C TV TEL **MARTA:** Peachtree Center.

Rates: Mon–Thurs, $59–$109 single; $69–$119 double; Fri–Sun, $49–$69 single; $59–$79 double. Suites $145. Extra person $10. Children under 18 stay free in parents' room. AE, CB, DC, DISC, MC, V. **Parking:** Free.

An 8-story cream stucco building that forms a courtyard around its swimming pool, the Clarion has recently completed a $5 million renovation. Public areas, hung with architectural and historic prints of Atlanta, include a wide resort-like mezzanine with comfortable furnishings. Rooms, 90% of them with balconies, are charmingly decorated in about 20 different color schemes—all of them lovely; they have traditional cherrywood furniture, pretty floral-print bedspreads, and framed botanical prints gracing the walls. In-room amenities include remote-control cable TVs offering pay-movie options (they're housed in handsome armoires) and AM/FM alarm-clock radios.

Dining/Entertainment: The Courtyard Café, a very pretty garden-motif restaurant decorated with botanical prints, has outdoor balcony seating overlooking the pool. It's open for all meals. A similarly decorated and very comfortable lounge adjoins.

Services: Room service during restaurant hours, airport shuttle.

Facilities: Medium-sized outdoor pool and sundeck, gift shop. For a $10 fee, guests can use the nearby Phoenix Health Club, offering a full complement of Paramount machines, indoor track, treadmills, stair machines, Lifecycles, free weights, aerobics classes, cross-country ski machines, rowing machines, racquetball/basketball/volleyball courts, sauna, and whirlpools.

Comfort Inn, 101 International Blvd., at Williams St., Atlanta, GA 30303. ☎ **404/524-5555** or toll free **800/535-0707** or **800/228-5150.** 257 rms, 3 suites. A/C TV TEL **MARTA:** Peachtree Center or Omni.

Rates: $59–$139 single; $69–$149 double (Rates may be higher during major conventions or special events). Extra person $10. Children 18 and under free in parents' room. AE, CB, DC, DISC, ER, JCB, MC, V. **Parking:** $6 (self only).

A chain of moderately priced hotels created by the Quality Inn group in 1981, Comfort Inns are based on the theory that a low-cost hotel needn't be a no-frills hotel. This 11-story property, opened in 1985, is a good example. It's garnered three-star ratings from both Mobil and AAA. Entered via a lobby with a fountain, it offers appealing rooms with oak furnishings, maure or teal carpeting, color-coordinated floral-print bedspreads and drapes, and watercolors depicting scenes of France on grasspaper-covered walls. Each room has both a desk and a table with two chairs (or sleeper sofa), a full-length mirror on the closet door, remote-control cable TV offering Spectravision movies, and an AM/FM alarm-clock radio. The Greyhound bus station is just across the street, the Omni Coliseum two blocks away.

Dining/Entertainment: Bistro 101, the on-premises eatery, is rather charming, with tables amid potted ferns and copper cookware on the walls. Many seats overlook the pool. It offers typical American fare. In the adjoining Blind Zebra Bar, sporting events are aired on the TV (proximity to the Omni Coliseum attracts many sports-minded guests).

Services: Room service during restaurant hours.

Facilities: Electric shoeshine machines on each floor, a nice-size outdoor pool/sundeck with adjoining whirlpool, "Discover Atlanta" video machine in the lobby, gift shop, airport shuttle.

Days Inn Downtown, 300 Spring St., at Baker St., Atlanta, GA 30308. ☎ **404/523-1144** or toll free **800/DAYS-INN.** Fax 404/577-8495. 262 rms. A/C TV TEL **MARTA:** Peachtree Center.

Rates: $79–$129 single; $89–$139 double (rates may be higher during major conventions or special events). Extra person $10. Children under 18 free in parent's room. Reduced rates may be available if you reserve at least 30 days in advance. AE, DC, DISC, MC, V. **Parking:** $6 (self only).

This very central Days Inn allows visitors to stay in the heart of the business district at a very moderate cost. The rooms, decorated in a burgundy/mauve/forest-green color scheme, have handsome oak furnishings and grasspaper-style wall coverings. In-room amenities include remote-control cable TVs (with free HBO and Spectravision pay movies), safes, and AM/FM alarm clock radios. Some rooms have refrigerators, and those on floors 3 to 10 have balconies. Although you don't get all the luxury-hotel frills here, accommodations are clean and spiffy-looking, facilities very ample. A Wendy's restaurant adjoins the property. There's also a comfortable lounge in the hotel, open 5pm to midnight, where sporting events are aired. And a large outdoor pool is a plus.

Quality Inn Habersham, 330 Peachtree St. NE, between Baker St. and Ralph McGill Blvd., Atlanta, GA 30308. ☎ **404/577-1980** or toll free **800/241-4288.** Fax 404/688-3706. 91 rms. A/C TV TEL **MARTA:** Peachtree Center or Civic Center.

Rates (including extended continental breakfast): Sun–Thurs, $80–$90 single; $90–$100 double. Fri–Sat, $59 single; $69 double. Extra person $10. Children 18 and under free in parents' room. AE, CB, DC, DISC, ER, JCB, MC, V. **Parking:** Free (self only).

Just a few blocks from the center of downtown, this pleasant hotel offers a lot for its price range. From a cozy lobby lounge with velvet-upholstered sofas to cheerful hallways adorned with ficus trees, its public areas are well cared for and aesthetically pleasing. The mauve-carpeted rooms, with navy blue bedspreads, are large and nicely furnished, each equipped with a desk, two armchairs or a sofa, a remote-control cable TV with free HBO, wet bar/refrigerator, and an in-room coffeemaker. Marble baths are amply supplied with shampoo, soaps, toothpaste, mouthwash, and deodorant.

Dining/Entertainment: In a comfortably furnished room off the lobby, complimentary continental breakfast—danish, rolls, bagels, sausage, biscuits, juice, fresh fruit, cold cereals, tea or coffee—is served each morning. There's a TV here, should you care to watch the "Today" show over the morning meal. Or, weather permitting, you might breakfast outdoors at patio tables.

Services: Room service is available from about a dozen area restaurants (you'll find a comprehensive menu in your room). *USA Today* is free in the lobby.

Facilities: A workout room with exercise bikes, free weights, treadmill, stair machine, rowing machine, Universal multi-station exercise machine, and sauna.

Ramada Hotel—Downtown Atlanta, 175 Piedmont Ave. NE, at International Blvd., Atlanta, GA 30303. ☎ **404/659-2727** or toll free **800/228-2828.** Fax 577-7805. 467 rms, 6 suites. A/C TV TEL **MARTA:** Peachtree Center.

Rates: Mon–Thurs, $79–$150 single; $89–$160 double. Fri–Sun, $65 per room. Extra person $10. Children 12 and under free in parents' room. Packages available via the toll-free number. AE, CB, DC, DISC, MC, V. **Parking:** Free (self only).

This 6-story hotel opened in the early 1960s, its 7-story addition 10 years later. It's a particularly nice property, entered via a large lobby with intimate, lamplit seating areas. Much of the staff has been here since the hotel's inception, always a sign of a well-run operation. Recently renovated rooms offer AM/FM alarm-clock radios and remote-control cable TVs with free HBO and ESPN. Easy access to all interstates is a plus.

Dining/Entertainment: The Pantheon, a pretty plant-filled restaurant-in-the-round, serves typical American fare at all meals. A lounge called Raphael's adjoins. And complimentary coffee is available in the lobby weekdays from 7 to 9am.

Services: Room service 6:30am to 2pm and 5 to 10pm, airport shuttle, complimentary toiletries on request at the front desk.

Facilities: Lobby gift shop, large outdoor swimming pool with nicely landscaped sundeck. An exercise room is under construction at this writing.

Inexpensive

Travelodge Atlanta Downtown, 311 Courtland St. NE, between Baker St. and Ralph McGill Blvd., Atlanta, GA 30303. ☎ **404/659-4545** or toll free **800/578-7878.** Fax 404/659-5934. 71 rms. A/C TV TEL **MARTA:** Peachtree Center.

Rates (including continental breakfast): Mon–Thurs, $68–$74 single; $76–$86 double. Fri–Sun, $44–$49 per room. Extra person $8. Children under 18 free in parents' room. AE, CB, DC, DISC, ER, MC, V. **Parking:** Free (self only).

Operated by the Clark family since 1964, this small TraveLodge offers a moderately priced hotel alternative in the heart of downtown. Its teal-carpeted rooms look clean and fresh. Each is equipped with an AM/FM radio, a personal safe, and a remote-control cable TV with free HBO. VCRs and rental movies are available at the front desk.

Complimentary continental breakfast—juice, coffee, and doughnuts—is served in the lobby each morning; there's a 24-hour eatery just down the street, and numerous other restaurants are within walking distance. Free daily newspapers are another plus. Facilities include an outdoor pool and sun deck. And TraveLodge guests can use the extensive facilities of the nearby Peachtree Center Athletic Club for $10 a day, (see Ritz-Carlton write-up above for details).

2 Midtown

Midtown hotels tend to be low-key, catering to tourists and their families rather than conventioneers. Joggers and other outdoor enthusiasts will appreciate proximity to Piedmont Park. The Woodruff Arts Center is also in this section of town.

Very Expensive

 Occidental Grand Hotel, 75 14th St., between Peachtree and W. Peachtree Sts., Atlanta, GA 30309. ☎ **404/881-9898** or toll free **800/952-0702.** Fax 404/888-8669. 228 rms, 18 suites. A/C MINIBAR TV TEL **MARTA:** Arts Center.

Rates: Sun–Thurs, $149–$230 single or double (range depends on floor and view). Fri–Sat, $112 Suites $395–$1,500. Extra person $20. Children under 18 stay free in parents' room. Inquire about packages. AE, CB, DC, DISC, ER, JCB, MC, V. **Parking:** $11.50 self or valet.

The late 1992 opening of the Occidental Grand (part of a Madrid-based chain of first-tier properties) brought unprecedented glamour and Old-World elegance to Atlanta's midtown hotel scene. It has already hosted the Emperor and Empress of Japan, the Queen of Norway, and the King of Finland in its Royal Suite and become a haunt of visiting celebrities such as Tony Bennett, Beverly Sills, Isaac Stern, and Jimmy Buffett. Its 19 floors, defined by vast arched

---

Frommer's Cool for Kids: Hotels

Residence Inn Buckhead (see p. 93). This place has not only a swimming pool but also accommodations with fully equipped kitchens—a potential money-saver when you're traveling with family. Rates here include breakfast, and there are barbecue grills and picnic tables on the premises. It's like having your own Atlanta apartment, with parking at your door. The property also contains basketball, volleyball, and paddle-tennis courts, and VCRs and movies can be rented at the front desk.

Westin Peachtree Plaza (see p. 66). The Westin Kids' Club provides many perks for families: kits filled with children's bath products and activities; kiddie furniture such as high-chairs, potty seats, cribs, and bed rails; special children's restaurant and room-service menus, and more—all at no extra charge. And there's a swimming pool on the premises.

windows, are housed in an imposing 53-story polished-granite building that also contains luxury residences and plush offices. Guests pass from the porte cochère entranceway to a soaring marble-floored 3-story atrium lobby with a sweeping curved stairway appropriately reminiscent of *Gone With the Wind*. A massive Baccarat crystal chandelier (which originally graced a turn-of-the-century Paris hotel) sparkles brightly overhead.

Earth-toned residential-look accommodations—done up in soft beiges, ochres, and gold—are suitably luxe, with fleur-de-lis swagged curtains framing large windows, tapestried armchairs at terra-cotta-hued marble desks, handsome armoires, and gilt-framed artworks illumined by gallery lights. Beds are embellished with upholstered headboards and shimmery gray-blue chintz spreads with gold dust ruffles. All rooms are equipped with sofas, remote-control cable TVs (offering free HBO, Spectravision pay movies, and tourism-information channels; VCRs and rental movies are available), AM/FM alarm-clock radios, three phones (bedside, desk, and bath), and safes. Gorgeous marble baths contain scales, terry robes, hair dryers, upscale toiletries, and linen hand towels.

Dining/Entertainment: The magnificent Florencia Restaurant, one of Atlanta's most notable nighttime dining venues, is detailed in Chapter 6, where you'll also find mention of several other Occidental eateries. The beautiful Café Opera—with its tapestried banquettes, potted palms, white marble tables set with fresh flowers, and an oil mural evoking 1920s European café society—serves all meals. At Overtures, on the mezzanine overlooking the lavishly marbled grand staircase, a pianist entertains from 3:30pm to midnight daily. This brass-railed balcony facility is the setting for daily afternoon teas, and, along with the Café Opera, sumptuous Sunday champagne brunches. And the softly lit and very simpatico Segovia Bar—with its raised burl panels of Carpathian elm inset with hand-tooled suede, elegantly draped floor-to-ceiling windows, plush furnishings arranged in intimate seating alcoves, and handsome marble columns—is open for business lunches as well as Spanish tapas and sherries until closing at midnight Sunday to Thursday, 1am Friday and Saturday.

Services: 24-hour room service, 24-hour concierge, nightly bed turndown with gourmet chocolate, *USA Today* and/or newspaper of your choice delivered to your room daily, foreign currency exchange, complimentary shoeshine, limo rental, complimentary round-trip transport via town car from 7am to 7pm to downtown, Buckhead, and points in between.

Facilities: Full-service unisex hair/beauty salon (massage, makeovers, facials, and more; inquire about "days-of-beauty" packages), extensive business services, gift shop, health club (with a full complement of Nautilus equipment, exercise bikes, stair machines, treadmills, free weights, aerobics classes, large indoor pool with adjoining outdoor sun deck, whirlpool, steam, sauna). Kids enjoy a special program which includes a toiletries box with baby shampoo and a rubber duck, child-size robes, milk and cookies at nightly turndown, board games, and children's movie videos and video games.

Expensive

 Marriott Suites, 35 14th St. NE, between Peachtree and W. Peachtree Sts., Atlanta, GA 30309. ☎ **404/876-8888** or toll free **800/228-9290.** Fax 404/876-7727. 254 suites. A/C TV TEL **MARTA:** Arts Center.

Rates: Mon–Thurs, $159 single; $174 double. Fri–Sun, $79 per room, $94 with full breakfast for two. No extra person charge. Discounted rates and packages may be available through the toll free number. AE, CB, DC, DISC, ER, MC, V. **Parking:** $8 (self or valet).

It would be hard to come by a more simpatico place to stay than this very hospitable, all-suite hotel. It's obvious a great deal of planning has gone into meeting guests' needs and providing a luxurious residential atmosphere here. Each spacious suite, attractively decorated in a mauve/dusty aqua color scheme, offers a full living room with a convertible sofa, an extra phone on the desk (phones here are equipped with call waiting and voice-mail messaging), a wet bar/refrigerator, and a big console TV. Both this TV and the one in your bedroom are remote-control cable sets offering free HBO and Spectravision pay movies, plus video account review, checkout, and message retrieval. Bedrooms, set off from living room areas by lace-curtained French doors, are furnished in glossy traditional mahogany pieces. Most have king-size beds. Additional in-suite amenities: coffeemakers, AM/FM alarm-clock radios, hair dryers, and irons and full-size ironing boards. Closets have full-length folding-mirror doors, and large marble baths adjoin dressing rooms. Jimmy Carter was a guest here during the Ethiopian peace negotiations which took place at the Carter Center.

Dining/Entertainment: Off the palm court-style lobby is the plant-filled, lavender-and-teal Windows, serving lavish buffet break-fasts (everything from blintzes to Belgian waffles) and à la carte lunches and dinners daily. Steak and seafood are featured, along with lighter items—sandwiches, burgers, salads, etc. In the adjoining bar/lounge area, inexpensive cocktail-hour hors d'oeuvres are offered Monday through Friday.

Services: Room service between 6 and 9:30 a.m. and 5:30 and 11 p.m., nightly bed turndown on request with Godiva chocolates, airport shuttle, *USA Today* delivered to your door each morning.

Facilities: Gift shop, health club (with an array of Universal exercise equipment, stair machine, exercise bikes, free weights, Lifecycle, treadmill), connecting indoor and outdoor swimming pools (both ample for laps) and a nicely landscaped sun deck nestled in the treetops (the pool's on the third floor), whirlpool, coin-op washer/dryer.

Sheraton Colony Square Hotel, 188 14th St. NE, at Peachtree St., Atlanta, GA 30361. ☎ **404/892-6000** or toll free **800/422-7895.**

Midtown/Georgia Tech Accommodations

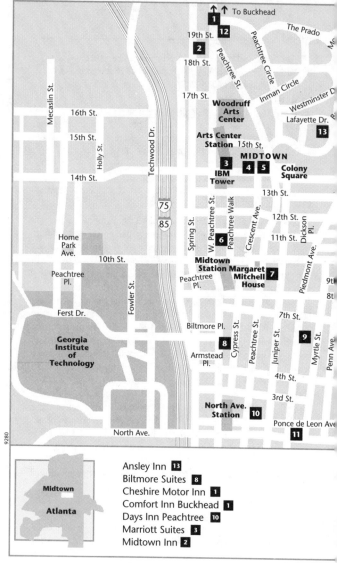

Ansley Inn **13**
Biltmore Suites **8**
Cheshire Motor Inn **1**
Comfort Inn Buckhead **1**
Days Inn Peachtree **10**
Marriott Suites **3**
Midtown Inn **2**

Fax 404/876-3276. 430 rms, 31 suites. A/C TV TEL **MARTA:** Arts Center.

Rates: Mon–Thurs, $129–$159 single; $149–$179 double. Fri–Sun, $89 per room, per night, including continental breakfast. Colony Club $149–$179 single; $169–$199 double. Extra person $20. Children 18 and

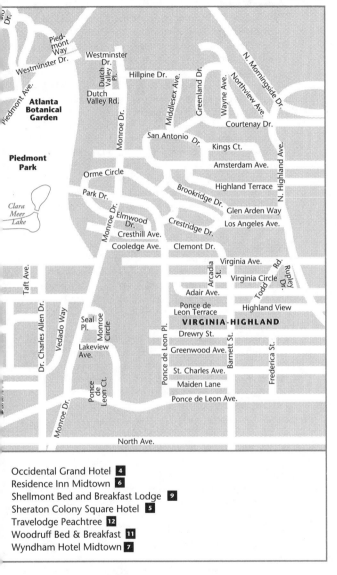

0 ——— 300 m
——— 330 y
N

Occidental Grand Hotel **4**
Residence Inn Midtown **6**
Shellmont Bed and Breakfast Lodge **9**
Sheraton Colony Square Hotel **5**
Travelodge Peachtree **12**
Woodruff Bed & Breakfast **11**
Wyndham Hotel Midtown **7**

under free in parents' room. AE, CB, DC, DISC, MC, V. **Parking:** $7.50 self, $10 valet ($10 Fri–Sun).

Built in 1974 as an opulent anchor of the Colony Square complex (which includes a mall of 20 shops and restaurants), this theatrically themed property is very popular with entertainers playing at the adjacent Woodruff Arts Center. Sheraton Colony Square has hosted Willie Nelson, Frank Sinatra, Dionne Warwick, and Linda Ronstadt, not to mention Presidents Reagan, Ford, and Carter. It's also a great choice for tennis and jogging enthusiasts, since Piedmont Park is just a few blocks away.

Rooms are simply gorgeous, decorated in earth tones with plush armchairs and hassocks, beautiful marble desks, and silk throw pillows on the beds. In a handsome armoire, you'll find your remote-control cable TV with free HBO and Spectravision pay movies. Other in-room amenities include alarm clocks, AM/FM radios, walk-in closets, full-length mirrors, electric shoe buffers, and, in the baths, upscale toiletries and cosmetic mirrors. A silk ficus tree in each room is a nice residential touch.

Floors 18 and 19 comprise the Colony Club, a hotel-within-a-hotel with its own luxurious concierge-staffed lounge offering bountiful buffets at breakfast and cocktail hour. Guests on these floors enjoy upgraded amenities, nightly bed turndown, and copies of the *Wall Street Journal* and *USA Today* delivered to their doors each morning.

Dining/Entertainment: The oak-columned 14th Street Bar & Grill, which has a full-size hot-air balloon over the bar, serves American fare at all meals. In the cozy lamplit Lobby Bar, complimentary hors d'oeuvres are served with cocktails from 4 to 8pm nightly. There are many good restaurants in the Mall, including The Country Place (details in Chapter 6).

Services: Room service 6:30am to 1am, concierge, airport shuttle.

Facilities: Business services, nice-size outdoor pool and sun deck, workout room (with stair machines, Lifecycles, a rowing machine, and a multi-station Universal machine). The mall offers a copy shop, shoe repair, photo shop, clothing and shoe stores, a drug store, florist, and more.

Wyndham Hotel Midtown, 125 10th St. NE, just east of Peachtree St., Atlanta, GA 30309. ☎ **404/873-4800** or toll free **800/822-4200.** Fax 404/870-1530. 162 rms, 29 suites. A/C TV TEL **MARTA:** Midtown.

Rates: Mon–Thurs, $135 single; $145 double; $155 for an Executive King. Fri–Sun, $69 per room. Suites $165–$500. Extra person $10. Children 12 and under free in parents' room. AE, CB, DC, DISC, JCB. **Parking:** $9 self, $9.50 valet.

An 11-story Georgia red-brick building, faced with bronze glass, the luxuriously appointed Wyndham opened in 1987. Its rooms, many with bay windows, are furnished in mahogany pieces and decorated in mauve/beige/forest green color schemes. Each has an armchair and hassock, a handsome armoire concealing a remote-control cable TV (offering free HBO and pay movie channels), a bedside AM/FM alarm-clock radio, and a coffeemaker. There are hair dryers and cosmetic mirrors in the bath. Executive King rooms feature separate parlors with sofas, extra TVs and phones, refrigerators, and stocked wet bars.

Dining/Entertainment: An art nouveau entranceway heralds the spacious, marble-floored Juniper Street Café, featuring buffet breakfasts and lunches as well as an à la carte menu at lunch and dinner. A lunchtime pasta bar offering three pastas, three sauces, and about a dozen toppings is a unique feature. There's outdoor seating at umbrella tables. Inside, tables set with white linens are lit by shaded lamps at night. The adjoining Butler's bar and lounge, furnished with comfortable leather chairs, specializes in premium wines by the glass.

Services: Comprehensive business services (including complete audiovisual setups), airport shuttle, room service 5 to 11pm, complimentary *USA Today* at front desk.

Facilities: 7,000-square-foot fitness center offering Nautilus equipment, steam and sauna, whirlpool, large indoor pool, aerobics classes.

Moderate

 Residence Inn Midtown, 1041 W. Peachtree St., at 11th St., Atlanta, GA 30309. ☎ **404/872-8885** or toll free **800/331-3131.** Fax 404/872-8885, ext. 1805. 66 suites. A/C TV TEL **MARTA:** Midtown.

Rates (including continental breakfast): Suites $119 one bedroom, $149 two bedrooms. Rates are reduced off season and for stays of more than six nights. AE, DC, DISC, MC, V. **Parking:** Free (self only).

Marriott's excellent Residence Inns are designed to offer travelers the ultimate in homeyness and hospitality. Staying here is like having your own apartment in Atlanta. This particular inn occupies a 7-story brick building with green-awninged windows fronted by a landscaped courtyard. A very inviting lobby, softly lit, with plush sofas and Persian rugs on oak floors, sets a warm tone. Superb housekeeping is in evidence everywhere; the place is gleaming.

Accommodations, off pristine peach hallways with white doors, are spacious suites decorated in soft pastel hues with accents of burgundy and forest green. Handsome oak and mahogany furnishings are mostly antique reproductions, such as Chippendale-style beds, and both bedrooms and living rooms (the latter with Casablanca-style fans overhead) have their own TVs (remote-control cable sets with free HBO) and telephones. Kitchens are fully equipped and provided with gratis coffee, tea, sugar, cream, and microwave popcorn (the maid does your dishes). All rooms have full-length mirrors and French doors leading to balconies, and many have large walk-in closets.

Dining/Entertainment: An extended continental breakfast—muffins, croissants, fresh fruit, juice, yogurt, cereal, pancakes, and tea or coffee—is included in the rates; it's served in a pleasant breakfast room off the lobby, where hot tea and coffee are provided all day. Monday to Thursday night from 5:30 to 7:30pm, there are gratis beer-and-wine parties in the lobby with a wide array of hot and cold hors d'oeuvres. And every Wednesday night there's a complimentary barbecue dinner. All of these events provide a pleasant opportunity to meet and mingle with fellow guests. In addition, there's an on-premises restaurant/bar, **The Vortex,** serving sandwiches and salads.

Services: Complimentary grocery-shopping service, free newspapers daily.

Facilities: Coin-op washers/dryers, rooftop Jacuzzi, complimentary membership at a nearby health club.

Inexpensive

Biltmore Suites, 30 Fifth St. NE, at West Peachtree St., Atlanta, GA 30308. ☎ **404/874-0824** or toll free **800/822-0824.** Fax 404/458-5384. 60 suites. A/C TV TEL **MARTA:** North Avenue.

Rates (including continental breakfast): studios and one-bedroom suites (for one or two people) $75–$110; two-bedroom suites (for up to four) $140–$165; penthouses and tri-level honeymoon/anniversary suites $225–$250. AE, DISC, MC, V. **Parking:** $5 (self only).

A majestic 10-story brick building with a white-columned facade, its courtyard entrance shaded by stately oaks and magnolias, the Biltmore has a rich and glamorous history. Built in 1924 (as a hotel-cum-luxury apartment complex) by Coca-Cola heir William Candler, it played host in its heyday to everyone from *GWTW* stars Vivien Leigh and Olivia de Havilland to Presidents Franklin Roosevelt and Dwight Eisenhower. Closed in 1982, its apartment section was refurbished as an elegant all-suite hotel in 1986. The property is on the National Register of Historic Places. The hotel today is popular with actors and musicians performing at the Woodruff Arts Center, and the cast of Cirque de Soleil stayed here when they were in town.

A mahogany-paneled elevator whisks guests to the lovely suites, all of which offer fully equipped kitchens, dining areas, and (except in some studios) living rooms. Very residential in feel, they're traditionally furnished (largely in 18th-century style cherrywood and mahogany pieces) with area rugs strewn on glossy oak floors and gilt-framed Chinese art and botanical prints adorning the walls. Lion-head door knockers, 10-foot ceilings, hand-carved crown moldings, multipaned windows, brass bathroom fixtures, and French doors are additional enhancements. All accommodations are spacious and provide such in-room amenities as cable TVs, AM/FM radios, and alarm clocks. All but studios feature extra TVs and phones in the living rooms, and the stunning penthouse suites (as well as some two-bedroom suites) contain Jacuzzis.

Dining/Entertainment: Complimentary continental breakfast (bagels, toast, English muffins, pastries, juice, and tea or coffee) is served daily in a charming breakfast room off the lobby.

Services: Room service from dozens of area restaurants (there's a menu in your room), airport shuttle, complimentary shuttle from 7 to 11am and 4 to 8pm to anywhere within a five-mile radius of the property.

Facilities: Gratis health club privileges at the North Side Athletic Club, with an indoor/outdoor Olympic-size pool, a full complement of Pyramid workout machines, treadmills, Stairmasters, Lifecycles, rowing machines, free weights, aerobic classes, and tennis (for a fee); coin-op washer/dryer.

Days Inn Peachtree, 683 Peachtree St., between 3rd St. and Ponce de Leon Ave., Atlanta, GA 30308. ☎ **404/874-9200** or toll free **800/DAYS-INN.** 141 rms, 1 suite, A/C TV TEL **MARTA:** North Avenue.

Rates: $59–$89 single; $72–$109 double. Suites $125–$199. Extra person $10. Children under 18 free in parents' room. Weekend rates and packages available via the toll-free number. Super Saver rate of $49 a night may be available if you reserve at least 30 days in advance. AE, DC, DISC, MC, V. **Parking:** $5 (self only).

You'll realize this Days Inn is something special from the moment you enter its uniquely charming lobby with Persian rugs on Saltillo-tile floors and an 18th-century-style brass chandelier suspended from a lofty mahogany ceiling. The property occupies a 1924 building that was originally a select boarding house for young men. The hotel is across the street from the Fox Theatre, and since many of its entertainers (not the stars, but backup groups and musicians) stay here, it's not unusual to hear some pretty professional-sounding music emanating from the lobby's grand piano.

The rooms, decorated in teal, mauve, and burgundy, have handsome mahogany furnishings and grasspaper-covered walls hung with nautical- or equestrian-themed prints. All feature AM/FM alarm-clock radios and remote-control cable TVs with free HBO and pay-movie channels; some have comfortable, velvet-upholstered sofas.

Dining/Entertainment: Bridgetown Grill, a terrific Caribbean restaurant (see Chapter 6), adjoins the property, as does a Wendy's. Complimentary wine, cheeses, and hot hors d'oeuvres are served at a cocktail party in the lobby every Thursday night; coffee is served in the lobby throughout the day.

Services: Complimentary *Atlanta Journal-Constitution* daily at the front desk, airport shuttle.

Facilities: Coin-op washers/dryers.

Midtown Inn, 1470 Spring St. NW, at 19th St., Atlanta, GA 30309. ☎ 404/872-5821. Fax 404/874-3602. 176 rms, 3 suites. A/C TV TEL **MARTA:** Memorial Arts Center.

Rates: Mon–Thurs, $65–$75 single; $75–$85 double. Fri–Sun, $49–$59 per room. Executive Kings $85 single; $95 double; parlor suites $125–$175. Extra person $10. Children under 18 free in parents' room. AE, DC, DISC, ER, MC, V. **Parking:** Free (self only).

The Midtown Inn welcomes guests in a large, inviting lobby with copper-mirrored columns. Rooms are clean, well-maintained, standard motel accommodations with burgundy carpets and color-coordinated floral bedspreads. All offer dressing areas, remote-control cable TVs with free HBO, and coffeemakers. Rooms designated Executive Kings are larger and equipped with AM/FM alarm-clock radios and sofas. There are also parlor suites—one- or two-bedroom accommodations whose adjoining parlors are equipped with sofa beds.

Dining/Entertainment: The plant-filled Spring Street Café, overlooking the pool, serves breakfast, lunch, and dinner. In the comfortable adjoining Spirits Lounge, sporting events are aired on a large-screen TV. **Note:** A new poolside restaurant and bar are in the works at this writing.

Services: Gift shop, complimentary shuttle to MARTA and local attractions (daily 7am to 11pm).

Facilities: Exercise room, pool with two sundecks.

Budget

★ $ **Cheshire Motor Inn**, 1865 Cheshire Bridge Rd. NE, between Wellborne Dr. NE and Manchester St. NE, Atlanta, GA 30324. ☎ **404/872-9628** or toll free **800/827-9628**. 58 rms. A/C TV TEL **MARTA:** Lindbergh (about a mile away; you can catch a bus to the station in front of the hotel).

Rates: $35–$42 single. $6 each additional person. Children under 12 stay free in parents' room. AE, DC, DISC, MC, V. **Parking:** Free.

This is my favorite kind of budget hotel, a small property run for decades by caring private owners (the Lacy family) who proffer homelike hospitality and many personal touches. On attractively landscaped, woodsy grounds, the Cheshire offers rooms that are spacious, immaculate, and cozy. Recently redecorated in teal and mauve, with traditional cherrywood furnishings, they have textured beige walls hung with pretty landscape prints and shimmery striped bedspreads. In-room amenities include remote-control cable TVs with free HBO movies. Some rooms have sofas. In the bath, you'll find shampoo, a toothbrush, toothpaste, and a razor. A big plus is a famous Atlanta restaurant, the Colonnade, on the premises, serving authentic southern food (see details in Chapter 6). Services include free newspapers (*USA Today* and the *Atlanta Journal-Constitution*) and coffee in the lobby each morning.

Comfort Inn Buckhead, 2115 Piedmont Rd. NE, between Lindbergh Dr. and Cheshire Bridge Rd., Atlanta, GA 30324. ☎ **404/876-4365** or toll free **800/221-2222**. Fax 404/873-1007. 177 rms, 5 suites. A/C TV TEL **MARTA:** Lindbergh (about three-fourths of a mile north; bus #31 stops at the door).

Rates (including continental breakfast): $49–$58 single; $55–$63 double. King rooms $5 extra. Suites (for five to eight people) $75–$90. Extra person $5. Children 12 and under stay free in parents' room. AE, CB, DC, DISC, MC, V. **Parking:** Free.

Poised on the border between midtown and Buckhead, this Comfort Inn has rather nice rooms decorated in peach/mauve/turquoise color schemes, with grasspaper-like wall coverings and oak-look furnishings. Large king-bedded rooms contain desks, recliners, and pull-out sofas. And suites offer full living rooms, wet bars, and refrigerators. In-room amenities include remote-control cable TVs with free Showtime and pay-movie stations, AM/FM alarm-clock radios, and phones that provide push-button access to dozens of services (the weather, sightseeing and restaurant information, Federal Express, even your horoscope). Local calls are free, and there's no service charge for credit-card calls. A free copy of *Newsweek* in your room is another plus. Doughnuts, juice, tea, and coffee are served in a pleasant room off the lobby each morning.

Dining/Entertainment: Surprise, surprise! One of Atlanta's finest restaurants, the Chef's Cafe, leases space on the property. See details in Chapter 6.

Services: Coffee served in lobby all day.

Facilities: Small outdoor pool and sundeck.

Travelodge Peachtree, 1641 Peachtree St. NE, at I-85, Atlanta, GA 30309. ☎ **404/873-5731** or toll free **800/255-3050.** Fax 404/874-5599. 56 rms. A/C TV TEL **MARTA:** Arts Center.

Rates: $43–$59 single; $49–$69 double (rates may be higher during major conventions or special events). Extra person $4. Children under 18 free in parents' room. AE, CB, DC, DISC, ER, JCB, MC, V.

A small property housed in a 3-story yellow concrete building, the TraveLodge Peachtree offers a convenient location (the hotel is on the airport shuttle route) and low rates. The rooms, decorated in teal and mauve, with grasspaper-covered walls and mahogany furnishings, are equipped with remote-control cable TVs offering HBO movies. There's no on-premises restaurant, but an International House of Pancakes is a block away, and coffee and doughnuts are served in the lobby each morning. There's a small pool and sundeck out back.

Bed & Breakfasts

★ **Ansley Inn**, 253 15th St. NE, at Lafayette Dr., Atlanta, GA 30309. ☎ **404/872-9000** or toll free **800/446-5416.** Fax 404/892-2318. 33 rms, 1 cottage. A/C TV TEL **MARTA:** Arts Center.

Rates (including continental breakfast): $89–$500 single or double; two-bedroom cottage (sleeps six) $200. Extra person $10. AE, DC, DISC, ER, MC, V. **Parking:** Free.

Far and away my favorite accommodation in Atlanta, the Ansley Inn is in every way a delight. Occupying a 1907 yellow-brick Tudor mansion, this former estate of department-store magnate George Muse is located in one of the city's most beautiful and chic residential areas, Ansley Park. Ancient magnolias and white oaks shade the inn's front lawn.

The Persian-carpeted dining room is furnished with a long English Chippendale-style table and Empire sideboards; two turn-of-the-century Italian crystal chandeliers are suspended from a beautiful arched ceiling carved with fruit motifs. It adjoins a handsomely furnished living room, with Chinese rosewood horseshoe-back chairs and a pair of plush Regency-style tufted-leather Chesterfield sofas in front of an 8-foot ceramic-tile fireplace. Pale peach walls in the Italian marble-floored hallways are hung with changing art exhibits, and lavish floral arrangements top a stunning swan table. Classical music or traditional jazz played downstairs during the day further enhances the inn's ambience, which is refined but never haughty.

The rooms, all named for Ansley Park streets, also have oak floors, some strewn with Oriental rugs. Painted in pastel colors or rich jewel tones typical of the Tudor period, with glossy white trim, they're elegantly furnished in antique pieces and reproductions. Your accommodation might have a brass bed or an 18th-century mahogany four-poster, crystal lamps, swag-curtained windows, or a cushioned window seat overlooking the park. Some rooms have lofty cathedral ceilings and working fireplaces, and all feature marble-topped oak wet bars, comfortable armchairs with hassocks, remote-control cable TVs, AM/FM clock radios, and full baths with whirlpool tubs. You'll find a terry-cloth robe in the closet. The 1,300-square-foot cottage has a fully equipped kitchen, two bedrooms, and a living room with a working fireplace.

Most importantly, the Ansley Inn's charming staff offers warm hospitality and gracious service to guests, creating a friendly, home-like atmosphere that will make your stay a memorable experience.

Dining/Entertainment: Complimentary breakfast includes croissants, muffins, dry cereal, pastries, fresh fruit, juices, hot chocolate, and tea or coffee. Complimentary refreshments (coffee, tea, plus cheeses, fresh-baked cookies, and/or crudites with dip) are served in the living room every afternoon.

Services: Newspaper of your choice delivered to your door daily, 24-hour concierge, room service from area restaurants.

Facilities: Complimentary membership at two local health clubs. The inn itself is building a large outdoor pool/sun deck at this writing.

★ **Shellmont Bed And Breakfast Lodge**, 821 Piedmont Ave. NE, at 6th St., Atlanta, GA 30308. ☎ **404/872-9290.** 4 rms plus carriage house. A/C **MARTA:** North Avenue or Midtown.

Rates (including continental breakfast): $70 single; $80 double in main house. $90 single; $100 double in carriage house. Extra person $15. **Note:** children 12 and under allowed in the carriage house only. AE, DC, MC, V. **Parking:** Free.

This charming 2-story Victorian mansion looks, from the outside, like a Wedgwood fairy-tale house embellished with cream-colored ribbons, bows, garlands, and shells. It was designed by noted Atlanta architect Walter T. Downing for Dr. W. P. Nicholson as a present for the doctor's new bride, hence the wedding-bell newel post on the stairway. The building dates to 1891 and is on the National Register of Historic Places. When innkeepers Ed and Debbie McCord purchased it in 1982, they were only the second owners. The property was, however, considerably down at the heels by that time. The McCords have done a superb job on its restoration, not only in repairing all the functional aspects, but in meticulously researching original paint colors, stencil designs, woodwork, and period furnishings and reproducing them with 100% accuracy.

Breakfast is served on fine china in a lovely dining room with a floor-to-ceiling mantel fireplace. Guests might while away an evening reading (the McCords keep a fairly extensive library) before a blazing fire in the oak-furnished living room. The walls of this room are covered in hand-printed silk-screen Victorian-reproduction wallpaper, the windows hung with lace curtains. There's also a downstairs parlor that was originally a music room (carved instruments adorning the mantelpiece honor the room's original function) and, Ed's favorite room, the Moorish-influenced, Kilim-carpeted "Turkish corner," with its inverted-dome ceiling.

Up the stairway (its landing graced by an exquisite five-paneled stained-glass window that the McCords believe is an authentic Tiffany) are the four guestrooms. They have gorgeous beds (perhaps you'll have an Eastlake or a bed with a 6-foot oak headboard embellished with carved ribbons and bows), leaded-glass or bay windows with floral-motif balloon curtains, Oriental rugs strewn on hand-oiled hard pine floors, and framed botanical prints on the walls. All have private baths, but no TVs or phones (local calls are free on house phones). The other accommodation, in an adjoining carriage house, offers a master bedroom, full modern bath, fully equipped kitchen, living room, and dressing area. It is equipped with a phone and TV.

Fronted by a small garden, the Shellmont has both a front porch and a lovely veranda out back with wicker rocking chairs overlooking a flower garden and fish pond.

Dining/Entertainment: Daily breakfast, included in rates, of fresh-squeezed juice, fresh and dried fruits, homemade pastries, cereal, and tea or coffee. Coffee and tea are available throughout the day in an upstairs nook, where you'll also find an ice machine, phone, and desk.

Services: Ed and Debbie live on the premises and offer all the services of a hotel concierge, daily chamber service, and fruit and fresh flowers in your room daily.

Woodruff Bed & Breakfast Inn, 223 Ponce de Leon Ave. NE, at Myrtle St., Atlanta, GA 30308. ☎ **404/875-9449** or toll free **800/473-9449.** Fax 404/875-2882. 10 rms, 2 suites. A/C TV (on request) TEL **MARTA:** North Avenue.

Rates (including full breakfast): $65–$125 single; $75–$150 double. $129 for two rooms with a shared bath (for up to four people); $109–$150 for a two-room Jacuzzi suite. AE, DISC, MC, V. **Parking:** Free.

The 3-story white-brick Victorian house, built in 1906 by an Atlanta physician, went on to a more interesting incarnation in the 1950s when Miss Bessie Woodruff bought the property and turned it into a successful house of ill repute. Officially, it was a licensed massage facility (the "girls" actually wore white nurses' uniforms), and some of Atlanta's most prominent politicians came by frequently to relieve the tensions of public office. Current owners Joan and Doug Jones not only honored Bessie by naming their bed and breakfast for her, they've displayed, in public areas, light boards that were used to keep track of the rooms in use, framed photographs of Bessie (she was a beauty), and her old love letters.

The first floor, entered via a foyer with beautiful beveled-glass doors, has a cozy plant-filled parlor with a bay window; it's furnished with turn-of-the-century antiques, including a plush Empire sofa and an English piano. The dining room, with leaded-glass windows, features a massive oak table under a crystal chandelier. Pine floors, in rooms and public areas, are waxed and buffed to a high gloss and strewn with Oriental rugs. The rooms, all but three with private baths, contain a mix of 19th- and early 20th-century English antiques, along with pieces one might categorize as "grandma's house" furnishings. Beds have ruffled comforters and lots of pillows. Your accommodation might have stained-glass or bay windows, an overhead fan, or French doors leading to a porch furnished with rocking chairs. The house itself also offers a large front porch overlooking the oak-shaded lawn. Guests in Jacuzzi suites enjoy complimentary flowers and champagne on arrival.

Dining/Entertainment: Rates include a full breakfast—eggs and bacon, fresh fruit, orange juice, jumbo muffins, cereal (on request), and tea or coffee.

Services: Free daily newspaper; magazines and books available.

Facilities: Cable TV with VCR in the parlor.

3 Buckhead

Buckhead hotels combine the quiet residential appeal of midtown accommodations with the luxury of downtown properties. Many of Atlanta's best restaurants are close by. In my opinion, it's the optimum hotel location.

Very Expensive

⭐ **Hotel Nikko Atlanta,** 3300 Peachtree Rd., just east of Piedmont Rd., Atlanta, GA 30326. ☎ **404/365-8100** or toll free **800-NIKKO-US.** Fax 404/233-5686. 418 rms, 22 suites. A/C MINIBAR TV TEL **MARTA:** Lenox.

Rates: Mon–Thurs, $150–$190 single; $170–$210 double. Fri–Sun, $119–$169 per room. Nikko floor $220 single; $240 double. Suites $435–$1,500. Extra person $25. Children under 16 stay free in parents' room. AE, CB, DC, DISC, ER, JCB, MC, V. **Parking:** $15.

The towering Hotel Nikko offers a winning combination of 18th-century American architecture and Japanese attention to aesthetic detail. An exquisite flower arrangement graces the entrance foyer, and the lobby is a sublime setting overlooking a 9,000-square-foot garden with traditional plantings, rock formations, and splashing waterfalls created by noted Kyoto landscape architects. A collection of museum-quality Japanese art, spanning four centuries, is displayed throughout the hotel.

Rooms, decorated in subtle hues (peach, teal, mocha, café-au-lait) are furnished in 18th-century mahogany reproductions, with crane-motif headboards, fresh orchids, and Japanese prints in black lacquer frames providing Eastern nuance. Every luxury is provided: three phones (bedside, bath, and desk), remote-control cable TVs with Spectravision movie options, AM/FM alarm-clock radios, terry robes, and baths equipped with hair dryers, TV speakers, cosmetic mirrors, and scales. You'll even find an umbrella in your closet. The Nikko floors (23–25) comprise a concierge level where guests enjoy upgraded amenities, services of a private concierge, and use of a very elegant lounge (complete with working fireplace)—the setting for extended continental breakfasts, afternoon teas, a large array of cocktail-hour hors d'oeuvres, and evening desserts and cordials. Gratis use of a charming conference room off the lounge is an additional benefit.

Dining/Entertainment: Kamogawa, Atlanta's premier Japanese restaurant, offers a uniquely authentic dining experience (see Chapter 6, "Atlanta Dining"). The delightful Cassis, with soaring arched windows overlooking the Japanese garden, is also much acclaimed for its sophisticated and eclectic cuisine (main courses run the gamut from risotto of porcini mushrooms to Maryland crab cakes); all meals are served here, including a Japanese breakfast and lavish Sunday brunch. A pianist entertains daily from 5 to 8pm in the plush Lobby Bar, also the setting for English-style afternoon teas. Weather permitting, a Japanese tea is also served afternoons in a tranquil garden with pagoda seating on the third floor. And a jazz trio performs nightly in the Library Bar, a handsome mahogany-paneled setting with tapestried wing chairs and tufted-leather sofas before a blazing fireplace.

Services: Complimentary overnight shoeshine, 24-hour room service, 24-hour concierge, babysitting, toys/activities for children, massage, airport shuttle, complimentary shuttle within a 2-mile radius of the hotel.

Facilities: Comprehensive business center, fully equipped health club, with TVs and VCRs on the exercise bikes, Life Trim equipment, stair machines, aerobics videos, steam, and sauna; a lovely outdoor pool and sun deck. Lenox Square and Phipps Plaza shopping malls are two blocks away.

Ritz-Carlton Buckhead, 3434 Peachtree Rd. NE, at Phipps Dr., Atlanta, GA 30326. ☎ **404/237-2700** or toll free **800/241-3333.** Fax 404/239-0078. 524 rms, 29 suites. A/C TV MINIBAR TEL **MARTA:** Lenox.

Rates: Mon–Thurs, $159–$219 single or double. Fri–Sun, $119 single or double. Club Floor, $249 single or double. Children under 12 stay free in parents' room. Inquire about packages. AE, DC, DISC, JCB, MC, V. **Parking:** $8 self, $12 valet.

From the mahogany-paneled lobby, with antique Oriental carpets on white marble floors and cut-crystal French chandeliers, to public areas graced with Regency and Georgian antiques and an outstanding collection of 18th- and 19th-century paintings and sculpture, every inch of this hotel bespeaks unexampled luxury. And the quality of service fully matches the sumptuous surroundings.

The exquisite rooms, all with large bay windows, are decorated in two color schemes: moss green/ecru and mauve/cream. Furnishings include a burled-walnut armoire (which houses a remote-control cable TV with HBO) either a sofa or armchairs upholstered in raw silk,

18th-century-reproduction beds, beautiful Chinese lamps, and Federalist mirrors. Framed botanical prints and historical lithographs adorn the walls; baths amply supplied with fine toiletries contain scales, phones, and makeup mirrors; and a fully stocked refrigerator/ bar is concealed in a handsome cabinet. You'll find a terry robe in your closet.

Floors 18 and 19 are the hotel's Club Floors, with a deluxe private concierge-staffed lounge in which lavish complimentary buffets are served daily at breakfast and cocktail hour. Complimentary drinks and snacks are also available here throughout the day; a full English tea is served every afternoon, cordials and chocolates at night.

Dining/Entertainment: The Dining Room at the Ritz-Carlton Buckhead is one of Atlanta's premier restaurants; as such it is covered extensively in Chapter 6. The Lobby Lounge, its mahogany-paneled walls hung with 18th- and 19th-century portraits and sporting scenes, centers on a glowing oak-log fire. It is the setting for afternoon English-style teas. A classical pianist plays from 3 to 5pm daily, and jazz artists entertain evenings. From 5 to 7:30pm, 11 different martinis are featured on a special drink menu. The three-tiered Café, an all-day dining room, its mahogany-paneled walls hung with equestrian-themed paintings, is also a repository of art and antiques. Its classic haute-cuisine menu includes light health-conscious choices. A lavish buffet brunch is served here every Sunday. In the adjoining Café Bar, there's music for dancing Friday and Saturday nights from 8:30pm to 12:30am. And Expresso's, on the lower level, with indoor seating as well as outdoor umbrella tables on a poplar-shaded courtyard, serves full breakfasts and lunch specials weekdays from 7am to 3pm.

Services: Limousine on request, airport shuttle and shuttle to nearby malls, newspaper delivered to your door each morning, 24-hour room service, nightly bed turndown with gourmet chocolates, currency exchange, concierge, 1-hour pressing, on-premises seamstress, personalized shopping, complimentary shoeshine.

Facilities: Full business center, swimming and fitness center, steam and sauna rooms, Jacuzzi, gift shop, hair salon, tobacconist, fur boutique.

★ **Swissôtel,** 3391 Peachtree Rd. NE, between Lenox and Piedmont Rds., Atlanta, GA 30326. ☎ **404/365-0065** or toll free **800/63-SWISS.** Fax 404/233-8786. 348 rms, 17 suites. A/C MINIBAR TV TEL **MARTA:** Lenox (complimentary transport to/ from station).

Rates: Mon–Thurs, $149–$210 single; $170–$235 double. Club Level $210 single; $280 double. Fri–Sun, $109 per room; $165 Club Level. Extra person $25. Children under 16 free in parents' room. AE, CB, DC, DISC, ER, JCB, MC, V. **Parking:** $11 valet, $6 self.

Opened in 1991, the Zurich-based Swissôtel (it's owned by Swissair) added a new aesthetic dimension to Atlanta's hotel scene. Its postmodern European architecture and interior spaces utilize Bauhaus elements, notably exemplified in a pristine white porcelainlike tile

Buckhead Accommodations

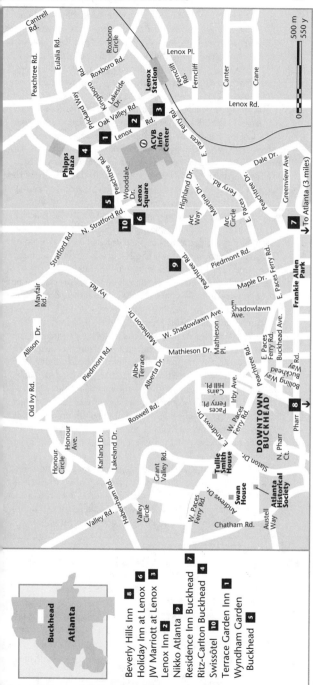

Beverly Hills Inn **8**
Holiday Inn at Lenox **6**
JW Marriott at Lenox **3**
Lenox Inn **2**
Nikko Atlanta **9**
Residence Inn Buckhead **7**
Ritz-Carlton Buckhead **4**
Swissôtel **10**
Terrace Garden Inn **1**
Wyndham Garden Buckhead **5**

Information ⓘ

exterior with a graceful piano curve. An impressive lobby, with floor-to-45-foot-ceiling windows and a grand staircase, is warmed by the extensive use of reddish Australian lacewood paneling. Hallway carpets are designed after a Paul Klee painting, and original works by internationally known contemporary artists—Rauschenberg, Chagall, Schnabel, Stella, and many others—grace restaurants and public spaces. This is a visually exciting hotel.

Rooms are uniquely furnished in Biedermeier-style birds-eye maple pieces with black lacquer accents and capacious leather-topped desks. Color schemes—subtle tone-on-tone gray and lavender hues—are enhanced by interesting modernistic lamps and mirror frames and splash-of-color elements such as sienna velvet armchairs or chaise lounges. Armoires house remote-control cable TVs (with Spectravision/HBO movie options and video checkout), and all rooms are equipped with terry robes, three phones (with call waiting, voice-mail messaging, and computer jacks), and AM/FM alarm-clock radios. Baths offer cosmetic mirrors, TV speakers, hair dryers, and upscale biodegradable toiletries. Especially nice are corner king rooms (ask for one when you reserve). The 21st and 22nd floors comprise a concierge-staffed Club Level with a plush private lounge, the setting for gratis continental breakfasts, afternoon teas, cocktail hour hors d'oeuvres, and late-night pastries. Guests on these floors enjoy special services such as nightly bed turndown.

Dining/Entertainment: Opus, the hotel's acclaimed premier restaurant, is detailed in Chapter 6. The charming semicircular Café Gamay shares Opus's distinguished kitchen, offering its lunch menu throughout the day. In good weather, the café has patio dining. And sandwiched between these fine eateries is the posh art deco Lobby Bar, offering light fare and nightly piano entertainment.

Services: Concierge, complimentary shuttle to any destination in a 2-mile radius (including MARTA and the plush upscale Lenox Square and Phipps Plaza Malls), multilingual staff, airport shuttle, 24-hour room service, daily newspaper delivery, complimentary shoeshine.

Facilities: Gift shop, unisex hair salon/spa, car rental desk, airline desk (Swissair), 24-hour business/communications center. A small but nicely equipped health club offers treadmills, stair machines, rowing machines, exercise bikes, free weights, a multi-station Nautilus machine, a lap pool, sauna, steam room, and aerobics studio.

Expensive

⭐ **JW Marriott At Lenox,** 3300 Lenox Rd. NE, at E. Paces Ferry Rd., Atlanta, GA 30326. ☎ **404/262-3344** or toll free **800/228-9290.** Fax 404/262-8603. 323 rms, 48 suites. A/C MINIBAR TV TEL **MARTA:** Lenox.

Rates: Mon–Thurs, $139–$180 for up to four people. Fri–Sun, $119 per room. Club Level rooms $200. AE, CB, DC, DISC, ER, MC, V. **Parking:** $7 self, $9 valet.

This luxurious Marriott, with an interior modeled after Atlanta's historic Swan House (see Chapter 7), is enchanting from the moment you step inside its elegant marble-floored entranceway under a silver-leafed coffered ceiling. The residential-style lobby divides into a series of beautifully appointed, cozy living rooms furnished with plush sofas and Chippendale pieces, its gracious ambience enhanced by classical music and exquisite flower arrangements.

Rooms are charmingly furnished with Chippendale-style mahogany pieces, the walls hung with gilt-framed watercolors of Buckhead mansions. Picture windows offer panoramic vistas. Handsome mahogany armoires house remote-control cable TVs with free HBO and Spectravision pay movie channels, minibars, and AM/FM alarm-clock radios. Each room has three phones (bath, beside, and desk—with voice-mail messaging and computer jacks), lavish marble baths are equipped with scales and hair dryers, and you'll find an iron and ironing board in your closet. Floors 23 to 25 comprise the Concierge Level, which features a gorgeous concierge-staffed private lounge, setting for a substantial buffet breakfast, afternoon cocktails and hors d'oeuvres, and late-night liqueurs and chocolates. The Marriott connects from an interior door to the Lenox Square Mall, and the even posher Phipps Plaza Mall is within walking distance.

Dining/Entertainment: The exquisite Swan Room is designed to suggest an 18th-century English garden, with pale-yellow walls, Chinese Chippendale-style chairs, and English Axminster carpeting. At night, special lighting creates a leaf design on the tablecloths, evoking an elegant dinner in the woods. Serving American/Continental fare, the Swan Room is open for all meals; reasonably priced weekend buffet brunches are especially popular. The clubby Ottley's, with Persian runners on bare oak floors and mahogany-paneled walls hung with equestrian-themed art, offers piano bar entertainment Wednesday to Saturday evenings. Light fare is available. And yet another plush setting for cocktails/light fare is the cozy Lobby Lounge, with comfortable sofas and armchairs before a working pagoda-style fireplace backed by Brazilian marble.

Services: 24-hour room service, multilingual concierge staff, nightly bed turndown, airport shuttle, 1-hour dry cleaning, *USA Today* delivered to your room each morning.

Facilities: Large indoor pool in a setting patterned after a Roman bath, health club (offering Stairmasters, treadmills, free weights, Lifecycles, a multi-station Universal machine, steam, and sauna), car rental desk, full business center, pastry shop, Lenox Square Mall (the largest in the Southeast) adjoining.

★ **Terrace Garden Inn,** 3405 Lenox Rd. NE, between Peachtree and E. Paces Ferry Rds., Atlanta, GA 30326. ☎ **404/261-9250** or toll free **800/866-ROOM.** Fax 404/848-7301. 357 rms, 7 suites. A/C TV TEL **MARTA:** Lenox.

Rates: Mon–Thurs, $135–$155 single; $150–$170 double. Fri–Sun, $89–$129 per room. Club level $175 single; $190 double. Extra person $15. Children under 18 free in parents' room. AE, DC, DISC, MC, V.

Parking: $4 per night for the first two nights, no charge for additional nights (self only, covered garage).

This is an especially lovely hotel that offers abundant services and facilities plus a great location (the Lenox Square Mall is just across the street). Antique furnishings, exquisite flower arrangements, ficus trees, and planters of greenery grace the public areas, and sprightly classical music replaces the usual din of Muzak. Rooms are elegantly residential in decor, furnished with French country and 18th-century-reproduction mahogany pieces (some have four-poster or brass beds); they're decorated in three attractive earth-toned color schemes with accents of moss green, sienna/cream, or mauve. Most rooms have balconies, and all offer extra phones in the bath, AM/FM alarm-clock radios, and remote-control cable TVs with free HBO and Spectravision pay movies. Phones are equipped with call waiting and computer jacks. Rooms with king-size beds have plush armchairs with ottomans.

Guests on Club floors enjoy additional amenities: a bilevel lounge with a concierge on duty; complimentary continental breakfast, cocktails, and hors d'oeuvres; free pressing and shoeshine services; upgraded in-room toiletries, terry robes, umbrellas, and nightly bed turndown with gourmet chocolates and liqueurs. The Terrace Garden's charm and graciousness have attracted numerous celebrity guests, from Presidents Carter, Nixon, and Reagan, to tennis star Andre Agassi and show-biz luminaries Elizabeth Taylor, Red Skelton, and Willie Nelson.

Dining/Entertainment: On two levels, The Café, one of Atlanta's prettiest hotel dining rooms, is garden-themed, with gilt-framed botanical prints on white-trimmed mauve walls, tapestried bamboo chairs at flower-bedecked tables, and lots of leafy greenery. A window wall on the upper level overlooks the pool. The fare is American/Continental. Open daily from 6:30am to 11pm. The cozy, equestrian-themed Corner Hearth Lounge offers seating in plush chairs and sofas around a vast stone-walled, copper-hooded fireplace (ablaze in winter).

Services: Room service from 6:30am to 11pm, free daily newspaper, airport shuttle, concierge.

Facilities: Avis car rental desk, United Airlines desk, gift shop. The extensive Health & Racquet Center offers racquetball, an indoor pool, Nautilus equipment, Lifecycles, stair machines, steam, sauna, and Jacuzzi. There's also an outdoor swimming pool with waterfalls cascading over bronze dolphins and fish sculptures.

Moderate

Holiday Inn At Lenox, 3777 Peachtree Rd. NE, between Lenox and Piedmont Rds., Atlanta, GA 30326. ☎ **404/264-1111** or toll free **800/HOLIDAY.** Fax 404/233-7061. 293 rms, 4 suites. A/C TV TEL **MARTA:** Lenox.

Rates: Mon–Thurs, $89–$109 single or double. Fri–Sun, $69–$79. Extra person $10. Children under 18 stay free in parents' room. AE, DC, DISC, ER, JCB, MC, V. **Parking:** Free.

Conveniently located adjacent to the Lenox Square Mall, this 11-story Holiday Inn recently redecorated all of its rooms in soft teal, beige, and terra cotta hues, with attractive striped damask bedspreads and drapes. Furnished in oak-trimmed beige Formica pieces, they're equipped with AM/FM alarm-clock radios, coffeemakers, phones with computer jacks, and remote-control cable TVs with free HBO and pay-movie options, plus, uniquely, Game Boy (your kids will be thrilled). Most also have small refrigerators. Future plans call for the top three floors to be converted to a concierge level.

Dining/Entertainment: The Brentwood Café, a pretty dining room with a wall of windows and fresh flowers on every table, serves American fare at all meals.

Services: Room service 7am to 2pm and 5 to 10pm (Pizza Hut also delivers), airport shuttle, free *USA Today* in restaurant, free van transport within three miles of the hotel.

Facilities: Outdoor pool and sundeck, coin-op washer and dryer, business center. Guests can use a nearby health club called Gold's Gym for a small fee; it offers stair machines, treadmills, Lifecycles, free weights, and a full complement of Body Master equipment.

★ **Residence Inn Buckhead,** 2960 Piedmont Rd. NE., between Pharr Rd. and Lindbergh Dr., Atlanta, GA 30305.

☎ **404/239-0677** or toll free **800/331-3131.** Fax 404/262-9683. 136 suites. A/C TV TEL **MARTA:** Lindbergh or Lenox (each about a mile away); buses stop half a block away.

Rate: Mon–Thurs, studio suites (for up to four people) $109; penthouse suites (for up to six) $144. Fri–Sun, studio suites $79; penthouse suites $119 (subject to availability). Reductions are available for stays of seven nights or longer. AE, DC, DISC, MC, V. **Parking:** Free.

This home-away-from-home was designed to meet the needs of travelers making extended visits, but it's marvelous even if you're only spending a single night. It's like having your own luxurious apartment, with a private entrance and a large, fully equipped kitchen containing a refrigerator (it makes ice), dishwasher (the maid does your dishes), sink, stove, microwave oven, toaster, coffeemaker, and table settings for four. The kitchen is stocked with complimentary tea and coffee, sugar, cream, and microwave popcorn, and there's plenty of counter space for preparing meals.

Accommodations—which include comfortable living-room areas—are decorated in mauve or smoky blue color schemes, with pretty floral-print bedspreads and very nice watercolors and botanical prints on the walls. Among your in-room amenities are clocks, AM/FM radios, and remote-control cable TVs with free HBO (VCRs and movies can be rented). About half the suites have working fireplaces (during winter, logs are available from the front desk). The most luxurious accommodations are duplex penthouses with vaulted ceilings, full dining-room/office areas, two baths, and living-room fireplaces.

The Residence Inn is located on five attractively landscaped acres backed by woods, and the suites are in 2-storey cream stucco chalets. You can park right outside your door.

Dining/Entertainment: One of the most salient features here is the cathedral-ceilinged Gatehouse Lounge. A TV, small library, a stereo, and a big sectional sofa facing a blazing fireplace are among its amenities. The Gatehouse provides many opportunities to mingle with fellow guests over breakfast (a buffet of fresh fruits, cereals, yogurt, pastries, juice, tea, and coffee) and at cocktail-hour parties on Monday, Tuesday, and Thursday from 5 to 7pm (featuring gratis beer, wine, and hot and cold hors d'oeuvres); Wednesday a full barbecue or buffet dinner is served during those hours.

Services: Airport shuttle, complimentary shuttle service within a 3-mile radius of the property at specified hours, complimentary grocery shopping, free daily newspapers in lounge.

Facilities: Outdoor pool and sundeck with adjoining whirlpool; coin-op washers and dryers; outdoor barbecue grills; on-premises basketball, volleyball, and paddle-tennis courts; and complimentary use of an extensively equipped health club nearby (with every kind of workout equipment, a Junior Olympic indoor pool, an outdoor pool, jogging, track, tennis/racquetball/squash courts, and much, much more).

Wyndham Garden Hotel Buckhead, 3340 Peachtree Rd. NE, between Lenox and Piedmont Rds., Atlanta, GA 30326.

☎ **404/231-1234** or toll free **800/WYNDHAM.** Fax 404/231-5236. 221 rms, 10 suites. A/C TV TEL **MARTA:** Lenox.

Rates: Mon–Thurs, $109 single; $119 double. Fri–Sun, $79 single or double. Suites $169–$219. Extra person $10. Children under 14 stay free in parents' room. AE, CB, DC, DISC, JCB, MC, V. **Parking:** $4 (self or valet).

Designed with the business traveler in mind, this is an equally viable choice for the tourist. Entered via an attractive cherrywood-paneled lobby with an oak parquet floor, it houses comfortable teal-carpeted guest rooms fitted out with pretty ochre/sienna/teal-striped bedspreads and drapes, traditional mahogany furnishings (including large desks), upholstered recliner chairs, closets with louver doors, and ecru faux-silk walls hung with botanical prints. Large king-bedded rooms are especially desirable. In-room amenities include AM/FM alarm-clock radios, coffeemakers (coffee and tea are supplied), phones with 25-inch cords and computer jacks, hair dryers, and remote-control cable TVs with free Showtime movies.

Dining/Entertainment: The garden-themed bi-level Savannah Room, with swagged floral-print curtains, flower-bedecked tables amid planters of greenery, and a wall of windows overlooking a brick patio, serves all meals. The menu features steak, seafood, pastas, pizzas, and quesadillas. Beauregard's, a handsome lounge where

19th-century equestrian prints are displayed on mahogany-wainscoted walls, is furnished with plush sofas, club chairs, and wing chairs; it serves complimentary hors d'oeuvres weekdays from 5 to 7pm.

Services: Room service 5 to 10pm, airport shuttle, complimentary *USA Today* and Atlanta paper at front desk, free courtesy van to/from Lenox Square Mall, Phipps Plaza, and the Lenox MARTA station. The front desk supplies gratis toothbrushes, toothpaste, razors, shaving cream, deodorant, and other bath amenities you may have neglected to pack.

Facilities: Pleasantly secluded pool and sundeck bordered by trees, gift shop. Guests enjoy free use of the adjacent state-of-the-art Sports Life Fitness Center, offering a full complement of Body Masters, Cybex, David, and LifeCircuit machines, Stairmasters, treadmills, Lifecycles, free weights, massage, steam, sauna, aerobics classes, child care, basketball/racquetball courts, indoor track, and more. Buckhead's posh shopping malls are close by.

Inexpensive

Lenox Inn, 3387 Lenox Rd. NE, between Peachtree and E. Paces Ferry Rds., Atlanta, GA 30326. ☎ **404/261-5500** or toll free **800/241-0200.** Fax 404/261-1640. 174 rms, 6 suites. A/C TV TEL **MARTA:** Lenox.

Rates: Sun–Thurs, $64 single; $69 double. Fri–Sat, $59.95 per room. Extra person $5. Children under 18 stay free in parents' room. AE, CB, DC, MC, V. **Parking:** Free.

Considering all you get here, in a great location just across the street from Lenox Square Mall, the Lenox Inn is a great bargain. Under the same ownership as the adjacent Terrace Garden Inn and sharing many of its facilities, the Lenox offers accommodations in four 2- and 3-story cream-trimmed brick buildings with shuttered windows. They have a kind of quaint colonial look. Rooms are pristinely charming, decorated in mauve and forest green, with cherrywood doors, 18th-century-reproduction mahogany furnishings, cream-colored walls, and drapes in a pretty floral pattern. Amenities include remote-control cable TV (with Spectravision pay movies and free HBO), AM/FM alarm-clock radios, and a full complement of toiletries in the bath. Some baths have extra sinks in dressing rooms, and rooms with king-size beds offer steambaths. Only one building has an elevator, by the way; ask for it, or a first-floor room elsewhere, if stairs are a problem.

Dining/Entertainment: A choice of a complimentary continental breakfast (homemade muffins, juice, and tea or coffee) or a large buffet breakfast ($6.25) is offered in a cozy, cherry-paneled restaurant with a working fireplace. Guests also gather here for complimentary cocktails and hors d'oeuvres nightly from 5:30 to 6:30pm. In summer there are occasionally gratis poolside cookouts/buffets with an open bar. And guests can charge meals at the Terrace Garden (see listing above) to their rooms at the Lenox.

Services: Airport shuttle, complimentary newspaper (*Atlanta Journal Constitution*) at front desk, free local calls. Room service is available via a menu compiled from local restaurants.

Facilities: Two outdoor swimming pools, health-club facilities of the Terrace Garden Inn next door at no charge.

Bed & Breakfasts

★ **Beverly Hills Inn,** 65 Sheridan Dr. NE, just off Peachtree Rd., Atlanta, GA 30305. ☎ **404/233-8520** or toll free **800/331-8520.** Fax 404/233-8520, ext. 18. 18 suites. A/C TV TEL **MARTA bus:** No. 23 at the corner.

Rates (including continental breakfast): $74–$90 single; $90–$120 double for a one-bedroom suite. $120–$140 for a two-bedroom suite accommodating up to four people. Extra person $7. Children under 12 stay free in parents' room. Reductions available for stays of a week or more. AE, CB, DC, DISC, JCB, MC, V. **Parking:** Free.

Housed in a Wedgwood green 1920s California-style building, with forest-green shutters and window awnings, this charming B&B is located on a sedately residential tree-lined street. British owner/host Mit Amin offers warm hospitality to guests. On the first floor is a cozy parlor/library where a decanter of port is available all day. Another library is downstairs in the sunny garden room, which has a skylit conservatory area filled with plants.

Rooms are cheerful and attractive, decorated in an eclectic period mix of antiques (many of them English pieces) and collectibles, with very pretty floral fabric bedspreads and curtains, oak floors strewn with area rugs, and framed botanical prints on the walls. Some have canopied beds. All are equipped with kitchenettes (the maid does your dishes), TVs, and AM/FM alarm-clock radios. Private balconies are entered via French doors. Several supermarkets are within easy walking distance, should you want to cook in your room, but the area also abounds with good restaurants. Classical music played in public areas enhances the residential ambience, as do dozens of flourishing plants.

Dining/Entertainment: An extended continental breakfast—bagels, rolls, pastries, fresh fruit, juice, yogurt, tea, and coffee—is served in the garden room. Or, in good weather, you can enjoy the morning meal at umbrella tables on the front lawn.

Services: You'll find a half bottle of burgundy in your room on arrival; four daily newspapers are complimentary; free local calls.

Facilities: Lounge with Xerox and fax machines, complimentary washer/dryer, complimentary membership privileges at the nearby Buckhead Towne Club, a state-of-the-art facility offering two outdoor swimming pools, Lifecycles, Stairmasters, saunas, Jacuzzi, a full complement of Nautilus equipment, racquetball, and squash.

4 Georgia's Stone Mountain

Georgia's Stone Mountain Park, just 16 miles east of downtown Atlanta, is a recreation area with 3,200 acres of lakes and wooded parkland. It is, in itself, a major travel destination, visited by over six million tourists annually. **Note:** There's a one-time $5 parking fee to enter the park.

Expensive

 Evergreen Conference Center and Resort, One Lakeview Dr., Stone Mountain Park, Stone Mountain, GA 30086. ☎ **404/879-9900** or toll free **800/722-1000.** Fax 404/469-9013. 220 rms. 29 suites. A/C TV TEL

Rates: $100–$140 single; $125–$160 double; rates depend on view. Extra person $20. Children under 18 free in parents' room. Inquire about packages when you reserve. AE, CB, DC, DISC, ER, MC, V. **Parking:** Free (self only).

Geared primarily to business travel, the Evergreen is also a good choice for vacationers. A turreted stucco lakefront "castle" nestled in a fragrant forest of pine, its lodgelike lobby centers on a massive stone fireplace backed by cherry paneling. Balconied rooms are large and luxuriously appointed, decorated in neutral tones and furnished with floral-tapestried armchairs and 18th-century American reproduction mahogany pieces. Each contains a remote-control cable TV (concealed in a handsome armoire) with free HBO and Spectravision pay movies and an AM/FM alarm-clock radio.

Dining/Entertainment: The stunning Waterside Restaurant, under a 35-foot rotunda, offers lake, mountain, and treetop views. Buffets are offered at all meals in addition to à la carte regional American fare. Even breakfast can get fancy here, with entrées such as quail eggs and sautéed quail with grits. It's open daily from 6:30am to 11:30pm. Both Ivy's, a plush window-walled lounge offering complimentary cocktail-hour hors d'oeuvres, and Vista, a wicker-furnished lobby lounge, overlook the pool. Classical music is played in all public areas and restaurants here. The poolside snack bar, open seasonally, is called Splash.

Services: Complimentary *USA Today* at front desk, 24-hour room service, airport limo, concierge (tickets for all park attractions sold at the concierge desk).

Facilities: Two nightlit tennis courts, two 18-hole championship golf courses, full business/meeting facilities, gift shop, health club (with indoor swimming pool, whirlpool, Universal multi-station machine, free weights, treadmill, rowing machine, Lifecycle, and stair machines), large outdoor pool, whirlpool, baby wading pool, and sun deck.

Inexpensive

Stone Mountain Park Inn, Stone Mountain Park, Stone Mountain, GA 30086 ☎ **404/469-3311** or toll free **800/277-0007.** Fax 404/498-5691. 89 rms, 3 suites. A/C TV TEL

Rates: $49–$99 for one or two people (rates vary seasonally). Extra person $10. Children under 12 stay free in parents' room. Honeymoon suites $115, including a bottle of champagne and breakfast. Golf, tennis, and other packages available. AE, CB, DC, MC, V. **Parking:** Free (self only).

This charming inn, built in 1965, is housed in a two-story white-colonnaded brick building that wraps around a central courtyard. Rooms, decorated in taupe and Williamsburg blue, are lovely, featuring Chippendale-reproduction walnut and mahogany furnishings and turn-of-the-century-style ceiling fan/lighting fixtures. Most have large vanity/dressing room areas and spacious parlors with comfortable sofas and armchairs. Walls are covered in pretty floral-motif papers and hung with framed Williamsburg sampler embroideries. Honeymoon suites offer king-size, four-poster canopied beds. Remote-control cable TVs are equipped with free HBO. Almost all accommodations have courtyard-facing balconies or patios with rocking chairs. The inn prides itself on offering warm southern hospitality.

Dining/Entertainment: A winding staircase leads from the lobby to the inn's attractive dining room. Its floor-to-ceiling windows overlook verdant scenery, and there's balcony seating facing the mountain sculptures. All meals here are buffets (very reasonably priced) featuring southern fare.

Services: Limited room service during restaurant hours, airport limo; tickets for all park attractions sold across the street.

Facilities: The park itself offers everything in the way of recreational activities, including two 18-hole championship golf courses (see Chapter 7 for details). On the premises: coin-op laundry, business services, very large outdoor pool/sundeck in a woodsy setting.

A Campground

Family Campground, Stone Mountain Park, P.O. Box 778, Stone Mountain, GA 30086. ☎ **404/498-5710.**

Rates: $13 for a tent site, $14 for site with water and electricity, $15 for full hookup. Rates cover two people; additional people pay $2 per night. Children 11 and under stay free. AE, DISC, MC, V.

A very large campground, with sections for pop-ups, RVs, and tents, this is a great place to stay. Nestled in the woods, the area has many sites overlooking the lake, especially in the tent section. All have barbecue grills, and picnic tables are scattered throughout. Public facilities include a dining pavilion, playgrounds, laundries, and showers. The park's beach is close by.

5 | Druid Hills/Emory University/Brookhaven

Though not a happening section of town in terms of restaurants or attractions, this area, east of midtown and Buckhead, offers good value for your hotel dollar. And if you have a car, the properties listed below are only about a 10-minute drive from the center of things.

Moderate

Courtyard By Marriott, 1236 Executive Park Dr., off N. Druid Hills Rd., Atlanta, GA 30329. ☎ **404/728-0708** or toll free **800/321-2211.** Fax 404/636-4019. 133 rms, 12 suites. A/C TV TEL **MARTA bus:** in front of the hotel.

Rates: Sun–Thurs, $86 single, $96 double. Fri–Sat, $69–$75 per room. Suites $99 single; $109 double. Extra person $10. Children under 18 stay free in parents' room. Reduced rates offered for stays of seven days or more. AE, CB, DC, DISC, MC, V. **Parking:** Free (self only).

Housed in a 4-story cream stucco building, in an attractively landscaped setting of trees, shrubbery, and well-tended flower beds, the Courtyard represents yet another kind of link in the Marriott chain. It's a limited-service (no bellhops, though you can get a luggage cart), moderately priced lodging. But don't picture a spartan, no-frills atmosphere. This is a beautiful property with a pleasant, plant-filled lobby and very nice rooms indeed.

Furnished with substantial oak pieces, the rooms have ecru walls hung with gilt-framed floral prints, brass lighting fixtures, and pretty print bedspreads. They're decorated in two color schemes—muted green or mocha-and-mauve, both with sienna accents. All rooms feature large desks, nice-size dressing-room areas, full-length folding-mirror closet doors, 25-foot phone cords, remote-control cable TVs with free HBO and On-Command pay movie channels, bedside AM/FM alarm-clock radios, and hot-water dispensers so you can make tea or coffee (both available free at the front desk) in your room. Suites—a good bet for families—have full sofa-bedded living rooms with extra phones and TVs plus small refrigerators.

Dining/Entertainment: A delightful lobby restaurant, with seating around a fireplace and overlooking a verdant garden, serves breakfast, lunch, and dinner daily. Prices are very low. A comfortable bar/lounge adjoins.

Services: Airport shuttle, room service at dinner.

Facilities: Medium-size outdoor pool, indoor whirlpool, poolside gazebo (nice for picnicking), lobby vending machines which supply necessaries, coin-op washers and dryers. A workout room is equipped with a multi-station Universal machine, exercise bike, and stair climber.

Emory Inn, 1641 Clifton Rd. NE, between Briarcliff and N. Decatur Rds., Atlanta, GA 30329. ☎ **404/712-6700** or toll free **800/933-6679.** Fax 404/712-6701. 107 rms. A/C TV TEL **MARTA bus:** No. 6 Emory stops in front of the hotel.

Rates: Sun–Thurs, $84–$98 single. Fri–Sat, $64–$74 per room for up to four people. $10 each additional person. Children under 12 stay free in parents' room. AE, CB, DC, DISC, MC, V. **Parking:** Free (self only).

Owned by Emory University, this totally delightful hotel is bordered by 14 acres of woodland property. Though it's quite centrally located—just 6 miles from downtown—it's peaceful out here; you'll wake to birds singing every morning. This sense of tranquillity is enhanced by classical music played in public areas which include a charming lobby and a cozy living room/lounge with a working fireplace. Rooms, furnished in Early American-style knotty-pine pieces, are attractively decorated in pale peach or apricot color schemes with teal accents. Many overlook the woods. Amenities include remote-control cable TVs (with free HBO and Spectravision pay movies), AM/FM alarm-clock radios, and phones with voice-mail messaging and computer jacks. **Note:** An expansion is underway at this writing adding 200 new rooms and a new restaurant and lounge.

Dining/Entertainment: The lovely Emory Café, with bamboo and wicker garden furnishings and fresh flowers on every table, serves buffet and à la carte American/continental fare at all meals. There's also outdoor seating for dining or cocktails in a beautiful flower garden.

Services: Airport shuttle, room service during restaurant hours, complimentary *USA Today* in lobby, complimentary morning coffee, complimentary shuttle service to Lenox Square Mall and local MARTA stations.

Facilities: Coin-op washers and dryers, medium-sized L-shaped swimming pool/sun deck bordered by flower beds, Jacuzzi. Guests enjoy gratis use of a vast fitness complex on campus with an indoor pool, 12 night-lit tennis courts, basketball, indoor track, racquetball, a full complement of Nautilus equipment, and much more.

Budget

Budgetel Inn, 2535 Chantilly Dr. NE, just off Cheshire Bridge Rd., Atlanta, GA 30324. ☎ **404/321-0999** or toll free **800/428-3438.** Fax 404/636-3384. 92 rms, 10 suites. A/C TV TEL **MARTA bus:** No. 47 bus stops at the corner weekdays.

Rates: $35.95–$47.95 single. Each additional person pays $7. Children 18 and under stay free in parents' room. AE, CB, DC, DISC, MC, V. **Parking:** Free (self only).

This hotel, part of a Milwaukee-based chain, offers great value to price-conscious travelers. Its small lobby is clean and cozy; its rooms are immaculate and well tended. Furnished in oak pieces, with attractive teal carpets, mauve bedspreads, and nicely chosen prints adorning ecru walls, all rooms have recessed windows (with screens) that can actually be opened—a welcome alternative to air conditioning. In-room amenities include dressing areas, coffeemakers, 25-foot phone cords, computer jacks, and remote-control cable TVs with Spectravision and Showtime movie stations. Ten larger rooms, called leisure suites, offer refrigerators, microwave ovens, hairdryers, and sofa beds. Coin-op washers and dryers are on the premises. There's no restaurant, but a sweet roll, juice, and coffee are delivered to your room gratis each morning. Local calls are free.

6   Off I-20

Though fairly far out east of town, these two properties are located right off I-20, allowing you to zip into downtown Atlanta in about 10 to 15 minutes by car.

Budget

Econo Lodge, 2574 Candler Rd., just off I-20 at exit 33, Atlanta, GA 30032. ☎ **404/243-4422** or toll free **800/424-4777.** 60 rms. A/C TV TEL **MARTA bus:** Bus #15 stops in front of hotel.

Rates: $32–$100 single; $38–100 double. Extra person $4. Children under 12 free. AE, DC, MC, V. **Parking:** Free.

The Econo Lodge slogan is "Spend a night, not a fortune," and that's just what you can do very happily here. The property opened in 1989, so its oak-furnished rooms are spiffy-looking and attractive, with plum carpeting and curtains and color-coordinated mauve-and-green floral-design bedspreads. You get a remote-control, 25-inch TV with HBO, and some rooms with king-size beds even have wet bars with sinks and cabinets. The property is just a 10-minute drive from downtown. A Long John Silver's and a Wendy's adjoin the Lodge, numerous other eateries are close by, and free coffee, juice, and doughnuts are served in the lobby each morning.

Motel 6, 2565 Wesley Chapel Rd., off I-20, Atlanta, GA 30035. ☎ **404/288-6911.** 100 rms. A/C TV TEL

Rates: $28.99 single; $34.99 double. Each additional person $3. Children under 18 stay free in parents room. AE, CB, DC, DISC, MC, V. **Parking:** Free

Located in Decatur, Motel 6 offers all you *really* need in the way of accommodations at a very low cost. And it has a swimming pool. Most of the rooms have two double beds (10 have one double bed), and all offer satellite TVs with free HBO. Dudley's, a western-style restaurant and lounge on the premises (it's like a cowboy version of "Cheers"), serves up steaks, salads, burgers, and sandwiches. It also has an oyster bar. Open till 3 or 4am every night, its entertainment options include three pool tables, a large-screen TV on which sports events are aired, and friendly conversations with locals.

6

Atlanta Dining

1	Downtown	103
•	Frommer's Smart Traveler: Restaurants	110
2	Midtown	112
•	Frommer's Cool for Kids: Restaurants	112
3	Buckhead	125
4	Virginia-Highland/Little Five Points	140
5	Sweet Auburn	145
6	Decatur	146
7	Chamblee	147
8	Specialty Dining	148

ALTHOUGH I LIVE IN ONE OF THE NATION'S TOP RESTAURANT TOWNS—NEW York—most of the year, believe it or not I have occasional cravings for various only-in-Atlanta culinary creations—soft-shell crab in lemony red-pepper coulis at Pano and Paul's, baked cheese-stuffed figs wrapped in Parma ham at Partner's, fried oysters at the Ocean Club, Rocky's baked rigatoni with chicken balsamico, macaroni and cheese at the OK Café, Oreo cheesecake (the world's best) at Mick's . . . and many delectable others. This is a town that has gastronomically arrived while continuing to nurture its grits-and-greens roots. Atlanta dining options run the gamut from superb ethnic dishes (Chinese, Thai, and Cajun, to name a few) to the most sophisticated contemporary and traditional haute-cuisine fare. All that and sugar-cured smoked ham with redeye gravy, too!

Atlantans love to dine out. Reservations, where accepted, are always a good idea—in some places, imperative.

How to Read the Listings

Listings are divided first by location, then alphabetically by price. I've used the following price categories: **very expensive** (dinner is over $45 per person for a full meal, including a glass of wine, tip, and tax), **expensive** ($35 to $45), **moderate** ($25 to $35), **inexpensive** ($15 to $25), and **budget** (under $15).

Keep in mind that the above categories refer to dinner prices, and some very expensive restaurants offer more affordable lunches (most notably City Grill) or early-bird dinners. Also, I'm going under the assumption that you're not stinting when you order. Some restaurants, for instance, have main courses ranging from $12 to $20. In most cases, you can dine for less if you order carefully.

Note: MARTA stations are listed where they are within walking distance. If you need bus-routing information, call **848-4711.**

1 Downtown

Your choices here range from the ultra-elegant City Grill to the world's largest drive-in.

Very Expensive

⭐ **City Grill,** 50 Hurt Plaza, at Edgewood Ave. ☎ **524-2489.**
  Cuisine: CREATIVE/AMERICAN. **Reservations:** Recommended.
  MARTA: Peachtree Center. **Parking:** Complimentary valet parking.
  Prices: Appetizers $5–$8.50 at lunch, $6.50–$8.50 at dinner; main courses $9–$13.50 at lunch, $16–$25 at dinner. AE, CB, DC, MC, V.
  Open: Lunch Mon–Fri 11:30am–2:30pm; dinner Mon–Sat 5:30–10:30pm, Sun hours vary (call ahead).

Atlanta's most opulent restaurant, City Grill opened in 1988 and immediately became a mecca for downtown power-lunchers and a high-society enclave at dinner. For openers, no dining room in town can match its architectural splendor. Ensconced in the lavishly refurbished Hurt Building, designed in 1912 to be the largest and most magnificent office building in the South, it is entered via a marble-walled Rotunda with a rosette- and gold-leaf-adorned dome. Downstairs seating, amid potted palms, is in upholstered teal or moss-green neoclassical Georgian-, Sheraton-, and Queen Anne–style chairs at oversized tables covered in white linen. Murals of misty pastoral scenes adorn the walls, graceful European candelabra chandeliers glitter overhead, and floor-to-ceiling windows are framed by gold draperies. An aisle flanked by lofty gilt-topped columns and a staircase with an oak banister lead to balcony seating.

It's all rather grand, but don't be intimidated. Service is very relaxed and amiable, and you can dress as you like.

City Grill's resplendent setting provides a fitting backdrop for the dazzling creations of executive chef Roger Kaplan. A recent menu (they change daily) included appetizers of Southern-fried quail served with black pepper biscuits (spread with raspberry and blackberry preserves) and smothered in sage-sausage cream gravy; plump and piquant barbecued Long Island oysters served atop a salad of fried corn niblets tossed with apple-smoked bacon, spinach, bell peppers, and radicchio; and hickory-fired portabello mushrooms, accompanied by a deep-fried sun-dried tomato risotto, with a nugget of fresh mozzarella buried in its center, and fried leek garnish. A main course of crispy softshell crabs was served with crunchy lobster slaw on yellow tomato-champagne vinaigrette. Tender duck, slow-smoked on maple chips, came with a savory vidalia onion pudding studded with toasted pecans and celery and topped with onion rings and wild mushrooms; it was sauced with ruby grape vinaigrette and garnished with fresh grapes. And Kaplan paired pan-seared farm-raised Canadian salmon with a crisp potato ring (a mix of puréed potatoes, cream cheese, and sautéed shiitake mushrooms and vidalia onions) topped with a layer of sautéed spinach and a five-caviar sauce. And yes, it's all as good as it sounds, as are pastry chef Mark Anstey's creations—try a moist chocolate pecan soufflé served warm on vanilla crème anglaise with a topping of chocolate ganache and three scoops of banana ice cream. Or, on a lighter note, a lemon tart on citrus pastry crust served with sabayon sauce, raspberry coulis, and fresh fruit garnish. City Grill's extensive cellar is stocked with over 400 wines (most of them French and Californian) in all price ranges, with about 20 selections available by the glass. Do consult friendly wine steward Alan Olegniczak.

Morton's of Chicago, 245 Peachtree Center Ave., at Harris St. ☎ 577-4366.

Cuisine: STEAK AND SEAFOOD. **Reservations:** Required. **MARTA:** Peachtree Center. **Parking:** Free valet parking at dinner on Harris Street, between Peachtree Center Avenue and Courtland Street.

Prices: Appetizers $7.95–$8.95; main courses $15.95–$29.95. AE, CB, DC, MC, V.

Open: Mon–Sat 5:30–11pm, Sun 5–10pm.

The Morton's chain of gourmet steak houses was founded in 1978 by one-time *Playboy* executive vice-president Arnie Morton, who was also instrumental in developing the Playboy Club concept. His restaurant empire has been as successful as his bunny business, and it's no wonder: These are truly great steak houses. A keynote of every Morton's is a star-studded clientele. Here the cream stucco walls are lined with photos of famous beef eaters like Bob Hope, Liza Minnellii, Mickey Mantle, Robert Duvall, Frank Sinatra, and Vice President Al Gore. One night, 15 Atlanta Falcons descended on the restaurant like a swarm of locusts and consumed 56 appetizers in five minutes prior to double and even quadruple steak orders. They worked up a tab of $3,000! As for the Braves, they always order up 24-ounce steaks all around.

Few restaurants offer more in the way of solid comfort. Much of the seating is in roomy horseshoe-shaped cream leather booths at tables adorned with white linen and fresh flowers. Bronze pig-motif candle lamps (Mr. Morton's whimsical encouragement to make a pig of yourself) cast a soft glow. An exhibition kitchen is hung with copper pots, and wines are stored in a brick-walled rack.

There's no printed menu. Servers in flowing white aprons roll up carts laden with several cuts of meat, a cooked chicken, and a frisky live lobster. What you see is what you get. Do start off with an appetizer—perhaps lump crabmeat cocktail with remoulade sauce, smoked Pacific salmon, or broiled sea scallops wrapped in bacon with apricot chutney. Main course choices include succulent prime midwestern beefsteaks—porterhouse, sirloin, rib eye, or double filet mignon—prepared to your exact specifications—plus lemon oregano chicken, lamb chops, Sicilian veal chop, whole baked Maine lobster, broiled swordfish sauce béarnaise, and prime rib. Side orders such as flavorfully fresh al dente asparagus in hollandaise sauce, sautéed spinach with mushrooms, or hash browns are highly recommended, and portions are huge, so you can share. A loaf of onion bread on every table is complimentary. Leave room for dessert—perhaps a lemon, Grand Marnier, or chocolate soufflé. There is, of course, an extensive wine list.

Expensive

⭐ **Chow Downtown,** 303 Peachtree Center Ave., at Baker St., in the Peachtree Center Complex. ☎ **222-0210.**

Cuisine: CONTEMPORARY AMERICAN. Reservations: Recommended. **MARTA:** Peachtree Center. **Parking:** Use the lot on Baker St. between Courtland St. and Peachtree Center Ave.; validated after 5pm and on weekends.

Prices: Appetizers $4.95–$7.95; main courses $5.95–$8.95 at lunch and brunch, $9.95–$18.95 at dinner. AE, DC, MC, V.

Open: Mon–Thurs 11:30am–10:30pm, Fri 11:30am–11:30pm, Sat 6–11:30pm, Sun 11am–10pm. Lunch/brunch menus are in effect through 3pm, cocktails and desserts are served 3 to 6pm, dinner from then on.

Virginia-Highlands' immensely popular Chow opened this sleek and sophisticated downtown location in 1993, and it was an immediate hit with the convention crowd (large parties are easily accommodated here), lunching office execs, and savvy locals seeking a simpatico setting for leisurely dinners. Its casual-elegant ambience (wear a suit or jeans, no one cares) is conducive to long, convivial conversations over good food and wine. A stunning interior features a bare oak parquet floor, alabaster hanging lamps, potted palms, and black-lacquer-trimmed birch wall panels stained a rich redwood hue. Wraparound windows create a Park Avenue café effect (the owners are transplanted New Yorkers) enhanced by seating in beautifully upholstered banquettes and bamboo/rattan chairs at polished black granite tables (candlelit at night). Further adornments include museum-quality paintings, gorgeous flower arrangements, and country baskets overflowing with herbs, breads, fruits, and vegetables. On cool nights, the breezy patio under sail-like white canvas awnings is one of my favorite Atlanta venues.

I love Chow's eclectic menu, which proffers such varied appetizers as smoked Maine trout served with sliced cucumbers, crusty bread, and sour cream; delicate crisp-fried wonton filled with minced shrimp, turkey, and Oriental vegetables, served with spicy mustard; and piquant southwestern black bean cakes with chunky avocado/tomato salsa and sour cream. For your main course consider grilled tuna marinated in sherry, ginger, soy, and garlic, served with a medley of fresh vegetables; a hearty Mediterranean-style dish of garlicky chicken chunks sautéed with crushed tomatoes, black olives, and toasted pine nuts, served over linguine and topped with fresh parmesan; or tri-color ravioli stuffed with ricotta and parmesan in smoked salmon-cream sauce. At lunch, a blackened salmon salad is highly recommended. And the brunch menu adds eggs, waffles, and other breakfasty fare. Desserts range from crème caramel (with a sprinkle of toasted almonds and a dollop of whipped cream) to a rich Oreo-crusted ice cream cake drizzled with chocolate sauce. Chow's wine list features 35 by-the-glass selections as well as single malt scotches and liqueur-laced coffees.

★ **Dailey's,** 17 International Blvd., just east of Peachtree St. ☎ **681-3303.**

Cuisine: CONTEMPORARY AMERICAN. **Reservations:** Not accepted; arrive off-peak hours. **MARTA:** Peachtree Center. **Parking:** Street only, which is difficult in the heart of downtown.
Prices: Appetizers $6.75–$8.95; main courses $5.95–$10.50 at lunch, $14.95–$22.50 at dinner. AE, CB, DC, MC, V.
Open: Lunch Mon–Sat 11am–2:30pm; dinner Sun–Thurs 5:30–11pm, Fri–Sat 5:30pm–midnight.

Entered via a cozy bar, Dailey's is one flight up a majestic staircase reached via a lushly planted walkway. It's a beautiful room, a former warehouse with a 20-foot peaked ceiling crisscrossed with dark wooden beams, exposed brick walls, and pine-plank floors. Two immense brass and fluted-glass train-station lamps are hung on chains from the beams, but they cast little light; Dailey's is romantically dim, with candles aglow on tables covered in white linen. English carousel horses on brass poles are centerpieces, but attention tends to be riveted on a spotlit stage—the marble-topped dessert bar (more about that later).

Waiters, all very efficient and gracious, elucidate the blackboard menu. And a wonderful menu it is, highly original and frequently changing to include new creations and market-fresh specialties. Both appetizers and main courses run a wide gamut. On my last visit the former included escargots baked in garlic butter; flaky strudel stuffed with cheeses, artichoke hearts, and prosciuttini ham, topped with basil-garlic butter; and a signature dish—steamed broccoli dipped in parmesan-cheese batter and deep-fried. A main dish of swordfish steak was marinated in mustard sauce, rolled in cracked black peppercorns, grilled, and served with mustard-cognac sauce. Other excellent choices for the main course were large grilled Gulf shrimp dredged in grated coconut and served in tangy sweet-and-sour sauce, and fresh salmon filet wrapped in edible rice paper in soy balsamic sauce. Portions are huge and accompanied by a choice of fresh vegetables or new potatoes roasted in garlic-parsley butter; doughnutlike deep-fried yeast rolls served with whipped herb butter; and a large salad. There's a small but well-chosen wine list.

You simply mustn't pass up the above-mentioned dessert bar, where a pastry chef is stationed at all times to explain an array of irresistible oven-fresh temptations. My favorite is the delectable apple caramel pie—cinnamon apples on a walnut crust, topped with brown-sugary streusel, vanilla ice cream, and ginger-caramel sauce. You can also opt for dessert and after-dinner drinks in the downstairs bar, where a pianist plays nightly. At lunch, similar main courses are supplemented by burgers, omelets, salads, stuffed baked potatoes, and sandwiches.

 Ocean Club, International Blvd., between Peachtree St. and Peachtree Center Ave. in the Peachtree Center Complex. ☎ **688-9330.**

Cuisine: SEAFOOD. **Reservations:** Accepted at dinner only. **MARTA:** Peachtree Center. **Parking:** Complimentary validated parking at lot across the street after 5pm.

Prices: Appetizers $5.95–$6.50 at lunch, $5.95–$10.95 at dinner; main courses $6.95–$10.95 at lunch, $9.95–$17.95 at dinner. AE, DC, MC, V.

Open: Mon–Thurs 11am–10pm, Fri 11am–11pm, Sat 5–11pm.

The Ocean Club is another winner for noted Atlanta restaurateur Michael Tuohy (see Chefs' Café below). Its seaside-evocative, casual-chic interior is both sophisticated in concept and warmly inviting. Decorated in soft beachy colors—peach, coral, turquoise, sand, periwinkle—with zippy angled windows, its walls are adorned with whimsical fish-themed watercolors, painted-wood sculptures, oversized ceramic plates, and a "day-at-the-beach" mural by artist Sidney Guberman. Wooden furnishings are wash-painted in turquoise, the tables covered with brown butcher paper and set with white cloth napkins. Seating runs the gamut from intimate booths divided by glass partitions to stainless-steel stools at a mosaic-tiled oyster bar. Light jazz makes a perfect audio backdrop.

Everything here is just scrumptious. Raw oyster lovers will relish a platter of fresh seasonal varieties (the seafood equivalent of a wine tasting), though the plump and juicy deep-fried ones served with chili aioli are also a heady culinary experience. Another good appetizer choice is house-smoked salmon cake spiced with red pepper, cilantro, cumin, and chili; it's served with black bean sauce and cilantro-lime sour cream. And Ocean Club pastas are noteworthy; try linguine tossed with clams, garlic, lemon, and parsley in white wine sauce. But the star feature is fresh fish—a daily-changing variety, served with a choice of unique savory sauces—hot pepper-sesame vinaigrette, jalapeño tartar, grilled pineapple salsa, spicy remoulade, black bean (cooked with ham for a smoky flavor), and others. Order two or three of these condiments with a grilled fish du jour—perhaps Alaska king salmon or swordfish. Main courses come with fresh al dente vegetables, and your choice of mashed (yummy) or baked potato or saffron rice. There are also nightly specials such as sautéed softshell crab crusted with ground pine nuts and parmesan cheese with mustard sauce and risotto. And lunch or dinner, you can opt for a light meal— a crabcake sandwich or even a hamburger. A carefully constructed wine list is supplemented by microbrewery specialty beers that go well with seafood. And desserts (always great at Tuohy restaurants) range from a light-as-air key lime pie served with mixed berry sauce to a decadently rich coconut-pecan cake with cream cheese frosting served with fresh peach compote and raspberry garnish.

The Pleasant Peasant, 555 Peachtree St., between Linden and Merritts Aves. ☎ 874-3223.

Cuisine: CONTINENTAL **Reservations:** Not accepted. **MARTA:** North Avenue. **Parking:** Free self and valet parking.
Prices: Appetizers $3.75–$4.50 at lunch, $3.75–$6.50 at dinner; main courses $6–$9 at lunch, $10–$19 at dinner. AE, CB, DC, DISC, MC, V.
Open: Lunch Mon–Fri 11:30am–2:30pm, dinner nightly 5:30pm–midnight.

Housed in a former drugstore, the Pleasant Peasant has all the elements of a typical New York Soho pub—exposed brick walls, white-tile floors, and a cream-colored pressed-tin ceiling. At night, the dining room is subtly (let's say romantically) lit by hurricane lamps on white-linen-covered tables. During the day, you can see that a large ficus and other greenery thrives in the sunshine streaming through a large skylight.

The menu, presented at your table on a blackboard, changes daily. At a recent dinner, there were appetizers of shrimp southwestern (five large Gulf shrimp baked in phyllo pastry with cumin/cayenne/chili-flavored cream cheese, served with piquant salsa) and homemade fettuccine tossed with fresh basil, spinach, tomatoes, parmesan cheese, garlic butter, and toasted almonds. Among the main courses: honey-sweetened duck in cilantro/jalapeño/lime sauce with macadamia nuts; char-grilled rack of lamb sliced into chops and served with spicy

Downtown Dining

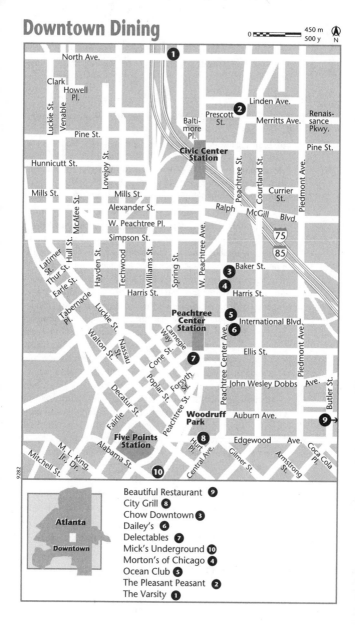

Beautiful Restaurant	**9**
City Grill	**8**
Chow Downtown	**3**
Dailey's	**6**
Delectables	**7**
Mick's Underground	**10**
Morton's of Chicago	**4**
Ocean Club	**5**
The Pleasant Peasant	**2**
The Varsity	**1**

apple-butter barbecue sauce; and baked corn husks stuffed with thick fresh salmon filets. Sound good? You better believe it. All main courses include a big salad served with cheese toast and two vegetables—perhaps fresh asparagus and roasted red potatoes.

Lunch offers similar fare, along with fabulous soups (for example, classic French onion or creamy mushroom-hazelnut), omelets, and sandwiches. At either meal, do order a dessert such as apple-walnut pie with a brown-sugary crust, served warm and topped with cinnamon ice cream.

Inexpensive

Mick's, In Underground Atlanta, at the corner of Pryor and Alabama Sts. ☎ 525-2825.

Cuisine: AMERICAN **Reservations:** Not accepted. **MARTA:** Five Points.

Prices: Appetizers $3.95–$6.50; main courses $6.95–$12.95 (burgers, salads, and sandwiches $3.95–$7.95). AE, CB, DC, MC, V.

Open: Mon–Thurs 1am–11pm, Fri–Sat 1am–1am, Sun noon –10:30pm

My favorite of the Underground eateries is Mick's, an imposing turn-of-the-century-themed 2-story restaurant in Humbug Square. It's fronted by a gaslit wraparound porch enclosed by black wrought-iron fencing, a marvelous venue for viewing indoor "street" action while sipping vodka-spiked pink lemonade. The main dining room, done up in Victorian-saloon red and black, has whitewashed brick walls hung with Early American patchwork quilts. It's a casual but very simpatico setting with candlelit tables and large candelabra chandeliers overhead. Upstairs is a cozy bar, furnished with cushioned wicker chairs amid potted palms. There's also café seating on both levels, the upper actually outdoors on a patio overlooking the fountain plaza. Mick's is great for anything from a snack to a full meal. Nachos here are as good as nachos get—piled high with melted Monterey Jack, cheddar, and jalapeños. Hand-mixed guacamole and french fries smothered in cheddar cheese and homemade chili are also excellent. A superb house specialty is a hefty platter of hickory-grilled baby back ribs served with fries. Yet another option is Southern fried chicken fingers served with savory peach and honey-mustard dipping sauces and fries or pasta salad. Whatever you order, do leave room for dessert—perhaps the rich, silky-smooth chocolate-cream pie

---

Frommer's Smart Traveler: Restaurants

1. Eat your main meal at lunch; prices are lower then and you can enjoy gourmet main courses for much less than they'd cost at dinner.

2. Hotel breakfasts tend to be very pricey. Consider a hotel or B&B accommodation where rates include breakfast.

3. Some accommodations listed in this book have fully equipped kitchens: for families, especially, these can represent substantial savings.

4. Atlanta has many lovely parks. Occasionally buying picnic food and lunching alfresco will save money as well as affording you a relaxing break from sightseeing.

topped with whipped cream, or the buttery, brown-sugary streusel-topped fruit cobbler crowned with vanilla ice cream.

Mick's has additional locations at 557 Peachtree St. (☎ 875-6425), the Lenox Square Mall. (☎ 262-6425), and 2110 Peachtree Rd. (☎ 351-6425).

Budget

Delectables, 1 Margaret Mitchell Sq., at the corner of Carnegie Way and Fairlie St. ☎ 681-2909.

> **Cuisine:** AMERICAN **Reservations:** For large parties only. **MARTA:** Peachtree Center. **Parking:** In nearby lots only, not validated.
> **Prices:** Small plates $2.95–$3.95; main courses $4.75–$7.50. No credit cards.
> **Open:** Mon–Fri 11am–2pm.

Down a flight of steps from the Atlanta-Fulton Public Library, Delectables is the charming domain of society caterers Cary and Nancy Smith. Though service is cafeteria-style, the setting is elegant. Pale peach walls are hung with photographs of Atlanta's original library, built in 1890; menus are propped on music stands; and tables, amid potted ficus trees, are covered in floral chintz and adorned by sprigs of flowers in bud vases. Food is served on quality china, and silver cutlery comes wrapped in thick white linen napkins. There's also a patio landscaped with terra-cotta planters of foster holly, kale, and ferns. Classical music plays in the background.

As for the fare, Delectables is not a misnomer. Everything here is made from fresh, first-quality ingredients. In cold months, order up a hearty bowl of chili, with chunks of coarse-ground beef tenderloin and beans, served with a cheddar corn muffin, grated cheese, and chopped onion. Caesar salads here are usually topped with grilled salmon or chicken. More filling choices range from pasta pesto tossed with shrimps and scallops to tenderloin of beef with horseradish sauce, served with a salad of ziti tossed with Gouda cheese and broccoli. There are terrific sandwiches, too, like lemon tarragon chicken salad on whole wheat. Homemade desserts include fabulous raspberry-almond tarts topped with powdered sugar and white chocolate macadamia nut brownies. Iced tea is served with fresh mint, and coffees (including cappuccino and espresso) are brewed from freshly ground beans. No alcoholic beverages are served.

The Varsity, 61 North Ave., at Spring St. ☎ 881-1706.

> **Cuisine:** AMERICAN. **Reservations:** Not accepted. **Parking:** Free.
> **Prices:** Everything is under $5. No credit cards.
> **Open:** Sun–Thurs 9am–11:30pm, Fri–Sat 9am–1:30pm.

Atlanta grew up around the Varsity, the world's largest drive-in restaurant, opened in 1928 by Frank Gordy and today run by his daughter Nancy Simms. It's de rigueur to visit this fast-food mecca—its greasy feasts are an essential element of the Atlanta experience. A 150-foot stainless-steel counter is the hub of the operation, behind which red-shirted cooks and counterpeople rush out thousands of orders.

It's a constant chorus of "What'll ya have?" with customer responses translated into such esoteric orders as "walk a dog sideways, bag of rags" (a hot dog with onions on the side and potato chips). It takes 200 employees to process the ton of onions, 2,500 pounds of potatoes, 2 miles of hot dogs, and 300 gallons of chili consumed here by some 16,000 hungry customers each day. The Varsity's interior is spartan, with tiered seating consisting in the main of large, windowed rooms with Formica tables. Five big TVs are always on.

Order up a chili dog or a couple of chili burgers (they're only two ounces each), with fries, onion rings, and a frosted orange (it's a creamy frozen orange drink). Barbecued pork, homemade chicken salad, and deviled-egg sandwiches are other options. And since none of this is health food (though it's all fresh and made from scratch), don't resist the fried apple or peach pie à la mode for dessert.

2 Midtown

Many Midtown restaurants are a little less flashy than those in downtown or Buckhead, perhaps because they're primarily patronized by local people rather than tourists. But to this rule, the first two listings are glamorous exceptions.

Very Expensive

 Florencia, at the Occidental Grand Hotel, 75 14th St., between Peachtree and W. Peachtree Sts. ☎ **881-9898.**

Cuisine: CONTEMPORARY AMERICAN/CONTINENTAL. **Reservations:** Recommended. **MARTA:** Arts Center. **Parking:** Complimentary valet parking.

Frommer's Cool for Kids: Restaurants

The Varsity (see p. 111) The greasy feasts of the world's largest drive-in restaurant are of course big kid-pleasers.

Gorin's (see p. 124) This place offers the best kind of fast food—everything is homemade and fresh, prices are low, you can have quiche while the kids eat grilled cheese, and there are yummy ice-cream sundaes for dessert.

Fellini's (see p. 138) The New York–style pizza Fellini's serves is a treat that will please everyone. There's an outdoor patio upstairs.

Mick's (see pp. 110) If you're looking for real sit-down meals in pleasant surroundings, the four locations of this excellent chain all serve the simple foods kids love at moderate to budget prices.

The OK Cafe (see p. 137) This casual, low-priced restaurant serves excellent home cooking–style food, and has a special brunch menu Saturday and Sunday.

Prices: Appetizers $6.50–$12; main courses $18–$23. AE, CB, DC, DISC, ER, JCB, MC, V.
Open: Mon–Sat 6–11pm.

The signature restaurant of the deluxe Occidental Grand Hotel is a warmly intimate dining room proffering a winning combination of solid comfort, culinary excellence, and deft, professional service. Pale oak walls, with panels of burled carpathian elm and pleated fabric, are hung with gilt-framed oil paintings and collections of antique mirrors. Seating is in high-backed tapestried chairs and roomy forest-green leather booths. And the romantic glow of silk-shaded silver candle lamps on elegantly appointed white-linened tables is augmented by flickering sconces, gorgeous crystal chandeliers (suspended from a recessed gilded-parchment ceiling), and a fire ablaze in the massive hand-carved limestone hearth. A stunning flower arrangement atop a marble table forms a visual centerpiece.

Talented chef Scott Dangerfield changes his menus seasonally. When last I dined, appetizers included savory escargots sautéed with shallots, garlic, shiitake mushrooms, and herbs, finished with a touch of cream, and served over black squid-ink pasta; sugar-cured gravlox, infused with beet juice to create a rosy fringe and served with zingy minted marscapone and lemony fennel salad brushed with grapeseed oil; and quick-seared foie gras and smoked duck wrapped in a speckled wild rice crêpe topped with a sprinkling of duck cracklings. In the nouveau southwestern mode, the versatile Dangerfield additionally offered spicy grilled shrimp atop black bean cakes with green (cilantro/jalapeño) and red (saffron/tomato) sauces, a dollop of sour cream, and sevruga caviar. A main course of roasted rack and loin of lamb came poised on a goat cheese and spinach pie with a rosemary-garlic-brushed buttery phyllo crust; the plate was further embellished with baby carrots and crunchy shoestring potatoes. And pan-seared North Atlantic salmon was ringed with steamed green-lip New Zealand mussels drizzled with pesto, "leaves" of quick steamed roma tomatoes, and spinach cappelini tossed with pesto. Every dish was delicious and exquisitely presented on Villeroy & Boch china. A loaf of hot, crusty country bread came with three butters (herbed, salmon, and plain). And desserts ranged from a classic chocolate soufflé to a scrumptious warm strudel filled with cheese and amaretto-splashed bing cherries, served on zabaglione dotted with dried cherries. There were complimentary petit fours as well. Ask the wine steward to recommend wines that complement your main course selections; Florencia's impressive list includes Spanish wines, sherries, and ports.

Note: A quarterly event here is a black-tie cigar connoisseur's dinner—a seven-course prix-fixe repast accompanied by premium selections of cigars, vintage wines, ports, and cognacs.

Expensive

 Bistango, 1100 Peachtree St., at 12th St. ☎ **724-0901.**
Cuisine: CREATIVE MEDITERRANEAN. **Reservations:** Recommended.
MARTA: Midtown. **Parking:** Complimentary valet parking.

Prices: Appetizers $5.95–$6.95 at lunch, $6.95–$8.95 at dinner; main courses $7.95–$16.95 at lunch, $12.95–$18.95 at dinner. AE, CB, DC, MC, V.

Open: Lunch Mon–Fri 11:30am–2:30pm; dinner Mon–Thurs 5:30–10:30pm, Fri–Sat 5:30–11pm.

Entered via an elegant bar/lounge (the perfect place for posttheater cocktails and desserts), Bistango is a simpatico setting for the Mediterranean culinary creations of noted Atlanta chef Tom Coohill. Toting an impressive resume ranging from a Michelin three-star restaurant in France to Los Angeles' chic Ma Maison, he came to local prominence as the original executive chef of the illustrious City Grill (described above). His upscale midtown bistro is dramatic in design. Sun-drenched by day via floor-to-ceiling windows, softly lit by night, its earth-toned interior centers on a massive alabaster chandelier suspended from a 35-foot octagonal skylit dome. An elaborate dried-flower arrangement in subtle wildflower hues graces a central cherrywood pedestal, and art deco elements include a bold geometrically patterned carpet, colorful Matisse-like cut-out motifs embellishing chandeliers and upholstery (very apt, since Matisse lived in Nice), and period cherrywood furnishings and wainscoting. Large white-linened tables are luxuriously spaced. In good weather, you can also dine al fresco on a lovely outdoor patio with green marble tables under canvas umbrellas.

Coohill's seasonally changing menus range from the French and Italian Rivieras to the Costa Brava. I most recently experienced Tom's refreshing summer fare, which included appetizers of ravioli filled with Gorgonzola and oven-dried tomato served with a compote of tomato chunks and sautéed arugula in light virgin olive oil; thin slices of Parma ham served with canteloupe and a crostini spread with dried figs; and alderwood-smoked salmon, grilled, chilled, and served over a gazpacho-like summer salad tossed with goat cheese in balsamic vinaigrette. A main course of grilled scampi—made with plumply sweet New Zealand prawns—was served atop a chewy saffroned risotto spiced with Moroccan chilies and studded with morsels of stewed tomato, asparagus, and rock shrimp. Pasta dishes included a marvelous vegetarian lasagne—egg and spinach pasta layered with grilled Mediterranean vegetables, wild mushrooms, and fresh mozzarella and romano cheeses, roasted crunchy and brown. A thick grilled pork chop stuffed with oven-dried tomatoes, crisp sautéed spinach, and romano cheese was served with chunky mashed red bliss garlicky potatoes and sautéed shiitake mushrooms in a pork jus. Also notable: Tom's lavish version of a salad Niçoise replete with big filets of pinkly rare alderwood-smoked tuna. Bistango's wine list is first-rate, and pastry chef Rebecca Thompson offers ethereal endings, such as a buttery bread pudding afloat on rich caramel sauce studded with golden raisins, topped with fresh whipped cream, and garnished with berries. Desserts here are de rigueur.

★ **The Country Place,** 1197 Peachtree St. NE, at 14th St., in the Colony Square complex ☎ **881-0144.**

Cuisine: CREATIVE AMERICAN. **Reservations:** Not accepted. **MARTA:** Arts Center. **Parking:** Free validated parking in the Colony Square lot. **Prices:** Appetizers $4.75–$8.25; main courses $6.95–$10.50 at lunch and brunch, $10.95–$19.95 at dinner (burgers, salads, and sandwiches $7.95–$8.95). AE, CB, DC, MC, V.
Open: Lunch Mon–Fri 11:30am–2:30pm, Sun brunch 11am–3pm; dinner Sun–Thurs 5:30–11pm, Fri–Sat 5:30pm–midnight.

This charming low-key restaurant just across from the Woodruff Arts Center is a local favorite for pre-theater dining and post-theater desserts and cocktails. Its attractions include a pianist and singer Tuesday through Saturday nights, great food, friendly service (waitstaff is casually attired in blue jeans and long white aprons), and a winning mellow ambience. At night soft lighting emanates from shaded table lamps poised atop booth dividers (very residential in feel), while a wall of French windows makes for sun-drenched daytime lunches. Floors are terra-cotta, walls and columns embellished with beautiful, hand-painted blue-and-white Portuguese tiles. Diners are seated in comfortable upholstered bamboo chairs, banquettes, and booths amid planters of greenery, potted palms, and big ceramic urns. Consider adjourning to the awninged piano bar/lounge for after-dinner drinks.

The kitchen is innovative and exciting, predictable only in its commitment to quality. A Country Place dinner might begin with a trio of crisp sautéed crabcakes seasoned with cumin and chili powder, served with fresh salsa; baked elephant garlic with marinated goat cheese, roasted plum tomatoes, and rounds of hickory-grilled French bread; or a hearty red bean/bacon/cheddar soup topped with sour cream. A recent menu offered main courses of hickory-grilled pork medallions in Dijon mustard sauce, served with steamed new potatoes and sugar snap peas; grilled salmon, juiced with lemon, accompanied by garlicky pan-sautéed spinach and smoked couscous studded with tasty morsels of carrot and corn; and a deliciously healthy platter of grilled vegetables (baby artichokes, peppers, and portobello mushrooms in garlic basil vinaigrette) served with couscous salad and goat cheese. Desserts are of the not-to-be-missed variety, like berry crème brûlée or apple strudel cheesecake on buttery graham cracker crust topped with whipped cream and warm caramel sauce. At lunch there are great salads, sandwiches, and burgers in addition to regular main courses. And the brunch menu adds options such as crabcakes benedict and apple-walnut French toast. The wine list features many premium selections by the glass.

South City Kitchen, 1144 Crescent Ave., between 13th and 14th Sts. ☎ 873-7358.

Cuisine: CONTEMPORARY SOUTHERN. **Reservations:** Recommended after 6pm. **MARTA:** Arts Center. **Parking:** Free in lot behind restaurant.

Prices: Appetizers $5.50–$7.50; main courses $5.95–$11.25 at lunch (most are under $10), $13.75–$18.50 at dinner ($6.95–$8.95 for sandwiches and light fare). AE, CB, DC, DISC, MC, V.

Open: Sun–Thurs 11am–11pm, Fri–Sat 11am–midnight.

Fronted by a brick patio lined with pear trees, South City Kitchen is cozily ensconced in a converted two-story house with charming dining areas upstairs and down. On the lower level, light filters in through large windows and a bustling marble-countered exhibition kitchen serves as a visual focus. My favorite spot, however, is a pristine pine-floored alcove painted pale yellow with glossy white trim. Working fireplaces on both floors, large floral arrangements, bay windows, a changing art show, and candlelit white-linened tables further enhance this friendly restaurant's appeal. Weather permitting, patio seating is also very pleasant.

The seasonally changing menu reflects widely varied Southern influences, and the food is enhanced by its presentation on creamy white Royal Doulton platters or in big china bowls. A basket of fresh-baked buttermilk biscuits and corn muffins accompanies all main courses. Start off with a steaming bowl of creamy she-crab soup replete with jumbo lump crabmeat and enlivened by a shot of sherry. A crabcake appetizer is served with zingy cayenne hollandaise and three-bean relish in a light vinaigrette. Also tempting: a Tex-Mex-style quesadilla layered with grilled chicken, jack cheese, and roasted poblano pepper, served with chunks of avocado, cilantro salsa, and a dollop of spiced sour cream. "New South" salads might include arugula with fresh Georgia peach slices and garlicky grilled croutons in a pecan-studded gorgonzola dressing. And main courses are likely to range from jambalaya to pastas—such as fettuccine tossed with fresh seafood, chopped tomatoes, and andouille sausage in white wine cream sauce garnished with fresh-shaved parmesan—to tangy barbecued swordfish served atop creamy cheese grits. A rather extensive and lovingly constructed wine list includes small signature acquisitions and other unusual finds, plus 20 or more premium wines available by the glass. And daily-changing desserts always feature a fruit cobbler topped with vanilla bean ice cream. There's usually crème brûlée as well.

Moderate

 Chefs' Café, 2115 Piedmont Rd., between Lindbergh Dr. and Cheshire Bridge Rd. ☎ **872-2284.**

Cuisine: CONTEMPORARY AMERICAN. **Reservations:** Recommended.

MARTA: Lindbergh.

Prices: Appetizers $4.50–$7.50 at dinner, $2.95–$5.95 at brunch; main courses $10.95–$16.95 at dinner, $4.95–$10.95 at brunch. AE, CB, DC, DISC, MC, V.

Open: Sun–Thurs 6–10pm, Fri–Sat 6–11pm, Sun brunch 11am–2:30pm.

Though unpretentiously located adjacent to a Comfort Inn, this charming café lacks nothing in the way of culinary sophistication. Chef Georges Màrtin creates main courses that are both innovative and tantalizing, using only the finest and freshest of ingredients. Menus change frequently to take advantage of seasonal specialties: All fish is fresh and local farmers grow specialty greens and produce to the restaurant's specifications. The setting is lovely—textured peach walls are hung with whimsical oil paintings of rotund chefs pursuing crabs and other would-be food sources, soft lighting emanates from candles and faux-stone wall sconces, and flower-bedecked tables are covered in crisp white linen.

Appetizers here might include grilled pancetta-wrapped oysters on a bed of orange salsa cruda, and exquisitely light Gulf Coast crabcakes served with tomato butter. As for main courses the Chefs' Café makes a superb spicy paella replete with scallops, shrimp, littleneck clams, saffron rice, chorizo sausage, peas, peppers, tomatoes, and mushrooms. Grilled lamb loin is served with rosemary aioli chilled white bean salad, and ratatouille. And steamed salmon topped with julienned butterfly leeks, sautéed crisp vegetables, and grilled new potatoes is served with fresh tarragon-and-saffron-flavored sauce. Beautiful plate presentations further enhance your meal, as does a carefully constructed (mostly Californian) wine list, with 35 premium wines available by the glass.

Do not pass up the delectable desserts, such as a classic tarte Tatin topped with cinnamon ice cream, the lightest-and-creamiest-ever lemon cheesecake, brioche bread pudding in bourbon-caramel sauce, and rich Frangelico-flavored Belgian chocolate pâté studded with pistachios and served afloat an espresso crème anglaise. Brunch main courses range from crab cakes Benedict to smoked Irish salmon on a toasted bagel with herbed cream cheese and capers.

Taste of New Orleans, 889 West Peachtree St., at 8th St.
☎ 874-5535.

Cuisine: NEW AMERICAN CREOLE. **Reservations:** Recommended at dinner. **MARTA:** Midtown. **Parking:** Free in adjoining lot.
Prices: Appetizers $2.95–$4.95; main courses $5.99–$7.99 at lunch, $8.95–$16.95 at dinner. AE, CB, DC, MC, V.
Open: Lunch Mon–Fri 11:30am–2pm; dinner Mon–Thurs 6–10pm, Fri–Sat 5:30–11pm.

Taste of New Orleans offers a comfortable setting for owner/chef John Beck's lighter version of Créole cookery. A slightly austere gray and burgundy interior, with vertical aluminum blinds and glass-brick partitions, is warmed by soft sconce lighting and candlelight. Whimsical New Orleans–themed paintings and posters adorn pale gray walls, and an actual street lamp fronting a mural of a French Quarter brick-walled garden creates a trompe l'oeil effect.

Begin with an appetizer of delicious Long Island oysters en brochette; lightly battered, they're wrapped in bacon, deep-fried, and served on a piquant remoulade. Seafood gumbo and oyster/andouille sausage soup are also first rate here. Delicate, fluffy crawfish cakes (available as an appetizer or main course) are seasoned with garlic, hot sauce, fresh basil, and romano cheese and served with jalapeño tartar sauce on tomato buerre blanc. When crawfish are out of

Midtown/Virginia-Highland Dining

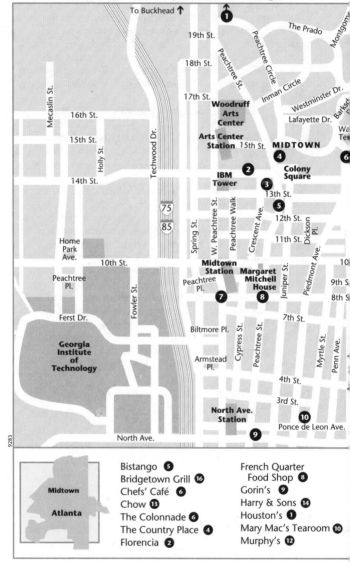

To Buckhead ↑

19th St.

18th St.

17th St.

The Prado

Montgome

Peachtree Circle

Peachtree St.

Inman Circle

Westminster Dr.

Lafayette Dr.

Mecaslin St.

16th St.

15th St.

14th St.

Holly St.

Techwood Dr.

Woodruff Arts Center

Arts Center Station 15th St.

MIDTOWN

Barksd

Wa
Ter

MIDTOWN

IBM Tower

Colony Square

13th St.

12th St.

11th St.

W. Peachtree St.

Spring St.

Peachtree Walk

Crescent Ave.

Dickson Pl.

Piedmont Ave.

Home Park Ave.

10th St.

Peachtree Pl.

Fowler St.

Ferst Dr.

Midtown Station

Peachtree Pl.

Margaret Mitchell House

Juniper St.

9th S.

8th S

Biltmore Pl.

Georgia Institute of Technology

Armstead Pl.

Cypress St.

Peachtree St.

7th St.

Myrtle St.

Penn Ave.

4th St.

3rd St.

North Ave. Station

Ponce de Leon Ave.

North Ave.

9283

Midtown

Atlanta

Bistango ⑤
Bridgetown Grill ⑯
Chefs' Café ⑥
Chow ⑬
The Colonnade ⑥
The Country Place ④
Florencia ②

French Quarter Food Shop ⑧
Gorin's ⑨
Harry & Sons ⑭
Houston's ❶
Mary Mac's Tearoom ⑩
Murphy's ⑫

season, Beck offers crab/shrimp seafood cakes. The same applies to his superb seafood etouffée. Blackened grouper (crispy here, not charred) is dusted with Créole spices and lightly brushed with Dijon mustard, topped with hollandaise and toasted almonds, and served with a boiled red potato and a medley of fresh vegetables. And though fresh seafood is featured, you can also opt for tender Long Island duck,

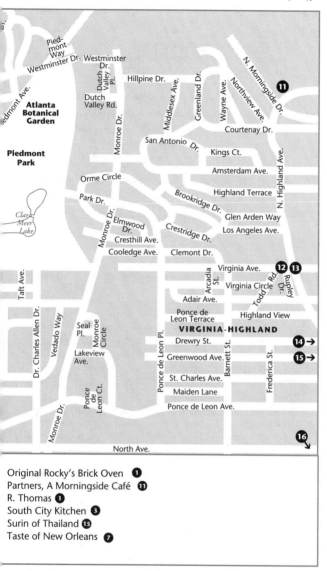

300 m
330 y

Atlanta Botanical Garden

Piedmont Park

Clara Meer Lake

VIRGINIA-HIGHLAND

Original Rocky's Brick Oven ❶
Partners, A Morningside Café ⓫
R. Thomas ❶
South City Kitchen ❸
Surin of Thailand ⓯
Taste of New Orleans ❼

deboned, roasted, and glazed with a semisweet Grand Marnier orange sauce on a bed of pecan rice. The restaurant's velvet pies and classic bread pudding are renowned, but I like to check the dessert specials, which often include lighter options. The wine list is reasonably priced, with many by-the-glass offerings. Luncheon fare includes chicken andouille po-boys, jambalaya, and salads.

Inexpensive

The Colonnade, 1879 Cheshire Bridge Rd. NE, between Wellborne
Dr. and Manchester St. ☎ **874-5642.**

Cuisine: SOUTHERN. **Reservations:** Not accepted. **Parking:** Free.
Prices: Main courses $6–$9 at lunch, $8–$14 at dinner. No credit cards.
Open: Lunch Mon–Sat 11am–2:30pm; dinner Mon–Wed 5–9pm.
Thurs–Sat 5–10pm, Sun 11am–9pm. **Closed:** Dec 24–25, Labor Day.

This Atlanta institution, established in 1927, offers some of the most
authentic and savory southern specialties in town. It has an enormous
local clientele of devoted regulars—many of whom look like they
might enjoy a birthday greeting from Willard Scott any day—and
some of the waitstaff have worked here for decades. Though comfortable, the Colonnade is totally unpretentious, a vast room with
English prints on charcoal-slate walls and seating at butcher-block
tables. A cozy bar with a working fireplace adjoins, a nice place to sit
if you have to wait for a table.

At lunch or dinner, you might order fresh-from-the-oven turkey
with dressing (they roast about a dozen a day), sugar-cured ham in
redeye gravy, or roast leg of lamb, all of which are served with a choice
of two vegetables—you may choose from among homemade whipped
potatoes, black-eyed peas, macaroni and cheese, sweet-potato soufflé,
lima beans, greens, fried okra, and others. Homemade cornbread and
yeast rolls accompany all main courses. In addition to menu listings,
there are fancy specials ranging from Cornish game hens to frog legs
and low-priced blue-plate specials. Everything is fresh and made from
scratch, including desserts like the yellow cake topped with ice cream
and drenched in semisweet hot fudge. Portions are very large.

★ **French Quarter Food Shop,** 923 Peachtree St. NE, just north
of 8th St. ☎ **875-2489.**

$ **Cuisine:** CAJUN. **Reservations:** Not accepted. **MARTA:** Midtown.
Parking: Free. Near Comedy Act Theater at lunch; between Franklin
Printing and Stein Club, just north of the restaurant, at dinner.
Prices: Appetizers $1.95–$5.95; po-boy sandwiches $4.95–$6.25; main
courses $4.95–$8.95 at lunch, $4.95–$12.95 at dinner. AE, MC, V.
Open: Lunch Mon–Fri 11am–2pm, Sat 11:30am–2:30pm; dinner Mon–
Thurs 6–10pm, Fri–Sat 6–11pm.

This little eatery is so 100% authentic that I rank it among Atlanta's
best restaurants. Cajun owners Tony and Missy Privat (they met in
a Louisiana cooking school) grew up on this cuisine and know its
every nuance. Their restaurant is small and unpretentious (almost a
joint), with black and white checkerboard tile floors and gray walls
hung with French Quarter–themed art, a Louisiana state map, and
Mardi Gras beads. Patio seating out front is heated in cool weather,
and enclosed by plastic flaps in cold weather. The clientele ranges
from folks in jeans to the conservatively suited business crowd. Arrive early to avoid a wait for seating.

Everything here is just scrumptious. Gumbo is dark, rich, and
spicy, thickened with roux and replete with savory chunks of

andouille sausage. Velvety oyster-andouille bisque is another superb soup. Traditional red beans and rice are slow-simmered in andouille and ham hock stock, and two other Cajun signature dishes—crawfish etouffée and jambalaya—reach their culinary apogee here. Lightly battered fried oysters, plump and juicy, with a choice of two remoulade sauces, one hot, one cold (ask for both), are in the not-to-be-missed category. Oyster po-boys are also great, as is the muffaletta—a grilled sandwich on sesame boule stuffed with ham, Genoa salami, provolone, Swiss cheese, and a relish of coarsely chopped black and green olives, marinated mushrooms, and artichoke hearts. And one of the best things I ever tasted was a special here of fried soft-shell crab stuffed with bechamel-sauced crawfish in a roasted garlic cream sauce. For dessert, there's excellent crème caramel, but the pièce de résistance is nutmeg/cinnamon-flavored bread pudding. Studded with crushed pineapple, pecans, and raisins, it's smothered in fresh whipped cream and buttery bourbon sauce. The French Quarter serves beer and wine. A small on-premises shop sells Louisiana food products.

Houston's, 2166 Peachtree Rd., at Colonial Homes Dr. in the Brookwood Square Shopping Center. ☎ 351-2442.

> **Cuisine:** AMERICAN. **Reservations:** Not accepted; arrive off-peak hours. **Parking:** Free.
>
> **Prices:** Appetizers $5.95–$6.95; burgers and salads $5.95–$8.95; main courses $8.25–$16.95. AE, MC, V.
>
> **Open:** Sun–Thurs 11am–11pm, Fri–Sat 11am–midnight.

Part of an Atlanta-based chain with restaurants throughout the country, Houston's has created an immensely popular dining format. It's a simple approach: They serve lavish portions of fresh, first-quality fare in very simpatico surroundings. The spacious dining room has a rustic ambience, with exposed brick walls and a crisscross of rough-hewn rafters under a skylight ceiling. Seating is in roomy burgundy leather booths at bare oak tables, with cozy lighting emanating from shaded table lamps. If you're in a rush, there's counter seating; and weather permitting, you can dine on the patio at tables with red umbrellas.

Thick, hickory-grilled burgers, made from choice chuck meat, are served with skillet beans, fries, or coleslaw. The same fixings come with barbecued chicken or tender, meaty ribs. But my favorite main course is the salad of sliced grilled chicken (big chunks), tossed with chopped greens and julienned tortilla strips in a honey-lime vinaigrette, garnished with a light peanut sauce. Marvelous too are appetizers such as creamed spinach and artichoke hearts in parmesan cream sauce. Beverages range from premium wines by the glass to mixed drinks made with premium liquors, fresh-squeezed juices, and natural spring water.

For dessert you can indulge in a huge, chewy brownie topped with vanilla ice cream and Kahlúa. A second location is in Buckhead at 3321 Lenox Rd., at E. Paces Ferry Rd. (☎ 237-7534). Menu and hours are the same.

Mary Mac's Tearoom, 224 Ponce de Leon Ave. NE, at Myrtle St. ☎ 876-6604.

Cuisine: SOUTHERN. **Reservations:** Not accepted. **MARTA:** North Avenue. **Parking:** Free on premises.

Prices: Main courses $5–$8 at lunch, $6–$10 at dinner; junior plates (you can order them if you're 9 or 90) $3. No credit cards.

Open: Lunch Sun–Fri 11am–3pm, dinner Mon–Sat 5–9pm.

In business since 1945, Mary Mac's is a quaint and colorful Atlanta institution, a bastion of classic southern cuisine that is patronized by everyone from truck drivers to bank presidents. Jimmy Carter often came by for lunch when he was governor as does Zell Miller, and the state legislature can almost be said to meet here. Cream-colored walls in the four dining rooms are covered with photos of famous clients and Atlanta sites (including the original house used for Tara in *Gone with the Wind*), along with murals of the Carter Center and the city skyline. Schoolroom lights hang overhead. Service is friendly and very southern. You'll find a glass of pencils on your table; check off menu items you desire (they change daily) and hand your selections to your server.

Among the famous main courses are fried chicken dredged in buttermilk and flour, fried rainbow trout from the North Georgia mountains, and chicken pan pie topped with thick giblet gravy. All main courses come with a choice of side dishes. You might select corn bread with pot likker (a scrumptious broth made with chicken drippings and turnip greens), black-eyed peas, whipped potatoes, steamed okra, macaroni and cheese, or sweet-potato soufflé. Fresh-from-the-oven corn and bran muffins and yeast rolls are served with lunches; at night there are hot cinnamon buns as well. Desserts include Georgia Peach cobbler and pound cake topped with strawberries and whipped cream. There's a full bar.

★ **Original Rocky's Brick Oven Pizza & Pasta,** 1770 Peachtree St. NE, at 26th St. ☎ 876-1111.

Cuisine: ITALIAN/PIZZA. **Reservations:** Not accepted. **Parking:** Free.

Prices: $7.95 for an individual pizza; $14.95 for a pie serving two to three people; $17.95 for a pie serving four; $9.95 for pasta dishes. AE, MC, V.

Open: Mon–Thurs 5–11:30pm, Fri–Sat 4pm–midnight, Sun 4–11pm.

When I want pizza I want to be in Atlanta—at Rocky's—where irrepressible ex-Brooklynite Bob Russo (his father was Rocky) creates the best pies I've ever had. He makes his own mozzarella fresh every day, grows his own herbs and tomatoes, uses garlic lavishly, and bakes the pies in a hickory- and oakwood-burning oven from Milan, but none of that explains the culinary magic here. Let's just say, when it comes to pizza, Bob is Escoffier.

Rocky's is comfortable and candlelit, with seating in dark-green leather booths. Walls are brightly painted with Sicilian donkey-cart motifs, whimsical cubist fruits, and a fish frieze. An enticing garlicky aroma emanates from the display kitchen, and opera and Italian classical music enhance a convivial atmosphere; it's not unusual for local opera singers to stand up and belt out arias here. In fact, Rocky's attracts a lot of media people and celebrities. Bob set up a large-screen TV when pal John Amos (along with other notables, including Atlanta Mayor Bill Campbell) came by to watch the premiere of his new TV sitcom. And though things didn't work out, Julia Roberts and Keifer Sutherland had their first date here. In addition to its cozy interior, Rocky's has a rustic screened patio with umbrella tables (it's heated in winter by a fireplace), and additional totally al fresco seating framed by trellising.

Bob specializes in pizzas from various provinces of Italy. My favorites are the chicken bianca oreganato (topped with sautéed chicken breast, virgin olive oil, fresh oregano and rosemary, white wine, garlic, lemon juice, red onions, and Gorgonzola and mozzarella cheeses) and the Rudolph Valentino, with sweet-onion sauce and rosemary-seasoned roasted new potatoes. The perfect pizza accompaniment is homemade zinfandel (Bob's grandfather's recipe) served with a slice of fresh peach. Do consider ordering a salad of homemade mozzarella layered with ripe tomatoes, finely chopped onion, and fresh basil in extra-virgin olive oil drizzled with balsamic vinegar. Or ask for a bowl of spinach in oil and garlic with fresh tomatoes and roasted almonds (it's not on the menu). Rocky's baked pasta balsamico is another unforgettable dish—a baked rigatoni quattro formaggio arrayed with chicken tenderloins and smothered in a chicken-broth/white-wine sauce enhanced by aged black balsamic wine vinegar, extra virgin olive oil, and fresh rosemary and garlic. Finally, cioppino here is a hearty amalgam of fresh clams, New Zealand mussels, Gulf shrimp, bay scallops, fresh grouper, and marinated calamari served over homemade linguine with zesty marinara sauce in a round nest of wood-fired Italian bread. Desserts, such as tira misu and chocolate soufflé, are first rate. Kids get free gelato.

Note: For hotel pizza delivery, dial **262-ROCK.**

R. Thomas, 1812 Peachtree St. NW, between Collier Rd. and 26th St. ☎ **881-0246.**

Cuisine: AMERICAN. **Reservations:** Not accepted. **Parking:** Free in lot behind restaurant.

Prices: $5.95–$8.95 for main courses, sandwiches, salads, omelets, and burgers. AE, MC, V.

Open: Daily 24 hours.

Richard Thomas is king of late-night Atlanta, his 24-hour eatery a mecca for postdisco/posttheater crowds and actors unwinding after performances. Tom Cruise, Madonna, Emilio Estevez, Halle Berry, John Amos, and Val Kilmer have all dined here after hours. They come, like everyone else, to relax on the beautiful plant-filled tented patio, which is festively lit by multicolored globe lights strung overhead. Don't get the idea this is a fancy place, however. It's super-casual. Comfort is the keynote, enhanced by good music—light jazz or rock—and a friendly waitstaff. Thomas is an avid gardener. His premises are so lushly planted with pansies, petunias, rose bushes, geraniums, irises, sunflowers, and more—that passersby have stopped in thinking it was a nursery. He also maintains an aviary here of doves, canaries, parakeets, cockatiels, and parrots. Open year round, the patio is cooled by fans in summer and cozily warmed in winter by 12 heaters.

Nature-loving Thomas is health and ecology conscious. He serves free-range chickens and steroid-free lean beef, grows his own fresh herbs, and squeezes fresh fruit and vegetable juices. Everything is made from scratch. Come by for breakfast any time—perhaps a California omelet stuffed with shrimp, crabmeat, cheddar, and avocado, served with freshly made home fries. There are pasta dishes (for example, blue cheese tortellini with eggplant and sundried tomatoes), terrific salads, sandwiches (ranging from grilled vegetables to hickory-grilled chicken with cheddar sauce, both served on organic five-seed bread with cole slaw and home fries), homemade soups, tacos and quesadillas, and oven-baked citrus-marinated chicken dinners. For dessert, you can indulge in anything from raspberry white-chocolate cheesecake to bananas Foster. There's a full bar.

Budget

Gorin's, 620 Peachtree St., between Ponce de Leon and North Aves. ☎ **874-0550.**

Cuisine: AMERICAN/ICE CREAM. **Reservations:** Not accepted. **MARTA:** North Avenue. **Parking:** Difficult on street; a parking lot is nearby.

Prices: Everything under $5. No credit cards.

Open: Mon–Fri 9:30am–5pm, Sat–Sun 10am–5pm.

Gorin's homemade ice cream is Atlanta's answer to Häagen-Dazs. And Gorin's locations, which also serve food in an ice-cream-parlor setting, are a great choice for casual meals with the kids. Not only is the ice cream homemade, sandwich meats and salads are also freshly prepared on the premises. Menu selections include a classic Reuben sandwich with Thousand Island dressing, ham and cheese with honey mustard on grilled egg bread, an almond chicken salad platter served with potato salad, and homemade soups. For dessert there are oven-fresh cakes and, of course, ice cream, over 200 flavors—everything from amaretto almond to peach cobbler. Light ice creams, frozen yogurts, sherbets, and sorbets are also served, as, of course, are milk shakes, malts, ice-cream sodas, and sundaes. In nice weather you can indulge at umbrella tables on the front patio.

A few blocks from this location is **Gorin's Diner,** at 1170 Peachtree St., at 14th St. (☎ **892-2500**). Similar fare—but with a broader menu including items such as grilled Cajun chicken with remoulade sauce—is served here in a re-creation of a classic American diner, complete with stainless-steel facade, gleaming neon, and checkerboard-tile floors. Open Sun–Thurs 7am–midnight, Fri–Sat 7am–2am. Check your phone book for other locations.

3 Buckhead

Buckhead contains the majority of Atlanta's posh dining venues.
Note: There's another **Morton's of Chicago** (see description above
in "Downtown" listings) at 3379 Peachtree Rd., between Stratford
Rd. and Wooddale Dr. (☎ **816-6535**). It's open for lunch Mon–
Fri 11:30am–2:30pm; dinner Mon–Sat 5:30–11pm, Sun 5–10pm.

Very Expensive

 Bone's, 3130 Piedmont Rd. NE, a half-block below Peachtree Rd.
☎ **237-2663.**

Cuisine: STEAK AND SEAFOOD. **Reservations:** Essential. **Parking:**
Complimentary valet parking.
Prices: Appetizers $6.95–$10.95 at lunch, $8.95–$11.95 at dinner; main
courses $7.95–$24.95 at lunch, mostly $19.95–$26.95 at dinner. AE,
CB, DC, MC, V.
Open: Lunch Mon–Fri 11:30am–2:30pm; dinner nightly 6–11pm.
Closed: Most major holidays.

Atlanta's most famous steak house, Bone's receives great reviews not
only at home ("best steaks," raves *Atlanta* magazine) but in countless national publications, including the *New York Times, Esquire,*
and *GQ.* It's a top power-lunch venue for the expense-account crowd
(as many deals as steaks are cut here), which is provided with notepads
and phones at the midday meal. And celebrity stories abound. When
Bob Hope dined here, everyone respected his privacy until he rose
to leave; then the entire dining room stood up and gave him a standing ovation. During his presidency, George Bush came in for dinner
one night, booking six surrounding tables for Secret Service men (they
ate, too). Ted Turner conducted a *Fortune* magazine cover-story
interview here over lobster. And Chuck Mangione once gave an
impromptu concert in the lounge.

The setting is traditional masculine-clubby, with deep-red leather
chairs at tables covered in crisp white-linen, wide-plank oak floors,
and globe-light fans overhead. Patinated wainscoted walls are covered with vintage museum-quality photographs depicting the history
of Atlanta (do take a tour after you dine; it's a fascinating display),
and caricatures of local personalities. Sports events are aired on the
TV in the comfortable lounge.

As noted for its seafood as for its steaks and chops, Bone's flies
Maine lobster in daily and serves fresh Gulf Coast crabmeat and
shrimp. As for the steak, it's prime aged, corn-fed Iowa beef, butch-
ered on the premises. A good beginning here is a salad of crabmeat,
romaine and iceberg lettuce, chunks of avocado, mushrooms, and
hearts of palm in a classic vinaigrette. Thick, juicy lamb chops (two
9-ounce chops, served with mint jelly) and tender char-grilled steak
and prime-rib main courses are prepared to your exact specification
and served in more-than-ample portions. Lobster is a specialty; request a steak-lobster combo if you so desire. Other seafood dishes
range from grilled salmon with sautéed crawfish to sautéed crabcakes.

Of the side dishes, I like the sea-breeze baked potato, brushed with egg and rolled in kosher salt to seal in moistness. Sautéed snow peas and fried onion rings are also great. Similar entrées are available at lunch, along with salads and sandwiches.

The wine gallery at Bone's houses over 500 selections; international in scope, it highlights French and California wines. There are rich desserts like mountain-high pie—layers of chocolate chip, rum raisin, and vanilla ice cream on a crème-de-menthe-soaked brownie, topped with chocolate sauce, whipped cream, and meringue. And finally, at this unabashedly macho enclave, a cigar humidor is brought to your table on request after dinner.

⭐ **Chops,** 70 W. Paces Ferry Rd., at Peachtree Rd. ☎ 262-2675.
Cuisine: STEAK AND SEAFOOD. **Reservations:** Highly recommended.
Parking: Complimentary valet parking at W. Paces Ferry entrance.
Prices: Appetizers $3.50–$7.95 at lunch. $3.95–$8.50 at dinner; main courses $8.50–$13.95 at lunch, $14.75–$29.50 at dinner. AE, CB, DC, DISC, MC, V.
Open: Lunch Mon–Fri 11:30am–2:30pm; dinner Mon–Thurs 5:30–11pm, Fri–Sat 5:30pm–midnight, Sun 5:30–10pm.

This very popular Atlanta steak house is an extremely elegant version of its clubby genre. Soft lighting emanates from art deco alabaster chandeliers. A coffered ceiling and columns are handsomely paneled in California redwood, as is the retro-look marble-topped bar. Trilevel seating is in comfortable upholstered redwood armchairs or roomy black leather semicircular banquettes at crisply white-linened tables. And moss green carpeting beautifully complements the redwood paneling and furnishings. USDA prime midwestern beef is aged in a glassed-in case, with additional cuts of meat displayed on a marble sideboard. And white-hatted chefs can be seen busily broiling, steaming, and sautéeing clams, oysters, and lobsters in an exhibition kitchen. Seafood is a real option here, not an afterthought as in most steak houses. Chops serves only the freshest fish and seafood, expertly and innovatively prepared.

A good beginning here, in fact, is seafood, perhaps Maryland softshell crab, lightly battered in seasoned flour and quick-fried crisp, served with lemon-mustard and red-pepper coulis. A recommended seafood main dish is boneless whole rainbow trout with diced lemon croutons, capers, and mushrooms. Meat main courses will require a hearty appetite (or doggy bags), for example, a 22-ounce portion of triple cut lamb loin chops, a 24-ounce porterhouse steak, or a hearty serving of roast prime rib of beef au jus in creamy horseradish sauce. All the meats are fork tender, juicy, and delicious, prepared exactly as ordered. Traditional à la carte side dishes like creamed spinach, jumbo asparagus hollandaise, cottage fries, or a skillet of steak mushrooms are a must. A large selection of wines is, of course, available, and if you have room for dessert the chocolate chip butterscotch pie is noteworthy. At lunch, delicious sandwiches are options.

⭐ **The Dining Room,** at the Ritz-Carlton Buckhead, 3434 Peachtree Rd. NE, at Phipps Dr. ☎ 237-2700.

Cuisine: EUROPEAN HAUTE CUISINE. **Reservations:** Essential, and as far in advance as possible. **MARTA:** Lenox. **Parking:** Complimentary valet parking.
Prices: Four-course prix-fixe dinner $56, $80 with appropriate wines with each course. AE, CB, DC, MC, V.
Open: Mon–Sat 6:30–11pm.

One of Atlanta's most highly acclaimed restaurants, the Dining Room is the domain of brilliantly talented chef Guenter Seeger. Internationally renowned, Seeger received the coveted Michelin Star rating for his restaurant in the Black Forest of Germany—one of the few restaurants outside of France, to be so honored. His traditional European haute-cuisine creations (with American regional overtones) are magical, drawing the maximum of flavor from the very freshest of ingredients. A network of Georgia farmers grow organic produce to his meticulous specifications; a San Antonio ranch does the same with venison; and fresh fish and seafood are flown in daily from Maine, Florida, and Louisiana waters.

Seeger's refined cuisine is a gem in a worthy setting. The Dining Room's mahogany-paneled walls are hung with a museum-quality collection of gilt-framed British hunt paintings. Diners sink into comfortable silk-upholstered armchairs and banquettes at elegantly appointed tables adorned with stunning arrangements of Hawaiian flowers—tropically hued orchids, birds of paradise, and anthurium. Shaded table lamps provide soft lighting, and background music is classical. Service is impeccable ("The waiters, the wine steward, all move in a well-orchestrated dance," raved one reviewer), but never haughty.

A four-course dinner here is as harmonious as a string-quartet concerto, each course complemented by appropriate wines and liqueurs. Menus change daily. On a recent visit, such a meal began with delicately cubed tuna ceviche with cilantro and osetra caviar garnish in extra-virgin olive oil. It was followed by grapefruit-garnished Gulf red snapper in a croustade of thinly sliced potatoes with citrus vinaigrette. Next came a crispy fan of rosemary-garnished duck breast with date purée in caramelized sherry-vinaigrette sauce. And dessert was a heavenly fig tart topped with vanilla ice cream and garnished with fresh mint and raspberries. Everything is sensational, and presentations, on white German Hutschenreuther china platters, are works of art. A very comprehensive list of over 300 wines is dominated by French and California selections, but also offers many German and Italian vintages. Master Sommelier Michael McNeill, one of only 23 master sommeliers in the United States, oversees wine selections and confers daily with Seeger to match wines for his prix-fixe menus.

⭐ **The Hedgerose Heights Inn,** 490 E. Pacos Ferry Rd., at Maple Dr. ☎ 233-7673.
Cuisine: CLASSIC EUROPEAN. **Reservations:** Required. **Parking:** Free.
Prices: Appetizers $7.50–$8.95; main courses $17.50–$23.50. AE, CB, DC, MC, V.

Open: Tues–Sat 6:30–10pm, with two staggered seatings at 6:30, 7, and 7:30pm and 9, 9:30, and 10pm.

For over a decade a shining star in the galaxy of Atlanta's formal dining rooms, Hedgerose Heights is as charming as it is celebrated. It's entered via a gemlike little bar, where a hostess provides a warm welcome and escorts you to your table. Occupying a former Buckhead town house, the inn is living room–cozy, with pristine white wainscoting and intricately carved moldings framing peach and forest-green walls. Graceful arched niches contain exquisite flower arrangements, an ornate fireplace is filled with lush greenery, and the garden motif is further enhanced by botanical prints. Crystal chandeliers glitter overhead, and seating is in comfortable armchairs at elegantly appointed white-linened tables lit by shaded lamps.

Owner-chef Heinz Schwab, the son and grandson of chefs, trained in the classic European tradition, apprenticing from age 16 in the resort restaurants of his native Switzerland. His cooking garners only superlatives from food critics ("virtually flawless" raved New York's Mimi Sheraton). Menus change frequently. A recent carte offered these wonderful appetizers: delicate mousse of goose and duck liver studded with grapes and green peppercorns, garnished with cornichons and cocktail onions, and served with crisp toast; crabmeat-stuffed raviolis (plain and spinach) glossed with noisette butter; and, one of Schwab's unique creations, a tasty poached leek terrine served chilled with truffle vinaigrette. A main course of sautéed red snapper, Provence style, was enhanced with red and yellow peppers, plump sundried tomatoes (made here, the best I've ever had), mushrooms, artichokes, and black olives. A game special—medallions of venison with field mushrooms, sautéed spaetzle, lingonberries, chestnut purée, burgundy-poached pear, and white wine–poached apple—seemed to combine the world's most ambrosial foods on a single plate. Also very memorable here were sautéed breast of pheasant with porcini mushroom sauce; roast duck, lushly prepared with apple, foie gras, and calvados sauce and served with lacy-crisp potato pancakes; and roast rack of lamb accompanied by fresh pasta. A very extensive wine list (over 300 selections, many available by the glass) offers choices in several price ranges. For dessert, I never pass up the soufflés (flavors change nightly), which is all that a soufflé could ever aspire to. But there are sumptuous others such as a thin bittersweet chocolate cup filled with soft frozen cappuccino cream and Irish whiskey/hazelnut cream sauce dusted with powdered sugar. You can, by the way, come in just for appetizers or dessert and cappuccino in the bar.

★ **Kamogawa,** in the Hotel Nikko, 3300 Peachtree Rd., just east of Piedmont Rd. ☎ **841-0314.**

Cuisine: JAPANESE. **Reservations:** Highly recommended, especially for tatami rooms. **MARTA:** Lenox. **Parking:** Complimentary valet parking.

Prices: Appetizers $3.50–$12.25; main courses $7.75–$19.75 at lunch, $16.75–$28.50 at dinner; prix-fixe complete lunch $6.75; kaiseki dinner $50, $70, or $100. AE, CB, DC, JCB, MC, V.

Open: Lunch daily 11:30am–2pm, dinner nightly 6–10:30pm.

Built by temple craftsmen from Kyoto, Kamogawa has an understated decor authentically reflective of traditional Japanese interior design. Its clean lines derive from simple materials—rice paper, bamboo, pale cedar paneling, and granite pathways. And in lush contrast, large windows overlook a classic Japanese garden—a serene backdrop of waterfalls, carefully placed rocks and plants, and a "teahouse" structure meant for meditation. It's the perfect setting for a cuisine more subtle and refined than you're likely to have experienced at other Japanese restaurants in this country. If you have four or more in your party, I suggest reserving a tatami room for which you'll remove your shoes at the door and dine in luxurious privacy seated on floor cushions. It's less confining than a table and there's a pit for your legs, so you don't have to sit cross-legged. Flawless service is provided by graceful kimonoed waitresses.

Dining at Kamogawa, you'll experience exquisite nuances of food preparation and presentation. Every aesthetic element is considered. An appetizer of grilled salmon with shiitake mushrooms, for instance, comes wrapped in an artistically knotted leaf secured by a bamboo skewer; it's served on a lovely ceramic fan with a cherry blossom. And dobinmushi—an exotically herbed consommé infused with shrimp, chicken, oyster mushrooms, and gingko nuts—is served in a delicate ceramic spouted pot from which the soup is poured into a beautiful little dish and sipped. The visual and tactile elements of the pottery subtly heighten gustatory sensations. All main courses are served with steamed rice and marinated Japanese pickles. One of my favorites is filets of yellowtail tuna basted with teriyaki sauce and grilled to a crisp, aromatic flavor enhanced by ginger and shredded burdock root. A unique delicacy is nasu dengaku—a deep-fried eggplant dish; the cooked pulp is scooped out, mashed with sweet rice wine and a soupçon of miso sauce, stuffed into the shell, and served caramelized with ginger and shrimp garnishes. And a sushi course is de rigueur. Especially marvelous is the "dynamite" roll filled with avocado, yellowtail tuna, seaweed, scallion, and finely minced cucumber flavored with miso/mayonnaise/five-pepper sauce. Plum wines and sake are essential accompaniments to this sublime fare, though your server can also recommend appropriate French and California wines. Dessert is fresh fruit and green-tea ice cream. A specialty here is the prix-fixe kaiseki dinner, an esoteric ceremonial meal with multiple courses selected by the chef. I heartily recommend it to adventurous diners.

103 West, 103 W. Paces Ferry Rd., off Peachtree Rd. ☎ **233-5993.**
Cuisine: FRENCH-INFLUENCED CONTEMPORARY AMERICAN. **Reservations:** Recommended. **Parking:** Complimentary valet parking.
Prices: Appetizers $6.50–$12.50; main courses $15.50–$26.75 (most under $20). AE, CB, DC, DISC, MC, V.
Open: Mon–Sat 6–11pm.

Unrestrained Victorian opulence is the keynote of 103 West, from its porte-cochère entranceway lit by 19th-century coach lights to its posh interior with rose silk moiré wall coverings, Venetian sky-painted domes, Aubusson tapestries, and fleur-de-lis-patterned Axminster carpeting. Walls are hung with gilt-framed mirrors and oil paintings. Plants in ornately carved urns grace faux-marble columns, and arched windows are framed by heavy silk draperies. A pianist entertains during dinner. This theatrical setting provides the perfect backdrop for chef Dean Pogel's stellar performances. Under his auspices, 103 West has garnered dozens of awards for its excellent food, exquisite presentations, and extensive wine list (over 600 wines, 54 of them available by the glass).

Begin your meal with an appetizer of thick, scallion-studded crab cakes topped with a nest of sautéed shredded leeks, the cakes afloat on a basil-flavored beurre blanc sauce ringed with red-pepper rouille. Also superb are shrimp- and lobster-filled ravioli in lobster bisque garnished with cilantro and sour cream. Main courses—all accompanied by a beautiful bouquetière of vegetables—include roasted duck breast with peppered red wine sauce and a gratin of turnips and plums; Dover sole rolled with lemony garlic butter, dredged in brioche crumbs, and quickly deep-fried; and pinkly juicy roast rack of lamb seasoned with rosemary. The dessert menu offers many temptations—a luscious crème brûlée, hot soufflé Grand Marnier served with cold vanilla sauce, double-rich chocolate apricot cake with homemade ice cream, and baby chocolate truffles in a cookie basket, among others—but most tempting is the sampler of six.

⭐ **Opus,** At Swissôtel, 3391 Peachtree Rd. NE, between Lenox and Piedmont Rds.☎ **365-6395.**

Cuisine: CONTEMPORARY AMERICAN. **Reservations:** Recommended. **MARTA:** Lenox. **Parking:** Complimentary valet parking.
Prices: Appetizers $4.75–$5.75 at lunch, $5.25–$9.75 at dinner; main courses $7.50–$12.75 at lunch, $14.75–$22 at dinner. AE, CB, DC, DISC, ER, JCB, MC, V.
Open: Lunch Mon–Fri 11:30am–2:30pm; dinner Mon–Thurs 6–10pm, Fri–Sat 6–11pm.

Swissôtel's widely acclaimed premier restaurant, Opus is an elegant setting evocative of plush European resorts with soaring ceilings, Bauhaus-style furnishings, potted palms, and museum-quality Cartier-Bresson photographs adorning rich-toned Australian lacewood walls. Leather hides suspended from a latticed window treatment add a dramatic note. At night piano music filters in from the lobby.

Culinary wizard Ken Vedrinski creates a world of wonders utilizing only the finest and freshest ingredients. His magical menus change frequently. On a recent visit I began with a refreshing chilled celery-root soup made with chicken stock, finished with crème fraîche, and enhanced by chunks of blue crabmeat and a sprinkle of oesetra caviar. It was succeeded by a potato-crusted lump crabcake splashed with vermouth and citrus juices. A main course of crisp-skinned roasted duck breast served with duck jus-rhubarb sauce had been slow-marinated in herbs and garlic; it was served with a mousseline of parsnips and creamed potatoes, apple cubes poached in port wine,

Buckhead Dining

0 |■■■■| 500 m
         550 y   ◈N

Information ①

Bone's **13**
The Buckhead Diner **12**
Chops **6**
The Dining Room **17**
Fellini's Pizza **4**
The Fish Market **8**
Hedgerose Heights Inn **11**
Kamogawa **15**
Kudzu Café **9**
La Fonda Latina **4**
The OK Cafe **2**
103 West **5**
Opus **16**
Pano & Paul's **1**
Peasant Restaurant & Bar **14**
Pricci **10**
Rib Ranch **7**
The Swan Coach House **3**

9284

and red cabbage that had been braised in duck fat and bacon for a scrumptious smoky tang. Another choice that evening was grilled Florida pompano that had been dusted and pan-seared in exotic spices (cumin, chilies, etc.) and drizzled with curry oil; a chutney-like relish of peaches, roasted pimientos, vidalia onions, cucumber, tomato, cilantro, and lime made a cool contrast. And roast Wild Copper River salmon, in a savory sauce of finely chopped shallots, truffle butter, rosemary, and cepe mushrooms, came with fava beans and wisps of fried potato. For dessert, a soufflé-like flourless chocolate cake, served warm on chocolate-marbleized caramel-lime sauce, was ambrosial. Ditto a crème brûlée served with honey-caramelized phyllo, fresh berries, and passionfruit sauce. Vedrinski's food presentations are aesthetically exquisite, and the restaurant's extensive wine list—which features many by-the-glass selections—is very reasonably priced.

⭐ **Pano & Paul's,** 1232 W. Paces Ferry Rd. ☎ **261-3662.**
Cuisine: AMERICAN/CONTINENTAL. **Reservations:** Recommended.
Parking: Free.
Prices: Appetizers $4.75–$9.50; main courses $15.95–$27.95. AE, CB, DC, DISC, MC, V.
Open: Mon–Thurs 6–10:30pm, Fri–Sat 6–11pm.

When Pano and Paul opened their deluxe dining emporium in 1979, they brought big-city sophistication to Atlanta's restaurant scene. For over a decade, they've continued to dazzle the dining public with dependable but ever-exciting culinary creations garnering countless awards, from Mobil's four stars to the International Wine Festival's Gold Medal for Best Restaurant Wine List. Well-heeled Atlanta business and society people consider the place a kind of posh private club.

And very posh it is, with intimate canopied booths framed by forest-green velvet curtains; delicate vases of fresh-cut flowers on rose damask-clothed tables lit by pink silk-shaded lamps; floral-patterned wall fabrics hung with ornate gilt-framed mirrors; and antique chandeliers and wall sconces. Tuxedoed waiters provide deft service, and a pianist entertains nightly in the opulent adjoining piano bar; consider adjourning to one of its plush burgundy velvet sofas for dessert or after-dinner drinks.

The kitchen, under executive chef Paul's expert direction, never rests on its laurels but stays apace—and ahead—of current food trends. Dinner here might begin with an appetizer of spinach- and ricotta-filled tortellini tossed in browned butter with fresh sage leaves and walnuts. Or you might opt for house-smoked salmon on a potato pancake. In season, be sure to order a main course of soft-shell crabs, lightly battered and sautéed crisp, a succulent treat served with white lemon butter, and red-pepper coulis. Also highly recommendable is the grilled filet of lightly smoked salmon with Pommery honey cream on a bed of sesame spinach. Yet another main course suggestion: crisp Chinese-style roast duck in orange-ginger sauce, served with wild rice, a spring roll, and sugar snap peas. The wine list is distinguished and desserts are lush—from a classic crème brûlée to

Kahlúa-flavored ice-cream pie with Oreo crust, topped with bourbon-flavored whipped cream, roasted pecans, and chocolate sauce.

Expensive

The Peasant Restaurant & Bar, 3402 Piedmont Rd. NE, a block north of Peachtree Rd. ☎ **231-8740.**

> **Cuisine:** CONTEMPORARY AMERICAN. **Reservations:** Not accepted.
> **Parking:** Valet parking is complimentary.
> **Prices:** Appetizers $4.75–$8.25; main courses $50–$10.50 at lunch/brunch, $9.95–$19.50 at dinner. AE, DC, DISC, MC, V.
> **Open:** Lunch Mon–Fri and Sun brunch 11am–2:30pm; dinner Sun–Thurs 5:30–10pm, Fri–Sat 5:30pm–11pm.

The Peasant group owns 18 restaurants in Atlanta, many of which are described above (Mick's, The Country Place, Pleasant Peasant, Dailey's, even the posh City Grill). All of them offer marvelously unique menus and venues and waitstaff so gracious and efficient that I can spot a Peasant-trained waitperson at any Atlanta restaurant. The setting here is romantic, with candlelit tables amid potted palms. Walls, hung with large gilt-framed mirrors, alternate glossy black lacquer paneling with beautiful fleur-de-lis fabric. Shaded table lamps, English landscape paintings, French antiques, and lovely dried-flower arrangements add residential charm. There's an elegant bar area (come by some afternoon for hors d'oeuvres and cocktails), and a glass-walled conservatory section is verdant with lush plantings.

You might begin your meal here with a grilled quesadilla stuffed with shrimp, black beans, melted cheddar and Monterey Jack cheeses, and jalapeños, served with guacamole and sour cream. Another notable appetizer is sea scallops in a hot and spicy soy-chili sauce, with black beans on a bed of crisp-fried spinach leaves. Main courses come with delicious cheese toast and a huge salad. A good choice is pan-sautéed boneless chicken breast topped with Jarlsberg cheese sauce and accompanied by roasted tomatoes, hickory-grilled mushrooms, and savory onion-flavored homemade mashed potatoes. Grilled grouper (seafood is always fresh here) is served with avocado slices, roasted tomatoes, and butter-browned couscous tossed with mushrooms, macadamia nuts, and ginger. And extra-thick and juicy pork chops are stuffed with black beans, rice, and melted cheddar and garnished with avocado slices and fresh-fruit salsa. The brunch menu adds options such as crabcake eggs Benedict served with hash browns or challah French toast stuffed with strawberry cream cheese. This is a sumptuous cuisine, and portions are huge. Desserts are no exception, with lavish offerings like caramel-butter pecan pie on pecan cookie crust, slathered with whipped cream, and topped with warm caramel and pecans. The wine list features California wines; about a dozen premium selections are offered by the glass.

Pricci, 500 Pharr Rd., at Maple Dr. ☎ **237-2941.**

> **Cuisine:** ITALIAN REGIONAL. **Reservations:** Recommended. **Parking:** Valet parking is complimentary.

Prices: Appetizers $3.95–$6.50 at lunch, $4.95–$7.95 at dinner; pizzas and calzones $6.50–$8.50 at lunch or dinner; main courses, $8.25–$11.50 at lunch, $14.75–$21.50 at dinner (pastas $10.50–$12.95). AE, CB, DC, DISC, MC, V.

Open: Sun–Thurs 11am–11pm, Fri 11am–midnight, Sat 5pm–midnight.

One of Atlanta's hottest restaurants, Pricci is strikingly glamorous. Part of the drama ensues from an exhibition kitchen where a team of white-hatted chefs are engaged in culinary frenzy and a rosy glow emanates from the oak-fired pizza oven. A theatrical interior utilizes curved vaulted ceilings, gorgeous terrazzo marble floors, art deco–look chrome and brass dividers, rich decorative woods such as African turtle shell sapelle and East India rosewood, and stunning, whimsical hand-blown lighting fixtures. Crisply white-linen-covered tables, potted palms, and lavish floral arrangements add traditional panache.

Pricci's fare is the hearty cuisine of Italy's Tuscan, Ligurian, and Milanese regions. Your meal might begin with a crisp Gorgonzola-and walnut-filled risotto on fresh tomatoes or, perhaps, beef tenderloin carpaccio drizzled with creamy mustard and served with shaved parmesan and arugula salad. My preference, though, is to begin with one of the thin-crusted oak-fired pizzas such as the rustica, topped with fresh-grilled tuna, thinly sliced grilled fennel, black olives, fresh mozzarella and capers. Among the pasta dishes (available as appetizers or main courses) I love the arrechiette (small ear-shaped pasta) tossed with roast chicken, braised baby greens, crushed red pepper, and pecorino-romano cheese. More substantial main courses include spicy Tuscan seafood stew filled with chunks of fresh fish, shrimps, mussels, scallops, and tomatoes in herbed white wine broth; it's served with garlicky bruschetta. Or you could opt for juicy baby lamb shank in Barolo wine sauce, served with pastina, sliced artichokes, and roasted garlic. Two desserts were especially memorable—a caramelized upside-down apple tart with homemade vanilla ice cream and the most chocolatey ever flourless torte made with valrhona French cocoa and served with double-chocolate ice cream and whipped cream on crème anglaise. Get both; sharing is bliss. The lunch menu lists focaccia sandwiches, pastas, salads, pizzas, and calzones. The award-winning wine list highlights every wine-producing region of Italy and features a good selection of grappas—clear after-dinner wines made from distilled sediment of the wine-making process. Try one that is infused with macerated fruit.

Moderate

Atlanta Fish Market, 265 Pharr Rd., between Peachtree Rd. and N. Fulton Dr. ☎ **262-3165.**

Cuisine: SEAFOOD. **Reservations:** Accepted. **Parking:** Complimentary valet parking.

Prices: Appetizers $3.50–$8.85; main courses mostly $12.50–$15.95 (luncheon sandwiches $7.95–$9.95). AE, CB, DC, DISC, ER, MC, V.

Open: Lunch Mon–Fri 11:30am–2:30pm; dinner Mon–Thurs 5:30–11pm, Fri–Sat 5:30–midnight, Sun 4–10pm. The Geechee Crab Lounge and Porch are open daily from 2:30–5:30pm for light fare and desserts.

Like the Buckhead Diner (under the same ownership, details below), for consistency the Atlanta Fish Market offers a winning combination of glamour (you might note anyone from Madonna to Gov. Zell Miller among the fish fanciers) and laid-back casual ambience. Housed in a brick building inspired by a 1920s Savannah train station, it is fronted by a covered veranda furnished with rocking chairs. Diners pass through an antique revolving door into a dramatic interior space, where vast globe lights ringed by brightly colored stars are suspended from a lofty 24-foot beamed ceiling, creating an airy dining-in-outer-space sensation. Plush leather booths lit by art deco sconces contrast with distressed-look pine tables and wide-plank pine floors. Potted palms add a traditional note. And wall treatments vary from exposed brick, to whimsical mermaid- and fish-themed wallpaper, to painted yellow clapboard. To the rear, a bustling exhibition kitchen is fronted by display cases of fresh seafood on ice and backed by a mural of famous Georgia people and places. Another venue is the 1990s room—an elegant glass-walled café with exterior cedar shutters filtering the sunlight. The Geechee Crab Lounge is low lit and pubby. And there's also a cozy enclosed Porch area—very southern in feel with a sloped corrugated-tin ceiling, exposed brick walls, and windows hung with Venetian blinds and café curtains. On the premises you can glance into a glass-walled fish-cutting room or shop at a fancy food boutique. But enough description. Let's eat.

A vast daily-changing menu proffers appetizers such as barbecued oysters topped with applewood-smoked bacon; deep-fried calamari drizzled with aioli and served with a rich, spicy marinara nuanced with crushed red pepper; and big fluffy broiled Dungeness crabcakes served with tartar and red mustard sauces. A list of over a dozen fresh catch items can be ordered charbroiled or steamed; they're served with steamed vegetables, creamy mashed potatoes, and tartar sauce. Or you can opt for daily specials: I recently enjoyed a sautéed swordfish that had been dredged in ground cashews and black peppercorns to form a flavorful crust; it was served on white corn cheese grits with haricots verts and mushrooms poached in white wine. There are pasta dishes and salads as well. Desserts include an apple crumb tart with streusel topping served warm with cinnamon ice cream and a rich chocolate toffee crunch pie drenched in caramel sauce, garnished with fresh fruit, and topped with whipped cream and morsels of toffee.

★ **The Buckhead Diner,** 3073 Piedmont Rd., at E. Paces Ferry Rd. ☎ 262-3336.

Cuisine: AMERICAN. **Reservations:** Not accepted; arrive off-peak hours. **Parking:** Complimentary valet parking.

Prices: Snacks, sandwiches, and salads mostly $4.50–$9; main courses $7.95–$12.50 at lunch, mostly $10.95–$14.50 at dinner. AE, CB, DC, DISC, MC, V.

Open: Mon–Sat 11am–midnight, Sun (including brunch) 11 am–10pm.

This nouvelle-diner-chic reconstructed roadhouse is *the* place to see and be seen in Atlanta, attracting a stream of celebrities year after year, including Princess Stephanie of Monaco, who stood patiently in line waiting for a table, then returned for another meal a few days later. And local boy Elton John comes in regularly. As sleek as a Thunderbird convertible, the Buckhead was designed to the tune of $1.5 million by Pat Kuleto, who has also done interiors for noted California restaurateur Wolfgang Puck. Its exterior glitters with stainless-steel and neon tubing. Inside there's a trompe-l'oeil Italian marble floor, a "bar car" inspired by the opulence of the Orient Express, and a gorgeous counter of Honduran mahogany with ebony, cherrywood, and bird's-eye maple marquetry detail. Bustling white-hatted chefs behind the counter comprise an exhibition-kitchen area. Most diners, however, opt for the more intimate transom-windowed, upholstered mahogany booths. As in the bar, a vaulted ceiling evokes a luxury railroad dining car. Lighting emanates from beautiful art deco fixtures, and classic recorded jazz (Louis Armstrong, Ella Fitzgerald) creates an ambience evocative of an earlier era.

Charming young chef Daniel O'Leary has created a contemporary American menu that highlights southern and southwestern cookery. That means main courses are a mix of Mom and modern: for example, thick-cut grilled smoked pork chops with spinach, cheese grits, and blackeyed pea salsa; crispy fried oysters and scallops with shoestring potatoes and jalapeño coleslaw; and a grilled cheese sandwich of Jarlsberg and cheddar with plum tomato, scallions, and grainy mustard on three-cheese bread. Many low-priced little snack items—like crispy calamari, quesadillas, and tamarind-glazed baby back ribs with fried plaintains and black bean mango salsa—make grazing fun here. Both the menu and the wine list change seasonally, the latter always offering many selections by the glass. Desserts are great, ranging from peach bread pudding with Southern Comfort–flavored cream to upside-down apple pie topped with homemade cinnamon ice cream.

Kudzu Café, 3215 Peachtree Rd., at E. Shadowlawn Ave.
☎ 262-0661.

Cuisine: CONTEMPORARY SOUTHERN. **Reservations:** Not accepted.
Parking: Complimentary valet parking.
Prices: Appetizers $3.95–$6.95; main courses $8.95–$15.95 at lunch and brunch (burgers, sandwiches, and salads $6.50–$7.95), $8.95–$19.95 at dinner. AE, MC, V.
Open: Lunch Mon–Sat 11am–4:30pm, Sun brunch 11am–2:30pm; dinner Mon–Thurs 4:30–11pm, Fri–Sat 4:30pm–midnight, Sun 2:30–11pm.

Themed after a vigorous vine that flourishes in the South, the Kudzu Café brings new vigor to traditional southern cookery. And in similar mode, its thoroughly contemporary sage, green, and burgundy interior has southern roots (wooden Venetian blinds, a plant-filled oak-floored porch area cooled by overhead fans and lit by gaslight sconces, and a display of museum-quality historic photographs of the old South on exposed brick columns). Dining room floors are covered with specially designed kudzu-motif carpeting, sprigs of sculpted metal kudzu vine embellish the walls, and you'll also spot the curly kudzu leaf on menu covers, lampshades, and server's vests. Most seating is in comfortable leather booths lit by shaded lamps, though some diners prefer to perch on stools at an oval bar overlooking a busy display kitchen. If you bring the kids, they can retreat to a small room with video games while you linger over coffee. Background music is mellow rock and oldies.

If you've been hankering after fried green tomatoes since the movie came out, you'll find them here battered with cornmeal and served with chunky Créole tomato sauce. Other good beginnings include crisp calamari served with chili and lime-caper tartar sauces or a salad of crunchy battered crayfish tossed with mixed greens in a piquant balsamic vinaigrette topped with fried turnip greens. Main courses such as hickory-grilled smoked pork chops with spicy applesauce and southern-style barbecued chicken, though delicious, are, for me, merely pretexts to garner the accompanying vegetables—hickory-grilled corn on the cob, apple cider slaw studded with golden raisins, sugar snap peas, sautéed spinach, and chunky red skin mashed potatoes nuanced with horseradish. You get two with your main course but I always order extras or simply opt for a vegetable plate. At lunch or brunch, a hickory-grilled turkey burger served with cranberry mayonnaise and fries is noteworthy. The dessert of choice is hot peach bread pudding with rum sauce. A small list of California wines—all offered by the glass or bottle—is supplemented by a good choice of American beers.

Inexpensive

 The Ok Cafe, 1284 W. Paces Ferry Rd., at Northside Dr. in the West Paces Ferry Shopping Center. ☎ 233-2888.

Cuisine: AMERICAN. **Reservations:** Not accepted. **Parking:** Free.
Prices: Lunch and dinner burgers, salads, and sandwiches $4.50–$6.95; blue-plate specials $8.50–$8.95 at lunch; $9.50–$10.50 at dinner. AE, MC, V.
Open: 24 hours.

Though it was actually built in 1987, it's hard to believe this isn't an authentic 1950s rural Georgia roadhouse, transported "back to the future" by some magical force. A low yellow cement-block building, with striped aluminum awnings and a green shingled roof, it's heralded by the requisite neon roadhouse sign. Within, seating is in roomy leather booths at old-style Formica tables, windows are shaded with Venetian blinds and framed by retro-look curtains, the jukebox is stocked with oldies, and waitresses are attired in white diner uniforms. Shaded table lamps further enhance the cozy ambience.

As for the food, it evokes memories of Mom, with blue-plate specials such as meat loaf, fried catfish with Cajun ketchup, and roast turkey with cornbread dressing (they change seasonally), all served with scrumptious homemade corn muffins and two side dishes—your choices including, among many others, creamy macaroni and cheese made with six cheeses (the best I've ever had), collard greens, lima beans, sugar snap peas, and sweet potatoes seasoned with nutmeg and cinnamon, studded with honeyed pecans, and topped with a cornflake crust. Excellent sandwiches, burgers, and salads are additional options, not to mention old-fashioned thick shakes and malteds served in the tumbler. And do leave room for dessert, be it homemade hot apple pie topped with brown sugar, pecans, cinnamon, and a scoop of vanilla ice cream, or hot fudge cake—an ultramoist, ultrachocolaty brownie smothered in fresh whipped cream, nuts, strawberries, hot fudge, and vanilla ice cream. The OK is also a great place for country-style breakfasts and brunches. Stop in for griddle cakes with Granny Smith apples and pecans or a three-egg omelet (with a filling of smoked turkey, leeks, and Monterey jack) served with grits and homemade biscuits.

⭐ **The Swan Coach House,** 3130 Slaton Dr. NW, at the Atlanta History Center. ☎ **261-0636.**

Cuisine: AMERICAN. **Reservations:** Not accepted.
Prices: Main courses $6–$8. MC, V.
Open: Mon–Sat 11:30am–2:30pm. **Closed:** Jan 1, Memorial Day, July 4, Thanksgiving, and Dec 25.

When you visit the Atlanta History Center in Buckhead (see Chapter 7, "What to See and Do in Atlanta," below), plan a lunch at this delightful restaurant. Tables are adorned with lovely flower arrangements, walls are covered in exquisite fruit-and-flower-motif fabric, crystal chandeliers glitter overhead, and multipaned windows overlook wooded grounds. A vast gift shop and art gallery adjoin the dining room.

The menu mirrors the ambience, featuring ladies' fork-luncheon fare such as salmon croquettes topped with white caper sauce and served with a spiced peach, vegetables, and congealed salad (chopped apples, pecans, and walnuts in a lime-jello mold). Or you might opt for chicken salad in pastry timbales served with cheese straws and creamy frozen fruit salad. There's even chicken à la king. Fresh muffins accompany all main courses. For dessert, order lemon chess pie or a French silk swan—a meringue base filled with chocolate mousse and whipped cream, topped with slivered almonds, and garnished with a swan-shaped cracker. There's a full bar; drinks like peach fuzz and mint julep are featured. **Note:** You don't have to be visiting the AHC to dine here; it has a separate entrance.

Budget

Fellini's Pizza, 2809 Peachtree Rd., at Rumson Rd. ☎ **266-0082.**

Cuisine: PIZZA. **Reservations:** Not accepted. **Parking:** Free.
Prices: $1.10–$2.50 for a slice; $7.50–$12.50 for a medium pie, with additional toppings $1–$1.50; $4.50–$5 for calzones. No credit cards.
Open: Mon–Sat 11:30am–2am, Sun noon–midnight.

You won't get chèvre or cilantro on your pies here, but you will get traditional toppings like anchovies, Italian sausage, meatballs, pepperoni, fresh mushrooms, and onions piled on cheesy New York–style pies with thin, doughy crusts that exude the heavenly aroma of fresh-baked bread. Fellini's is a classic pizza joint, and a darned good one. It's a wacky place, very atypical for Buckhead. It occupies a converted gas station. Most of the seating is at white-canvas umbrella tables on a large outdoor patio shaded by a scalloped yellow awning. It centers on a tiered fountain topped by an angel, and there are statues of angels, the god Pan, gargoyles, and King Tut here and there. At night, citronella candles and strings of colored lights overhead make for a festive ambience. The patio is lit by gas heaters in winter, but when the heat is wilting, you can retreat to a cheerful air-conditioned interior space with red plastic booths, brick walls painted bright jade and coral, and exposed overhead pipes painted yellow, lavender, rose, and orange.

The pizzas, regular and thick-crusted Sicilian, are made with only the freshest ingredients. Other options are immense calzones stuffed with fillings like sausage and cheese and a tasty salad of lettuce, mushrooms, onions, green peppers, mozzarella, tomatoes, and black olives in creamy Italian dressing. Beer and wine are available.

There are additional locations at 422 Seminole Ave. in Little Five Points (☎ 525-2530) and in midtown at 923 Ponce de Leon Ave. (☎ 873-3088).

$ **La Fonda Latina,** 2813 Peachtree Rd. NE, between Rumson Rd. and Sheridan Dr. ☎ 816-8311.

Cuisine: SPANISH. **Reservations:** Not accepted. **Parking:** Free in lot behind restaurant.
Prices: Appetizers $2.50–$3.95; main courses $3.50–$7.95. No credit cards.
Open: Sun–Thurs 11:30am–11pm, Fri–Sat 11:30am–1am.

Funky and festive, La Fonda is brightly painted in tropical resort hues (turquoise, raspberry, pink, orange, chartreuse, sunny yellow, lavender), with hibiscus, palm trees, parrots, and other colorful island motifs adorning every inch of wall space. It comprises a small interior dining area with an open kitchen, an outdoor patio under a striped awning, and an awninged, open-air rooftop patio with seating in wooden booths amid lots of plants. Outdoor areas are heated in winter and cooled by large fans in summer. Well-chosen Spanish and Brazilian music enhances the mood.

The food is both fresh and refreshingly authentic. You might simply order up a bottle of vino blanco and a delicious ensalada mixta (tuna, black olives, lettuce, onions, and peppers in a classic vinaigrette you can soak up with Cuban bread). Grilled quesadillas layered with cheddar, Monterey jack, sautéed shrimp, and tomato salsa come with yellow rice and black beans. The paella—yellow rice cooked with herbed baked chicken, calamari, shrimp, chorizo sausage, peppers, onions, and pimientos—is heartily satisfying here. Ditto mesquite-grilled chicken served with rice and black beans. La Fonda does a marvelous gazpacho as well. And I'm also partial to sandwiches on crusty Cuban bread stuffed with roast pork, ham, swiss cheese, mayo, mustard, and mojo sauce, served with rice and beans. There are flans for dessert.

Note: There's another location in Little Five Points at 1150B Euclid Ave., off Colquitt Ave. (☎ 577-8317).

The Rib Ranch, 25 Irby Ave. NW, just west of Floswell Rd. between W. Paces Ferry Rd. and E. Andrews Dr. ☎ 233-7644.

Cuisine: TEXAS BARBECUE. **Reservations:** Not accepted. **Parking:** Free in a few spaces here; paid parking across the street.
Prices: Barbecue sandwiches $3.45–$7.25; platters $6.50–$15.95; ribs $6.95–$19.50; children's plates $2.50. MC, V.
Open: Mon–Sat 11am–11pm, Sun noon–10pm.

Fronted by a Texas flag awning shading a few picnic tables, the Rib Ranch is your archetypical Lone Star rib joint. The cozy interior, with dark-stained pine floors and café-curtained windows, is cluttered with long horn skulls, neon beer signs, license plates, and university football banners suspended from a low-beamed ceiling. Tables are covered with red and white checker cloths. And, of course, the jukebox is stocked with country tunes.

Come here for fork-tender Texas-style ribs that have been slow-cooked over hickory wood and basted with tangy sauce. The beef ribs are the most truly Texan, but the pork ribs are equally delicious. Don't bother with the chicken; it's undistinguished. There are all kinds of side dishes, the best being spicy Brunswick stew—a mix of tomato, shredded pork and beef, okra, onions, and lima beans. Also noteworthy: authentic all-beef chili, crisp fresh-made onion rings, and homemade sweet and creamy coleslaw. Beer is the beverage of choice, and you can have a brownie or blackberry cobbler for dessert.

4 Virginia-Highland/Little Five Points

Make a meal in this charming district the occasion to see a nontouristy part of Atlanta. Come a little early, so you can browse in the area's great little shops and boutiques.

Expensive

★ **Partners, A Morningside Café,** 1399 N. Highland Ave., between N. Morningside and University Drs. ☎ 876-8104.

Cuisine: CROSS-CULTURAL. **Reservations:** Limited reservations accepted Tuesday through Thursday only; otherwise, arrive early to avoid a wait. **Parking:** Free in a lot across the street.
Prices: Appetizers $4.95–$8.95; main courses $14.95–$17.95.
Open: Tues–Thurs 5:30–11pm, Fri–Sat 5:30–11:30pm.

Alix Kenagy is the culinary genius behind Partners' innovative international menu, and I simply can't pile on enough accolades for the exquisite dining experience she offers. If I lived in Atlanta, I'd be such a regular patron she'd have to put up a brass plaque behind my seat. A former fashion editor, Alix has an artistic flair equal to her kitchen skills. She's designed a warmly intimate setting for Partners. Distressed-look earth-toned walls are hung with beautiful large oil landscapes and paintings of golden angels. Lovely flower arrangements, bare yellow-pine floors, Georgia heart-pine cabinets (one of them ajar to reveal big loaves of crusty country bread), lace-curtained front windows, and candlelit white-linened tables complete the cozy picture. Partners crackles with excitement every night, and Alix is always on hand to greet guests, a charming hostess at a great party. There's a small exhibition kitchen in the back.

Menus—clipped to cedar boards made from naturally fallen Vermont trees—change frequently to reflect market specialties. A recent meal here began with large squares of red-pepper and natural-pasta raviolis, stuffed with Maine lobster and shiitake mushrooms, splashed with sherry, and served on basil oil and champagne beurre blanc sauces with a garnish of oven-dried flying fish roe. Another choice that evening: fresh mission figs stuffed with Gorgonzola and ricotta cheeses, wrapped in Parma prosciutto, baked, and served with a dice of fresh melon marinated in sweet vermouth and a drizzle of balsamic vinegar. A main course of Tuscan grilled pork tenderloin—dry-rubbed with herbs and cracked peppercorns—was served in a fan of slices around soft parmesan polenta garnished with a ribbon of fresh-shaved asiago and tomato coulis. A pair of outwardly crisp, inwardly succulent Delaware crabcakes was enhanced by a roasted pepper/ chipotle-zapped reduction sauce. And Alix's pastas—such as a mix of grilled free-range chicken, charred poblano peppers, golden brown corn kernels, sweet onion, and tomatoes in tequila cream over roasted-red-pepper pasta—are always outstanding. However happily replete, do not pass up Partners' ethereal desserts. Isn't there always room for the likes of a Belgian chocolate pâté flecked with coins of white chocolate on a puddle of hazelnut crème anglaise with a tumble of raspberries? The wine list is about 98% Californian, with many exciting discoveries from boutique wineries and an ample by-the-glass selection. Turn to the friendly, wine-savvy waitstaff for guidance.

Moderate

Chow, 1026¹/₂ N. Highland Ave. NE, at Virginia Ave. ☎ **872-0869.**

> **Cuisine:** CONTEMPORARY AMERICAN. **Reservations:** Not accepted.
> **Parking:** Free behind restaurant on Highland, north of Virginia.
> **Prices:** Appetizers $4.50–$7.95; main courses $5.95–$7.95 at lunch/ brunch, mostly $9.95–$14.95 at dinner. AE, DC, MC, V.
> **Open:** Lunch Mon–Fri 11:30am–3pm; brunch Sat–Sun 11am–3pm; dinner Sun–Thurs 6–10:30pm, Fri–Sat 6–11:30pm.

At the very hub of Atlanta's arty Virginia-Highland area, Chow evokes the casual chic of New York's trendy Soho district. Glossy cream walls function as gallery space for quality artworks, large halaphane lamps are suspended from a high pressed-tin ceiling (very Big Apple), and bare oak floors further an uncluttered less-is-more ambience. However, the setting is warmly inviting rather than stark. Highly polished black granite tables are candlelit and adorned by exquisite flower arrangements, the soft lighting is flattering, and a rough-hewn stone wall adds rustic charm. In good weather, outdoor balcony seating under a striped awning is very popular.

Chow has always attracted a sophisticated clientele. Movie people tend to come by when they're doing films in town (Morgan Freeman was a regular during *Driving Miss Daisy*), and other visiting celebs have included Harry Connick, Jr., Mel Harris, Piper Laurie, and, during Super Bowl, Buffalo Bills quarterback Jim Kelly.

Everything on the menu is fresh and prepared from scratch. Dinner might begin with rosemary- and thyme-marinated garlic cloves served with feta cheese spread and toasted French bread croutons; a platter of hummus dip with pita bread, plump black olives, and cucumber slices; or lightly battered fried calamari with a spicy chunky-tomato marinara sauce. Main courses include many pasta dishes such as Gulf shrimp and sea scallops tossed with linguine in olive oil, garlic, fresh-grated parmesan, and parsley. Also featured is fresh seafood. Try the sautéed Cyprus grouper in lemon-butter sauce served with yellow rice and a bed of spinach topped with plum tomatoes and a generous crumble of feta cheese. The lunch menu features delicious salads, half-pound burgers with toppings like Monterey jack and jalapeños, overstuffed sandwiches, pasta dishes, and quesadillas. And Chow is, without a doubt, the most exciting Sunday brunch venue in town (one local critic described its regulars as a cult). Selected lunch menu items are augmented by breakfasty omelets, strawberry French toast, and Belgian waffles. There's a full bar, and a large selection of wines and aperitifs are offered by the glass.

Harry & Sons, 820 N. Highland Ave., between Greenwood Ave. and Drewry St. ☎ **873-2009.**

Cuisine: THAI/ITALIAN. **Reservations:** Not accepted. **Parking:** Free in lot behind restaurant.

Prices: Appetizers $4–$7; main courses $4.95–$7.95 at lunch and brunch, $7.95–$14.95 at dinner. AE, DISC, MC, V.

Open: Lunch Mon–Sat 11:30am–2:30pm; Sun brunch 10am–2:30pm; dinner Mon–Thurs 5:30–10:30pm, Fri–Sat 5:30pm–1am.

Under the same ownership as Surin of Thailand (see below), this comfortable neighborhood restaurant offers great food in a friendly, casual setting. Owners Harry and Carolyn House count their employees as extended family (hence the name), and that warm relationship is clearly reflected in the happy mien of everyone who works here. The room is simpatico and bistrolike, with bare wood floors, exposed brick walls hung with mirrored beer advertisements, a row of black leather booths lining an upper tier, fans and peach-bulbed lamps suspended from a high white ceiling, and tables (candlelit at night) covered with paisley cloths. It's one of my favorite places for relaxed schmoozy meals—most notably Sunday brunches.

The Thai and Italian menu provides diverse dining choices. For instance, you might start off with wings of angels (battered, deep-fried Thai-style deboned chicken wings stuffed with pork, shrimp, straw mushrooms, and onions) or with fried calamari in a tangy red sauce. Thai main courses include chicken panang in red curry paste—a savory (but mild) mix of chili peppers, peanuts, lemongrass, galanga (a gingerlike root), lime peel, fresh Thai basil, and other spices—

served over saffroned rice. And in the Italian mode, there's a delicious grilled shrimp scampi served over angelhair pasta tossed with garlic butter, oregano leaf, and chunks of fresh tomato. At night there's a satay (kebab) grill at the bar. Entrees are served with big soft yeasty buns—the perfect foil for spicy fare. And speaking of spicy, if you want hot dishes toned down, be sure to tell your server; the kitchen will accommodate. There's a full bar, and first-rate desserts range from a refreshing mint-garnished key lime trifle topped with whipped cream to a rich amaretto chambord cheesecake on a buttery almond-graham cracker crust. The brunch menu offers items such as eggs benedict, pecan waffles, and sourdough French toast that has been dipped in orange-flavored egg batter. Request your coffee laced with amaretto.

★ **Surin of Thailand,** 810 N. Highland Ave., at Greenwood Ave. ☎ 892-7789.

Cuisine: THAI. **Reservations:** Not accepted. **Parking:** Free in lot behind restaurant. If that's full there's paid parking close by.
Prices: Appetizers $3–$5.95; main courses $4–$6.50 at lunch, $6.50–$14.95 at dinner. AE, DISC, MC, V.
Open: Mon–Fri 11:30am–11:30pm, Sat noon–11:30pm, Sun noon–10:30pm.

This pristinely charming Thai restaurant opened in 1991 to rave reviews, and it has continued to enjoy hearty acclaim for its scrumptious and very authentic fare. It's a very comfortable sitting, with bare oak floors and candlelit tables covered in royal blue linen cloths. Colorful Thai banners (depicting a golden Buddha, a Thai dancer, and other familiar imagery) are suspended from a lofty pressed-tin ceiling, and cheerful yellow walls are hung with striking color photographs of Thailand taken by Carolyn House (one of the owners). During the day, light streams in through a wall of windows overlooking the street.

The same menu is offered throughout the day, with specials at both meals. All sauces are made from scratch, and everything—including seafood—is fresh and delicious. There are many tempting appetizers, my favorites of which are chef Surin Techarukpong's perfectly crispy mee-krob—a pungent rice noodle dish sauced with tamarind and garnished with plump shrimp, egg, and bean sprouts—and his exquisite deep-fried edible "baskets" filled with shrimp, chicken, and corn, served with a piquant vinegar-chili-peanut sauce. Other good choices are satays (kebabs) of chicken or beef in spicy peanut sauce served with cucumber salad; tender poached rice paper rolls, stuffed with minced pork, shrimp, bean sprouts, and fresh Thai basil, served with hot peppery plum sauce; and a subtly spiced yum yai salad of romaine lettuce, shredded carrot, hard-boiled egg, cucumber, shrimp, and chicken in a light sweet and sour peanut dressing. Main courses include a hearty chicken curry with potatoes, carrots, and other vegetables in an unsweetened coconut milk sauce. And if it's on the specials menu, opt for neur nam tok—strips of grilled beef tenderloin seasoned with lime, hot serrano chili peppers, fresh basil, fish sauce, and green onion; it's eaten rolled in cabbage leaves. This is a complex cuisine in which each dish yields a kaleidoscopic spectrum of spicy flavors. Beverage choices include exotic drinks like mango daiquiris, sake, a small wine list, and creamy-sweet Thai herbal iced tea. For dessert there's homemade coconut ice cream as well as mango, green tea, and ginger versions—all fittingly light and cooling finales. On weekends, arrive early or late to avoid a wait for seating.

Inexpensive

Bridgetown Grill, 1156 Euclid Ave. NE, between Moreland and Colquitt Aves. ☎ **653-0110.**

Cuisine: CARIBBEAN. **Reservations:** Not accepted. **MARTA:** Bus Nos. 3, 6, and 48 stop here. **Parking:** Free in a lot on Seminole Ave. behind restaurant.
Prices: Appetizers $1.50–$4.50; main courses $4.50–$5.95 at lunch, $5.50–$12.95 at dinner. AE, MC, V.
Open: Sun–Thurs 11:30am–10:30pm, Fri–Sat 11:30am–midnight. (Dinner menu begins at 5pm.)

I adore long, leisurely weekend lunches, comfortably ensconced in a roomy white wooden booth of Bridgetown's airy skylit patio. Lush tropical plantings and a Caribbean-style beach bar nestling in the corner further enhance the island ambience. And since it's heated in winter, this sun-dappled setting can be enjoyed year round. The interior is also simpatico, with saltillo-tile floors and exposed brick walls hung with Haitian folk art painted on oil drums. At night, candlelight sets the mood.

To get things going, order up delicious flaky-crusted Jamaican patties stuffed with spicy ground beef or shredded vegetables. Bay scallops ceviche, marinated in lime, jalapeños, and cilantro, comes garnished with mandarin oranges, tomato wedges, and pineapple chunks. And you can't go wrong with a basket of jerk chicken wings. Jerk chicken is a specialty here, seasoned in a mix of spices that yield an explosion of subtle flavors with every bite. You can order it grilled in a sandwich; as a main course served with raspberry-tamarind sauce (like all main courses here, it comes with salad, black beans, and rice); or in a terrific salad tossed with greens, grated Monterey Jack cheese, fresh mushrooms, tomatoes, pineapple chunks, and orange sections in mango vinaigrette dressing. Also available jerk-seasoned are grilled pork chops with honey apricot glaze, sautéed plump Gulf shrimp served with chipotle pepper sauce, and grilled filet of salmon in Scotch bonnet pepper butter. After such hearty fare, I think a light coconut flan is the best dessert choice, but there are richer options such as creamy key lime pie and chocolate cheesecake with raspberry sauce. Beverages include beer and wine, as well as nonalcoholic ginger beer, an excellent foil for spicy fare. Pitcherfuls of tropical coolers are also available.

There's another Bridgetown Grill at 689 Peachtree St., at 3rd Street (☎ 873-5361). It's open Sunday to Thursday 11am to 11pm, Friday to Saturday 11am to midnight.

Murphy's, 997 Virginia Ave. NE, at N. Highland Ave. ☎ 872-0904.

Cuisine: AMERICAN. **Reservations:** Not accepted. **Parking:** A few on-site spots, otherwise street only. Evenings you can park at the Texaco station across the street.

Prices: Appetizers $2.95–$6.95; main courses $4.25–$6.25 at lunch and for breakfast/brunch fare, $4.75–$11.95 at dinner. AE, MC, V.

Open: Mon–Thurs 7am–10pm, Fri 7am–12:30am, Sat 8am–12:30am, Sun 8am–10pm (Sat–Sun brunch served from 8am–2pm).

Murphy's, originally a wine-and-cheese shop that evolved into a restaurant and bakery, today comprises a cozy warren of rooms separated by French doors. Charming and innlike, its interior, softly lit by sconces and shaded table lamps, has low-beamed ceilings, exposed wine racks, walls adorned with a collection of framed mirrors, and beautiful dried-flower arrangements here and there. Sunny during the day (there are lots of windows), the restaurant is candlelit at night. A large open-air patio, cooled by fans suspended from an aqua ceiling, nestles in a lush garden. And up front is the now-expanded bakery-cum-shop, a rustic cracker-barrel setting with baskets suspended from rough-hewn pine rafters overhead and maple cabinets and glass display cases overflowing with pastries, gourmet foods, crusty fresh-baked breads, charcuterie and salad items, and luscious-looking cakes. You can sit at the counter here and bask in the heavenly aroma of fresh coffee being ground. Classical music and light jazz enhance the ambience.

Everything here is fresh. At lunch and dinner there are haute-deli sandwiches such as basil-flavored chicken salad tossed with mayo and sour cream and served with lettuce, tomato, and sprouts on whole wheat; deep-dish quiches served with salad; hearty homemade soups; and entrées running the gamut from tortellini tossed in a fresh-herb cream sauce with artichokes, peas, and julienned spinach to grilled fresh Georgia trout topped with pecan butter. Breakfast/brunch items are also wide-ranging, including omelets, Mexican breakfasts rolled in tortillas, Belgian waffles, French toast, and bagel-and-lox platters. Irish potatoes—large chunks sautéed with onions, peppers, and zucchini, seasoned with Cajun spices—are a specialty. And luscious fresh-baked desserts range from peanut butter pie layered with chocolate ganache and topped with white chocolate mousse to an Irish whiskey bundt cake served with vanilla bean ice cream. Beer and wine are available.

5   Sweet Auburn

Budget

The Beautiful Restaurant, 397 Auburn Ave., at Jackson St. ☎ 233-0080.

Cuisine: SOUTHERN/SOUL FOOD. **Reservations:** Not accepted.
MARTA: King Memorial. **Parking:** Free.
Prices: Everything, except steaks, under $5. No credit cards.
Open: Daily 7am–8:30pm.

It's not really all that beautiful, but this tiny eatery—one of a chain of soul-food cafeterias run by the Perfect Church—is a very good place for a lunch break when you're touring the Sweet Auburn district of Atlanta (see Chapter 8). There's seating in a few orange plastic booths and at long Formica tables; counterpersons are also attired in orange, and orange curtains frame the windows. A few plants and shell hangings constitute the sole attempt at decoration. You don't come here for ambience but for hearty homemade southern fare. There's always a choice of meat dishes—baked pork chops, baked chicken in thick gravy, barbecued beef tips, meat loaf—plus a half dozen or so side dishes. These might include collard greens, candied yams, black-eyed peas, baked macaroni, lima beans, and spiced rice, all of them delicious. Fresh-baked corn bread is served with all main courses. And there are homemade desserts such as peach cobbler, sweet-potato pie, and banana pudding topped with vanilla wafers, along with an intriguing southern specialty called red velvet cake— a rich chocolate cake that is dyed red with food coloring! No alcoholic beverages are served. Good southern-style breakfasts here, too.

6   Decatur

Budget

Thumbs Up, 254 W. Ponce de Leon Ave., near Commerce Dr.
☎ 377-5623.

Cuisine: AMERICAN. **Reservations:** Not accepted; arrive off-peak hours. **Parking:** Street only.
Prices: Appetizers $2.25–$5.25; main courses $3.95–$5.25 at breakfast, $3.95–$6.50 at lunch, $4.95–$10 at dinner. No credit cards.
Open: Breakfast Mon–Fri 7:30–10:45am, Sat–Sun 8am–2pm; lunch Mon–Fri 11am–3pm; dinner Mon–Fri 6–10pm.

This tiny, somewhat funky Decatur restaurant consists of 10 tables and a counter in a small front room and five additional tables and another counter in the high-ceilinged, raspberry-colored back room. In the front section, sunshine streams in through a café-curtained corner window, and shelves are aclutter with knickknacks, old radios, and cameras. I prefer the back room, away from the hectic counter/grill activity.

Breakfast is the most popular meal here, featuring items like scrambled eggs with fresh herbs and cream cheese, homemade multigrain biscuits, and the house specialty, O'Brien spuds—baked potatoes chopped into large chunks, sautéed with onions, peppers, and spices, and topped with melted cheddar. Thick slabs of challah French toast served with powdered sugar, butter, and pure Vermont maple syrup are another tempting option. Ditto Belgian waffles and buckwheat cakes. But lunch and dinner also merit consideration. At lunch you might order sandwiches, salads, or main courses such as smoked barbecued chicken served with homemade potato salad and spicy black beans. Dinner features similar choices, along with some Mexican specialties (like smoked chicken burritos and grilled spinach and cheese quesadillas), pastas (such as angel hair tossed with spinach, shrimp, and red peppers in a garlicky white wine sauce), and nightly specials—perhaps a pinkly juicy $1^1/2$-inch thick blackened salmon steak. Wine and beer are available, and the homemade Key lime pie and peanut-butter torte are delicious.

7   Chamblee

Inexpensive

★ **Honto,** 3295 Chamblee-Dunwoody Rd., between Buford Hwy. and Peachtree Industrial Blvd. ☎ **458-8088.**

Cuisine: CANTONESE. **Reservations:** For large parties only. **Parking:** Free.

Prices: Appetizers $1.60–$3.95; main courses mostly $6–$11, $3.50–$4.50 for lunch specials served with soup, fried rice, and egg rolls; dim sum items $1.75–$5.50 per plate. AE, MC, V.

Open: Sun–Thurs 11:30am–9:45pm, Fri–Sat 11:30am–10:45pm; special dim sum meals Sat–Mon 11am–2pm.

Almost all the restaurants listed in this book are very centrally located, but this one's well worth an extra 10 minutes on the road. *Atlanta* magazine calls it the city's best Chinese restaurant. Honto isn't a fancy place. Large and well lit, it has peach walls hung with Chinese art and dining areas separated by carved golden arches. The most important aspect of its decor, however, is a row of pink strips of paper marked with Chinese characters that inform diners (those who can read Chinese) of fresh seafood and other market specialties available on any given day. Ignore the printed menu; instead, put yourself in the expert hands of chef Johnny To, indicating the amount you wish to spend and any food preferences (for shrimp, beef, lobster, or pork dishes), and let him create a feast for you.

On a recent visit, seasonally fresh main courses included delectably tender sautéed beef with snow peas, thinly sliced carrots, and oyster mushrooms in a brown sauce; crispy fresh pan-fried pompano, garnished with cilantro, in a delicately seasoned soy sauce; a superb dish of clams steamed in garlic butter and served in a piquant cilantro-flavored broth (it comes in a big cast-iron pot); and sautéed Dungeness crab with ginger or black-bean sauce. Though these dishes may sound prosaic, you'll find they are exquisitely flavored and very unique. Every morsel is a delight, and many morsels there are—portions are vast. This is also a great place for dim sum (Chinese tea lunch) meals consisting of numerous appetizer-size dishes.

8 Specialty Dining

Most of the establishments listed in this section have been described in detail elsewhere in this chapter. They're noted here for special attributes and/or because they are the best in their category. Check out specific listings above for details.

Local Favorites

For authentic southern cooking, Atlanta residents flock to the unpretentious **Colonnade,** 1879 Cheshire Bridge Road NE (☎ 874-5642).

If you grew up in Atlanta, chili dogs at the **Varsity,** 61 North Ave. (☎ 881-1706), the world's largest drive-in restaurant, are as much a part of your heritage as *Gone With the Wind.*

And the "in" place to see and be seen is the **Buckhead Diner,** 3073 Piedmont Rd. (☎ 262-3336).

Hotel Dining

Atlanta's premier restaurant is a hotel dining room—the ultraelegant **Dining Room** at the Ritz-Carlton Buckhead, 3434 Peachtree Rd. NE (☎ 237-2700). Its cuisine is renowned nationally.

Also notable: the warmly intimate **Florencia** at the Occidental Grand Hotel (☎ 881-9898), a plush oak-paneled precinct with a working fireplace.

Hotel Dining with a View

Nikolai's Roof, atop the Atlanta Hilton at 255 Courtland St. (☎ 659-2000), offers superb French/Russian cuisine and 30th-floor skyline views.

The **Sun Dial,** a revolving restaurant-cum-aerie on the 72nd floor of the Westin Peachtree Plaza, 210 Peachtree St. (☎ 589-7506), offers the most breathtaking city views in town. You can enjoy the panorama for very low prices at lunch Monday to Saturday (most main courses are $6 to $9). Sunday the Sun Dial sets out a lavish buffet brunch ($19.50 prix fixe, including a glass of champagne).

Light, Casual, and Fast Food

You don't need a suit and tie at **Original Rocky's Brick Oven Pizza & Pasta,** 1770 Peachtree St. (☎ 876-1111), but you won't get better food if you spend 10 times as much in the most plush surroundings. Jeans and such are also acceptable at **Houston's,** 2166 Peachtree Rd. (☎ 351-2442), specializing in hickory-grilled burgers, chicken, and ribs (great salads, too); **Thumbs Up,** 254 W. Ponce de Leon Ave. (☎ 377-5623), featuring great omelets with homemade O'Brien spuds; **Murphy's,** 997 Virginia Ave. NE (☎ 872-0904), a cozy, innlike neighborhood hangout; **R. Thomas,** 1812 Peachtree St. NW (☎ 872-2942), offering hearty sandwiches on multi-grained bread, and fresh-squeezed juices in a lushly planted patio.

Pre- and Post-Theater Dining

If you're attending a show at the Woodruff Arts Center—Atlanta's major performance facility—valet park at **The Country Place,** 1197 Peachtree St. NE (☎ **881-0144**) or **Bistango,** 1100 Peachtree St. (☎ **724-0901**), have dinner, walk to the theater (a block away), and return post-theater for desserts (especially yummy at both of these places) or after-dinner drinks. The Woodruff's excellent on-premises restaurant is closed for renovations at this writing. Call **872-2284** to see if it's back in operation when you visit.

Breakfast/Brunch

One of the best things in life has to be a leisurely Sunday brunch. You sip champagne, maybe read the funnies, and hang out for a couple of hours eating and schmoozing. Reservations are suggested at all the establishments listed below. Hotel dining options all feature validated free parking. **Note:** You won't get an alcoholic drink on Sunday until 12:30pm.

The **Occidental Grand Hotel,** 75 14th St. (☎ **881-9898**), serves up a sumptuous buffet brunch—complete with ice carvings and freely flowing champagne—every Sunday from 11:30am to 2:30pm at **Overtures** and **Café Opera** (see descriptions in Chapter 5). Fare varies weekly. A typical spread might include a carving station for prime rib and honey-baked ham, an array of jumbo shrimp and crab claws, imported and domestic cheeses, smoked fish, seafood terrines, fresh fruits, bagels, fresh-baked breads and pastries, salads (ranging from saffron rice and sausage to Thai shrimp curry), egg and waffle dishes, a choice of hot main courses such as mesquite-grilled New York strip steak and pepper-seared swordfish, and a large selection of desserts. Price is $32 per person. Reservations suggested.

Though it doesn't offer a specific brunch menu, for laid-back sun-dappled brunches, you can't beat the patio at **Bridgetown Grill,** 1156 Euclid Ave. (☎ **653-0110**), which opens at noon on weekends. A meal here is like a mini-vacation in the Caribbean.

The **Ritz-Carlton Buckhead,** 3434 Peachtree Rd. (☎ **237-2700**), serves an exquisite brunch in its stunning triple-tiered **Café** every Sunday from 11:30am to 2:30pm. The buffet boasts a caviar station, no less, as well as a carving station, an array of smoked fish, main courses such as grilled chicken with wild mushrooms in madeira sauce, fresh fruits and cheeses, salads, vegetables, egg dishes, breakfast meats, pâtés and terrines, fresh-baked breads, and dozens of cakes and pastries. A pianist entertains. Price is $35 for adults, $17.50 for children 12 and under.

The **Ritz Carlton Atlanta,** 181 Peachtree St. (☎ **659-0400**), offers an equally impressive buffet downtown ($28 for adults, $14 for children 12 and under), in its intimate crystal-chandeliered **Café.** A gorgeous 100-item Pacific Rim spread, served every Sunday from 10:30am to 2:30pm, includes such exotica as sushi, dim sum, and Chinese, Japanese, Thai, and Vietnamese main courses—along with omelet stations and traditional American breakfast fare, of course. A pianist entertains.

A delightful plan is to drive out to Stone Mountain for the day, eat yourself into oblivion at the **Evergreen Conference Center and Resort's Waterside Restaurant,** in Georgia's Stone Mountain Park (☎ 879-9900), and then walk off a few thousand calories on the park's wooded paths. A bountiful buffet, served Sunday from 11:30am to 3pm, includes hot main courses, carved-meat stations, an omelet station, blintzes, eggs Benedict, Belgian waffles, homemade breads, fresh fruit and cheeses, vegetables, a complimentary glass of champagne, and a wide array of desserts. Adults pay $16.95, children 6 to 11 pay $8.50, under 6 free.

Chef's Café, 2115 Piedmont Rd. (☎ 872-2284), has a special brunch menu Sunday between 11am and 2:30pm. It features main courses ($4.95 to $10.95) like smoked Irish salmon on a toasted bagel with herbed cream cheese, red onion, chopped egg, and capers; crab-cakes Benedict, topped with poached eggs in tomato hollandaise and served with hash browns; and brioche French toast with orange-pistachio butter and maple syrup.

The **OK Cafe,** 1284 W. Paces Ferry Rd. (☎ 233-2888), offers a special brunch menu Saturday and Sunday from 10am to 3pm. The setting is casual, prices are low (main courses $3.95 to $7.95), and the food is delicious. Options include: blue-plate specials such as roast turkey and dressing served with a fresh-baked corn muffin and two vegetables (perhaps sweet-potato soufflé and collard greens); sour-dough French toast; and griddle cakes with Granny Smith apples and pecans. Wear your jeans.

Japanese Breakfast

Tired of the same old bacon and eggs? The **Westin Peachtree Plaza,** 210 Peachtree St. (☎ 659-1400), offers a traditional Japanese breakfast in its **Café** restaurant daily from 6 to 11:30am (reservations suggested). Priced at $10.50, it consists of grilled salmon, rice, miso soup, pickled vegetables, roasted seaweed, rice, and green tea. A more elaborate breakfast is $15.

A very similar meal is offered Monday to Friday from 7am to 10pm at **Kamogawa** in the **Hotel Nikko,** 3300 Peachtree Rd. (☎ 365-8100). Price is $19.50.

Afternoon Tea

This gracious southern city is the perfect place to enjoy the very civilized custom of afternoon tea. The following hotels offer the most exquisite venues for this leisurely repast.

The **Ritz-Carlton Buckhead,** 3434 Peachtree Rd. NE (☎ 237-2700), serves tea in its lobby lounge from 3 to 5pm daily. A pot of freshly brewed tea (your choice of about 10 varieties) comes with traditional tea sandwiches (smoked salmon, chive and egg, cucumber and cream cheese, or ham and asparagus), fresh-baked scones with Devonshire cream and fruit preserves, English tea bread, and a miniature fruit tart. A classical pianist provides tranquil background music. Price is $15. Reservations recommended.

The **Ritz-Carlton Atlanta,** 181 Peachtree St. (☎ **659-0400**), not to be outdone by its uptown relative, serves an identical tea in its mahogany-paneled, Persian-carpeted lobby lounge daily from 2:30 to 4:30pm. It, too, features a pianist. Price is $12. Another option here is a $7.50 minitea including tea, sandwiches as above, chocolate-dipped strawberries, and petits fours.

The **Hotel Nikko,** 3300 Peachtree Rd. (☎ **365-8100**), also serves a traditional English tea daily from 3 to 5pm in its stunning Lobby Bar overlooking a Japanese rock garden. A full tea—including finger sandwiches, cakes, pastries, and scones with Devonshire cream—is $13.25.

The **Occidental Grand Hotel,** 75 14th St. (☎ **881-9898**), hosts elegant afternoon teas in its softly lit mezzanine-level facility, **Overtures,** daily from 3 to 5pm. Seated in plush tapestried armchairs and couches, guests enjoy a choice of imported teas with tea sandwiches, fresh-baked scones with Devonshire cream and fruit preserves, fruit tartlets, and tea breads. Cost is $14. A pianist entertains.

Late Night/24-Hour

R. Thomas, mentioned above under "Light, Casual, and Fast Food," never closes. Its plant-filled patio, warmed by heaters in winter, is Atlanta's favorite late-night locale. And you can eat food like Mom's round the clock at the **OK Cafe,** also noted above.

Picnic Fare and Where to Eat It

A great choice is **Pano's Food Shop,** an adjunct of the **Atlanta Fish Market** restaurant at 265 Pharr Rd. (☎ **262-3165**). Here, you can pick up fish smoked on the premises, wines, marvelous fresh-baked breads (everything from foccacia to onion bagels), whole roasted chickens, salads such as roma tomatoes with goat cheese or haricots verts tossed in vinaigrette with mushrooms and walnuts, marinated grilled vegetables, cold cuts, side dishes (perhaps asiago-stuffed roasted red potatoes), and fresh-baked desserts.

Another possibility, though it's a little out of the way, is the **DeKalb Farmer's Market,** 3000 E. Ponce de Leon Ave. (☎ **277-6400**)—450 varieties of cheese alone! See Chapter 9 for details.

Good places to picnic: Georgia's Stone Mountain Park, Piedmont or Grant Park, Château Elan, and Yellow River Wild Game Ranch (all described in Chapter 7).

Dim Sum

Trader Vic's at the **Atlanta Hilton & Towers,** 255 Courtland St. (☎ **659-2000**), serves a dim sum lunch weekdays from 11:30am to 2pm. Small platters—such as lotus-wrapped sticky rice, black mushroom, and Chinese sausage; delicate pan-fried pot stickers; steamed pork dumplings encased in egg-noodle skin; and crisped jumbo Gulf prawns—are $2.50 to $2.95.

A more extensive dim sum menu is offered at **Honto,** 3295 Chamblee-Dunwoody Rd. (☎ **458-8088**), Saturday through Monday from 11am to 2pm. Plates are $1.75 to $5.50.

Tapas

The ultra-elegant **Segovia Bar** at the **Occidental Grand,** 75 14th St. (☎ **881-9898**), provides a stunning setting for the delectation of *tapas*—the currently *très chic* "little dishes" of Spain. Sink into a plush burgundy velvet sofa and order up a selection—perhaps crispy fried calamari with garlicky aioli, piquant stuffed turnovers, hot garlic shrimp in olive oil, and spicy red fried sausage. Spanish wines, sherries, and ports are the accompaniments of choice with these savory samplings.

7

What to See & Do in Atlanta

	Suggested Itineraries	154
•	Did You Know?	154
1	The Top Attractions	155
•	Did You Know?	157
•	Frommer's Favorite Atlanta Experiences	162
2	More Attractions	183
3	Cool for Kids	193
4	Organized Tours	201
5	Sports & Recreation	202

P EOPLE USED TO SAY ATLANTA WAS A GREAT PLACE TO LIVE, BUT YOU wouldn't want to visit. I'm happy to report that this is no longer the case. Atlanta offers numerous attractions—from one of the nation's most scenic parks to important black history landmarks, from a presidential center to a puppetry center. The area is rich in Civil War sites, and, in a related area, in *Gone With the Wind* memorabilia.

The best way to tackle it all is to read the comprehensive descriptions below and plan a personalized itinerary for your trip, allowing ample time to experience your selected sights. It's much more satisfying to see a few things in depth than to race around helter-skelter trying to see everything. There is no ideal agenda for everyone. The optimum plan depends on your interests, the amount of time you have, and whether or not you're traveling with kids. (**Note:** Don't pass up the attractions listed below as being of special interest to kids because you've reached man's estate; most of them will appeal to all age groups.) Do be sure to dress comfortably; tight shoes could sour you on the Taj Mahal. Visiting places near one another on the same day conserves time and energy. And I think taking long breaks (perhaps a 2-hour lunch or a picnic in the park) adds a lot to one's enjoyment.

MARTA stops close to attractions are listed where applicable. If you need bus-routing information, call **848-4711.**

Suggested Itineraries

If You Have One Day

Head up to Buckhead and visit the Atlanta History Center—pretty much a full day's activity with house tours, museum exhibits, and woodland trails to explore. Have lunch at the Swan Coach House on the premises. If you have extra time (and energy) in the afternoon, take a stroll around this beautiful neighborhood where almost every home is a mansion. From the History Center go south on Andrews

Did You Know?

- Atlanta has the largest mall in the Southeast (Lenox Square).
- Atlanta has the tallest escalator in the Southeast (at MARTA's Peachtree Center station—192 feet).
- Atlanta has the tallest hotel in the Western Hemisphere—the 723-foot, 73-story Westin Peachtree Plaza.
- Not a single scene from the movie *Gone With the Wind* was filmed in Georgia, though a few bushels of Georgia red clay were transported to the Hollywood set to add verisimilitude.
- Hartsfield is the world's third-busiest airport and is consistently ranked among the best airports in the world. Eighty percent of the United States population is within a three-hour flight of Atlanta.

Drive and/or west on West Paces Ferry Road. If the weather is not right for a leisurely stroll, head downtown to Underground Atlanta, see the shops and sights, and have dinner at Mick's.

If You Have Two Days

Follow the suggestions above on the first day. On the second day, get up early, go over to Auburn Avenue (see walking tour in Chapter 8), and visit the Martin Luther King, Jr., National Historic Site and surrounding attractions. In the afternoon, time and energy permitting, head over to Grant Park and see Cyclorama and/or Zoo Atlanta.

If You Have Three Days

On your first two days, you should see as many of the sights described above as a comfortable pace allows. If the weather is fine on the morning of your last day, nothing could be more pleasurable than a day at Georgia's Stone Mountain Park. There's much to do and see here. In summer, be sure to stay late and see Lasershow.

On the other hand, if it's cold or rainy, plan a morning tour of the Carter Presidential Center or CNN Center, possibly doing the other in the afternoon. If you're traveling with kids, spend the day at the Fernbank Museum of Natural History instead.

If You Have Five Days or More

Take it easy. Over the first four days, juggle the above suggestions as you see fit. On the fifth day, if you have kids, or you just like this kind of thing, now's the time for a little R&R. Go to Six Flags Over Georgia, White Water, or the marvelous Yellow River Wildlife Game Ranch. Civil War buffs should take in the Big Shanty Museum and Kennesaw Mountain/National Battlefield Park (both can be done in one day). Or do the Day 3 activity you didn't choose.

1   The Top Attractions

These may or may not be the top attractions to you, and nowhere is it written that you have to see them all. Give equal consideration to attractions listed elsewhere in this chapter when planning your itinerary.

⭐ **Atlanta History Center**, 130 W. Paces Ferry Rd., at Slaton Dr. ☎ 814-4000.

Originally dedicated to "preserving, protecting, and displaying information on the history of Atlanta," the Atlanta History Center has, in recent years, expanded its concept to encompass Georgian and southern history as well. The Center, which is operated by the Atlanta Historical Society, maintains a vast collection of photographs, maps, books, newspaper accounts, furnishings, Civil War artifacts, decorative arts, and Margaret Mitchell memorabilia. It occupies 32 woodland acres, with self-guided walking trails and five historical gardens. Plan to spend the better part of a day here; there's much to do. And call ahead, or inquire on the premises, about the comprehensive schedule of lectures, films, festivals, book signings, gardening symposia, workshops for adults and children, and other events that take place here on a regular basis; activities range from sheep-shearing demonstrations to decorative arts forums. When you call, also check on house-tour times for the day of your visit. Plan to have lunch at the delightful **Swan Coach House** restaurant on the premises (details in Chapter 6).

Note: House-tour tickets are limited and can only be purchased on the day of your visit. Arrive early to avoid disappointment.

Begin your visit at the **Atlanta History Museum,** an $11-million, 83,000-square-foot, two-story facility that opened in 1993. Neoclassic in design (to harmonize with the Swan House), it was built with native materials such as locally quarried granite and Georgia heart-pine flooring; its interior is painted to evoke Georgia clay. Here you can purchase tickets and get information about historic-house tours (see below) and other on-premises activities. The museum's major permanent exhibit, "Metropolitan Frontiers: Atlanta, 1835–2000," traces Atlanta's history from the days of Native American and rural pioneer settlements to the coming 1996 Olympics. Displays, enhanced by hands-on discovery areas and informative videos, include hundreds of photographs, documents, and artifacts; an entire 1890s shotgun house; a fire engine that was used in Atlanta's great fire of 1917 (when 50 city blocks were ravaged by flames); a rare 1920 Hanson Six touring car; and a model of Atlanta's most complex interstate intersection, known locally as "Spaghetti Junction." This permanent installation is augmented by changing exhibits dealing, for the most part, with black history, the Civil War, folk crafts, and *Gone With the Wind.* For example, "Gone for a Soldier: Transformed by War, 1861–1865" focused on the personal experiences—often misery, boredom, and horror—of Confederate and Union soldiers. And "The Herndon's: Style and Substance of the Black Upper Class in Atlanta, 1880–1930" told the story of Alonzo Herndon, a former slave who became the city's first black millionaire. A museum gift shop sells items ranging from southern crafts and Civil War memorabilia to Robert E. Lee T-shirts. And the **Coca-Cola Café**—an old-time soda shoppe decorated with vintage Coke advertisements and offering patio seating overlooking a dense woodlands—serves light fare.

Also on the Center's grounds is the **Swan House,** the 1928 estate of Edward Hamilton Inman, scion of an old Atlanta family and owner of one of the world's largest cotton brokerages. The house and gardens were designed by renowned architect Philip Trammell Shutze and are considered his finest residential work. The "swan" motif originated with Mrs. Inman, inspired by a pair of 18th-century swan console tables that you'll see in the dining room. The house is interesting not only architecturally but for its eclectic contents and furnishings, which comprise a veritable museum of decorative arts. Mr. Inman died three years after the house was completed at the age of 49, but his wife, Emily, lived here until her death in 1965.

Swan House is fronted by a classical colonnaded porte cochère, leading to a circular entrance hall with Ionic columns and a dramatic floating stairway. The formal gardens include terraced lawns and waterfalls, retaining walls with recessed ivied arches, and fountain statuary. In the entrance hall, you'll notice that the fanlight over the door centers on a swan, announcing the theme of the house. The grand stair hall is furnished with 18th- and 19th-century English console tables, needlework side chairs, and a Chinese lacquer coromandel screen, one of many chinoiserie touches in the house.

The wood-paneled library centers on a 17th-century limewood overmantel intricately carved with swags of fruit and flowers. The red silk Scalamandré sofa is typical of the oversized pieces that were a hallmark of 1920s interior design. Nineteenth-century Federalist mirrors reflect Mr. Inman's taste (she liked swans, he liked eagles). The 18th-century Dutch tall-case clock, ornamented with marquetry, plays excerpts from hymns every half hour.

A Tabriz carpet graces the walnut floor of the living room. The room is painted mint green, a popular 1920s color, and its ceiling and moldings display elaborate Georgian plasterwork. The mantel is flanked by columns with carved Corinthian swan capitals, while two Venetian blackamoor tables (held up by carved Nubian slaves) are surmounted by Federalist mirrors (swans and eagles again).

Family china (including a lavender Royal Doulton set custom-made for Tiffany) is displayed in the Aubusson-carpeted dining room. Here walls are covered in hand-painted chinoiserie paper, windows draped in silk rainbow plaid taffeta silk. Note the rococo marble-topped swan tables. The Inmans took their morning meal in a charming octagonal breakfast room, with windows overlooking woodland scenery and a beautifully detailed vaulted ceiling.

Did You Know?

- Atlanta has 32 streets named Peachtree.

- Georgia's major agricultural crop is peanuts, not peaches.

- Atlanta's earliest street lights burned whale oil.

- Atlanta University—including Morehouse, Spelman, Clark, and Morris Brown colleges—is the world's largest predominantly black higher-education complex.

- The world's largest bas-relief sculpture (Stone Mountain—90 feet by 190 feet) and the world's largest painting (Cyclorama, utilizing 20,000 square feet of canvas) are in Atlanta.

- Georgia Tech's Yellow Jackets set a world record football score in 1916—222 to 0 (they were the zero).

- Because it has received over $250 million from Coca-Cola. Emory University is known as "Coca-Cola U."

- *Fortune Magazine* rates Atlanta the nation's "best place to do business."

Upstairs, Mrs. Inman's bedroom is furnished with a high-post bed and a silk-upholstered Sheraton settee. Her adjoining faux-marble bathroom has a toilet hidden in a rattan chair (a Victorian holdover) and a huge-headed shower which must have provided heavenly cascades of water.

As you tour the house, you'll also see many museum-quality 17th- and 18th-century English paintings. And on the upstairs level is the Philip Shutze Collection of Decorative Arts—a marvelous array of china, silver, furnishings, textiles, rugs, and objets d'art. A must for aficionados, it can be seen only on tours weekdays at 11:15am and 3:15pm or by appointment. Half-hour tours of the house itself take place throughout the day on a continual basis.

Tullie Smith Farm depicts the life of Georgia's mid-19th-century farmers. A 2-story "plantation-plain" house built in the early 1840s, it was brought here along with period outbuildings in 1969. The farm was originally located outside 1864 city limits, so it survived Atlanta's destruction during the Civil War. This was no Tara-like colonnaded mansion—just an everyday farmhouse whose occupants lived in rustic simplicity. The "plantation-plain" style derives from English architecture. It features a gabled roof with twin chimneys and a full front porch with a room at one end to lodge travelers and itinerant parsons. In premedia days, travelers were an important source of news.

In the Hall Room (today set up as a dining room, though rooms in the 19th-century did not have such defined functions), the furnishings are handcrafted, some of them painted with pigments made of buttermilk and Georgia red clay. A pine cabinet decorated with punched-tin sand-dollar-motif panels served as a "pie safe" in which leftover food was stored. The drop-leaf table is set with a mixture of pearlware and transferware from Staffordshire, England. Some children's toys are displayed.

A bedroom has a rope bed with a feather mattress and a crib which was always occupied by the youngest baby. Here, demonstrations are given on a spinning wheel, and you'll learn that the term *spinster* derives from the fact that unmarried women had so much time to spin. A basket of pomander balls was typical—the 19th-century answer to today's air fresheners.

In a back room, there are weaving demonstrations, and a display shows natural materials used to dye yarns. During cooler months, demonstrations of 19th-century hearth cookery (Brunswick stew, corn bread) take place in the whitewashed kitchen, where game and herbs hang from the rafters. Additional outbuildings are a barn, corncrib, root cellar, blacksmith shop, and smokehouse. The gardens and grounds are authentic to the period. Costumed docents give tours throughout the day, and there are frequent demonstrations of 19th-century farm activities.

Leave some time to stroll the gardens, most notably the forested mile-long **Swan Woods Trail.** It includes plants native to Georgia and the Garden for Peace where you will see a sculpture by noted Soviet artist Georgi Dzhaparidze and Atlanta artist Hans Godo Frabel.

Admission: $7 for adults, $5 for seniors and students 18 or older, $4 for children 6–17, under 6 free. General admission includes the museum and gardens. House tour tickets are $1 additional per house, free for children under 6.

Open: Mon–Sat 10am–5:30pm, Sun and some holidays noon–5:30pm. Ticket sales stop at 4:30pm. **Closed:** Thanksgiving, Christmas Eve, Christmas, and New Year's Day. **Note:** The tour schedule for various buildings is rather complex; call ahead to find out tour hours for each attraction on the day of your visit. **MARTA:** Take MARTA rail to Lenox station, from there bus no. 23 to Peachtree Street and West Paces Ferry Road, walk three blocks west on the latter.

⭐ **Birth Home of Martin Luther King, Jr.,** 501 Auburn Ave., at Hogue St. ☎ **331-3920.**

Note: Tickets for a tour of the house must be obtained at the Martin Luther King Center at 449 Auburn Avenue. Tours depart from the Center taking in sights en route to the house. In summer months, especially, tickets often run out early; arrive at 9:30am to optimize your chances of getting in. If summer crowds do prevent you from getting on a tour, you can view a slide presentation about the Birth Home at the Martin Luther King Center.

Martin Luther King, Jr. was born in this two-story Queen Anne–style house on January 15, 1929, the oldest son of a Baptist minister and an elementary school music teacher. His childhood was a normal one. He preferred playing baseball to piano lessons, liked to

---

Martin Luther King, Jr., National Historic Site

Under the auspices of the National Park Service is an area of about 10 blocks around Auburn Avenue, established in 1980 to "preserve the birthplace and boyhood surroundings of the nation's foremost civil rights leader." It includes King's boyhood home and the Ebenezer Baptist Church, of which King, his father, and his grandfather were ministers. Other Auburn Avenue attractions, not under NPS auspices, include the Martin Luther King, Jr., Center for Nonviolent Social Change (where King is buried) and the APEX Museum.

The area is known as Sweet Auburn. John Wesley Dobbs, maternal grandfather of Atlanta mayor Maynard Jackson, is the person who first called it such, after Oliver Goldsmith's *The Deserted Village,* the first line of which reads, "Sweet Auburn! loveliest village of the plains." Mayor Jackson says his grandfather called the area "sweet" because the keys to black liberation existed here in the form of "the three b's—bucks, ballots, and books."

See Chapter 8, "A Walking Tour of Sweet Auburn," for a walking tour of the area.

play Monopoly, and got a kick out of tearing the heads off his older sister's dolls. Nonviolence came later. To quote his sister, Christine King Farris, ". . . my brother was no saint ordained at birth, instead he was an average and ordinary man, called by . . . God . . . to perform extraordinary deeds."

King lived here through the age of 12, then moved with his family to a house a few blocks away. A visit provides many insights into the boyhood of, and formative influences on, one of the greatest leaders of our time. The house, built in 1894, was originally owned by a German family. The Rev. A. D. Williams, King's maternal grandfather and pastor of Ebenezer Baptist Church, bought it in 1909. Reverend Williams was active not only in the church, but in the community and early manifestations of the civil rights movement. He was a charter member of Atlanta's NAACP and led a series of black registration and voting drives as far back as 1917. He was instrumental in getting black officers on the Atlanta police force. Martin Luther King, Sr. moved in on Thanksgiving Day, 1926, when he married Williams' daughter Alberta. When Reverend Williams died in 1931, Martin's father became head of the household and also took over Williams' pulpit at Ebenezer Church.

The King family retained ownership of the house at 501 Auburn even after they moved away. Martin's younger brother, Alfred Daniel, lived here with his family from 1954 to 1963. In 1971, King's mother deeded the home to the Martin Luther King, Jr., Center. It has since been restored to its appearance during the years of Martin's boyhood. The furnishings, wallpapers, linoleums, and paint colors are all originals or similar period reproductions, and many personal items belonging to the family are on display. Christine was actively involved in the restoration, providing a wealth of detail about its former appearance, as well as anecdotal material about life in the King family.

Tours of the house, conducted by National Park rangers, begin in the downstairs parlor, where you'll see family photographs showing Martin Luther King as a child. The parlor was also used for choir practice, for the dreaded piano lessons, and as a rec room where the family gathered around the radio to listen to shows like "The Shadow." In the dining room, world events were regularly discussed over meals, and every Sunday, before dinner, each child was required to recite a newly learned Bible verse from memory. You'll also see the coal cellar (stoking coal was one of Martin's childhood chores); the children's play area; the upstairs bedroom of Martin's parents in which Christine, Martin, and Alfred Daniel were born, with a family physician attending; Reverend Williams' den, where he prepared his sermons and the family gathered for nightly Bible study; the bedroom Martin shared with his brother ("always in disarray," says Christine); and Christine's bedroom.

Admission: Free.

Open: Daily 10am–5pm. **Closed:** Thanksgiving, Christmas, and New Year's Day. **MARTA:** Take bus No. 3 from the Five Points MARTA station.

⭐ **Martin Luther King, Jr., Center for Nonviolent Social Change,** 449 Auburn Ave., between Boulevard and Jackson St. ☎ **524-1956.**

Martin Luther King's commitment to nonviolent social change lives on at this memorial and educational center under the direction of Coretta Scott King. On the premises is an information counter where you can find out about all Auburn Avenue attractions and obtain tickets to tour the King birth home (details above). A nongovernmental member of the United Nations, the center works with government agencies and the private sector to reduce violence within the community and among nations. It provides day care for low-income families, assists students in developing leadership skills in nonviolence, and holds workshops on topics like hunger and illiteracy. Its library and archives house the world's largest collection of books and other materials documenting the civil rights movement, including Dr. King's personal papers and a rare 87-volume edition of *The Collected Works of Mahatma Gandhi,* a gift from the government of India. Equally important, it is Martin Luther King's final resting place, a living memorial to an inspiring leader which is visited by tens of thousands each year, including heads of foreign governments.

Visitors are given a self-guided tour brochure. The tour begins in the Exhibition Hall, where memorabilia of King and the civil rights movement are displayed in an exhibit called "King: Images of the Drum Major." Here you can see his Bible and clerical robe, a handwritten sermon, a photographic essay on his life and work, the Grammy Award King won for his "Why I Oppose the War in Vietnam" speech, and, on a grim note, the suit he was wearing when a deranged woman stabbed him in New York City and the key to his room at the Lorraine Motel in Memphis, Tennessee, where he was assassinated. In an alcove off the main exhibit area is a video display on Martin Luther King's life and works. Additional exhibits—including a room honoring Rosa Parks (whose refusal to give up her seat on a city bus led to the Montgomery bus boycott) and another honoring Gandhi—are in Freedom Hall.

Outside is Freedom Plaza, where Dr. King's white marble crypt rests on a beautiful five-tiered Reflecting Pool, a symbol of the life-giving nature of water. The tomb is inscribed with his words: "Free at Last. Free at Last. Thank God Almighty I'm Free at Last." An eternal flame burns in a small circular pavilion directly fronting the crypt. The Freedom Walkway, a vaulted colonnade paralleling the pool, will eventually be painted with murals depicting the civil rights struggle. Located at the end of Freedom Walkway is the Chapel of All Faiths, symbolizing the ecumenical nature of Dr. King's work and the universality of the basic tenets of all the world's great religions.

A very important part of your visit is the Screening Room, where four excellent half-hour videos about Martin Luther King play continuously throughout the day. Enhanced by music that ranges from spirituals to rap, they show many of his most stirring sermons and speeches, including "I've Been to the Mountaintop" and "I Have a Dream"—speeches that are as much a part of America's heritage as the Gettysburg Address.

A store on the premises offers King memorabilia and a wide selection of books and cassettes. Inquire about events (including puppet shows for kids) and workshops taking place during your stay. Ranger talks focusing on the community and the civil rights movement take place frequently on Freedom Plaza. The annual Kingfest, held mid-May and mid-June, features music, theatrical performances, a kids' day, and many other events. And every October 2, Gandhi's birthday is celebrated with Indian food, music, and entertainment. A very nice cafeteria is on the premises.

Admission: Free. To see the videos, adults pay $1, children 6–12 pay 50¢, under 6 free.

Open: Daily 9:30am–5:30pm. **Closed:** Thanksgiving, Christmas, New Year's Day. **MARTA:** Take bus No. 3, from the Five Points MARTA station.

Apex Museum, 135 Auburn Ave., at Courtland St. ☎ **521-APEX.**

Opened in 1985, the APEX (African-American Panoramic Experience) Museum both chronicles the history of Sweet Auburn, Atlanta's foremost black residential and business district, and serves as a national African American museum and cultural center. In the museum's Trolley Car Theater, a replica of a turn-of-the-century train that ran on Auburn Avenue, you'll see a 12-minute multimedia presentation on the area's history narrated by Cicely Tyson and Julian Bond. Sweet Auburn history is also represented in tableaux such as a replica of the barbershop run by Alonzo Herndon and a re-creation of the Gate City Drugstore (Atlanta's first black pharmacy), including some original furnishings. There are also changing exhibits.

APEX is still in its infancy, but future plans call for its development into a major cultural force in the community, offering many

---

Frommer's Favorite Atlanta Experiences

Afternoon Tea at the Ritz-Carlton Buckhead   It's served in the lovely mahogany-paneled lobby lounge, where an oak-log fire crackles in the hearth and a classical pianist provides soothing background music. Fresh-baked scones with fruit preserves and Devonshire cream, finger sandwiches, English tea bread and tarts, and pots of your favorite tea.

A Chastain Park Amphitheatre Concert   Big-name entertainers perform under the stars, and everyone brings elaborate picnic fare. It's always a great evening.

Georgia's Stone Mountain Park   A leisurely day spent seeing the sights, including lunch or bountiful buffet Sunday brunch at the Evergreen Conference Center and Resort.

Yellow River Wildlife Game Ranch   A totally satisfying encounter of the four-legged kind. Bring a picnic lunch.

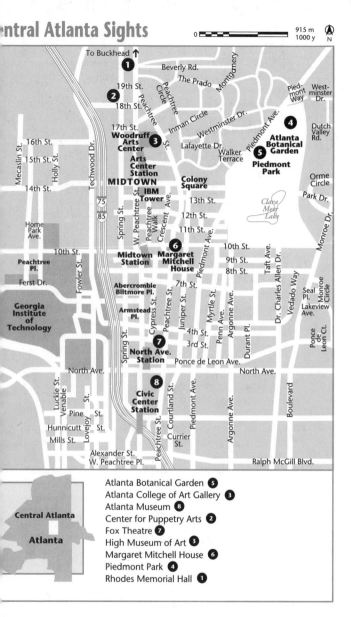

915 m
1000 y
N

Atlanta Botanical Garden 5
Atlanta College of Art Gallery 3
Atlanta Museum 8
Center for Puppetry Arts 2
Fox Theatre 7
High Museum of Art 3
Margaret Mitchell House 6
Piedmont Park 4
Rhodes Memorial Hall 1

programs for adults and children. Its aim is to "chronicle the history of the African American experience from early man in Africa to contemporary times." Do inquire about special events and workshops taking place during your visit to Atlanta.

Across the street from the APEX museum, at 100 Auburn Ave., is Herndon Plaza, where you can see a permanent exhibit on the Herndon family and changing shows of the works of African American artists.

Admission: $2 for adults, $1 for seniors and students, children under 5 free.

Open: Tues–Sat 10am–5pm, till 6pm Wed nights; also Sun 1–5pm Feb and June–Aug. **Closed:** Thanksgiving, Christmas, and New Year's Day. **MARTA:** Take bus No. 3 from the Five Points MARTA station.

Ebenezer Baptist Church, 407–413 Auburn Ave. ☎ 688-7263.

Founded in 1886, Ebenezer was a spiritual center of the civil rights movement during the years 1960 to 1968, when Martin Luther King, Jr., served as copastor. His grandfather, the Rev. A. D. Williams, dedicated the church to "the advancement of black people and every righteous and social movement." Williams's activist example was followed by his son-in-law and successor, Martin Luther King, Sr., who worked for voting rights and other aspects of black civil and social advancement. Later, Martin Luther King, Jr., would join his forebears in pursuing justice for black Americans. You can listen to a taped message on the history of the church and/or take a 10-minute guided tour. An ecumenical service takes place here every year during King week.

Admission: Free (donations appreciated).

Open: Mon–Fri 9:30am–noon and 1:30–4:30pm, Sun for services only at 7:45 and 10:45am. **MARTA:** King Memorial Station is about eight blocks away. You can also take a No.3 bus from anywhere on Peachtree Street.

★ Fernbank Museum of Natural History, 767 Clifton Rd., off Ponce de León Ave. ☎ 378-0127.

The largest museum of natural sciences in the Southeast, this architecturally stunning $42.8 million facility adjoins 65 acres of pristine forest. The building centers on a soaring 3-story, skylit Great Hall—a gorgeous Italianate brick atrium with spiral staircases, lofty columns subtly suggestive of a classical ruin, a delicate modernistic white steel barrel-vaulted construction overhead, and windows—some of them circular—embracing the verdant woodlands beyond. Architect Graham Gund has achieved one of the best integrations of interior/exterior space I've ever seen. Museum floors are imbedded with ancient fossil remains from the late Jurassic Period.

The major permanent exhibit, "A Walk Through Time in Georgia" uses the state as a microcosm to tell the story of the earth's development through time and the chronology of life upon it. Seventeen galleries here re-create landform regions from the rolling pine-forested foothills of the Piedmont Plateau to the mossy Okefenokee Swamp, from the Cumberland Plateau (where you can walk through a typical "limestone cavern") to the marshy Coast and Barrier Islands. Exhibits are enhanced by creative state-of-the-art films and videos, informational audiophones, interactive computers, sound

0 ▬▬▬▬▬▬ 915 m
1000 y

⊗ N

Mills St.
Alexander St.

Hull St.
Thur.
Earle St.
Tabernacle

Techwood
Williams St.
Spring St.
W. Peachtree

Peachtree Center Station

Walton
Luckie St.
Cone
Fairlie
Forsyth
Decatur St.

2

3

Baker St.

Harris St.

International Blvd.

Peachtree
Center Ave.

Ellis

John

Piedmont Ave.

8
Ralph McGill Blvd.

Highland Ave.

Wesley Dobbs **Ave.**

9 **10** Boulevard **11**
Auburn Ave.

Edgewood Ave.

4

Woodruff Park **5**

Five Points Station

M. L. King, Jr., Dr.
Mitchell St.
Alabama

6
Hunt

Gilmer St.

Armstrong
Coca Sq.

Peachtree St.

Central Ave.

Courtland St.

7

Decatur St.

12

M. L. King, Jr., Dr.

Memorial Dr.

Woodward Ave.

20

20

Central Ave.

Fulton St.
Richardson St.
Crumley St.
Glenn St.

Spring St.
Peachtree St.

Pullman St.

Washington St.

Capitol Ave.
Fraser St.
Martin St.

Richmond St.

Bass St.
Love St.

Terry St.

Little St.
South Ave.

Connally St.

Georgia Ave.

Grant St.

Sydney St.
13

Cherokee Ave.

14
15

Park Ave.
Boulevard

75
85

Ormond St.

Atlanta Ave.

Alonzo F. Herndon Home **1**
Apex Museum **5**
Atlanta History Center Downtown **3**
Birth Home of Martin Luther King, Jr. **11**
CNN Center **2**
Cyclorama **14**
Ebenezer Baptist Church **9**
Georgia State Capitol **7**
Grant Park **13**
Heritage Row **6**

High Museum of Art
  at Georgia-Pacific Center **4**
Martin Luther King, Jr., Center for
  Nonviolent Social Change **10**
Oakland Cemetery **12**
Scitrek **8**
Underground Atlanta **6**
World of Coca-Cola **6**
Zoo Atlanta **15**

effects, and old-fashioned field guides—not to mention over 1,500 fabricated plants and mounted specimens of birds and animals. Visitors travel back 15 billion years—to experience the origins of the universe (the Big Bang) and the formation of galaxies and solar systems—and into the future to consider the fate of our planet. It's a fascinating journey.

Another major permanent installation, "Spectrum of the Senses," comprises 65 participatory displays shown on a rotating basis—all of them designed by physicists to illustrate scientific principles. Here you can step into a life-size kaleidoscope, play with perspective, gaze into infinity, see physical evidence of sound waves, mix colors on a computer, blow giant bubbles, and see a steam fog tornado in formation. In Fantasy Forest, a colorful play area designed for preschoolers (ages 3 to 5), kids become bees and pollinate flowers, climb a treehouse, walk through a swamp, and play at being farmers. The state-shaped Georgia Adventure is a similar discovery room for ages 6 to 10. While you're here, be sure to catch a thrilling IMAX film (buy tickets as soon as you enter the museum; they sometimes sell out). And if it's a weekend, see if there are any programs going on at the Harris Naturalist Center, a cluster of science laboratories where visitors often get to examine items under an electron microscope.

Other museum attractions include a Caribbean coral reef aquarium, the Star Gallery (where 542 fiber-optic stars create a twinkling evening sky), and The World of Shells (a vast and beautiful collection). Permanent installations are augmented by traveling exhibits on subjects ranging from "Psychology: Understanding Ourselves, Understanding Others" to "Whales: Giants of the Deep." A museum store is stocked with entertaining and educational gifts and books, and there's a delightful on-premises restaurant with arched windows overlooking Fernbank Forest as well as outdoor patio seating.

Admission: $5.50 for adults ($9.50 inclusive of an IMAX Theater ticket), $4.50 for students and seniors ($7.50, inclusive of an IMAX Theater ticket), free for children 2 and under. IMAX Theater admission alone is $5.50 for adults, $4.50 for children, students, and seniors.

Open: Mon–Thurs and Sat 10am–5pm, Fri 10am–9pm, and Sun noon–5pm. **Closed:** Thanksgiving and Christmas.

★ **Cyclorama**, 800 Cherokee Ave., in Grant Park. ☎ **624-1071** or **658-7625.**

Though it sounds like something out of Disney World, this Cyclorama was created in the 1880s, and its concept—a huge, 360-degree cylindrical painting displayed on a rotating platform—dates back to a century earlier. Cycloramas were the rage of 18th- and 19th-century Europe, Russia, Japan, and later, the United States, depicting subject matter ranging from the splendors of Pompeii to Napoleonic battles. Enhanced by multimedia effects and faux-terrain dioramas extending 30 feet from the painting into the foreground, they were the forerunners of newsreels, travelogues, and TV war coverage.

The one you'll see here—a 42-foot-high cylindrical oil painting, 358 feet in circumference (on about 16,000 square feet of canvas)—depicts in meticulous detail the events of the Battle of Atlanta, July 22, 1864. It took 11 Eastern European artists, working in America in the studio of William Wehner, 22 months to complete. For

20th-century tourists, the concept itself is as interesting as the action depicted, and the restoration is incredibly impressive. Though painted on fine Belgian linen in the painstaking methodology of the 19th-century academies, the work suffered in moves from city to city, and later (when motion-picture epics made cycloramas passé) from neglect. Well-intentioned but incompetent attempts at restoration caused further damage, including the introduction of authentic Georgia red clay into the diorama battlefield area that brought in canvas-destroying beetles, vermin, and bacteria. In the 1970s, a severe storm waterlogged the painting, causing seemingly irreversible damage. But Mayor Maynard Jackson recognized the historic and artistic importance of Cyclorama; under his auspices $11 million was raised for its restoration. It took 2¹/₂ years for renowned conservator Gustav Berger and his crew to repair the damaged work, a process which included mending over 700 rips and tears in the canvas. In the auditorium itself the Cyclorama viewing is preceded by a 14-minute film about the Battle of Atlanta narrated by James Earl Jones.

The fascinating story of Cyclorama's development and restoration is related in a video format near the auditorium entrance. Cyclorama's central theme is General John B. Hood's desperate attempt to halt Sherman's inexorable advance into the city. Comprehensively narrated, and complete with music and sound effects including galloping horses and cannon fire, it vividly depicts the troop movements and battles of the day in which the Confederates lost 8,000 men, the Federals 3,722. A figure highlighted far beyond his historic importance is General John A. Logan of the Federal Army of Tennessee. He commissioned the painting at a cost of $42,000 as a campaign move in his bid for the vice presidency. He's shown gloriously galloping into the fray, bravely exposing himself and his men to enemy fire. The work was originally called *Logan's Great Battle.*

The building housing Cyclorama also comprises a museum of related artifacts, most importantly the steam locomotive Texas from the 1862 Great Locomotive Chase. Other exhibits include displays of Civil War arms and artillery, Civil War–themed paintings, portraits of Confederate and Union leaders, "life in camp" artifacts and photographs, and uniforms, as well as further elucidation of the Battle of Atlanta and Cyclorama. A bookstore on the premises is a repository of Civil War literature, including a sizable black history section.

Admission: $3.50 for adults, $3 for seniors, $2 for children 6–12, under 6 free (not recommended for very young children).

Open: Daily June–Labor Day 9:20am–5:30pm, the day after Labor Day–May 31 9:20am–4:30pm. Shows begin every half hour on the half hour starting at 9:30am. **Closed:** Thanksgiving, Christmas, New Year's Day, and Martin Luther King Day. **Bus:** Take Georgia Avenue bus No. 97 from Five Points Station.

★ **Oakland Cemetery,** 248 Oakland Ave. SE; main entrance at Oakland Ave. and Martin Luther King Dr. ☎ **688-2107.**

On the National Register of Historic Places, this outstanding 88-acre Victorian cemetery was founded in 1850. It survived the Civil War and remained the only cemetery in Atlanta for 34 years. Among the over 48,000 people buried here are Confederate and Union soldiers (including five Southern generals), prominent families and paupers, governors and mayors, golfing great Bobby Jones, and Atlanta's most famous personage, *Gone With the Wind* author Margaret Mitchell. There's a Jewish section (consecrated by a temple), a black section (dating from segregation days), and a potter's field. Two monuments honor the Confederate war dead. And standing at the marker that commemorates the Great Locomotive Chase, you can see the trees from which the Yankee raiders were hanged (Confederate conductor Captain William Fuller is buried here).

Almost every grave has a story. Real-estate tycoon Jasper Newton Smith had a life-size statue of himself erected on his grave so he could watch the city's goings-on into eternity. The sculptor originally gave Smith a tie, but Smith, who never wore one, refused to pay for the piece until the tie was chiseled off. Dr. James Nissen, Oakland's first burial, feared being buried alive; his will stated that his jugular vein be severed prior to interment. And John Morgan Dye was a baby who died during the siege of Atlanta; his mother walked through the raging battle to the cemetery carrying the small corpse. The smallest grave, however, is that of "Tweet," a pet mockingbird buried in his family's lot. You'll also learn about graveyard symbolism on the tour: a lopped-tree-trunk marker indicates a life cut short or goals unachieved, rocks on a grave denote a life built on a solid foundation, a shell means resurrection, and so on.

The cemetery is renowned not only for historical reasons, but as an outdoor "museum" of Gothic and classical-revival mausolea, bronze urns, stained glass, and Victorian statuary. Atlanta residents also view Oakland's rolling terrain as parkland; dozens of people actually jog here every day, and picnickers are a common sight. Every October, there's a celebration to commemorate the cemetery's founding, with turn-of-the-century music, food, and storytelling. Though you can visit whenever the cemetery is open, do try to come when you can take a guided tour. It's fascinating.

Admission: Free.

Open: Daily sunrise to 7pm (6pm in winter); Visitor Center Mon–Fri 9am–5pm. Purchase an informative self-guide walking tour map brochure at the Visitor Center for $1.25. **MARTA:** King Memorial. **Parking:** Inside the cemetery, near the Visitor Center.

★ **Georgia's Stone Mountain Park,** 16 miles east of downtown on U.S. 78. ☎ **498-5600.**

A monolithic gray granite outcropping (the world's largest), carved with a massive monument to the Confederacy, Stone Mountain is a distinctive landmark on Atlanta's horizon and the focal point of its major recreation area—3,200 acres of lakes and beautiful wooded parkland. It's Georgia's number-one tourist mecca and the third most visited paid attraction in the United States.

Over half a century in the making, Stone Mountain's neoclassic carving—90 feet high and 190 feet wide—is the world's largest piece of sculpture. Originally conceived by Gutzon Borglum, it depicts Confederate leaders Jefferson Davis, Robert E. Lee, and Stonewall Jackson galloping on horseback throughout eternity. Borglum started work on the mountain sculpture in 1923; after 10 years he abandoned it, due to insurmountable technical problems and rifts with its sponsors. He went on to South Dakota, where he gained fame carving Mount Rushmore. No sign of his work remains at Stone Mountain, but it was his vision that inspired the project. Augustus Lukeman took over in 1925, but three years later, the work still far from complete, the family that owned the mountain lost patience and reclaimed the property. It wasn't until 1963, the state having purchased the mountain and surrounding property for a park, that work resumed under Walter Kirtland Hancock and Roy Faulkner. It was completed in 1970.

The best view of the mountain is from below, but you can ascend a walking trail up and down its moss-covered slopes, especially lovely in spring when they're blanketed in wildflowers, or take the narrated tram ride to the top. There are picnic tables at the summit, along with a snack bar and a gift shop. Trams run about every 20 minutes in both directions.

A highlight at Stone Mountain is **Lasershow,** a spectacular display of laser lights and fireworks with animation and music. It begins in April (Friday, Saturday, and Sunday night at 9pm); from early May through Labor Day it can be seen nightly at 9:30pm; then it resumes its Friday-through-Sunday schedule during September; Friday and Saturday night only in October. Don't miss it.

Other major park attractions include: the **Stone Mountain Scenic Railroad** that chugs around the 5-mile base of Stone Mountain. The ride takes 25 minutes. Trains depart from Memorial Depot, an old-fashioned train station with a very attractive restaurant on the premises serving chicken dinners with all the fixings; on its walls hang mural-size oil paintings of Native Americans and settlers done in the 1930s. Fronting the depot are a barbecue snack bar, lemonade and funnel-cake concessions, an Olympic '96 souvenir shop, and a gem-panning trough.

The **Scarlett O'Hara,** a paddlewheel riverboat, cruises the 363-acre Stone Mountain Lake.

The **Antique Auto & Music Museum** is a jumble of old radios, jukeboxes, working nickelodeons, pianos, Lionel trains, carousel horses, and clocks along with classic cars such as a 1925 Ford Model T truck, a 1948 Tucker, a 1928 Martin built for World War I ace General Billy Mitchell out of airplane parts, and an electric car.

The 19-building **Antebellum Plantation** offers self-guided tours assisted by hosts in period dress at each structure. Highlights include an authentic 1830s country store; the 1845 Kingston House (it represents a typical overseer's house); the clapboard slave cabins; the 1790s Thornton House, elegant home of a large landowner; the smokehouse and well; a doctor's office; a barn, a coach house, and crop-storage cribs; a necessary; a cook house; and the 1850 neoclassical Tara-like Dickey House. The grounds also contain formal gardens and a kitchen garden. It takes at least an hour to tour the entire complex (a map is provided at the entrance), really a major Atlanta sightseeing attraction in itself. Often (especially in summer), there are crafts and cooking demonstrations, medicine shows, storytellers, and balladeers on the premises. You can even take a 20-minute horse-drawn carriage ride around the area ($5 for adults, $3 for children 3 to 11; free for children under 3).

Confederate Hall, an information center, houses a large narrated exhibit called "The War in Georgia," a chronological picture story of the Civil War.

At **Memorial Hall,** another information center, a 9-minute tape on Stone Mountain history and geology is shown throughout the day. A Civil War museum is upstairs.

Additional activities: golf (on a top-rated 36-hole course designed by Robert Trent Jones and John LaFoy), miniature golf, eight night-lighted Laykold tennis courts, a sizable stretch of sandy lakefront beach with wonderful water slides, 20 acres of wildlife trails with natural animal habitats and a petting zoo, carillon concerts, boating (rowboats, canoes, sailboats, and paddleboats), bicycle rental, fishing, hiking, picnicking, and more.

Stone Mountain Park is one of the most beautiful parks in the nation. Consider spending a few days of your trip here; it's a great place for a romantic getaway or a family vacation. On-site accommodations are detailed in Chapter 5, "Atlanta Accommodations." If you can only spare a day, it's an easy drive (about 30 minutes) from downtown.

Admission: There's a parking charge of $5 a day, $20 annually (one-time-only charge if you stay on the grounds); major attractions are $3 each for adults, $2 for children 3–11, free for children under 3. A ticket for all six major attractions is $13.50 for adults, $9 for children.

Open: Year round, gates open 6am–midnight. Major attractions are open fall and winter 10am–5pm, spring and summer 10am–9pm.
Closed: Attractions only are closed Christmas Day; park is open.
MARTA: Take a MARTA train to Indian Trail Station where you can transfer to a bus to Memorial Hall in the park.

The Jimmy Carter Library, N. Highland and Cleburne Aves.
☎ **331-3942.**

Opened in October 1986 on 30 acres of gardens, lakes, and waterfalls, this impressive presidential center library houses some 27 million pages of documents, memoranda, and correspondence from Jimmy Carter's White House years. There are also $1^1/2$ million photographs and hundreds of hours of audio- and videotapes, the latter documenting everything from meetings with world leaders to a footrace between the president and his daughter, Amy. The library's hilltop site is a historic one; it was from this spot that Sherman watched the Battle of Atlanta.

Georgia's Stone Mountain Park

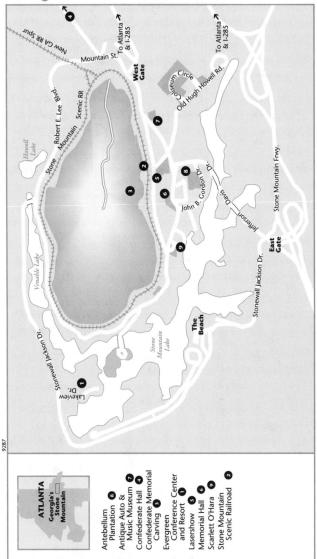

In the facility's extensive museum, you'll see an exact replica of the Oval Office during Carter's presidency, an exhibit enhanced by a recording of Carter speaking about his experiences in that office. A large display of "gifts of state" runs the gamut from a Dresden figurine of George and Martha Washington (a gift from Ireland) to a carpet from the Shah of Iran. You'll see the table setting used when the Carters entertained Chinese vice premier Deng Xiaoping and his wife in the State Dining Room; a video of artists such as the late pianist Vladimir Horowitz performing in the East Room; campaign memorabilia; and a large display devoted to the activities of Rosalynn Carter. A changing exhibit area houses art shows.

Other exhibits focus on Carter's support of human rights (there's a letter from Soviet dissident Andrei Sakharov and Carter's reply); his boyhood (his sixth-grade report card and a photo of the Plains High baseball team are two of the items on display); and his prepresidential life as a peanut farmer, governor, and state senator. Of course, the major issues of his administration—the Middle East; the nuclear threat and SALT II talks; terrorism; the advent of formal diplomatic relations with China; and the environment—are featured in displays as well.

There are informative videos throughout, including an interactive "town meeting" format in which visitors can ask Carter questions on subjects ranging from world affairs to his personal life. And a most interesting participatory video lets you choose your response to a terrorist crisis and learn the probable consequences of your choice.

Consider having lunch here. There's an attractive cafeteria on the premises with patio seating overlooking a Japanese garden and pond.

Admission: $4 for adults, $3 for seniors, free for children under 16.

Open: Mon–Sat 9am–4:45pm, Sun noon–4:45pm. **Closed:** New Year's Day, Thanksgiving, Christmas.

★ **Fernbank Museum of Natural History,** 767 Clifton Rd., off Ponce de Leon Ave. ☎ **378-0127.**

This brand-new $42.8 million museum is the largest museum of the natural sciences in the Southeast. It encompasses the 65-acre Fernbank Forest, the Fernbank Science Center (see details below under "Cool for Kids"), extensive gardens, greenhouses, and parklands. Be sure to see all these attractions when you visit.

In addition to its permanent exhibition area in a central Great Hall under a soaring 85-foot skylight, the museum has a 15,000-square-foot area for temporary traveling shows such as the Smithsonian's "Tropical Rainforest: A Disappearing Treasure." The major permanent exhibit, "A Walk Through Time in Georgia," uses the state as a microcosm to tell the story of the earth's development through time. Six regional galleries here re-create landform regions from the pine-forested Piedmont Plateau to the mossy Okefenokee Swamp.

In spacious discovery rooms children ages 3 to 5 can "pollinate" flowers and feed toy worms to mechanical baby birds. Older kids get to cast nets off a shrimp boat and sight birds from viewing platforms overlooking the "Blue Ridge Mountains." And, in the Robin Harris Naturalist Center, kids of all ages can watch scientists at work and categorize fossils, shells, and plant specimens they find along Fernbank's nature walks.

A highlight is an IMAX theater (the first in Georgia) which premiered the film *Mountain Gorillas,* shot in Rwanda, Africa. If you're not familiar with spectacular IMAX films (here shown on a screen measuring 52 feet by 70 feet), they're a not-to-be-missed attraction—a major thrill.

A pleasant dining room is on the premises, and a large museum shop focuses on educational merchandise.

CNN Center, Marietta St. at Techwood Dr. ☎ **827-2400.**

The CNN Center is headquarters for media magnate Ted Turner's 24-hour cable news networks, CNN, CNN International, and Headline News. During 45-minute guided walking tours, visitors get a behind-the-scenes look at the high-tech world of TV network news in action. You'll find the Tour Desk in the main lobby near the base of an 8-story escalator. While you're waiting for the tour to begin, have your photograph taken behind a CNN anchor desk replica.

Tours begin in an exhibit area where displays include MGM movie stills (Turner owns a portion of the MGM/RKO film library); a scaled-down model of the Galaxy 5 satellite that carries the signal for the company's networks; exhibits on Jacques Cousteau and *National Geographic* (both subjects of numerous specials on Turner-owned TBS); an exhibit on TBS sports (Turner owns the Atlanta Hawks and the Atlanta Braves); an exhibit on the Goodwill Games; a 12-monitor video wall that continuously airs all Turner networks; a display on the 24-hour cartoon network; a duplicate of MGM's Oscar for *Gone With the Wind;* and items involved in CNN's much-lauded coverage of the Gulf War.

On another level, visitors observe the CNN newsroom from a glass-walled viewing station. You'll see the domestic and international desks, and writers in the process of composing news scripts. On a monitor, you can observe what newscasters are up to during their breaks (often chomping sandwiches), and if a live broadcast is in progress, you can see CNN newscasters at work. Tour guides are knowledgeable and can answer virtually any question.

There are over a dozen restaurants and fast-food outlets on the premises, a variety of shops, and a movie theater. The Turner Store on the premises carries network-logo clothing and gift items, along with MGM movie memorabilia (this is your chance to buy a Rhett Butler jack-in-the-box or a *Gone With the Wind* beach towel). There are frequent exhibits, concerts, crafts shows, and other special events in the atrium lobby; ask your tour guide what's on.

Admission: $6 for adults, $4 for seniors, $3.50 for children 6–12; under 5 free (though the tour is not recommended for young children) they'll be bored. **Note:** Tickets are available on a first-come, first-served basis on the day of the tour. Arrive early for the tour you wish to take, since only 35 tickets are sold per tour, and they often sell out. Best bet is to reserve in advance via MasterCard or Visa.

Open: 45-minute tours are given daily every 15 minutes between 9am and 5pm; tickets go on sale at 8:30pm. **Closed:** New Year's Day, Easter, Memorial Day, July 4, Labor Day, Thanksgiving, and Dec

24–25. **MARTA:** Omni. **Parking:** There are many parking lots around the building.

⭐ **High Museum of Art,** 1280 Peachtree St. NE, at 16th St. ☎ **892-3600** or **892-HIGH** (24-hour information line).

The High Museum of Art, founded in 1926, opened its award-winning building in 1983. Designed by architect Richard Meier, this 135,000-square-foot, $20 million facility—part of the Woodruff Arts Center complex—is itself a work of art. A dazzling white porcelain-tiled edifice with an equally pristine white interior (the *New York Times* jokingly cautioned that visitors risk snow blindness on a sunny day), it houses four floors of galleries connected by semicircular pedestrian ramps girding a spacious, sun-filled, 4-story atrium. The north wall of this atrium is enhanced by a 62-foot-high jewel-toned ink drawing by Sol Le Witt. It's a very favorable setting in which to view art.

The permanent collection includes over 10,000 pieces, among them a significant group of 19th- and 20th-century American paintings. It features Hudson River school artists such as Thomas Cole and Frederic Church, as well as works by Thomas Sully, John Singer Sargent, and William Harnett. The Virginia Carroll Crawford Collection of American Decorative Arts comprehensively documents styles from 1825 to 1917. The Samuel H. Kress Foundation collection comprises Italian paintings and sculpture from the 14th through the 18th century. And the Uhry Print Collection contains important works by French impressionists and postimpressionists, German expressionists, and American 20th-century artists. Also notable are collections of sub-Saharan African art and works by noted 19th- and 20th-century American and European photographers.

In addition to its permanent collection, the museum hosts a number of traveling exhibitions each year, complemented by films, lectures, workshops, gallery talks, concerts, and other cultural events. Recent temporary exhibits have ranged from shows focusing on specific artists (Willem de Kooning, Mary Cassatt, Ansel Adams) to "Italian and Netherlandish drawings from the Steiner Collection" and "The Royal Art of Benin." Inquire at the desk about happenings during your stay, and call in advance to find out when you can take a free gallery tour. **Note:** There is a smaller branch of this museum at the Georgia-Pacific Center downtown (see "More Attractions," below).

Admission: $5 for adults, $3 for seniors and students with ID, $1 for children 6–17, children under 6 free. Free to all on Thurs 1–5pm.

Open: Tues–Sat 10am–5pm, Fri till 9pm, Sun noon–5pm. **Closed:** Mon, July 4, Thanksgiving, Christmas, and New Year's Day. **MARTA:** Arts Center. A parking garage is located on Lombardy Way between 15th and 16th Streets.

⭐ **Fox Theatre,** 660 Peachtree St. NE, at Ponce de Leon Ave.
☎ **881-1977** for box office, **876-2040** for tours.

Originally conceived as a Shriners' temple in 1916, this lavish, block-long Moorish-Egyptian fantasyland ended up as a movie theater when the Shriners realized their grandiose conception had far exceeded their budget. In 1927, they sold the "temple" to movie magnate William Fox, who amended their plans and created a peerless pleasure palace. The building was designed by French architect Oliver J. Vinour (he trained at the Ecole des Beaux Arts in Paris), who utilized design motifs of the Middle East in his creation, including replicas of art and furnishings from King Tut's tomb.

Atlanta's new theater opened in 1929 as a masterpiece of Oriental splendor, its Moorish facade, onion domes, and minarets an exotic contrast to the surrounding Victorian boardinghouses. A brass-trimmed marble kiosk imported from France served as a ticket booth. The 140-foot entrance arcade led to a lushly carpeted lobby with blue-tiled goldfish pools. And the auditorium was an Arabian courtyard under a twinkling starlit sky that could, with state-of-the-art technology, be transformed to a sky at sunrise or sunset and produce rain, fog, and snow. A striped bedouin canopy sheltered the balcony, and sequin- and rhinestone-studded stage curtains depicted mosques and Moorish horsemen. As the show began, a gigantic gilded 3,610-pipe Möller organ rose majestically from its vault, its rich chords accompanied by a full orchestra. A medley of popular songs, cartoons, a follow-the-bouncing-ball sing-along, a stage-show extravaganza by a bevy of Rockette-like chorines called the Fanchon and Marco Sunkist Beauties, and a newsreel preceded every main feature. At night there were dances in the Egyptian Ballroom, designed to replicate Ramses' temple. And even the men's lounge was exotically appointed with hieroglyphic adornments, winged scarab-motif friezes, bas reliefs of royal figures, and throne chairs.

Unfortunately, the Fox's opening coincided with the Great Depression, and it proved impossible to maintain its unstinting opulence. In 1932 the company declared bankruptcy and closed its doors. The theater reopened three years later for occasional concerts featuring cultural superstars such as Leopold Stokowski and Yehudi Menuhin. By the forties, it was a viable concern once more, and in 1947 the Metropolitan Opera began a 20-year stint of week-long performances here. An oversize panoramic screen was installed in the 1950s, along with a 26-speaker stereophonic system. But like monumental movie palaces nationwide, the Fox inevitably declined in the age of television. In 1975 its doors were padlocked once again.

An organization of concerned citizens calling themselves Atlanta Landmarks raised $1.8 million and saved the Fox from the wrecking ball in 1978, foiling Southern Bell's plans to purchase and demolish it to make way for a regional headquarters building. Ever since, it's been a thriving entity, featuring Broadway shows, headliners (Ray Charles, Liza Minelli, Ben Vereen), dance companies such as Alvin Ailey, and comedy stars such as Jay Leno and Whoopi Goldberg. A big event every summer is the Summer Film Festival, which features organ concerts, sing-alongs, and cartoons with classic and current blockbuster movies (see the "Calendar of Events" in Chapter 2 for details). Best of all, the theater has been restored to its former glory, its fabulous furnishings and fixtures, terrazzo-tile floors and elaborately stenciled ceilings, gilded columns and velvet draperies all refurbished or replaced with replicas.

To tour the Fox is to enter the fantasy world of Hollywood's heyday—a world in which dreams usually do come true and adventures abound. I guarantee you'll be caught up in its glamorous mystique.

Admission: Tours cost $5 for adults, $4 for seniors, and $3 for students.

Open: The Atlanta Preservation Center conducts walking tours of the Fox Theatre and its surrounding area Mon and Thurs at 10am and Sat at 10 and 11:30am. **MARTA:** North Avenue.

★ **Atlanta Botanical Garden,** in Piedmont Park, at Piedmont Ave. and the Prado. ☎ **876-5858.**

This delightful botanical garden, occupying 30 acres in Piedmont Park, was founded in 1977 and has since expanded considerably. It consists of three main sections. **The Gardens,** designed to be an inspiration to the local horticultural set, highlight plants that flourish in North Georgia's extended growing season. Displays in this section include a carnivorous plant bog, a rock garden, a dwarf conifer garden, a group of grass plots (helpful for Georgian homeowners choosing lawn grass), an English knot-designed herb garden, a tranquil moongated Japanese garden, a rose garden, and a fragrance garden built for the blind. These lovely gardens are enhanced by fountains, stone statuary, benches, and pagodas. Lunch is served Tuesday to Sunday from April through October on Lanier Terrace, overlooking the Rose Garden.

Two natural arboretum settings comprise 15 acres of hardwood forest. The **Upper Woodlands,** with a paved path, contains a fern glade, a camellia garden, gurgling streams, beautiful statuary, and a backyard wildlife habitat designed to show visitors how to attract wildlife to their own backyards. Still more rustic is **Storza Woods,** with an unpaved path. Both make for easy and very pleasant walks.

Most exciting is the 16,000-square-foot, glass-walled **Dorothy Chapman Fuqua Conservatory,** opened in 1989 to house rare and endangered plants from exotic climes. With 54 acres of irreplaceable rain forest being bulldozed every minute, facilities such as this provide a much-needed haven for technology-threatened plant species. Approached via an arbored promenade and fronted by a water lily pond, the conservatory has a revolving globe outside its entrance showing the many regions worldwide where plant life is endangered. An interactive video display enhances visitor understanding of exhibits.

The focal point of the conservatory is the misty Tropical Rotunda, housing fern collections, old-world succulents, cycads (the most primitive seed-bearing plants known), epiphytes (plants that don't require soil to grow), gorgeous orchids, carnivorous plants (always intriguing), a wide variety of begonias, and towering tropical palms. It's a lush and humid jungle, with brightly hued native birds warbling overhead, a splashing waterfall, and winding pathways lined with fragrant hibiscus, gardenias, and flowering jasmine vines. Of special interest is a double coconut palm seed from the Seychelles, the largest and heaviest seed in the plant kingdom. Its first 12-foot leaves have already begun to grow, but it will be 100 years before the tree reaches its full height.

The arid Desert House displays Madagascar succulents such as a unique family of spiky plants called Didieriaceae. Here, too, are "living stones" (desert succulents that nature designed to look like pebbles to protect them from being eaten by animals), tree aloes, caudiciforms (with swollen stems and roots for storing water), and conifers from Africa and the Canary Islands. Adjoining is an area for special exhibits.

The building also houses an orangery of rare tropical mango, papaya, star fruit, lychee, coffee, and citrus trees. And a new addition is an "Olympic" olive tree presented by Greece in honor of the 1996 event.

There are flower shows throughout the year, along with lectures and other activities. Call to find out what's on during your stay. A marvelous gift shop is on the premises; your purchases help support the garden. Audio tours ($2) are available in five languages.

Admission: $6 for adults, $4.75 for seniors, $3 for students with ID, free for children 6 and under. Admission is free every Thurs 1pm to closing. Parking is free on the premises.

Open: Tues–Sun 9am–6pm, till 7pm during daylight savings time.

Georgia State Capitol, Capitol Hill at Washington St.
☎ **656-2844.**

After the Revolutionary War, Georgia's capital, first situated in Savannah, moved to Augusta in 1786 and Louisville in 1796. In 1807, westward expansion of the state caused the capital to be moved to Milledgeville, a more central location, which remained the seat of Georgia government for 61 years. It wasn't until after the Civil War (1868) that Atlanta became, once and for all, the state capital; its present capitol building, completed July 4, 1889, was hailed as a testament to the city's recovery. Assuming office in the new building, Governor (and former Confederate general) John Brown Gordon eloquently expressed the sentiments of his constituency: "Built upon the crowning hill of her capital city, whose transformation from desolation and ashes to life . . . and beauty so aptly symbolizes the State's resurrection, this proud structure will stand through the coming centuries as a fit memorial to the indomitable will of this people." And so it does.

Modeled after the nation's Capitol, another neoclassical edifice atop a "crowning hill," its 75-foot dome, covered in gold leaf and topped by a statue of Freedom, is a major Atlanta landmark. The building is fronted by a massive 4-story portico with a pediment supported by six Corinthian columns set on large stone piers. Engraved on the pediment is the Great Seal of State, flanked by two figures representing Georgia agriculture and commerce. Inside the magnificent rotunda, with its soaring 237-foot ceiling, are busts of famous Georgians, including signers of the Declaration of Independence and the Constitution.

Tours begin in the entrance hallway of the main floor, this level also serving as an information center for city and state attractions. The governor's office is off the main hall. The tours take 45 minutes; allow at least another 30 minutes to browse around on your own after the tour. Highlights of the grounds are detailed in a brochure available at the tour desk. **Note:** For security reasons, your bag will be searched when you enter.

On the main floor, you'll see display cases of bullet-ridden Georgia Civil War flags and portraits of past governors. Flags suspended from the fourth-floor balustrades can be seen in the Hall of State Flags on this level in the south wing. Flags that have flown over Georgia (including the British flag and several flags of the Confederacy) are displayed in the Hall of Flags, to the north of the rotunda. Also in the north wing are additional governors' portraits, busts of famous Georgians, and a portrait of Dr. Martin Luther King, Jr., backed by the Lincoln Memorial.

Grand staircases in both wings rise to the fourth floor, where you'll enter the House of Representatives, and, across the hall, the Senate chambers. The legislature meets for 40 days, beginning the second Monday in January (it can also be called into special sessions); all of its sessions are open to the public. The fourth floor additionally houses the State Museum of Science & Industry, with exhibits on cotton, peach, and peanut growing; cases of mounted birds, fish, deer, insects, and other species native to Georgia; weaponry; rocks and minerals; Indian artifacts; and more.

Some events of note: The week before Thanksgiving is Indian Heritage Week at the capitol. A wattle-and-daub Indian dwelling is constructed in the rotunda, and there are Native American lecturers, music, and arts-and-crafts demonstrations. At Christmas, a beautifully decorated 40-foot tree adorns the rotunda. And on January 15, Dr. Martin Luther King, Jr's., birthday, there's an annual memorial program; local dignitaries, including the governor, give speeches, and King's family attends.

Admission: Free.

Open: Mon–Fri 8am–5pm, Sat 10am–4pm, Sun noon–4pm. Tours are given weekdays only at 10 and 11am and 1 and 2pm. **Closed:** Major holidays, including state holidays. **MARTA:** Georgia State. **Parking:** Lot behind the capitol building on Capitol Avenue is closed to the public during legislative sessions; other lots are on

M. L. King Drive at Central Avenue and on Courtland Street between M. L. King Drive and Central Avenue.

Underground Atlanta, bounded by Wall St., Central Ave., Martin Luther King, Jr., Dr., and Peachtree St. ☎ **523-2311.**

The site of Underground Atlanta is the historic hub of the city, centered on the Zero Milepost that marked the terminus of the Western & Atlantic Railroad in the 1800s. For many years a flourishing locale, the area became so congested in the early 1900s that permanent concrete viaducts were constructed over it, elevating the street system and routing traffic over a maze of railroad tracks. Merchants moved their operations up to the new level, using the lower level for storage space. For most of the 20th century, it remained a deserted catacomb. Then, in 1969, a group of Atlanta businesspeople decided to create an underground entertainment complex of restaurants, shops, and bars in a setting that retained the historic feel of the area. The idea was great, but perhaps the time wasn't right; the complex declined and closed after a little over a decade. Since 1989, however, it has, under the auspices of the Rouse Company (operators of New York's South Street Seaport, Baltimore's Harborplace, and Boston's Faneuil Hall), become one of Atlanta's most ballyhooed sightseeing extravaganzas.

Occupying 12 acres in the center of downtown, this $142 million entertainment mecca and spirited urban marketplace is heralded by a beacon of oscillating searchlights emanating from a 138-foot light tower, an outdoor staging area used for performances and concerts, and the cascading waters of Peachtree Fountain Plaza. It offers over 150 retail operations, restaurants, and nightclubs. Humbug Square—where street vendors and con artists flourished in the early 1900s—is again a colorful street market with turn-of-the-century pushcarts and wagons displaying offbeat wares. Specialty foods are sold in Packinghouse Row, a site on which meat packers and food wholesalers operated in the 1800s. Clustered around a section called Kenny's Alley, over a dozen restaurants and nightclubs (see Chapter 10, "Atlanta Nights") offer a wide spectrum of food and entertainment. And like Rouse projects everywhere, Underground has a food court purveying everything from egg rolls to stuffed baked potatoes.

Markers throughout the complex indicate historic sites. The Atlanta Convention and Visitors Bureau (☎ **577-2148**) maintains an information center at Underground on the corner of Pryor and Alabama streets. And the Olympic Experience, at the corner of Alabama and Peachtree streets (☎ **658-1996**) offers information about the upcoming Olympic games, exhibits, and a gift shop retailing official Olympic merchandise.

Admission: Free. There is a charge for parking in the garage on Central Avenue off Martin Luther King Drive, but it's reduced if you get your ticket validated at a store or restaurant.

Open: Mon–Sat 10am–9:30pm, Sun noon–6pm. Most restaurants and clubs stay open until midnight (or later) nightly.

MARTA: Five Points Station has a short pedestrian tunnel that connects directly with Underground Atlanta.

⭐ **Atlanta Heritage Row,** 55 Upper Alabama St., at Underground Atlanta. ☎ **584-7879.**

This informative and highly entertaining attraction tells the story of Atlanta from its humble beginnings as a wilderness village through its eventful 200-year history to its present-day status as an international city. It's divided into six themed sections. Your journey through history begins in "Origins" with the Cherokee and Creek Native Americans who resided near the Chattahoochee River for centuries before Europeans arrived. You'll view the virgin forest that surveyor Stephen Long saw in 1837 when he drove the Zero Mile Post stake marking the terminus of the Western & Atlantic Railroad. An 1845 train depot is re-created. Tableaux are enhanced with audio recordings; you'll hear Creek music and train whistles, even the sound of Long driving in the stake.

As you pass through the train station doorway, you'll enter the "Civil War" area. Amid bombed rubble, with shells bursting in the background, you'll hear readings of the poignant diaries of people who experienced the siege of Atlanta.

In "Atlanta Resurgens—the New South" (through 1895), skyscrapers go up as Atlantans begin recovering from the ravages of war. In a reconstruction of *Atlanta Constitution* editor Henry Grady's office you can hear excerpts from his famous speech advancing the ideals of the "New South." Another audio enhancement is Sousa's "King Cotton March," composed in honor of the 1895 Cotton States and International Exposition in Piedmont Park.

"Forward Atlanta" (through 1945) deals with the surge in the business community and prominent roles played by major companies. It also examines the Jim Crow Laws and the prosperous black-owned businesses and thriving music scene that developed in Sweet Auburn, partially because of the segregation laws. You can listen to 12 minutes of Atlanta blues and country-music greats like Fiddlin' John Carson and Bessie Smith. Displays include a walk-through 1920s trolley car, and a video takes you to the movie premiere of *Gone With the Wind.*

"Big League City" (through 1974) documents Atlanta's continued emergence as a business center and as the cradle of the civil rights movement. Stand behind Martin Luther King's pulpit here, while listening to his stirring "I Have A Dream" speech, and view a video of Mayor Hartsfield peacefully integrating the public schools. Also heralded in this section is the arrival of big-time sports in Atlanta.

Transportation and communications are the themes of the final "International City" area, focusing on the role of Turner Broadcasting and Delta Air Lines. You can step inside a 1970 Convair 880 Delta jet cockpit (photos inside contrast the infinitely more complex controls of a present-day jet) and listen to pilots conversing with the tower at Hartsfield International Airport. Baseball buffs will enjoy a video of Hank Aaron's record-breaking home run. The tour ends with a 15-minute high-tech, wide-screen video called *People: The Spirit of Atlanta,* a tapestry of songs, stories, and interviews with community leaders and ordinary citizens. Heritage Row was created by a prestigious committee of historians, and they've done a superb job.

Admission: Adults $3, children 13–18 and seniors $2.50, children 4–12 $2, 3 and under free.

Open: Tues–Sat 10am–5pm, Sun 1–5pm. **Closed:** Mon.

MARTA: Five Points. **Parking:** In garage on Central Avenue off Martin Luther King Dr.

The World of Coca-Cola, 55 Martin Luther King Dr. SW, at Central Avenue, adjacent to Underground Atlanta. ☎ **676-5151.**

This exposition-like attraction showcases "the world's most popular product." Its vast 3-story pavilion houses a vast collection of Coca-Cola memorabilia, along with numerous interactive displays, high-tech exhibits, and video presentations. A self-guided tour begins on the third level where visitors are greeted by a Rube Goldberg–like kinetic sculpture called a "Bottling Fantasy." Exhibits throughout trace the history of Coca-Cola from its 1886 debut at Jacob's Pharmacy in downtown Atlanta to its current worldwide fame. Highlights include: displays of antique bottling equipment; a recreation of Barnes Soda Fountain in Baxley, Georgia (ca. 1930) (a jukebox on the premises plays Coke-themed pop songs of yesteryear like "Sweet Coca-Cola Bush" sung by Shirley Temple); diverse advertising campaigns over the years (did you know that Maxwell House's "good to the last drop" was originally a Coke slogan?); Coke-themed toys, trays, school supplies, games, and the like; a video on the making of the "Hilltop Reunion" Coke commercial (it kicked off the "I'd Like to Teach the World to Sing" campaign); print ads featuring screen stars such as Jean Harlow Claudette Colbert, Clark Gable, and Cary Grant; and an interactive audio exhibit that lets you listen to Coke commercials sung by pop stars like Al Jarreau, Loretta Lynn, Jerry Lee Lewis, and the Supremes. A high-tech film on the third floor called *Every Day of Your Life* highlights Coca-Cola consumption in over a dozen countries on six continents—from Hong Kong's Taikoo Tower to the Masai Steppe of Africa. And, in case you've worked up a thirst by this time, you can sample unlimited amounts of 38 Coca-Cola Company beverages at Club Coca-Cola, including 18 international drinks that are not sold in the United States (for example, a pineapple/orange/banana beverage marketed only in Kenya). The tour ends in the first-floor gift shop, which vends a mind-boggling array of Coke-motif items—everything from T-shirts to Coke polar bears. There's much, much more; this experience is a total immersion in Coca-Cola.

Admission: Adults $3.50, seniors over 55 $3, children 6–12 $2.50, under 6 free.

Open: Mon–Sat 10am–8:30pm, Sun noon–5pm. **Closed:** New Year's Day, the second Mon in Jan, Easter, Thanksgiving, Christmas Eve, and Christmas Day. **MARTA:** Five Points. **Parking:** Garage on Central Avenue off Martin Luther King Drive.

★ **Michael C. Carlos Museum of Emory University**, 571 S. Kilgo St., near the intersection of Oxford and N. Decatur Rds. on the Main Quadrangle of the Emory Campus. ☎ **727-4282.**

Emory University's antiquities collection dates to 1875 and this intriguing museum to 1919, when it was founded to display the art and artifacts collected by Emory faculty in Egypt, Cyprus, Greece, Sicily, the Sea of Galilee, and the sites of ancient Babylon and Palestine. Today the museum also maintains collections of ancient art and archaeology of Rome, Central and South America, the Near East, and Mesoamerica; works of the native cultures of North America; and art and ethnology of Asia, Africa, and Oceania. And a sizable collection of works on paper encompasses illuminated manuscript pages, drawings, and prints from the Middle Ages and the Renaissance to the 20th century. It's all housed partly in a 1916 beaux-arts building which is on the National Register of Historic Places, its interior redesigned in 1985 by postmodernist architect Michael Graves. The remainder is in a 35,000 square foot exhibition space (also designed by Graves) that opened in 1993.

The first-floor galleries feature changing exhibits from the extensive permanent collection—objects that were part of the daily life of people from three continents as early as the third millenium B.C. They include Bronze and Iron Age clay pots, jugs, loom weights, and oil lamps from Palestine; Egyptian mummies, pottery, cosmetic containers, and headrests; Greek and Cypriot pottery, flasks, and statuary; and Mesopotamian pottery, coins, tools, sculpture, and cuneiform tablets inscribed with ancient writing. Also on this level: the Thibadeau Pre-Columbian collection, comprising over 1,300 objects spanning 2,000 years of creativity—gold jewelry, pottery, and statues, including many ceramic, volcanic stone, greenstone, and gold sculptures from ancient Costa Rica.

The upper floor is used for changing exhibits ranging in subject matter from Pueblo Indian pottery to impressionist art. This level also houses a café serving light fare. Throughout the museum, 210 plaster casts of ancient architectural elements—reliefs, friezes, column capitals, and decorative elements from temples and monuments—adorn hallway and lobby walls. There are many interesting workshops, lectures, films, and gallery tours here; call to find out what's on during your stay.

Admission: A donation of $3 is suggested.

Open: Mon–Thurs 10am–5pm, Fri 10am–9pm, Sat 10am–5pm, Sun noon–5pm. **Closed:** New Year's Day, Thanksgiving, and Christmas.

2 More Attractions

Château Elan Vineyards, exit 48 off I-85 in Braselton.
☎ **867-8200** or toll free in Georgia **800/233-WINE.**

Château Elan is a hilltop winery that replicates a 16th-century French estate surrounded by verdant countryside. Its first wines were produced in 1985, and already they have garnered 194 awards. There's much to do here. Guided tours are given daily between 11am and 4pm (call ahead for hours; you can also take self-guided tours from 5pm to closing).

On view are the crushing and pressing machines, oak barrels used to age and flavor wines, the cask room, and the bottling area. Tours conclude with a wine tasting. Vines ripen in July/August, so if you're here during harvesting in August and September, you'll actually see the winemaking procedure. About 300 tons of grapes are harvested and processed each year. The interior of the château, a stage-set version of a Paris street, has a quarry-stone floor, wrought-iron fences, and streetlamps. Walls are adorned with large murals depicting the history of winemaking and two Parisian sites—the train station Gare du Nord and the Place des Vosges. The building houses an art gallery offering changing exhibits by regional and national artists, displays of antique European winemaking equipment, and a wine market.

There are also two on-premises restaurants, so plan to dine here. Café Elan, open daily from 10am (closing hours vary; call before you go), features sandwiches, salads, and continental main courses like chicken sautéed with pecans in red-wine cream sauce for $5 to $7 at lunch, $13.50 to $17.50 at dinner. It's a charming setting, with seating under a green awning. The fancier Le Clos—with pale pink walls, lace-curtained French doors, and tables covered with crisp white linen—is open for dinner only Wednesday through Saturday evenings, with seatings at 6:30 7, 8, 8:45, and 9:15pm. A six-course prix-fixe meal for $65 features haute-cuisine main courses such as Barbarie duck breast with cerise sauce and Dover sole aux champignons meunière; appropriate wines with each course are included. Reservations are imperative. Men are requested to wear a coat and tie. There are also several restaurants at the adjoining Château Elan resort. And there are picnic areas on the lovely grounds; custom picnic baskets can be purchased here.

In addition to its interior attractions, Château Elan has nature trails along St. Emilion Creek (forested with tulip poplar, oak, hickory, and beech trees) and by Romanée-Conti pond. On select Saturday evenings between Memorial Day and Labor Day there's dancing to live music (oldies or country) in an adjoining outdoor facility called Le Pavillon. Admission is $20; you can order a picnic box in advance ($17.95 for two) or enjoy a themed buffet for $19.95 per person. Entertainment begins at 7:30pm, but you should arrive at least an hour earlier for dinner. In addition, there are numerous events at

Château Elan—call to find out what's on during your stay. A gorgeous 18-hole golf course, a full spa (consider a day of beauty here), and seven tennis courts are on the grounds. If all that's not enough to do, there are designer-outlet malls close by.

Admission: Free.

Open: Daily 10am–10pm. **Closed:** Christmas.

Big Shanty Museum, 2829 Cherokee St., Kennesaw. ☎ 427-2117.

On this site began the wild adventure known as "the Great Locomotive Chase." The Civil War had been under way for a year on April 12, 1862, when Union spy James J. Andrews and a group of 21 Northern soldiers disguised as civilians boarded a locomotive called the *General* in Marietta, buying tickets for diverse destinations to avert suspicion. When the train made a breakfast stop at the Lacy Hotel in Big Shanty, they seized the locomotive and several boxcars and fled northward to Chattanooga. The goal of these daring raiders was to destroy tracks, telegraph wires, and bridges behind them, thus cutting off the Confederate supply route between Virginia and Mississippi.

Conductor William A. Fuller, his breakfast interrupted by the sound of the *General* chugging out of the station, gave chase on foot, then grabbed a platform car and poled along the tracks. With him were a railroad superintendent and the *General's* engineer. At the Etowah River, Fuller and crew commandeered a small locomotive called the *Yonah* and made better progress. Meanwhile, the raiders tore up track behind them, and when the pursuers got close, the raiders slowed them down by throwing ties and firewood onto the tracks. Andrews, a very smooth talker, managed to convince station attendants en route that he was on an emergency mission running ammunition to Confederate general Beauregard in Mississippi. Fuller's chances of catching the *General* improved when he seized the southbound *Texas* and began running it backward toward the raiders, picking up reinforcements along the way and eventually managing to get a telegraph message through to General Danville Leadbetter, commander at Chattanooga. The chase went on, with Andrews sending uncoupled boxcars careening back toward Fuller as obstructions. Fuller, however, who was running in reverse, merely attached the rolling boxcars to his engine and kept on. At the wooden-covered Oostanaula Bridge, the raiders detached a boxcar and set it on fire in hopes of finally creating an impassable obstacle—a burning bridge behind them. But the *Texas* was able to push the flaming car off the bridge; it soon burned out, and Fuller tossed it off the track and continued.

By this time the *General* was running low on fuel and water, the *Texas* was hot on its heels, and the raiders realized that all was lost. Andrews gave his final command: "Jump off and scatter! Every man for himself!" All were captured and imprisoned within a few days. Some escaped, others were exchanged for Confederate prisoners of war, and the rest were hung in Atlanta, most of them at a site near Oakland Cemetery. Though the mission failed, the raiders, some of them posthumously, received the newly created Congressional Medal of Honor for their valor.

The Big Shanty Museum, occupying a building that was once the Frey cotton gin, houses the *General* (still in running condition, but don't get any ideas), exhibits of Civil War artifacts, memorabilia and photographs relating to the chase and its participants, and, for good measure, a *Gone With the Wind* exhibit. You can view a 20-minute narrated video about the chase, but if you really want the full story rent the Disney movie, *The Great Locomotive Chase,* starring Fess Parker as the dashing Andrews. To get here, take exit 118 off I-75N and follow the signs. It takes about a half hour. The museum is three miles from Kennesaw Mountain/National Battlefield Park (details below), so consider visiting both of these Civil War–related sights the same day.

Admission: $3 for adults; $2.50 for seniors, service people, and AAA members; $1.50 for children 7–15; children 6 and under free. Families pay a maximum of $12.

Open: Mar–Nov, Mon–Sat 9:30am–5:30pm; Dec–Feb, Mon–Fri 10am–4pm, Sat 10am–5:30pm, Sun noon–5:30pm.

Kennesaw Mountain/National Battlefield Park, Old Highway 41 and Stilesboro Rd., Marietta. ☎ 427-4686.

This 2,882-acre park was established in 1917 on the site of a crucial Civil War battle in the Atlanta campaign of 1864. A very popular attraction, it draws some two million visitors annually. The action began in June 1864. A few months earlier, Gen. Ulysses S. Grant had ordered Sherman to attack the Confederate army in Georgia, "break it up, and go into the interior of the enemy's country as far as you can, inflicting all the damage you can upon their war resources." In response to this order, Sherman's army, 100,000 strong, had been pushing back Confederate forces composed of 65,000 men under Gen. Joseph E. Johnston. By June 19, Union troops had driven Johnston's men back to a well-prepared defensive position on Kennesaw Mountain. Southern engineers had built a line of entrenchments in its rocky slopes allowing the Confederates to cover every approach with rifle or cannon. An Ohio officer later commented that if the mountain had been constructed for the sole purpose of repelling an invading army, "it could not have been better made or placed."

On June 27, following a few weeks of skirmishing, Sherman, underestimating the strength and still-feisty morale of the rebels, attempted to break through Confederate lines and annihilate them in a grand no-holds-barred assault from two directions. Confederate Gen. Samuel French described the onset of the attack thusly: "As if by magic, there sprang from the earth a host of men, and in one long, waving line of blue the infantry advanced and the battle of Kennesaw Mountain began."

Sherman's men were repelled by massive bursts of firepower and huge rocks rolling down the mountain at them. Federal casualties far outnumbered Confederate losses. Meanwhile, 8,000 Union infantrymen in five brigades attacked from another angle; in this battle the Union lost 3,000 men, the Confederates 500. Weeks of

Metropolitan Atlanta Sights

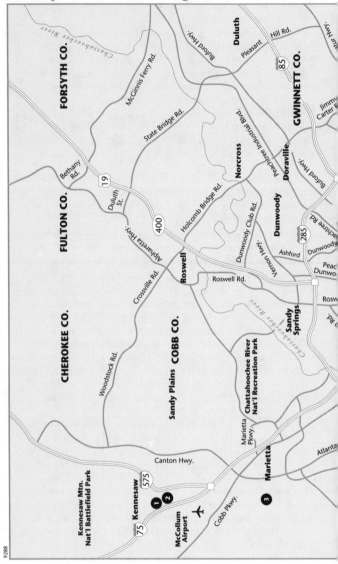

torrential rain, which had turned these battlegrounds into a muddy mire, added significantly to the misery quotient on both sides. There was no rain the day of the battle, but the day was swelteringly hot and muggy.

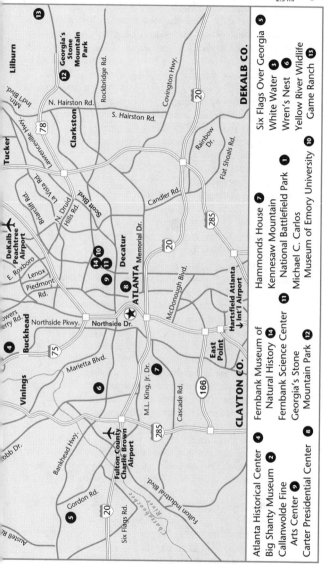

0 ┣▬▬▬▬┫ 4.0 km
        2.5 mi

Atlanta Historical Center ④	Fernbank Museum of Natural History ⑭
Big Shanty Museum ②	Fernbank Science Center ⑪
Callanwolde Fine Arts Center ⑨	Georgia's Stone Mountain Park ⑫
Carter Presidential Center ⑧	Hammonds House ⑦
	Kennesaw Mountain National Battlefield Park ①
	Michael C. Carlos Museum of Emory University ⑩
	Six Flags Over Georgia ⑤
	White Water ③
	Wren's Nest ⑥
	Yellow River Wildlife Game Ranch ⑬

Allow at least two hours for exploring. Start your tour at the **Visitor Center,** where you can pick up a map, watch a 10-minute slide show about the battle, and view exhibits of Civil War artifacts and memorabilia. You can drive weekdays (on weekends take a shuttle bus) or hike up the mountain to see the actual Confederate entrenchments and earthworks, some of them equipped with Civil War cannons and artillery. The trail is about one steep mile long, so wear comfortable shoes. Interpretive signs at key spots enhance the experience, and, weekends spring through fall, interpretive programs further elucidate the battle. You'll also want to drive to **Cheatham Hill,** site of some of the fiercest fighting. There are 16 miles of hiking trails for those who want a more extensive tour (trail maps are available at the Visitor Center), and picnicking is permitted in designated areas, some with barbecue grills. The scenery, by the way, is gorgeous, so even if Civil War battles are not your thing (that is, if you're reluctantly accompanying an enthusiastic spouse), it makes for beautiful hiking or driving.

Admission: Free.

Open: The visitor center is open daily 8:30am–5pm, till 6pm weekends June–Aug; front gate closes at 8pm Jun–Aug, 6pm the rest of the year. **Closed:** Christmas. **Directions:** I-75 north to Barrett Parkway (exit 116), then follow the signs.

High Museum Of Art, Folk Art and Photography Galleries,
30 John Wesley Dobbs Ave., at Peachtree St. NE. ☎ 577-6940.

This downtown branch of the High Museum of Art displays folk art and photography. Visitors can enter via an elegantly landscaped courtyard on John Wesley Dobbs Avenue or via the imposing lobby of the Georgia-Pacific building off Peachtree Street, itself the setting for Louise Nevelson's vast indoor environmental sculpture in white wood, *Dawn's Forest.* Spanning three levels, the 12,000-square-foot museum has beautiful walls paneled in an African wood called angré, and slate-covered pedestrian ramps affording visitors a view of the downtown skyline as they descend to the galleries.

The two levels of galleries provide approximately 5,000 square feet of exhibition space. The upper gallery has a barrel-vaulted ceiling with Plexiglas inserts allowing daylight to flood the space. And glass blocks in the slate floor permit light to filter down to the lower galleries, which evoke the galleries at the main museum. In addition to exhibits, the museum offers free films, lectures, concerts, and gallery talks (call for details). The Georgia-Pacific Building, by the way, occupies the hallowed site of the Loew's Grand Theatre, where *Gone With the Wind* premiered in 1939.

Admission: Free.

Open: Mon–Fri 10am–5pm. **MARTA:** Peachtree Center.

Atlanta History Center Downtown, 140 Peachtree St. NW, in
Margaret Mitchell Sq. ☎ 814-4150.

This downtown branch of the Atlanta History Center (see "The Top Attractions," above, for details) serves as an information station about Atlanta's (and the state of Georgia's) cultural offerings. It occupies the 3-story Hillyer Building, itself a historic site dating from 1911 and listed on the National Register of Historic Places. Upstairs, you can view any of 20 videos about Atlanta history. One called "Greetings from Atlanta,"—which traces the city's history from the days when Cherokee and Creek Indians roamed the pine forests to the present—provides a good overview. There are also changing exhibits and lectures here.

Admission: Free.

Open: Mon–Sat 10am–6pm. **Closed:** New Year's Day, Memorial Day, Labor Day, Thanksgiving, and Christmas. **MARTA:** Peachtree Center.

The Alonzo F. Herndon Home, 587 University Place, between Vine and Walnut Sts. ☎ **581-9813.**

Alonzo Herndon was born into the last decade of slavery in 1858. After emancipation, from age 13 to 20, he worked as a field hand and sharecropper, supplementing his meager income by selling peanuts, homemade molasses, and axle grease. He arrived in Atlanta in the early 1880s, where he worked as a barber and eventually owned several barbershops of his own. He acquired real estate with earnings from these shops. By 1895, with only a year of formal education and less than 40 years out of slavery, Herndon was the richest black man in Atlanta. In 1905, he began buying up insurance companies and reorganizing them. These became the nucleus of the Atlanta Life Insurance Company, today the nation's second-largest black-owned insurance company.

In 1910, Herndon built this elegant 15-room house in the beaux-arts neoclassical style with a stately colonnaded entrance. Today, visitors enter from the back. The tour begins in a receiving room with a 10-minute introductory video called *The Herndon Legacy*. Herndon and his wife, Adrienne McNeil, a drama teacher at Atlanta University, were the primary architects of the house, and construction was accomplished almost completely by black artisans. Since the home was occupied until 1977 by their son Norris, much of the original furniture remains, and there are family photographs throughout. Adrienne died about a week after the house was completed. Two years later, Herndon married Jessie Gillespie, who later became the vice president of Atlanta Life.

The tour takes you through the reception hall, where the butler greeted visitors; the music room with rococo gilt-trim walls and Louis XV–style furnishings; the living room, with a frieze on its walls depicting the accomplishments of Herndon's life; the dining room, furnished in late Renaissance style with family china and Venetian glass displayed in a mahogany cabinet; the butler's pantry; and the sunny breakfast room. Upstairs, you'll see Jessie Herndon's bedroom, with its Jacobean suite and Louis XV–style furnishings; Herndon's Empire-furnished bedroom, where a book from a Republican National Convention displayed on a table lets you know his political bent; the collection room (Norris collected ancient Greek and Roman vases and funerary objects); Norris's bedroom; a Victorian sitting room; and a guest bedroom.

Admission: Free (donations appreciated).

Open: Tue–Sat 10am–4pm, with tours on the hour. **Closed:** Mon, New Year's Day, July 4, Thanksgiving, and Christmas. **MARTA:** Vine City.

Atlanta College of Art Gallery, in the Memorial Arts Building of the Woodruff Arts Center, 1280 Peachtree St. NE. ☎ **898-1157.**

The Atlanta College of Art, housed in the Woodruff Arts Center complex, features an ongoing series of gallery shows. Some recent examples: "Subject Male Violence" (an installation of 80 study tables by Richard Bolton), "Make Yourself At Home: Race and Ethnicity in the American Family"; and "A Family Affair: Sexuality in the American Family." There are also faculty exhibitions, juried student shows, lectures, and concerts here. Call for details.

Admission: Free.

Open: Mon–Sat 10am–5pm; fall–spring Sun 2–6pm as well.
MARTA: Arts Center.

Atlanta Museum, 537 Peachtree St., between Renaissance Pkwy. and Linden Ave. ☎ **872-8233.**

If, like me, you love to come upon musty collections of curiosities, this will be a thrill. Antique dealer James Elliott, Sr., started his mini-Smithsonian in 1936; today, his son, James Elliott, Jr., is in charge of its 2,500 or so diverse exhibits. They're displayed in a 1900 Historic Register Victorian home that once belonged to the Rose family, founders of Four Roses liquor (when Georgia went dry in 1907, they moved to Tennessee). Mr. Elliott runs a cluttery antique shop on the first floor. The museum is upstairs.

Exhibits include: the throne of Haile Selassie, paw signatures of movie dogs, Franklin D. Roosevelt's fishing hat, personal articles (a coat, raincoat, camp mirror, tablecloth, and cigar box) that belonged to Adolf Hitler, a carved stone from King Tut's tomb, a lock of Napoleon's hair and a pair of chairs from his throne room (the latter were given to Admiral Dewey while on a goodwill tour of France), a World War II Japanese field telephone, a vase with an Egyptian curse, the desk on which the Georgia secession was written, General Custer's hairbrush, Davy Crockett's gun, furnishings and books that belonged to Margaret Mitchell, an original model of the cotton gin from Eli Whitney's shop, spoons made by Paul Revere, and a piece of root from the apple tree under which Robert E. Lee stood when he surrendered at Appomattox. Another collector of curiosities, Michael Jackson, once came in and tried to buy a thing or two, but Elliott wouldn't part with his treasures.

Admission: $3 for adults, $2 for children under 12 and seniors.

Open: Mon–Fri 10am–5pm, (hours may vary, call ahead).
MARTA: North Avenue or Civic Center. **Parking:** On the side and rear of the building.

Hammonds House, 503 Peeples St., at Lucille St. ☎ **752-8730.**

Occupying the 1857 Eastlake Victorian-style former home of Dr. Otis T. Hammonds, a black anesthesiologist and art patron, Hammonds House is a national center for the exhibition, preservation, research, and documentation of African American art and artists. The house was purchased with these aims in mind by the Fulton County Commission after Hammonds's death in 1985. Hammonds's extensive collection included works by African American and

Haitian artists, as well as African masks and carvings. On permanent display are paintings and prints by Romare Bearden and an exhibit of contemporary Haitian art. The facility also presents changing exhibits, including works from the permanent collection and shows of local and national artists.

Admission: $2 for adults, $1 for seniors and students.

Open: Tues–Fri 10am–6pm, Sat–Sun 1–5pm. **MARTA:** West End (4½ blocks away).

Callanwolde Fine Arts Center, 980 Briarcliff Rd. NE, north of Ponce de Leon Ave. ☎ 872-5338.

A magnificent Gothic/Tudor–style mansion, built for Coca-Cola heir Asa Candler in 1920, Callanwolde today serves as a fine-arts center for DeKalb County. Classes are given in pottery, painting, photography, drawing, and more, and there are numerous workshops for adults and children. Though it's a lovely setting for art students, I can't help wishing that some preservation committee had instead restored the house to its former grandeur and re-created its furnishings and appointments. As it is, most of the rooms are bare, and only Callanwolde's exquisite walnut paneling, beautifully carved ceilings and moldings, grand staircase, magnificent marble and stone fireplaces, and leaded-glass windows evoke its luxurious past.

The estate occupies 12 acres (originally 27) in the Druid Hills section of Atlanta, an area planned by Frederick Law Olmsted, designer of New York's Central Park. Its name derives from the Candler family's ancestral home, Callan Castle, in Ireland. *Callan* is the Irish name for Candler, and *wold* is an old English word for wood or forest. Visitors are welcome to peruse shows of local artists in the Petite Hall gallery upstairs; enjoy the lawns, formal gardens, and nature trails, which are maintained by the county; and participate in the many events here—concerts, storytelling festivals, dance performances (see the "Calendar of Events" in Chapter 2). Attending a function here is the best way to experience the estate.

Admission: Free. Guided tours, by special appointment only, cost $1.50 for adults, 50¢ for children under 12. If you're interested in a tour, call to arrange it as far in advance as possible.

Open: Mon–Fri 10am–9pm, Sat 10am–3pm.

Rhodes Memorial Hall, 1516 Peachtree St. NW, at Peachtree Circle. ☎ 881-9980.

Rhodes Hall is one of a few remaining pre–World War I Peachtree Street mansions. It was designed by Willis Franklin Denny (at the time Atlanta's leading residential architect) in 1903 as a residence for affluent Atlanta businessman Amos Giles Rhodes and his family. Its medieval baronial-cum-high Victorian Romanesque style was inspired by Rhineland castles. The granite exterior is replete with arched Romanesque windows, battlements and buttresses, parapets, towers, and turrets. A large Syrian-arched veranda wraps the east and north facades. And the interior is grandiose, with maple-bordered oak floors laid in herringbone pattern, mosaics surrounding the fireplaces, and a gracefully winding hand-carved Honduran mahogany staircase with nine stained-glass stairwell panels depicting "The Rise and Fall of the Confederacy." The house and stables originally occupied 150 acres of land and included servants' quarters, a carriage house, and other outbuildings. At the turn of the century, this site was in suburbia, an afternoon's drive from downtown.

Upon Rhodes's death in 1928, his residence was deeded to the state of Georgia in keeping with his desire to preserve it. The house was entered on the National Register of Historic Places in 1974. Today it is headquarters for the Georgia Trust for Historic Preservation and is in an ongoing process of restoration. To date, the original dining-room suite and some other furnishings are in place, and all the mahogany woodwork and decorated ceilings on the first floor have been restored. Original landscaping—with white and red cedars, dogwoods, banana trees, and a circular flower bed—is being re-created in the front yard.

Admission: $2 for adults, $1 for seniors and students, 50¢ for children under 12.

Open: Mon–Fri 11am–4pm. Tours are given on a continuous basis throughout the day. **MARTA:** Arts Center.

The Margaret Mitchell House, Peachtree and 10th Sts.
☎ 870-2360.

In Atlanta, *Gone With the Wind* comes up daily, and Margaret Mitchell is an almost-hallowed name. So it's rather surprising that only at this late date has restoration begun on the dilapidated turn-of-the-century Tudor-revival Peachtree Street apartment house where Mitchell lived with her husband, John Marsh, from 1925 to 1932 (they called it "The Dump") and wrote most of her epic novel. They even held their wedding reception there. Preservationists are currently raising money for the restoration, scheduled for completion in time for the 1996 Olympics. Since everyone comes to Atlanta seeking *GWTW*-related attractions, and few exist (the white-colonnaded mansion at 1401 Peachtree Street, where Mitchell grew up, was razed in 1952), it is estimated that the restored home will draw millions of visitors annually. Plans call for a re-creation of Mitchell's apartment and utilization of the rest of the building for a museum. At this writing, the project is in the earliest stages and not open to the public, but I include it for those who'd like to pass by and view the shrine.

Parks

Piedmont Park, Piedmont Ave. at 14th St. (main entrance).

Piedmont Park, the city's most popular and centrally located recreation area, was created at the turn of the century for the Cotton States Exposition. Its designer was Frederick Law Olmsted, America's most noted landscapist. "The beauty of a park," said Olmsted, "should be the beauty of fields, the meadow, the prairie, of green pastures, and still waters. What we want to gain is tranquility and rest of the mind." To this end, he transformed a woodsy meadow into a 180-acre parkland with a varied terrain of rolling hillsides, verdant lawns, and lush forest around beautiful Lake Clara Meer.

The park is the setting for many popular regional events, jazz and symphony concerts, art and music festivals, marathons, and more. It contains a large baseball field, tennis courts, a large public swimming pool, and paths for jogging, skating, and cycling. And the magnificent Atlanta Botanical Garden (see "The Top Attractions," above) is adjacent.

Admission: Free.

Open: Daily 6am–11pm. **MARTA:** Midtown or Arts Center.

Grant Park, bordered by Sydney St. and Atlanta Ave., Boulevard and Cherokee Ave.

Named for Confederate captain Lemuel P. Grant, who helped build Atlanta's defense line, Grant Park still contains vestiges of his fortifications. Grant also donated its 100 acres to the city for a park on this site. Near the intersection of Boulevard and Atlanta Avenue, you can see the remaining earthwork slopes of Fort Walker, a commanding artillery bastion with its original gun emplacements. Its cannons and caissons can be seen in the museum area of Cyclorama (see "The Top Attractions," above), one of Grant Park's two major attractions. The other is Zoo Atlanta (see "Cool for Kids," below).

Admission: Free.

Open: Daily 6am–11pm.

3 Cool for Kids

Though the following attractions are great choices if you're traveling with kids, don't pass them up if you're not. I especially love Wren's Nest, the Center for Puppetry Arts, the Yellow River Wildlife Game Ranch (visit in conjunction with Stone Mountain), and Zoo Atlanta (visit in conjunction with Cyclorama and Oakland Cemetery). In addition, be sure to take the kids to the Fernbank Museum of Natural History and the Martin Luther King, Jr. birth home and Center for Nonviolent Social Change (all described above).

★ **Zoo Atlanta,** 800 Cherokee Ave., in Grant Park. ☎ **624-5600**

This absolutely delightful 40-acre zoo dates from 1889, when George W. Hall (aka "Popcorn George") brought his traveling circus to town. Employee claims against Hall for back wages forced him to relinquish his menagerie, and the animal entourage was purchased by a prominent Atlanta businessman who donated the collection to the city as the basis for a zoological garden in Grant Park. It's grown considerably since then, but the real turnaround came in 1985, when the zoo began a still-ongoing multimillion-dollar renovation.

Today, Zoo Atlanta is a very exciting and creatively run facility, with animals housed in large open enclosures which simulate their natural geographical habitats. The zoo participates in breeding programs, many of them centering on endangered species. Signs, some translated into Swahili, use a cartoon format to inform visitors about environmental and conservational issues pertinent to wildlife. All areas are beautifully landscaped and adorned with animal sculptures. There are video displays in the Elephant Barn, Tiger Forest, and Gorilla museum, and safari carts throughout the zoo serve as educational stations. Do plan to catch entertaining and informative free animal shows in the Kroger Wildlife Theater, presented daily at 11:30am and 1:30 and 3:30pm May through September. Ditto the African Elephant Demonstration given daily year round at 11am, 1, and 3pm.

Flamingo Plaza is the first habitat you'll see upon entering the zoo. Farther on, **Masai Mara** houses elephants, rhinos, lions, zebras, giraffes, gazelles, and other African animals and birds. Its landscape resembles the plains of East Africa, with honey locust trees and yuccas; and the lion enclosure replicates an East African kopje (rocky outcropping). A café called the **Swahili Market** overlooks the zebras. Frequent animal demonstrations, African storytelling, and educational programs take place under the Elder's Tree in Masai Mara.

The lushly landscaped **Ford African Rain Forest** centers on four vast gorilla habitats separated by moats. Studies on gorilla behavior take place here, and there are often quite a few adorable babies. A gorilla named Willie B. is the zoo's mascot. Also in the section: a walk-through aviary of West African birds; small African primates (including drills—an endangered species—and Mona monkeys); and the Gorillas of Cameroon museum. Landscaping includes burned-out areas of forest and deadfall trees—gorillas do not live in manicured gardens.

Sumatran tigers (a very endangered species) and orangutans live in the **Ketambe** section, an Indonesian tropical rain forest with clusters of bamboo and a waterfall. Ketambe also includes a Reptile House and a special exhibit area, often used to house visiting animals.

A zoo train travels through the **Children's Zoo** area, a peaceful enclave where kids can pet baby llamas, sheep, pigs, and goats. There are aviaries here, too. In the works are **Okefenokee Swamp** and **Coastal Georgia** exhibits. There are shops and snack bars throughout the zoo and tree-shaded picnic areas in Grant Park.

Admission: $7.50 for adults, $6.50 for seniors, $5 for children 3–11, children 2 and under free. Strollers can be rented.

Open: Daily 10am–5:30pm, till 6:30pm during Daylight Savings Time. The admission booth closes an hour before zoo closing. **Closed:** New Year's Day, Martin Luther King Day, Thanksgiving, Christmas. **Directions:** By car, take I-75 south to I-20 east. Get off at the Boulevard exit and follow the signs to Grant Park. Or take a No. 31, 32, or 97 bus from the Five Points rail station.

★ **Wren's Nest,** 1050 Ralph Abernathy Blvd., two blocks from Ashby St. ☎ **753-7735.**

Named for a family of wrens that once nested in the mailbox, Wren's Nest is the former home of Joel Chandler Harris, who chronicled the wily deeds of Br'er Rabbit and Br'er Fox. It's been open to the public since 1913, when his widow sold it to the Uncle Remus Memorial Association. Harris's literary career began at the age of 13, when he apprenticed on *The Countryman,* a quarterly plantation newspaper. In four years spent learning journalism there, young

Harris spent many an evening hanging about the slave quarters, drinking in African folk tales and fables spun by George Terrell, a plantation patriarch who became the prototype for Uncle Remus. Sherman's army put *The Countryman* out of business, and Harris went on to other newspapers, working his way up to editorial writer at the *Atlanta Constitution* by age 28. There, plagued by writer's block one gloomy winter afternoon, he remembered the plantation stories of his youth and evoked Uncle Remus to fill his column. Enthralled readers clamored for more, and the rest is history.

The house itself is an 1870s farmhouse with a Queen Anne Victorian facade added in 1884. Harris lived here from 1881 until his death in 1908, doing most of his writing in a rocking chair on the wraparound front porch. On a 30-minute tour, including a slide presentation about Harris's life, you'll see much Uncle Remus memorabilia, including a carved wooden humidor depicting Br'er Fox arresting Br'er Rabbit for stealing beets, a gift from the town of Carlsbad, Austria. The stuffed great horned owl over the study door was a gift from Theodore Roosevelt, whose White House Harris visited. The original wren's nest mailbox reposes on the study mantel, and all of Harris's books, along with signed first editions of major authors of his day (Mark Twain and others) are displayed in a bookcase.

The house is restored to its 1900 appearance, and an interpretation center is in the works. Call ahead to find out when storyteller-in-residence Akbar Imhotep will be telling stories culled from African and African-American folklore; it's a real treat. Mid-June through mid-August, Akbar and storytellers perform daily at 11:30am and 12:30 and 1:30pm.

Joel Chandler Harris died at the age of 62 on July 3, 1908. He penned these words, which later appeared on his gravestone:

> I seem to see before me the smiling faces of thousands of children—some young and fresh—and some wearing the friendly marks of age, but all children at heart, and not an unfriendly face among them. And while I am trying hard to speak the right word, I seem to hear a voice lifted above the rest saying, "You have made some of us happy." And so I feel my heart fluttering and my lips trembling and I have to bow silently and turn away and hurry into the obscurity that fits me best.

Admission: $4 for adults, $3 for seniors and students 13–19, $2 for children 4–12, under 4 free; storytelling $1 per person additional.

Open: Tues–Sat 10am–4pm, Sun 1–4pm, with tours departing every 30 minutes on the hour and half hour. **Closed:** Mon, Jan 1, July 4, Thanksgiving, Dec 24 and 25. **Directions:** MARTA: West End (3 long blocks away); by car, Take I-20 to Ashby St., turn left on Ashby, right on Ralph Abernathy Blvd.; Wren's Nest is 2 blocks down on the left.

★ **Center for Puppetry Arts,** 1404 Spring St. NW, at 18th St. ☎ **873-3089,** box office **873-3391.**

If you're traveling with the kids, this is in the not-to-be-missed category. In fact, I wouldn't miss it even without kids in tow. The center is dedicated to expanding public awareness of puppetry as a fine art and to presenting all its international and historic forms. Opened in 1978, with Kermit the Frog cutting the official ribbon (he had a little help from the late Jim Henson), it contains a 300-seat theater, a 90-seat black-box theater, two smaller theaters, gallery space, and a permanent museum. The puppet shows are marvelous—sophisticated, riveting, full-stage productions with elaborate scenery. Some are family oriented (such as a production with puppet dinosaurs or *Beauty and The Beast*); others, with nighttime showings, are geared to adults. Call ahead to find out what's on; reservations are essential. You can also call a week or so in advance to enroll yourself or your kids in a puppet-making workshop here.

The museum area displays puppets ranging from ritualistic African figures to Punch and Judy. It's an excellent collection, one of the largest in North America, including turn-of-the-century Thai shadow puppets, Indonesian wayang golek puppets used to tell classic stories (a centuries-old tradition), Chinese hand puppets, rod-operated marionettes from all over Europe, original Muppets, a German puppet made of scarves, pre-Columbian clay puppets that were used in religious ceremonies circa A.D. 1200, Turkish shadow figures made of dried animal skins, and a Nigerian Yoruba puppet, among many, many others. The permanent collection is augmented by short-term exhibits such as a Bill Baird retrospective (he created the puppets used in *The Sound of Music*).

Admission: $3 for adults, $2 for children 14 and under; free if you see a show or take a workshop. Show prices vary; call ahead for details.

Open: Mon–Sat 9am–4pm. **Closed:** New Year's Day, Memorial Day, July 4, Labor Day, Thanksgiving, and Christmas. **MARTA:** Arts Center.

★ **Yellow River Wildlife Game Ranch,** 4525 Hwy. 78, Lilburn. ☎ **972-6643.**

This 24-acre animal preserve bordering the Yellow River is one of the most special places I've ever visited. Owner Art Rilling has created an environment that offers close encounters of the four-legged kind—a chance to view, pet, feed, and generally mingle with some 600 animals (always including quite a few babies) living in open enclosures, or right out in the open, along a one-mile oak- and hickory-shaded forest trail. Art knows every animal on the ranch by name and can give you chapter and verse on the personality, preferences, and in some cases, even romantic history of them. You'll feel like you're in a Disney movie when the deer (there are over 100 whitetail deer) sidle up and nuzzle you. The animals know they're among friends here and are highly socialized, so you have a unique chance to study them up close. Inhabitants include donkeys named

Rhett and Scarlett, the goats at Billy Goat Gruff Memorial Bridge (they climb it to get food at the top), dozens of rabbits in Bunny Burrows (kids can walk right into this enclosure and pet the bunnies), a wide assortment of interesting-looking chickens, a herd of buffalo, a crow, a skunk named General Sherman (we are in Atlanta, after all), and a groundhog named General Beauregard Lee who lives in a white colonnaded southern mansion complete with miniature satellite dish. You can get animal food in the gift shop at the entrance or buy it along the trail.

Bring your camera (or sketchbook), wear comfortable shoes, and do consider packing a picnic lunch; there are tables throughout the property, and one especially nice picnic area overlooks the river. An exciting time to visit is Sheep Shearing Saturday in mid-May.

Admission: $4.50 for adults, $3.50 for children 3–11, one child under 3 admitted free.

Open: Memorial Day–Labor Day daily 9:30am–dusk; till 6pm the rest of the year.

SciTrek (Science and Technology Museum of Atlanta),

395 Piedmont Ave., between Ralph McGill Blvd. and Pine St.
☎ 522-5500.

Opened in 1988, this museum offers hands-on adventures for adults and kids in science and technology. There are over 100 interactive exhibits, divided into categories.

In Electricity and Magnetism you can create a magnetic field to hurl a disc upward, change light into electricity, produce electric current using your own hand as a "battery," see how much electricity you can generate pedaling a bicycle (how many bulbs can you light up?), and test various metals for electrical conductivity.

In Light and Perception, a kinetic light sculpture lets you vary frequency, intensity, and revolutions to create an infinite variety of designs. You can also examine the range of your peripheral vision here, step inside a kaleidoscope, watch yourself on video while walking through a distorted room (demonstrating how the brain visually perceives things based on past experience), mix over 16 million colors (time permitting) on a computer, bend light beams, and look into infinity. This section houses my favorite exhibit, the frozen shadow room, in which you can "freeze" your shadow on a wall of light-sensitive phosphorous vinyl film; a bright flash causes the panel to glow except in the area your body shields from the light. It's lots of fun dancing and jumping to create shadow art on the wall.

Kidspace has simple exhibits geared to the 2- to 7-year-old set. Here the kids can paint their faces in a mirror, explore a crystal cave, blow enormous bubbles, squirt water to float toys downstream, play electronic instruments, make images on heat-sensitive liquid crystal with their hands, and use furnished play environments including an office, puppet theater, and a TV news/weather station. There are also very easy computer games.

Pulleys, levers, wheels, axles, and suchlike are explored in Mechanics. You can lift billiard balls with a screw auger, become a human gyroscope, and suspend a ball in the air using a Bernouilli blower (don't ask me to explain what that is; I'm low tech).

In Mathematica, a history wall portrays the achievements of major mathematicians from the 12th century to the present. Other hands-on displays here demonstrate various aspects of mathematics from the laws of planetary motion to probability theory. And Power Your Future provides a glimpse at technical innovations that will shape future electrical energy use.

Exhibits are supplemented by an ongoing series of lectures, demonstrations, workshops, and temporary shows. Phase II of SciTrek, now in the works, will highlight technology with many new permanent exhibits. An IMAX theater is also planned.

Admission: $7 for adults, $5.50 for seniors, students; and children 3-17, free for children under 3. There's parking at $4 per car.

Open: Tues–Sat 10am–5pm, Sun noon–5pm, with later hours on occasional selected evenings. Also open Mon 10am–5pm Memorial Day to Labor Day. **Closed:** Monday (except in summer), Thanksgiving, Christmas, Easter, New Year's Day. **MARTA:** Civic Center.

Fernbank Science Center, 156 Heaton Park Dr. NE, at Artwood Rd. (off Ponce de Leon Ave.). ☎ **378-4311.**

Owned and funded by the DeKalb County School System, this museum/planetarium/observatory, located adjacent to the verdant 65-acre Fernbank Forest, is part of the Fernbank Museum of Natural History (details above in "The Top Attractions"). Plan to visit the entire complex the same day. There's a 1^1/2-mile forest trail here, with trees (oaks, pines, magnolias, dogwoods, sweet gums, red maples, tulip poplars), shrubs, ferns, wildflowers, mosses, and other plants marked for identification. This unspoiled natural environment is home to many animals and birds, and a small pond teems with aquatic life.

The indoor facility houses museum exhibits such as: a video display on geological phenomena (volcanoes, earthquakes, mountain formation); a gem collection; development of life in Georgia from 500 million years ago to a million years ago; a complete weather station; fossil trees; the original *Apollo 6* space capsule and space suit (on loan from the Smithsonian); computer games; a replica of the Okefenokee Swamp, complete with sound effects; and replicas of dinosaurs that roamed Atlanta in prehistoric times. There are planetarium shows, and, at the Observatory, which contains the largest telescope in the world dedicated to public education, an astronomer gives a talk and lets visitors use the telescope.

If you're here on a Sunday, allow time to visit the nearby greenhouse, about 2^1/2 miles from the Center. A horticulturist gives a talk to visitors, and children can pot a plant and take it home. There are many workshops, lectures, tours, and films for adults and children on subjects ranging from nature photography to weather forecasting.

Admission: Free. Planetarium shows are $2 for adults, $1 for students, free for senior citizens. **Note:** Children under 5 are not admitted to the planetarium.

Open: Mon 8:30am–5pm, Tues–Fri 8:30am–10pm, Sat 10am–5pm, Sun 1–5pm. Planetarium shows at 8pm Tues–Fri and 3pm Wed and Fri–Sun. The Observatory is open Thurs–Fri 8:30 (or whenever it gets dark)–10pm, weather permitting. Forest trails are open Sun–Fri 2–5pm, Sat 10am–5pm, The Greenhouse is open Sun only 1–5pm. **Closed:** All school holidays.

Six Flags Over Georgia, the Six Flags exit off I-20 W.
☎ 948-9290.

One of the state's major family attractions, Six Flags offers a great day's entertainment. Arrive early (at least 15 minutes before opening), note where you've parked in the vast lot, and take 10 minutes or so to plan out your show schedule.

The park's eight themed areas reflect the historical heritage of the region, both southern (Cotton States, Confederate, Georgia, and Lickskillet) and European (France, Britain, Spain, and U.S.A). The Spanish section contains Bugs Bunny World which is especially geared to young children. The "wascally wabbit" is just one of the costumed Looney Tune characters (Sylvester, Porky Pig, Daffy Duck and others) that roam the park greeting kids.

Thrill rides include several wet ones such as Ragin' Rivers (two-person inflatable boats that careen down contoured water channels), a log flume, and Thunder River (a simulated whitewater rafting adventure). White-knuckler coasters include Ninja (the "black belt" of roller coasters that turns riders upside down five times and offers thrilling loops, dives, and corkscrew turns), the Georgia Cyclone (a classic wooden roller coaster with 11 dramatic drops, patterned after Coney Island's), the Great American Scream Machine (another classic wooden coaster), and Mind Bender, a triple-looper. Other highlights are the Great Gasp (a 20-story parachute jump), Splashwater Falls (plummet down a soaring 50-foot waterfall), and Free Fall (ever wonder what it would be like to fall off a 10-story building). A less dizzying adventure is Monster Plantation, a Disneyesque boat ride through an antebellum mansion haunted by over 100 animated monsters. There's much, much more.

Shows vary from year to year, but they usually include a major musical revue, a country music show, a water show, a golden-oldies show, thrill cinema adventures on a 180-degree screen, a magic show, a Don Rickles–style comic (much modified, of course) in the form of a sharp-tongued bird named Buford Buzzard, and an animated character show. In addition, headline performers such as the B-52's, Pam Tillis, Reba McEntire, and the Steve Miller Band play the 8,072-seat (with lawn seating for 4,000) Southern Star Amphitheatre.

There are restaurants and snack bars throughout the park, though you might consider bringing a picnic. Gift shops also abound.

Admission: $28 for adults, $19 for children ages 3–9, $14 for seniors (55 and over), under 3 free. Amphitheatre concerts are free with park admission.

Open: Weekends only Mar–mid-May, Sept, and Oct; daily Memorial Day–Labor Day. Gates open 10am daily; closing hours vary. **Parking:** $5.

White Water, Exit 113 off I-75 on North Cobb Pkwy., Marietta. ☎ **424-WAVE.**

Forty acres of wet, splashy fun await you at White Water, the largest water-theme park in the south. Its star attraction is the $1 million Tree House Island, a 4-story fantasy treehouse with over 100 different activities—curvy slides, net bridges, water cannons, chutes, etc. A giant 1,000-gallon bucket of water empties over the whole attraction every few minutes! Other park highlights include: Black River Falls, with two enclosed 400-foot flumes creating a twisting "river of darkness" enhanced by strobe lights; the "Atlanta Ocean," a 710,000-gallon pool generating continuous waves; 4-foot Bahama Bob-Slide, a group tube ride down a chute the length of two football fields; Caribbean Plunge, a 100-foot free-fall water flume drop; and Dragon's Tail Falls, which sends riders plummeting down a 250-foot triple drop at speeds up to 30 miles per hour. There's much more, including a special section for children 48 inches and under called Little Squirt's Island, offering 25 tot-size water attractions. Captain Kid's Cove, adjacent to it, has dozens of additional activities for kids 12 and under. Restaurants and snack bars are on the premises, as are rental lockers and shower facilities. Swimsuits are essential. Over 300 lifeguards and ride attendants are on staff.

Adjacent to White Water is **American Adventures** (☎ **424-9283**), an $8.5 million, indoor/outdoor family amusement park featuring 15 children's rides in Fun Forest (bumper cars, a small roller coaster, a tilt-a-whirl, and others); a classic carousel; a penny arcade with over 130 games; Professor Plinker's Laboratory—a large children's play area with ball crawls and nets to climb; 18-hole miniature golf; and Imagination Station—a creative play area with arts and crafts, costumes, children's shows, and games. It's all geared to children 12 and under. A 180-seat family-style restaurant is on the grounds. Admission to American Adventures is free (you pay per ride; a pass for unlimited rides is $12.99 for children 18 and under, $4.99 for adults; adults ride free with toddlers). The park is open 365 days a year (hours vary seasonally).

Admission: (to White Water): $17.99 for adults, $10.99 for children from age 3 and up to 48 inches tall; children under 3 and senior citizens free.

Open: Weekends only in May, daily Memorial Day–late summer and Labor Day weekend from 10am to late evening (closing hours vary). **Closed:** Sep–Apr.

4   **Organized Tours**

Sightseeing Buses

Gray Line of Atlanta, ☎ 767-0594.

This company offers several comprehensive tours aboard comfortable sightseeing buses. Departures are from the Hyatt Regency Downtown. Since departure times and prices are subject to change, call before you go.

All Around Atlanta is a 3¹/₂-hour excursion that takes in Peachtree Street, Peachtree Center (you'll see the city's notable downtown architecture), the capitol, Georgia Tech, Coca-Cola headquarters, the Governor's Mansion, the Martin Luther King, Jr., Historic District (his birthplace, tomb, church, and the King Center), the Woodruff Arts Center, Swan House, and Cyclorama. It's a great introduction to the city. Adults pay $15, children 6 to 11 pay $10, under 6 free. Departures are daily at 1pm.

The **Atlanta Grand Circle,** a 7¹/₂-hour tour, includes all of the above plus the city's grand homes, history-rich Five Points, the CNN complex, Underground Atlanta, and Georgia's Stone Mountain. Adults pay $25, children $18. Departures are daily at 8:30am.

The **Black Heritage Tour,** a 3¹/₂-hour trip, concentrates on the Sweet Auburn district, where Dr. Martin Luther King, Jr., spent his boyhood years. In addition, you'll visit the Herndon mansion and the world's largest predominantly black center for higher education—the Atlanta University complex. Adults pay $15, children $10. Departures are on Saturdays only, June–Labor Day, at 1pm.

Guided Walking Tours

The Atlanta Preservation Center, 156 7th St. NE, Suite 3. ☎ 876-2040.

This private, nonprofit organization is dedicated to "the preservation of Atlanta's architecturally, historically, and culturally significant buildings and neighborhoods," and offers 10 1¹/₂- to 2-hour guided walking tours in the city. Cost of each tour is $5 for adults, $4 for seniors, $3 for students, free for children under 5. Tours of the Fox Theatre District are given year round; the remaining tours are offered February through November only. Call for days and hours.

The **Fox Theatre District Tour** is a must. You'll explore in depth this restored 1920s Moorish movie palace, a theater whose auditorium resembles the courtyard of a Cairo mosque and whose architecture and interior were influenced by the discoveries at King Tut's tomb. The tour also includes turn-of-the-century buildings in the area.

The **Historic Downtown Tour** is an architectural survey of Atlanta's downtown edifices from Victorian buildings to modern high rises. You'll learn about the architects, the businessmen, and the prominent families who created the city's early commercial center.

The **Inman Park Tour** visits Atlanta's first garden suburb, where you'll see preserved and restored Victorian mansions. Highlights include the homes of Coca-Cola magnates Asa Candler and Ernest Woodruff and the interior of the Inman Park Methodist Church.

The **Underground Atlanta Tour** explores the city's historic hub—today a flourishing complex of shops, restaurants, and nightclubs.

The **Sweet Auburn Tour** focuses on the area black 20th-century entrepreneurs developed into a prosperous commercial hub. You'll also visit Martin Luther King's boyhood home and the church where he preached.

Walking Miss Daisy's Druid Hills explores the neighborhood that was the setting for the play and film *Driving Miss Daisy*. The gracious parklike area was laid out by noted landscapist Frederick Law Olmsted and contains many architecturally important homes.

West End, Hammonds House, and Wren's Nest Tour focuses on the home of Joel Chandler Harris (author of the Uncle Remus stories) and Hammonds House (a museum; details above), while also noting Victorian homes and churches in the West End area.

The **Ansley Park Tour** explores one of Atlanta's first garden suburbs (today a charming midtown neighborhood), partly designed by Frederick Law Olmsted. Its broad lawns, majestic trees, parks, and beautiful houses make for a lovely tour.

The **Piedmont Park Tour** focuses on the history of this Frederick Law Olmsted–designed park (it's like a mini-version of New York's Central Park). In previous incarnations, it was a farm, a Civil War encampment, a driving club, and the grounds for the 1895 Cotton States and International Exposition.

Finally, the **Vine City Tour** examines the cultural heritage of Atlanta's African-American community, visiting Paschal's Motor Lodge (birthplace of many civil rights strategies), Morris Brown College, the Herndon Home (built by a former slave), and Friendship Baptist Church.

5   Sports & Recreation

Spectator sports are a favorite pastime in Atlanta. This is, after all, the town where Hank Aaron (Atlanta Braves) made his record-breaking 715th home run, breaking Babe Ruth's record. Take a break from museum going and catch a Falcons, Braves, or Georgia Tech game. Or get out on a playing field, tennis court, or golf course yourself.

Spectator Sports

In addition to the suggestions listed below, check the papers to see what's on during your stay.

Georgia Dome, 1 Georgia Dome Dr., at International Blvd. and Northside Dr. ☎ **223-9200** for information, **249-6400** (Ticketmaster) or **223-8427** (the Dome box office) for charge tickets. Atlanta's $214 million, 71,500-seat domed megastadium, built to accommodate Super Bowl XXVIII in 1994 and Olympic events in 1996, is also the home of the Atlanta Falcons (NFL), who play 10 to 12 games here each year. A Falcons exhibition game in August 1992 was the dome's very first event. The facility combines with the adjacent 2-million-square-foot Georgia World Congress Center to form the world's largest entertainment complex. Its oval shape provides a close view of stadium action from every seat. It is also the site for the annual Peach Bowl, while other targeted events include the NCAA Final Four in 2002, the NBA All-Star Game, and the ACC Basketball Championship. The dome additionally hosts tennis matches, tractor pulls, college basketball, track and field events, Supercross events, and the SEC Championship Football game every December. Check the papers or call the above number to find out what's on during your stay.

Forty-five minute **tours of the Georgia Dome** (including the visitors locker and dressing rooms, press box, executive suites, sports lounge, and other areas of interest) are offered on the hour Tuesday to Saturday between 10am and 4pm, Sunday between noon and 4pm. Call **223-TOUR** for reservations and details. Adults pay $4, seniors and children 5–12 pay $2.50, under 5 free.

Prices: Vary with events. Tickets to Falcon games are $27, Peach Bowl tickets are in the $35 range.

Open: Year round. **MARTA:** Omni/Georgia Dome.

Omni Coliseum, 100 Techwood Dr. NW. at Marietta St.
☎ **681-2100.**

The 17,000-seat oval-shaped Omni Coliseum is home to the Atlanta Hawks (NBA), who play 41 games here during their fall-to-spring season, plus preseason and, with luck, playoff games. Call **827-3800** for information. Also fall through spring, the Atlanta Knights hockey team (IHL) plays 41 games here. In September, the Omni hosts NHL exhibition games. And WCW professional wrestling takes place year round here. At other times, the Omni is used for varied sporting and entertainment events, including Harlem Globetrotter games, college basketball, and tennis exhibitions. Call or check the papers to find out what's on during your stay.

Prices: Vary with events. Tickets to Hawks games are mostly in the $10–$35 range, Knights games $8–$16. For all events here, tickets are usually available through Ticketmaster (☎ **249-6400**).

Open: Year round. **Marta:** Omni.

Atlanta-Fulton County Stadium, 521 Capitol Ave. SW, between Fulton St. and Ralph David Abernathy Blvd. ☎ **522-7630** for information, **249-6400** to charge tickets.

The circular open-air Atlanta-Fulton County Stadium, built in 1965, has 52,710 seats. The Atlanta Braves (NL) play 81 games here during baseball season, plus exhibition games and, hopefully, playoffs. The 85,000-seat Olympic Stadium is being constructed across the street at this writing. After the 1996 Games, it will become the new home of the Atlanta Braves.

Prices: Baseball tickets are $5–$20. Parking is $7.

Open: Baseball season is Apr–early Oct. **MARTA:** Shuttle-bus service (fare is 85¢) operates between the stadium and downtown Atlanta (Five Points Station), starting 2¹/₂ hours before game time; call **848-4711** for shuttle-bus information.

Bobby Dodd Stadium/Grant Field, Georgia Institute of Technology, North Ave. and Techwood Dr. ☎ **894-5447.**

Since 1913, this 46,000-seat stadium has been the home of those "Ramblin' Wrecks from Georgia Tech"—the Yellow Jackets college football team. For ticket information call the above number. Charge tickets via Ticketmaster (☎ **249-6400**).

Prices: Tickets are $17–$21.

Open: Sept–Nov for football season. **MARTA:** North Avenue.

Motor Sports

Road Atlanta, Georgia Hwy. 53 between I-85 and I-985.

☎ **967-6143** for information, **249-6400** to charge tickets.

Situated on 1,000 scenic wooded acres about 50 miles north of downtown Atlanta, this is the Southeast's premier motor-sports facility. Its 2.5-mile Grand Prix racecourse offers a challenging combination of turns, elevation changes, and high-speed straights.

Events include sports car, motorcycle, vintage/historic, and go-kart racing, including the annual International Motor Sports Association (IMSA) Exxon WSC for prototype sports cars, AMA Pro motorcycle road races, and Sports Car Club of America (SCCA) America Road Race of Champions and SCCA Trans-Am. Tickets are available through the above number or Ticketmaster (☎ **249-6400**). You can camp free on the property if you're attending an event.

Prices: Tickets are $10–$45.

Open: Year-round season of events. **Directions:** Route 85N to Exit 49, make a left, and follow the signs.

Recreation

Atlanta's fine climate is very conducive to participation in outdoor sports, and facilities abound.

FISHING

The Fish Hawk, 279 Buckhead Ave. NE, between Peachtree and Piedmont Rds. ☎ **237-3473.**

The Fish Hawk is the largest supplier in Atlanta for quality tackle. It carries all manner of fishing gear and outdoor clothing and can also supply the requisite license ($7 for seven days, $13 for a trout-fishing license valid for one year). There's good trout fishing on the Chattahoochee River, just 10 minutes from the store, or in the North Georgia Mountains, about 1¹/₂ hours from here. Many lakes in the area are good for bass and striper, including Lake Lanier, a 38,000-acre reservoir about 45 minutes away. For saltwater fishing, you'll have to drive about five hours from Atlanta to the East Coast. Owner

Gary Merriman is extremely knowledgeable and can tell you where to find the fish you seek. He can also tell you all applicable state regulations.

For additional information, serious fisherfolk can write or call the Georgia Department of Natural Resources, Wildlife Resources Division, 2070 U.S. Hwy 278 SE, Social Circle, GA 30279 (☎ **404/918-6406.**)

Open: Mon–Fri 9am–6pm, Sat 9am–5pm.

GOLF

Georgia's Stone Mountain Park Golf Course, Stone Mountain Park. ☎ **408-5717.**

Stone Mountain's 36-hole Robert Trent Jones nationally ranked layout is a beautiful facility, some parts of it adjacent to the park's lake. To quote *Gene's Guide to Atlanta's Public Courses*, "Its narrow rolling fairways lead to well trapped, tiered bent grass greens. When the tees are back this course demands both strength and accuracy." I don't know what that means, but if you're a golfer I guess it communicates something. A pro shop is on the premises, and lessons are available. For weekends and holidays reserve the Tuesday prior to the day you want to play; other times it's first come, first served. A restaurant/clubhouse has a large deck overlooking the lake.

Admission: $38 green fees, including the cart. There is a fee of $5 per vehicle to enter the park.

Open: Mon–Fri 8am–dark, from 7am until dark weekends and holidays.

RIVER RAFTING/CANOEING/KAYAKING

Southeastern Expeditions, 2936-H N. Druid Hills Rd.
☎ **329-0433** or toll free **800/868-RAFT.**

Southeastern offers white-water adventures on the scenic Chattooga River in North Georgia (it's the one you saw in the movie *Deliverance*) and the Ocoee in Tennessee. Put-in points for both rivers are about a 2-hour drive from Atlanta. Trips vary in length (from a few hours to a few days) and difficulty. A favorite of mine is a sunrise trip on the Chattooga; you'll find the exquisite morning peacefulness of river and forest soon contrasted by the thrill of running some of the toughest rapids around. After lunch you can hike to the magnificent Opossum Creek Falls. Days like that are magical. The Chattooga offers Class II and III rapids in Section III and Class III, IV, and V rapids in Section IV. The roller-coasterlike Ocoee has Class III and IV rapids only. Kids must be at least 10 for easy trips, 12 or 13 for more difficult rapids. The company also offers canoeing and kayaking. All of these expeditions are immensely popular, so make your reservations as far in advance as possible.

Prices: Vary depending on length and difficulty, and weekends are more expensive than weekdays. Half-day trips begin at about $28, full-day trips at $47, both rates including lunch, equipment, a guide, and transportation from the outpost to the river.

Open: Rafting season is Apr 1–Oct 31, with occasional trips in Mar and Nov.

ROLLER SKATING AND BICYCLING

Skate Escape, 1086 Piedmont Ave. NE, at 12th St. ☎ **892-1292.**

Conveniently located close to Piedmont Park, Skate Escape offers all kinds of bicycles and skates for rent or sale, as well as helmets, bicycle locks, and accessories. You can also buy skateboards here.

Prices: Rental per hour $5 for single-speed or children's bikes. Conventional or in-line skates are $4 per hour, $12 per day. A driver's license or major credit card is required for ID, or you can leave a deposit of $100 for skates, $200 for bicycles.

Open: Mon–Sat 10am–7pm, Sun noon–7pm. **MARTA:** Midtown.

SWIMMING

Almost every Atlanta hotel features a swimming pool. In addition, there's a large public swimming pool in Piedmont Park.

TENNIS

Piedmont Park, Piedmont Avenue and 14th St. ☎ **872-1507.**

The City of Atlanta Parks and Recreation Department operates 12 outdoor hard courts at Piedmont Park, all of them lit for night play. No reservations are taken; it's first-come, first-served. There's free parking at the courts, and showers, lockers, and a pro shop are on the premises.

Open: Weekdays 10am–9pm (noon–9pm in winter), Sat–Sun 9am–6pm.

Prices: $1.50 per person per hour during the day, $1.75 per person per hour when courts are lit for night play.

Bitsy Grant Tennis Center, 2125 Northside Dr., between I-75N and Peachtree Battle Ave. ☎ **351-2774.**

Leased from the Atlanta Parks and Recreation Department are these 13 outdoor clay courts (6 of them lit for night play) and 10 outdoor hard courts (4 lit). Courts are available on a first-come, first-served basis. No reservations. There are showers, lockers, and a pro shop on the premises.

Open: Mon–Fri 9am–9pm, Sat–Sun 8am–5pm.

Prices: $2.50 per person per hour for clay courts, $1.50 per person per hour for hard courts.

A Walking Tour of Sweet Auburn

IT'S MY FEELING THAT YOU NEVER REALLY UNDERSTAND A CITY UNLESS YOU walk around it a bit. Atlanta's lovely climate makes walking tours a marvelous option just about year round. In addition to the tour below, consider the excellent guided walking tours listed in Chapter 7, "What to See and Do in Atlanta." Also, note that the following attractions detailed in that chapter comprise walking tours in and of themselves: Georgia's Stone Mountain Park, Kennesaw Mountain/National Battlefield Park, Oakland Cemetery, and the Atlanta Historical Society in Buckhead. Auburn Avenue is specially set up for a walking tour.

Start MLK, Jr., Center for Nonviolent Social Change, 449 Auburn Ave.

Finish Auburn Avenue and Courtland Street.

Time Allow at least half a day to explore this area thoroughly. If you want to include a tour of King's Birth Home (stop No. 3) start out early in the day.

Sweet Auburn includes the Martin Luther King, Jr., National Historic District, which comprises about 12 blocks along Auburn Avenue. A neighborhood that nurtured scores of 20th-century black businesspeople and professionals, it contains the birthplace, church, and gravesite of Martin Luther King, Jr. Under the auspices of the National Park Service, portions of Auburn Avenue are in an ongoing process of restoration as an important historic district. Eventually, many of the homes and businesses on the "Birth Home" block will resume their 1920s appearance. This tour provides insight into black history, the civil rights movement, and black urban culture in the South. If you're traveling with children, it's a wonderful opportunity to teach them about a great American. The major attractions are covered in detail in Chapter 7.

Begin your stroll at:

1. The Martin Luther King, Jr., Center for Nonviolent Social Change, 449 Auburn Ave., is an organization that continues the work to which King was dedicated—reducing violence within the community and among nations. Freedom Plaza, on the premises, is his final resting place. The center functions as an information station for area attractions. This is where you obtain tickets to view the Birth Home of Martin Luther King, Jr. (on weekends, especially, arrive early, since demand for tickets often exceeds supply). Here, too, you can take a self-guided tour of exhibits on King's life and the civil rights movement and see videos which include some of his most stirring speeches. Including the videos (which shouldn't be missed), plan to spend at least two hours at the center.

Now, for further orientation, proceed, a few blocks east to:

2. The Visitor Center, 522 Auburn Ave., between Howell and Hogue streets (☎ **331-3920**), where you can pick up a comprehensive area map/brochure provided by the

National Park Service and view a 15-minute slide show about the history of the community. Often, other relevant videos/slide shows are offered, as are occasional exhibits. This orientation center itself is the elegant restored turn-of-the-century home of two prominent black citizens, the Reverend Peter James Bryant, and, later, of developer Antoine Graves. The center is open Monday to Friday 9am to 5pm.

Cross the street and walk west a bit to:

3. **The Birth Home of Martin Luther King, Jr.,** 501 Auburn Ave., at Hogue St., where free half-hour guided tours are given on a continual basis September through May 10am to 5pm, the rest of the year 10am to 7pm. Get tickets at the MLK, Jr., Center listed above.

After you leave, note some turn-of-the-century homes in the area such as:

4. **The Double "Shotgun" Row Houses,** 472–488 Auburn Ave., two-family dwellings with separate hip roofs which were built in 1905 to house workers for the Empire Textile Company. They were so named because rooms were lined up in a row; if you so desired, you could fire a shotgun right through them.

At the corner of Auburn and Boulevard is:

5. **Fire Station No. 6,** one of Atlanta's eight original firehouses, completed in 1894. The 2-story Romanesque-revival building was situated to protect the eastern section of the city. Note the Italianate arched windows on the second story. A museum is in the works here for the future.

Refueling Stop

The Martin Luther King, Jr., Center for Nonviolent Social Change, 449 Auburn Ave., (☎ 526-8920), houses the **South Fork Restaurant,** a very nice cafeteria serving home-cooked southern fare. For about $5, you can dine here on fried chicken with biscuits, candied yams, and fresh veggies in pot likker. There's fresh-baked peach cobbler for dessert. Open daily 7:30am to 6pm. No credit cards.

Continuing west, a notable stop on your tour is:

6. **Ebenezer Baptist Church,** 407 Auburn Ave., founded in 1886, where Martin Luther King, Jr., served as co-pastor from 1960–68. Ten-minute guided tours are given throughout the day.

Refueling Stop

At the corner of Auburn Avenue and Jackson Street is another very good, and very inexpensive, southern/soul food cafeteria, the **Beautiful Restaurant** (☎ 223-0800). It's open daily from 7:30am to 8pm. No credit cards. See Chapter 6 for details.

Walking Tour—Sweet Auburn

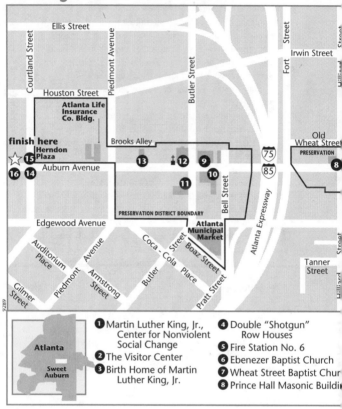

One block west is the:

7. Wheat Street Baptist Church, 365 Auburn Ave., built in the 1920s, but serving a congregation since the late 1800s. Auburn Avenue was originally called Wheat Street in honor of Augustus W. Wheat, one of Atlanta's early merchants. The name was changed in 1893.

Further west, on Auburn between Hilliard and Fort streets, is:

8. The Prince Hall Masonic Building, an influential black lodge led for several decades by John Wesley Dobbs. Today it houses the national headquarters of the Southern Christian Leadership Conference.

Refueling Stop

The corner of Auburn Avenue and Fort Street is the site of the famous **Auburn Avenue Rib Shack** (☎ 523-8315). There are only three booths and a counter, plus, in good weather, a few umbrella tables outside. Arrive early or late

9 Odd Fellows Building and Auditorium

10 Herndon Building

11 Butler Street YMCA

12 Big Bethel African Methodist Episcopal Church

13 Royal Peacock Club

14 APEX (Afro-American Panoramic Experience) Museum

15 Herndon Plaza

16 Auburn Avenue Research Library

to avoid a wait for seating. Everything is homemade—fabulous barbecued chicken, pork or beef ribs, potato salad, collard greens, candied yams, and more. Prices are low. Open Tuesday and Wednesday 11:30am to 4pm, Thursday 11:30am to 7pm, Friday 11:30am to 10pm, and Saturday noon to 10pm. Major credit cards are accepted. One drawback in summer: there's no air conditioning.

On the other side of the expressway, note:

9. The Odd Fellows Building and Auditorium, 228–250 Auburn Ave., another black fraternal lodge, which originated in Atlanta in 1870. Completed in 1914, the building later became headquarters for an insurance company.

Across the street is:

10. The Herndon Building, 231-45 Auburn Ave., named for Alonzo Herndon, an ex-slave who went on to found the

Atlanta Life Insurance Company. It was erected in 1924. By 1930, the Auburn business district supported 121 black-owned businesses and 39 black professionals.

Make a left and you'll see:

11. The Butler Street YMCA, built in the early 1900s.

Go back to Auburn Avenue, and across the street is:

12. The Big Bethel African Methodist Episcopal Church, at no. 220, originally built in the 1890s and then rebuilt in 1924 after a fire. In the 1920s, John Wesley Dobbs called the Bethel "a towering edifice to black freedom."

Farther along is:

13. The Royal Peacock Club, 184–186 Auburn Ave. Its walls painted floor to ceiling with peacocks, it presented top black entertainers such as Ray Charles, Aretha Franklin, and Dizzy Gillespie in its heyday. There is talk of restoring the club to its former glamour.

At Auburn Avenue and Courtland Street is:

14. The APEX (African-American Panoramic Experience) Museum, 135 Auburn Ave. (☎ **521-APEX**), featuring exhibits on the history of Sweet Auburn and changing exhibits relating to the African-American experience.

Cross the street to:

15. Herndon Plaza, where exhibits on the Herndon family can be seen.

If you'd like to do further research on the history of Auburn Avenue—or on any aspect of African-American history and culture—continue on to:

16. The Auburn Avenue Research Library on African-American Culture and History, 101 Auburn Ave. (☎ **730-4001**). A Heritage Center on the premises features special exhibits, workshops, seminars, lectures, and events. Open Monday to Thursday noon to 8pm, Saturday and Sunday 2 to 6pm; closed Friday.

9

Atlanta Shopping

1	Shopping Areas	214
2	Department Stores & Malls	219
3	Shopping around Town	221

ATLANTA IS THE SHOPPING MECCA OF THE SOUTHEAST. ITS VAST—AND VERY chic—malls serve not only locals but a large number of consumers who come from neighboring states just to shop. Buckhead boutiques such as Sasha Frisson can hold their own with the most fashionable emporiums of New York and Los Angeles. There are also browsable areas of quaint shops in Little Five Points and Virginia-Highland. This is a great town for antiquing, and I love the big old-fashioned downtown Macy's.

1 Shopping Areas

Chamblee's Antique Row

Antique Row, on Peachtree Road between Chamblee-Dunwoody and North Peachtree Rds. (☎ **458-1614**), is a quaint complex of over 30 shops located in historic homes, churches, and other buildings. Some of them date as far back as the 1800s. There are dealers of antique American and European furniture, glassware, pottery, Victoriana, Orientalia, wicker, collector toys, quilts, sports equipment, coke memorabilia, jewelry, architectural antiques, and crafts items. It's a great afternoon ramble. Hours vary with each store. Almost all are open Monday through Saturday from 10:30am to 5pm; most are open Sunday from 1 to 5pm as well. You can take a MARTA train to Chamblee Station; it's about three-fourths of a mile from the shops. On weekdays you can get the No. 132 Tilly Mill bus from there; on weekends walk or take a taxi.

Virginia-Highland

This charming area of town, centered on Highland Avenue between Virginia and Ponce de Leon Avenue, teems with antique shops, junk stores, trendy boutiques, and art galleries. Since you'll want to browse through all its shops in one excursion, they're grouped together here in the order in which you will find them while walking north through the neighborhood. Take a lunch break at Murphy's (see Chapter 6, "Atlanta Dining").

Antiques and Gifts

20th Century, 1044 N. Highland Ave., between Los Angeles and Virginia Aves. ☎ **892-2065.**

As its name implies, this shop specializes in international antiques and reproductions made during this century. The inventory is wide-ranging, including some terrific jewelry, Limoges porcelain boxes, whimsical clocks, art deco items, Belgian tapestries, and furnishings running the gamut from 19th-century reproductions to '50s blond wood pieces. Also in the mix: campy nostalgia items such as back issues of *Life* magazine, Elvis trading cards, and antique radios and telephones. Great browsing. Open Mon–Wed 11am–7pm, Thurs–Sat 11am–9pm, Sun noon–6pm. In summer the store stays open till 9pm Mon–Wed.

Affairs, 1401 N. Highland Ave., just below University Dr.
☎ **876-3342.**

This charming shop, its ambience enhanced by well-chosen classical and jazz tapes, offers many exquisite giftware items. Some examples: a mother-of-pearl toothbrush, a rabbit- or cow-shaped clock, one-of-a-kind picture frames, stuffed dolls and animals, beautiful dinnerware, and floral chintz-lined baskets. Affairs also carries French and Italian kitchenware and a full line of Crabtree & Evelyn products. Delightful browsing. Open Mon–Sat 10am–9:30pm, Sun noon–6pm.

Body and Bath

Natural Body, 1403 N. Highland Ave., just below University Dr.
☎ **876-9642.**

This very appealing shop invites you to pamper yourself with all manner of skin treatments, bubble baths, massage and body oils, potpourris, soaps, lotions, and cosmetics. All of their products are 100% natural, chemical free, and biodegradable, and none are tested on animals. They carry, among other lines, Kiehl (from New York), Aveda, Ahava (made in Israel with minerals from the Dead Sea), and Bindi (products made in India from ayurvedic herbs, roots, and flowers). Natural Body also runs a spa around the corner (☎ **872-1039**), offering massages, facials, aroma therapy, manicures, pedicures, and other beauty spa treatments. Open Mon 10:30am–6pm, Tues–Sat 10:30am–9pm, Sun noon–6pm.

Clothing Boutiques

Mitzi & Romano, 1038 N. Highland Ave., between Virginia and Los Angeles Aves. ☎ **876-7228.**

Mitzi Ugolini buys designer clothes in New York and California. Her clothing is fashion-forward—the kind that makes a statement instead of blending in with the crowd. Great jewelry and accessories, too. Prices are affordable. Open Mon 11am–8pm, Tues–Thurs 11am–9pm, Fri–Sat 11am–10pm, Sun noon–7pm.

Porter's, 994 Virginia Ave., just off N. Highland Ave. ☎ **874-7834.**

Stop by for carefully chosen men's clothing and men's and women's accessories, unique imported and designer ties for men, beautiful T-shirts, jewelry, and other lovely items. Open Tues–Thurs 11am–9pm, Fri–Sat 11am–10pm, Sun–Mon 12:30–6pm.

Mooncake, 1019 Virginia Ave. NE, just off N. Highland Ave.
☎ **892-8043.**

The ever-changing inventory of whimsical wearables for women here might include cloche and straw hats, black-printed cotton dresses, and oddments that range from ethnic and handcrafted jewelry to nomadic shoes from Turkey. The retro-style clothing looks vintage, but it's all new. You'll also find body and bath items, hair accessories, diaries, greeting cards, and carved wooden angels here. Open Apr–Dec Mon–Thurs 11:30am–9pm, Fri–Sat 11am–10pm; Jan–Mar Mon–Sat 11am–7pm.

Earth Angel, 1196 N. Highland Ave., at Amsterdam Ave.
☎ **607-7755.**

This very feminine and frou-frou shop is stocked with lacy wedding gowns, romantic and dressy frocks, beautiful lingerie, rosette-embellished ballet slippers, handmade antique-lace veils, hats decorated with antique flowers, ribbons, gift items such as potpourri and sachets, jewelry, and hair accessories, as well as upscale linens and towels. Open Mon–Sat 11am–7pm.

New Age

Atlantis Connection, 1402 N. Highland Ave., between University and Morningside Drs. ☎ **881-6511.**

Billing itself as a "metaphysical resource center," Atlantis Connection sells books (there's a comfortable reading balcony), audiotapes, CDs relating to meditation, channeling, self-help and recovery, Eastern philosophy, women's and men's spirituality, astrology, and angels. It also carries related items, such as crystals, incense, Chilean rain sticks, and Zuni fetishes, as well as New Age greeting cards and Native American and contemporary jewelry. Psychics are often on hand to do readings. Open Mon–Thurs 11am–9pm, Fri–Sat 11am–10pm, Sun noon–5pm.

An Art Gallery

Aliya Gallery, 1402 N. Highland Ave. NE, in the Highland Walk Center between University and Morningside Drs. ☎ **892-2835.**

Steve Fleenor and Gary Alembik (Gary lived a year in Jerusalem, hence the name Aliya), are the owners of this very lovely gallery. They represent 30 artists, both American and international, whose works range from contemporary paintings (abstracts, landscapes, and figurative), to pottery, sculpture, and jewelry. Open Mon–Fri 2–10pm, Sat noon–10pm, Sun 11:30–10pm.

Little Five Points

An area similar to Virginia-Highland (see above)—though a little funkier—Little Five Points reminds me of Berkeley in the 1960s. There are still authentic hippies here. It is also close to Virginia-Highland, so if you crave additional boutique browsing, both areas are easily covered in a few hours. While you're shopping here, plan a leisurely lunch at the delightful Bridgetown Grill (details in Chapter 6). Begin your shopping stroll at Euclid and Moreland avenues and proceed southwest along Euclid. Because shopping here is more of a browsing experience than a search for specific merchandise, stores in this area are listed in geographic order rather than by type of store.

Crystal Blue, 1168 Euclid Ave., between Moreland and Colquitt Aves.
☎ **522-4605.**

Wayne and Debbie Vaillancourt's esoteric emporium specializes in crystals and minerals touted for healing and other purposes. For example: black tourmaline promotes balance to the endocrine system, rose quartz perks up the kidneys and circulatory system, and meteorite helps reveal past lives from other planets and galaxies. Other items here include New Age books and cassettes, incense, chimes, chakra oils, and Acusphere exercise balls to stimulate acupuncture points. Open Mon–Sat 11am–7pm, Sun noon–6pm.

Stefan's, 1160 Euclid Ave., between Moreland and Colquitt Aves. ☎ **688-4929.**

Most of Stefan's merchandise is vintage clothing for men and women from the 1890s through the early 1960s, the rest accessories like belts, suspenders, cummerbunds, and glitzy period costume jewelry. There are 1950s net-skirt prom dresses, Mamie Eisenhower gowns, tuxedos, wedding gowns, Hawaiian shirts, and many many hats. Prices are low. Open Mon–Sat 11am–7pm, Sun noon–6pm.

Boomerang, 1145 Euclid Ave., between Moreland and Colquitt Aves. ☎ **577-8158.**

This eclectic shop carries funky furniture (it ranges from a 1950s Formica to handmade and painted contemporary pieces), and a wide array of gift items—pink French poodle salt and pepper shakers, Mona Lisa magnets, Indian cut-tin wall ornaments, hand-blown glass perfume bottles, Botticelli and Da Vinci shower curtains, tapestries, Chilean wood animals, and more. Open daily except Tues noon–6pm.

Rene Rene, 1142 Euclid Ave., between Moreland and Colquitt Aves. ☎ **522-RENE.**

Atlanta magazine, in a "best and worst" awards issue, once named Rene Rene the city's "best women's clothing" shop in the "funky club scene" category. It's true, but some of owner Rene Sanning's designs are more sophisticated—even possibly wearable for business. She even has high-fashion menswear in her line ("not for the IBM man," says Rene). Interesting accessories here, too, such as black gloves adorned with silk roses. Open Mon–Fri 11:30am–6:30pm, Sat 11am–7pm, Sun noon–6pm.

Throb, 1140 Euclid Ave., between Moreland and Colquitt Aves. ☎ **522-0355.**

Throb specializes in unconventional (to put it mildly) club wear for men and women. You can shop here for see-through vinyl minis, hot pants, bondage-look clothing, black fishnet and silver vinyl dresses, intergalactic plastic jewelry, leather lingerie, lingerie meant to be worn as outerwear, chartreuse wigs, and, to complete the look, wild hair dye and make-up colors. Open Mon–Sat 11am–7pm, Sun noon–6pm; summer hours are a little longer.

The Junkman's Daughter, 464 Moreland Ave., between Euclid and North Aves. ☎ **577-3188.**

This funky 8,000-square-foot store looks like a transplant from New York's East Village. Owner Pamela Mills, whose parents and grand-parents were in the salvage/junk-store business, inherited a bizarre assortment of family treasures, including cartons of Mickey Mouse toys, the remains of a perfume factory, and cases of stockings from World War II. This legacy formed the nucleus of her collection, which today includes a large array of costumes (everything from Elvis to a giant crayfish), Japanese military capes, '50s saddle shoes and crinolines, feather boas, leather jackets, antique furs, beaded and sequinned gowns, posters, cards, Elvis key chains, puppets from Sri Lanka, and toys (both antique and imported), not to mention a large selection of international masks and folk art, sequin-covered Haitian voodoo flags and bottles, and new and used tapes and CDs. The staircase leading to the mezzanine is in the shape of a 20-foot red high-heeled shoe. And a tattoo parlor and body-piercing operation are on the premises. Open Mon–Sat 11am–7pm, Sun noon–6pm.

A Cappella Books, 1133 Euclid Ave., at Colquitt Ave. ☎ **681-5128.**
This is the kind of offbeat bookstore that makes for great browsing. They carry new, used, and out-of-print books, many of them relating to counterculture, literature, history, and the arts. Signed editions here, too. Open Mon–Sat 11am–7pm, Sun noon–6pm, with extended hours spring and summer.

African Connections, 1107 Euclid Ave., between Colquitt and Washita Aves. ☎ **589-1834.**
This fascinating shop carries: soapstone carvings from Kenya; textiles, such as *asooke* cloth from Nigeria and *kente* cloth from Ghana; handcrafted jewelry from Africa, India, and Indonesia, as well as pieces made by African American jewelers using African materials; traditional and contemporary clothing from the Ivory Coast, Ghana, and Nigeria; traditional West African masks; Nigerian Fulani wedding bead necklaces; Indonesian and African baskets; and African ceremonial combs and medicine bowls. There's much more. Open Tues–Sat 11am–6pm, Sun 2–6pm.

Stone Mountain

Stone Mountain Village, just outside the West Gate of Georgia's Stone Mountain Park (bounded by Second and Main streets north and south, Poole St. and Memorial Dr. east and west; ☎ **879-4971**), is well worth a visit. It's been developing since the 1800s, and many of the 60-plus shops are housed in historic buildings (for example, a jewelry shop in a 160-year-old log cabin). Merchants here keep to a very high standard, and their wares are tasteful and of good quality. A lot of the stores specialize in antiques, crafts, and collectibles. Some examples: country furniture, canning jars, dried-flower wreaths, imported toys, handmade candles, dolls, baskets, homemade jams, potpourri, patchwork quilts and quilting fabrics, handcrafted dulcimers, Civil War memorabilia, and out-of-print books.

It's great fun to wander about this quaint village, and there's usually some festive event going on—perhaps an arts-and-crafts fair or live entertainment. During Christmas season, the streets are candlelit and the village becomes a magical place populated by St. Nick, elves, carolers, and harpists. Hours for most shops are Monday through Saturday from 10am to 5pm (Friday until 8pm); some also open Sunday from 1 to 5pm.

Stop for a meal at the nearby **Basket Bakery and Garden Café,** 6655 Memorial Drive, at Main Street (☎ **498-0329**). For breakfast there are croissants or ham-and-egg platters with homemade biscuits. Later, you can opt for sandwiches on fresh-baked breads, homemade salads, quiche, soups, and home-baked desserts. And the dinner menu highlights European specialties. Open Tues–Thurs 7am–9pm, Fri–Sat 7am–10pm, Sun for brunch only 11am–4pm. Major credit cards accepted.

2 Department Stores & Malls

So many malls, so little time. I've covered the most central shopping clusters only; there are many more in suburbia.

Macy's Peachtree, 180 Peachtree St., between International Blvd. and Ellis St. ☎ **221-7221.**

Opened in 1927, this downtown branch of Macy's is a department store in the grand tradition, its main floor featuring 30 lofty Corinthian columns, marble floors, and glittering crystal chandeliers. However, it's perfectly up to date when it comes to merchandise. Like most branches of Macy's nowadays, it has a Cellar—a street market with tiled brick floors and shops specializing in housewares. The mezzanine houses an Olympics shop, a shop selling Atlanta sports team merchandise, other Atlanta-themed merchandise, and shops based on current fads (like *Jurassic Park*). There's also a conveniently located visitor's center on the Cellar level; stop in for information on Atlanta attractions and a complimentary cup of coffee. Six floors of merchandise comprise everything you'd expect—clothing and shoes for the whole family, china, silver, bedding, the works. And dining options range from grilled seafood to a buttery hot cinnamon bun. Open Mon–Sat 10am–6pm, Sun noon–6pm. **MARTA:** Peachtree Center.

Underground Atlanta, Alabama St., between Peachtree St. and Central Ave. ☎ **523-2311.**

This 12-acre mix of colorful shops, nightclubs, and restaurants makes for a fun-filled day or evening. There are dozens of shops here, plus vendors in Humbug Square selling merchandise off antique pushcarts. Shopping options include numerous clothing shops for men, women, and children, running the gamut from upscale T-shirts at Dallas Alice, to unisex active wear at Gadzooks, to Victoria's Secret's sexy lingerie. Other interesting emporia include Art by God (fossils and rare mineral specimens), First World Bookstore (African-American literature), Kandlestix where candle-makers display their craft), Starlog (for futuristic and sci-fi stuff), and Antiquities Historical Galleries (for limited-edition, signed and numbered historical documents). Gift shops run the gamut from Georgia Grande General (Georgia-related gifts and crafts) to Papier D'Couleur (papier-mâché birds, fruits, and animals). And there are also novelty stores such as the bargain mecca, Everything's A $1. Other merchants here sell books, jewelry, shoes, music tapes and videos. You'll find branches of Warner Bros. Studio Store, Sam Goody, Nature Company Doubleday, and The Gap. And don't miss Olympic Experience, headquarters and retail outlet for the 1996 Games. Of course, eateries—from pizza and taco stands to elegant restaurants—abound. If you're driving, there's parking in a garage on Central Avenue off Martin Luther King Drive. Be sure to get your ticket validated inside for discounted parking. Open Mon–Sat 10am–9:30pm, Sun noon–6pm. **MARTA:** Five Points.

Lenox Square Mall, 3393 Peachtree Rd. NE, at Lenox Rd.
☎ **233-6767** or **800/344-5222.**

The vast upscale Lenox Square was built in 1959 and has since undergone three major expansions. And a fourth (170,000 square feet of merchandise space to house 50 or 60 new shops) is underway at this writing. Anchors include Neiman-Marcus, Macy's, and Rich's department stores, and the J. W. Marriott hotel. There are six movie theaters in the complex, 25 restaurants (including Mick's, detailed in Chapter 6, "Atlanta Dining"), and over 200 specialty shops. Among the best-known emporia are Ann Taylor, Victoria's Secret, Britches of Georgetowne, Burberrys, J. Crew, Warner Bros. Studio Store, a Metropolitan Museum of Art Store, Forgotten Woman, Benetton, Muse's, Cartier, Disney Store, The Sharper Image, Laura Ashley, The Limited, The Nature Company, Brooks Brothers, Banana Republic, the Gap, Polo/Ralph Lauren, B. Dalton, Waldenbooks, Radio Shack, Williams-Sonoma, Florsheim Shoes, Bally of Switzerland, Buster Brown, Hoffritz for Cutlery, F.A.O. Schwarz, and Louis Vuitton. Basically, you can purchase just about anything here, from a Siamese kitten to a diamond bracelet (there are 10 jewelry stores). A full complement of service shops are here as well—shoe repair, optician, locksmith, post office, airline offices, you name it. Open Mon–Sat 10am–9:30pm, Sun 12:30–5:30pm, with extended hours during the Christmas season. **MARTA:** Lenox.

Phipp's Plaza, 3500 Peachtree Rd. NE, at the Buckhead Loop.
☎ **262-0992.**

Atlanta's most exclusive shopping venue, Phipps Plaza serves the affluent Buckhead community. In 1992, it underwent a $140 million renovation/expansion, adding shops, spacious promenades, and grand interior courts. And another 550,000 square feet of merchandising space (which will include a Bloomingdale's and 130 specialty stores) is due to open in 1996. Phipps' 100-plus shops and restaurants are anchored by Lord & Taylor, Parisian (an Alabama-based department store), and Saks Fifth Avenue, and the exclusive Ritz-Carlton Buckhead hotel is adjacent. Its posh emporia include Gucci, Abercrombie & Fitch, Tiffany & Co., Mark Cross, Jaeger International, Adrienne Vittadini, A/X Armani Exchange, Ross-Simons (upscale jewelry, china, crystal, and silver), and Cole Haan for shoes. You'll also find chic boutiques selling ladies and men's apparel, luggage, jewelry, furs, home furnishings, shoes, and specialty gifts. The ambience is sedately elegant, and there's usually something special going on—perhaps an art or fashion show. First-class restaurants here include the highly recommended Peasant Uptown. Also on the premises: a restaurant complex called The Veranda Food Court and a 12-screen movie theater. Most stores are open Mon–Sat 10am–6pm, Thurs till 9pm. Some are also open Sun 12:30–5pm. **MARTA:** Lenox.

Mall at Peachtree Center, Peachtree St. at International Blvd. ☎ 614-5000.

Part of the vast 14-block Portman-designed Peachtree Center complex, this downtown mall offers 80 shops, restaurants, and services on three levels. It's location couldn't be more convenient—three adjoining hotels even offer direct access to it via indoor passageways. It's a very complete shopping center, with quality boutiques featuring shoes and clothing for the whole family, jewelry, toys, books, photographic equipment, office supplies, pharmaceuticals, tapes and CDs, and imported gifts—all in a smart setting of Italian marble, fountains, and greenery. There are branches of Muse's Department Store and Brooks Brothers. Services include florists, hairstylists, a Delta Air Lines desk, a travel agency, Federal Express, UPS, a dry cleaner, and an optician. As for dining, a food court dishes up everything from gyros to Mrs. Field's cookies, and full-service restaurants include some great choices: Chow, Downtown, Micks, The Ocean Club, and Morton's of Chicago (see Chapter 6, "Atlanta Dining"). Open Mon–Sat 10am–6pm, with some stores open Sun noon–5pm. **MARTA:** Peachtree Center.

3 Shopping around Town

Books

In addition to the independent bookstores in Atlanta, the nationwide chain stores of **B. Dalton** and **Waldenbooks** are represented (see "Department Stores and Malls" above). Most important, Atlanta has **Oxford,** a truly great book emporium.

Latitudes, Lenox Square Mall, 2393 Peachtree Rd. NE. ☎ 237-6144.

Latitudes offers a wide variety of atlases, globes, wall maps, road maps, and travel guide books, as well as travel accessories such as money belts, travel clocks, backpacks, toiletry kits, and kids' car games. Open Mon–Sat 10am–9:30pm, Sun noon–5:30pm. **MARTA:** Lenox.

Oxford Books, 360 Pharr Rd., between Peachtree and Piedmont Rds. ☎ 262-3333 or 800/476-3311.

The Oxford is the largest independent bookstore in the Southeast, and one of the best in the nation. It's a bibliophile's treasure trove, offering a vast selection of books on every subject plus sheet music, audio/videotapes, CDs, a comic-book shop, and out-of-town newspapers and magazines. It's also the scene of very frequent appearances by celebrated authors. Among those who have appeared to publicize new works (they sign books and give talks and/or readings) are Calvin Trillin, Erma Bombeck, Jimmy Carter, Armistead Maupin, performance artist Laurie Anderson, Lani Guinier, Andrew Young, John Grisham, James Earl Jones, and Robert Haas. You can peruse your newly purchased books over a sandwich and coffee at the Oxford Espresso Café on the premises. And while you're here, pick up a copy of the store's *Oxford Review,* a publication that includes book reviews and tells about upcoming author signings, writing workshops, poetry readings, lectures, songwriter's showcases, art exhibits, and other store-related events. Hours are Sun–Thurs 9am–midnight, Fri–Sat 9am–1am. Sun–Tues there's live music in the Café from 8:30pm to closing.

There's another immense store with vast inventory called **Oxford at Peachtree Battle,** 2345 Peachtree Rd. NE, at Peachtree Battle Ave., in the Peachtree Battle Shopping Center (☎ 364-2700). It, too, has an on-premises eatery, here called the Cup and Chaucer. Hours are the same as the above.

In the same shopping center is **Oxford Too** (☎ 262-3411), an additional 12,500 square feet of space housing a vast selection of used and bargain books, records, tapes, and CDs, collectible books, framed autographs, and a large comic collection. It's open Sun–Thurs 9am–10pm, Fri–Sat 9am–midnight.

A fourth **Oxford** store is at 1200 W. Paces Ferry Rd. and I-75 (☎ 364-2488). It offers a large selection of books in all categories, with special emphasis on books for children, home and garden, and travel. It's open Sun–Thurs 9am–10pm, Fri–Sat 9am–midnight.

Women's Clothing

See also "Department Stores and Malls," above, for more stores.

A Pea in the Pod, in the Phipp's Plaza Mall, 3500 Peachtree Rd., at Lenox Rd. ☎ 261-0808.

This cleverly named shop features maternity clothes, but we're not talking T-shirts with an arrow pointing to your stomach and the word *baby.* These are gorgeous clothes—the kind you wore when you weren't pregnant—including designer lines by Adrienne Vittadini, Carol Little, David Dart, and Joan Vass. They run the gamut from really elegant business garb (perfect for board meetings) to evening wear and chic sports clothing. In fact, the clothes are so beautiful that women who are not pregnant shop here as well. Open Mon–Sat 10am–9pm, Sun noon–5pm. **MARTA:** Lenox.

Sasha Frisson, 3094 E. Shadowlawn Ave. NE, between Peachtree and E. Paces Ferry Rds. ☎ 231-0393.

Without a doubt, the most high-fashion boutique in town. This is the stuff best-dressed lists are made of. Owners Emma Nassar and Laura Seydel carry only the smartest European and American designers—Moschino, Alberto Ferretti, Ritz Sadler, and Vestimenta, Chantal Thomass, Jacques Molko, Karl Lagerfeld, and others. Wonderful accessories and jewelry here, too. Prices are in the if-you-have-to-ask-it's-not-for-you category. This delightful and impeccably elegant boutique is located in a peach-brick 1930s house. There are other chic emporia occupying residential buildings on the same street if you feel like doing some upscale browsing. Open Mon–Sat 10am–6pm.

Factory Outlets

Tanger Factory Outlet, 198 Tanger Dr., at exit 53 off I-85N in Commerce. ☎ 706/335-4537.

Tanger is a bargain-hunter's paradise, with 45 factory-outlet stores on a 22-acre property. Included are Oneida, Harvé Benard, Liz Claiborne, Corning, American Tourister, Farberware, Gitano, Levi's, Reebok, Mikasa, L'Eggs, Hanes, Bali, Maidenform, Van Heusen, and the Paper Factory, among others. It's about a 50-minute drive from downtown. Open Mon–Sat 9am–9pm, Sun noon–6pm.

Farmer's Markets

Atlanta State Farmer's Market, 16 Forest Pkwy., Forest Park. ☎ 366-6910.

The State Farmer's Market is a vast 146-acre outdoor facility where stall after stall is piled high with produce. There are also vendors of meats, poultry, and fresh eggs; home-canned pickles, jams, and relishes; plants and flowers; and seasonal items such as pumpkins in October, holly and Christmas trees in December. It's a colorful spectacle. You can have a good meal at a restaurant on the premises. If you're driving, take I-75 south to exit 78; the market is on your left. Open 24 hours daily except Christmas.

DeKalb Farmer's Market, 3000 E. Ponce de Leon Ave., Decatur. ☎ 377-6400.

Even if you have no intention of purchasing comestibles, this incredible market, started in 1977 by Robert Blazer, merits a visit. A mind-boggling array of international food items is temptingly displayed in a 140,000-square-foot cedar-paneled building that harmonizes nicely with its wooded surroundings. It's about a 20-minute drive from downtown. International flags from Australia to Zaire are hung from the rafters. Tables are laden with mountains of produce from broccoli to bok choy, not to mention winter melons and water chestnuts, lily root, curry leaves, breadfruit, Jamaican jerk marinade, Korean daikon, a multiplicity of mushrooms, chick-pea miso, cheese fudge, a vast beer and wine section, dried fruits, plants and flowers, seafood, meat, poultry, every imaginable variety of fresh herbs and hot peppers, fresh-baked breads and pastries, stalks of sugarcane, 450 varieties of cheese, frog's legs, conch meat, quail, and so on. As you shop, you can nibble grilled red snapper, knishes, sections of grapefruit, Ecuadorian octopus, or whatever else is offered at sample tables throughout the facility. Open daily 9am–9pm.

10

Atlanta Nights

1	The Performing Arts	225
2	The Nightclub Scene	231
3	More Entertainment	238
4	Film & Video	238

THE ALLMAN BROTHERS DUBBED IT "HOT'LANTA!" THIS IS A CITY THAT sizzles after dark, with numerous music clubs featuring jazz, rock, country, and blues. It also offers a comprehensive cultural scene, including first-rate symphony, ballet, opera, and theater productions. And major artists headline regularly at Atlanta's many large-scale performance facilities.

To find out what's on during your stay, consult the "Weekend" section of Saturday's *Atlanta Journal-Constitution* or *Creative Loafing*, a free publication you'll see in stores, restaurants, and other places around town.

Tickets to many performances are handled by Ticketmaster. Call **249-6400** to charge tickets. **Note:** Oxford Bookstores (see Chapter 9) function as Ticketmaster outlets.

1 The Performing Arts

Major Concert/Performance Halls

Atlanta Civic Center, 395 Piedmont Ave. NE, between Ralph McGill Blvd. and Pine St. ☎ **523-6275** for general information, **873-5811** for information on Atlanta Ballet performances.

Built in 1968 to attract major performers, the Civic Center offers a wealth of entertainment options in its 4,600-seat auditorium. It hosts headliners such as Ray Charles, Sheena Easton, and comedian George Wallace. Broadway shows—and other plays—sometimes come here. And the center also presents contemporary Christian singers (Amy Grant, Michael English), gospel singers (Bobby Jones, Shirley Caesar, Daryl Coley), traveling symphonies and opera companies, local dance companies, TV evangelists, fashion shows, and body-builder contests. Quite a mixed bag.

The Civic Center is also the home of the Atlanta Ballet, a company founded in 1929 by Dorothy Moses Alexander. The oldest ballet company in the United States, it presents about six productions each season (Sept–Apr), ranging from classical ballets (for example, *Swan Lake* or *Romeo and Juliet*) to contemporary works by choreographers such as Twyla Tharp and Donald Bird.

Tickets to the ballet and other Civic Center performances are available through Ticketmaster (☎ **249-6400**). Call the Civic Center or check local newspapers and magazines to find out what's on during your stay.

Prices: Admission varies with performances. Tickets for the Atlanta Ballet are $5–$37.50, with discounts for students and senior citizens.

Open: Hours vary with performances. **MARTA:** Civic Center (about 5 blocks away); buses go to the door. **Parking:** Entrances to paid lot on Pine St. or Ralph McGill Blvd.

Coca-Cola Lakewood Amphitheatre, Fair Drive at the Lakewood exit of I-85. ☎ **627-9704, 249-6400** for tickets through Ticketmaster.

Opened in 1989, with Al Jarreau headlining, the $15 million Lakewood Amphitheatre accommodates 19,000 including 7,000 reserved seats and a sloping lawn that holds an additional 12,000. Needless to say, this vast facility is used for major shows. It offers a broad musical spectrum. Among those who have performed here are Rod Stewart, Eric Clapton, Michael Bolton, Janet Jackson, Bette Midler, Elton John, and the Allman Brothers. In addition, the Amphitheatre hosts music festivals such as Lollapalooza and Reggae Sunsplash. There are umbrellaed picnic tables on the grounds, and though you can't bring in food or drink, a wide variety of comestibles is available—imported beers, champagne, fruit and cheese, sandwiches, pizza, gourmet ice creams, and, of course, Coca-Cola. The amphitheatre is 3.5 miles south of downtown.

Prices: Prices vary with the performer.

Open: Early May to end of Oct; occasional events the rest of the year. Showtimes vary. **MARTA:** Lakewood/Fort McPherson (shuttle buses take patrons to and from the station). **Directions:** I-75 or I-85 south to Lakewood Freeway exit (88E or 88W) and follow the signs. **Parking:** Free.

Fox Theatre, 660 Peachtree St. NE, at Ponce de Leon Ave.

☎ **881-2100, 249-6400** to charge tickets via Ticketmaster.

Built in 1927, when movie theaters were conceived along lavish lines, the Fox is a Moorish-Egyptian extravaganza complete with arabesque arches, onion domes, and minarets. Its exotic interior reflects the Egyptomania of that decade—a phenomenon resulting from archaeologist Henry Carter's discovery of the treasure-laden tomb of King Tutankhamen. Throne chairs, scarab motifs, hieroglyphics, and falcon wings representing the Egyptian sun god are seen throughout the theater, and the auditorium evokes a Middle Eastern courtyard under a starlit azure sky. See Chapter 7, "What to See and Do in Atlanta," for details on the Fox's history, architecture, and interior design, as well as information on tours.

Every year there's an October-to-April "Best of Broadway" season, featuring six major New York shows with star casts. It's followed by a summer Broadway series, so you can see hit shows like *The Will Rogers Follies, Phantom of the Opera*, and *Cats* almost year round here. The Atlanta Ballet performs George Balanchine's *The Nutcracker* here every December. A wide spectrum of headliners plays the Fox—Keith Richards, Kenny Rogers, Stevie Wonder, Ray Charles, Liza Minnelli, Gladys Knight, George Strait, and legions of others. There's a major film festival every summer (see the "Calendar of Events" in Chapter 2 for details). The Coca-Cola International Series, September through April, offers diverse entertainment, a recent season including The Royal Ballet of Flanders, The Chieftains (Irish folk music), and *Nutcracker on Ice*, starring Olympic Skaters Oksana Baiul, Viktor Petrenko, and Brian Boitano. And the Atlanta Opera recently made the Fox its permanent home (see "Opera" below). Other happenings range from dance-company performances to fashion shows to closed-circuit boxing.

Prices: Admission varies with the performance.

Open: Hours vary with the performance. **MARTA:** North Avenue. **Parking:** Many paid lots are close by.

Bobby Dodd Stadium/Grant Field, Georgia Institute of Technology, North Ave. and Techwood Dr. ☎ **895-5400** for information, **249-6400** to charge tickets via Ticketmaster.

This 46,000-seat stadium, home of the "ramblin' wrecks from Georgia Tech," hosts occasional major headliners between football seasons. Jimmy Buffett, the Rolling Stones, and Pink Floyd are among those who've played here.

Prices: Vary with performer.

Open: For headliner concerts Dec–Aug. **MARTA:** North Avenue.

Road Atlanta, Georgia Hwy. 53, between I-85 and I-985.
☎ **967-6143** for information, **249-6400** to charge tickets via Ticketmaster.

Situated on 1,000 scenic wooded acres about 50 miles north of downtown Atlanta, this is the Southeast's premier motorsports facility. In between races, it offers lawn seating for up to 100,000 people for headliner concerts featuring artists such as Billy Ray Cyrus, Faith Hill, and Doug Stone.

Prices: $10–$45.

Open: Year round. **Directions:** Take Route 85N to exit 49, make a left, and follow the signs.

Georgia Dome, 1 Georgia Dome Dr., at International Blvd and Northside Dr. ☎ **223-9200** for information, **249-6400** (Ticketmaster) or **223-8427** (the Dome Box Office) to charge tickets.

Between sporting events, this 71,500-seat facility presents headliner concerts and country music shows. Among those who've played the domed megaspace are Paul McCartney, U-2, and Elton John and Billy Joel (a double bill!).

Prices: Vary with performer.

Open: Year round. **MARTA:** Omni/Georgia Dome.

Omni Coliseum, 100 Techwood Dr. NW., at Marietta St.
☎ **681-2100, 249-6400** to charge tickets via Ticketmaster.

The 17,000-plus-seat Omni is the Southeast's showcase arena for sports and entertainment. In addition to shows like Walt Disney's World on Ice, The Ringling Bros. and Barnum & Bailey Circus, and Sesame Street Live, the facility hosts about 40 major concerts a year, featuring headliners such as Bruce Springsteen, Elton John, ZZ Top, Travis Tritt, Whitney Houston, Eric Clapton, and Peter Gabriel. Call to find out what's on during your stay.

Prices: Vary with performer.

Open: Year round. **MARTA:** Omni.

Variety Playhouse, 1099 Euclid Ave., near Washita Ave.
☎ **521-1786** for information, **249-6400** to charge tickets via Ticketmaster.

Built in the 1930s as a neighborhood movie theater, the Variety today offers an eclectic array of live entertainment. For example, in recent months they've presented folk-rock artists such as Richard Thompson and Sarah McLachlan, blues artists such as Koko Taylor and NRBQ, and jazz artists such as Incognito and Joshua Redman. There are also frequent album-release parties here. It's definitely worth checking out. While you're in Little Five Points, plan dinner at the Bridgetown Grill (see Chapter 6, "Atlanta Dining").

Prices: Most tickets are in the $5–$20 range; they vary with the performer.

Open: Year round, whenever shows are booked. **Parking:** There's a lot on Euclid Ave., near Colquitt Ave., charging $2 a night.

Chastain Park Amphitheatre, in Chastain Park at Powers Ferry Rd. and Stella Dr. ☎ **231-5888** for information and to charge tickets.

This delightful 7,000-seat outdoor facility offers concerts under the trees from May to October. Everyone brings food; a picnic on the grass or at your amphitheatre seat is a tradition. Big-name performers are featured—stars like Fleetwood Mac, Tony Bennett, Melissa Manchester, John Mellencamp, James Taylor, The Temptations, George Benson, Stevie Nicks, and Liza Minelli. It's hard to get tickets, so order as far in advance as possible (months ahead if you can). See also listing for the Atlanta Symphony Orchestra "Summer Pops Concerts" below.

Prices: Vary with performers.

Theater

Alliance Theatre Company, Woodruff Arts Center, 1280 Peachtree St. NE, at 15th St. ☎ **892-2414.**

The Alliance Theatre Company, under the artistic direction of Kenny Leon, is the largest resident professional theater in the Southeast. On two stages, it produces about 10 plays a year. Many well-known actors have played these stages, among them Armand Assante, Jane Alexander, Richard Dreyfuss, Tony Roberts, Jean Smart, and Morgan Freeman. A recent season's productions included, among others, Lorraine Hansberry's *A Raisin in the Sun,* Alan Ayckbourn's *Dreams from a Summer House,* Dickens' *A Christmas Carol,* and Tony Kushner's *Angels in America: Millenium Approaches.*

The Alliance Lunchtime Theatre series comprises six one-act plays ranging from vaudeville to Shakespeare. The plays are presented on the Main Stage on designated Tuesdays and Thursdays between September and May. And the Alliance Children's Theatre presents plays geared to youngsters such as *Charlotte's Web* and *Klondike,* based on Jack London's novel *Smoke Bellew* (the season is September through April).

There's parking in the Arts Center Garage on Lombardy Way between 15th and 16th streets.

Prices: For most productions, $14–$34. Discounts to students and seniors and "rush tickets" are often available on the night of the performance. Lunchtime Theatre admission, $3. Children's Theatre productions are $8.

Open: Sept–May; occasional productions during the summer. **MARTA:** Arts Center.

Seven Stages Performing Arts Center, 1105 Euclid Ave., two blocks west of Moreland Ave. ☎ **523-7647.**

Seven Stages is a professional theater company "committed to providing the Atlanta community with issue-oriented plays whose themes provoke thought and discussion about social, political, interpersonal, or spiritual matters." Under the direction of Del Hamilton, it has been producing new and experimental works of international scope since 1979. Many worthy new works and new playwrights find a stage here, and both local and international acting groups supplement the resident company.

The center has two stages, the 100-seat Backdoor Theatre and the 300-seat Main Stage. Recent productions have included Polish emigre Janusz Glowacki's award-winning satire *Antigone in New York,* Frank McGinnis' *Someone Who'll Watch Over Me* (which enjoyed successful prior runs in London and New York), Samuel Beckett's *Waiting for Godot* and *End Game, Unquestioned Integrity* by Mame Hunt (about the Clarence Thomas hearings), and *My Children, My Africa* by South African playwright Athol Fugard. Not everything done here is avant-garde or controversial, however; the company has also performed Shakespeare, Molière, and Jacques Brel, and there are frequent children's-theater productions, such as the Berlin-based Grips Theatre and a puppet version of *Macbeth.* An on-premises gallery displays works of local artists.

Prices: $12–$14 for most shows; discounts available for students and seniors.

Open: Year round. **MARTA:** Inman Park. **Parking:** $2.

Opera

Atlanta Opera, Fox Theatre, 660 Peachtree St. NE, at Ponce de Leon Ave. ☎ **355-3311** or toll free **800/35-OPERA.**

Under the artistic direction of William Fred Scott, the Atlanta Opera, founded in 1979, offers three fully staged productions each summer at the Fox Theatre and performs additional operas and concerts at varied locations throughout the year. Principal performers are drawn from top opera companies from across the United States and Europe, and they are truly excellent. Three to five performances are given of each opera. A recent season's productions included Puccini's *Turandot,* Bellini's *Norma,* and Bizet's *The Pearl Fishers.* Future plans call for a more extensive season.

Prices: Tickets $15–$78, with half-price tickets for seniors and students on the day of performance only. Tickets can be difficult to obtain; charge them in advance if possible.

Open: Late May through Labor Day. **MARTA:** North Avenue. **Parking:** Many paid lots are close by.

Classical Music

Atlanta Symphony Orchestra, Woodruff Arts Center, 1280 Peachtree St. NE, at 15th St. ☎ **876-HORN** for Concert Hotline recorded information, **892-2414** (box office) for information and tickets.

Celebrating its 50th anniversary in 1994–95, the Atlanta Symphony Orchestra, under musical director Yoel Levi, is one of the most widely acclaimed in America. Complementing it is the 200-voice Atlanta Symphony Orchestra Chorus, enabling performances of large-scale symphonic-choral works.

The ASO's annual schedule is extensive. The main offerings from September to May are the **Master Season Series** and the **Light Classics Series.** Master Season concerts, held on selected Thursday, Friday, and Saturday evenings in the plush 1,762-seat Symphony Hall, feature world-renowed guest artists such as cellist Yo-Yo Ma, pianist Emanuel Ax, soprano Frederica Von Stade, baritone Thomas Hamson, violinist Shlomo Mintz, and conductor Robert Shaw, among many others. There are 24 different programs featuring the music of Bach, Rachmaninov, Mozart, Liszt, and others. The Light Classics Series, on selected Friday and Saturday evenings as well as Saturday mornings, are themed programs (such as **Broadway's Hottest Hits** or **Gershwin's Greatest**). Also held during this season is a series of **Family Concerts.** Geared to children, they might include anything from *The Story of the Magic Horn* (with the Magic Circle Mime Company) to a puppet première in collaboration with the Center for Puppetry Arts.

There are **Holiday Concerts** at Halloween, Thanksgiving, and Christmas, the latter always including Handel's *Messiah.* And four annual Saturday matinee classical music concerts at 2pm comprise a series called **Four @ 2.**

Classic Chastain Summer Concerts, held in the 7,000-seat Chastain Park Amphitheatre, begin at 8:30pm on Wednesday, Friday, and Saturday evenings between June and August. All except lawn seating is reserved. It's customary to bring elaborate picnics and wine—even candelabras—to these events. Artists such as Natalie Cole, Tony Bennett, John Denver, The Pointer Sisters, and The Beach Boys perform, most of them with the ASO. Another warm-weather event is **Summerfest,** which takes place for three weeks in July at Symphony Hall and is always themed—for example, **Mostly Tchaikovsky** or **Basically Beethoven.** There are also free concerts in parks throughout the Atlanta area on selected summer evenings. These run the gamut from full symphony performances to light classical repertoires.

Prices: Master Season Series tickets are $18.50–$45, Light Classics Series $17.50–$40, Family Concerts $13, Four @ 2 $17.50–$40, Classic Chastain Summer Concert Series $16–$40, Summerfest $17.50–$40.

Open: Year-round season includes Sept–May performances at Symphony Hall in the Woodruff Arts Center and summer concerts at Chastain and various Atlanta parks. **MARTA:** Arts Center. **Parking:** In the Arts Center Garage on Lombardy Way between 15th and 16th Sts.

Atlanta Chamber Players. ☎ 651-1228.

The Atlanta Chamber Players have been delighting audiences both here and abroad since 1975. Their highbrow repertoire includes a wide spectrum of classical and contemporary masterpieces, and each year they commission new works by leading composers. Call to find out if, and where, they'll be playing during your stay.

    Prices: Most concerts are $12, free for students with ID.

    Open: Fall-through-spring season.

Atlanta Boy Choir. ☎ 378-0064.

This choir of 175 boys ages 5 to 14 has been delighting Atlanta audiences since 1956. A frequent guest at the White House, the choir has toured extensively both in the United States and abroad, always to great critical acclaim. In 1989 it won a Grammy Award. In Atlanta the choir sings at the lighting of the capitol Christmas tree early in December and in local churches throughout the Christmas season. Several performances each year are given with the Atlanta Symphony Orchestra during its Master Concert season (Sept–May). And the choir frequently appears at other locations around town. Call the above number for schedule and ticket information.

    Prices: Vary with each performance.

---

2 The Nightclub Scene

Nightclubs come and go, so its always a good idea to call ahead. As we go to press, these are the major venues for varied nighttime revels.

Dance Clubs ────────────────

Velvet, 89 Park Pl. at John Wesley Dobbs Ave. ☎ 681-9936.

The hottest place to dance in Atlanta, Velvet has been featured in every national publication from *Interview* to *Details*. Its funky-opulent interior (*Details* called it "garish gothic") has exposed brick walls hung with ornate artworks, alabaster lighting fixtures over the bar, and plenty of Victorian red velvet and silk among its decorator embellishments. Many pop icons have partied here—RuPaul, Depeche Mode, U-2, sports stars David Justice and Dominick Williams, even Madonna. Monday night is Boy Brigade (the crowd is predominantly gay men); Wednesdays cater to Generation X with techno/house (the crowd is 18 to early 20s); Thursdays (Rebirth of Cool) feature acid, jazz, hip-hop, and house (a DJ alternates with live R&B bands); Friday is fashion night (don your best duds), featuring alternative dance music, fashion shows by local boutiques and designers, and parties (such as wig night); Saturday is gay oriented; and

Sunday night is the wildly popular "Disco Hell" (wear your bell bottoms). Pizza is available.

Prices: Cover charge is $3 Mon, $6 Wed, $7 Thurs, $5 Fri; Sat $5 before midnight ($7 after midnight), Sun $7 for ladies, $10 for men. Average drink is $3.50.

Open: Mon 10pm–2am, Wed and Fri–Sun 10pm–4am, Thurs and Sat 10pm–3am. **Closed:** Tues. **Parking:** Valet parking $5, self $3. **MARTA:** Five Points.

Masquerade, 695 North Ave. NE, just east of Boulevard. ☎ **577-8178.**

Housed in a century-old stone-walled Romanesque building—a former excelsior factory—Masquerade looks like the Bastille. Its interior, divided into three main areas, is adorned with factory remnants. Downstairs, a bar called **Purgatory**—under a lofty corrugated-tin ceiling with rough-hewn wood beams and exposed pipes—offers foosball, pool tables, pinball, video games, and a photo machine. Across the way, in **Hell**—a dark and dank stone-walled setting adorned with hanging chains—Wednesday is Club Fetish night (S&M), Thursday the music is 80s (they call it retro), Friday is "Rock & Rage" (industrial and guitar), Saturday is techno/high-energy, Sunday techno. Club-employed dancers perform on stages. Ascend the stairs to **Heaven** (not my conception, frankly), its walls painted blue with fluffy clouds; here live local and national acts perform (the latter have included Meat Loaf, Iggy Pop, Cheap Trick, Psychedelic Furs, and Ministry). In addition to these interior spaces there's a 4,000-seat outdoor **Music Park** behind the club, where bands such as Porno for Pyro, The Connells, The KMFDM, and 311 perform May through October (tickets available via Ticketmaster, **249-6400**). If you want to get away from the action, you can retreat to an al fresco bar with a tree-shaded wooden deck enclosed by a picket fence.

Prices: Cover $2–$5 in Hell and Purgatory ($4–$8 for ages 18–20), $2–$20 (depending on the performer) in Heaven; Music Park tickets vary with the performer.

Open: Wed–Sun 9pm–4am, and occasionally on Mon–Tues for special events. **Parking:** $3–$5.

Axys, 1150B Peachtree St. NE, at 14th St. ☎ **607-0922.**

Since I've been writing about Atlanta, this club—originally owned by Peter Gatien of the Limelight group—has taken on a new identity each edition. However, it's always one of the city's most elegant dance venues, so whatever form it takes it merits a visit. Occupying a 1919 baroque mansion, Axys is entered via a wrought-iron-enclosed garden, heralded by a fountain, with a row of flaming torchieres lighting the way to a reflecting pool. Inside, the dance floor is a million-dollar light and sound extravaganza, enhanced by multicolored mists and showers of confetti. The DJ plays every variety of international high-energy music, and there are occasional live concerts as well. Off the dance floor, you can relax on a plush sofa or play pool in the Gallery. Or you can observe the dance-floor frenzy from a balcony bar. Parties in the upper-level, glassed-in VIP Room have ranged from a birthday bash for Janet Jackson to the kickoff Superbowl party. And Madonna was in the house during a recent Atlanta visit.

Prices: Cover $5–$7. No drink minimum.

Open: Thurs, Fri, and Sun 10pm–4am, Sat 10pm–3am. Call about other nights. **Parking:** Valet parking $4. **MARTA:** Arts Center.

Rupert's, 3330 Piedmont Rd., just north of Peachtree Rd. in the Peachtree Crossing Shopping Center. ☎ **266-9866** or **266-9834.**

One of Atlanta's most popular clubs is Rupert's, a high-energy, live-music venue with state-of-the-art sound and lighting systems. Its interior is on the plush side, with gleaming mahogany paneling, silk wall coverings, mirrored columns, brass rails, and art deco lighting fixtures. Its clientele is upscale and chicly attired (though jeans are permitted). There's a top-flight show every night—a 10-piece band and six versatile star-quality vocalists performing everything from Motown to top-40 tunes, from blues to funk—with a DJ filling in between sets. Singers who perform here have a big local following.

The dance floor is right in front of the stage, and there are five bars downstairs. Rupert's has a pretty good visiting-celebrity quotient. Rod Stewart, Alec Baldwin and Kim Basinger, Cher, John Secada (he took the stage when the band performed "Just Another Day"), Eddie Murphy, and John F. Kennedy, Jr., are among those who've partied here while in Atlanta. A large $2 buffet is served Tuesday and Friday from 5:30 to 8pm.

Prices: $7 cover Fri–Sat, $4 Tues–Thurs. No cover if you arrive before 8pm.

Open: Tues–Thurs till 2am, Fri–Sat till 3am. Call ahead weeknights; sometimes the club is closed for private parties. **Parking:** Valet parking is $2, but you can park in the shopping center lot free if you wish.

Johnnys Hideaway, 3771 Roswell Rd., two blocks north of Piedmont Rd. ☎ **233-8026.**

Johnny's has been one of Atlanta's top night spots for over a decade. Its not glamorous, but the regular folks who frequent the club always seem to be having a super time. Ebullient owner Johnny Esposito, always on hand to greet his guests, is a well-known Atlanta character. The music is primarily big-band era to '50s/'60s oldies, and so is the crowd. Tunes progress through the decades as the night wears on, but the music is always mellow.

This is a place for serious dancing, and most of the clientele can execute a pretty proficient two-step or tango. And though it's unpretentious, there are celebrities who hang out here when in town (Tommy LaSorda, Arnold Palmer, Jake La Motta, and burlesque queen Tempest Storm). A silver ball rotates over the dance floor, and you're likely to see Glenn Miller on the video monitors. A reasonably priced menu lists items ranging from deli sandwiches to snack fare such as nachos and buffalo wings to steak and prime-rib main courses. Sunday at 6pm you can have a free spaghetti dinner. Special events here include Johnny's Tomato talent contests (about 1,500 women in Atlanta carry cards identifying them as "Johnny's Tomatoes"), bocci tournaments, and sing-alongs. Dress is casual.

Prices: Admission is free, but there's a two-drink minimum (at tables only) after 8pm nightly.

Open: Sun–Fri till 4am, Sat till 3am. **Closed:** Christmas. **Parking:** Free self and valet.

Sports Bars

Champions, at the Marriott Marquis, 265 Peachtree Center Ave., between Baker and Harris Sts. ☎ **586-6017.**

Champions, in several cities nationwide, is the quintessential sports bar. It's decorated with neon beer signs and a hodgepodge of athletically themed paraphernalia and memorabilia—a baseball autographed by Willie Mays, a 1962 Patterson-Liston fight poster, Duke Snider's baseball mitt, and more. The circular oak bar is plastered with thousands of baseball cards under a laminated surface, and 25 TV monitors, plus two large screens, air nonstop sporting events. (In those rare times when no game is on, they replay highlights.) But there's more to do than sit with your eyes glued to a TV set. You can test your skills on an 18-hole putting green; play Virtual Reality games, sports video games, or Full Court Frenzy (a coin-op basketball game); or shoot pool. Tuesday to Thursday there's laser karaoke. There are frequent promotions involving sports celebrities; they tend to stop in when in town. The menu features chili, nachos, salads, pastas, and burgers. Men outnumber women about five to one.

Price: No cover except during pay-per-view fights.

Open: Nightly till 2am. **MARTA:** Peachtree Center.

Damon's Clubhouse, 76 Wall St. near the Esplanade Fountains, above ground at Underground Atlanta. ☎ **659-RIBS.**

This simpatico sports bar at Underground is lots of fun. Out front, on a brick patio shaded by maples, jazz artists perform Friday and Saturday nights. Inside, the action centers on the comfortable Clubhouse, its walls hung with sporting paraphernalia like autographed sports-star photos, tennis rackets, hockey sticks, and the like. Windows are attractively shaded by Bermuda shutters, a kayak is suspended from the ceiling, and neon signage includes little tomahawks in honor of the Braves. Big roomy booths all provide great views of five large-screen TVs, on four of which a variety of sporting events are aired. The fifth monitor broadcasts an ongoing trivia game. Ask your server for a push-button set-up, and you can compete for prizes (I won a T-shirt and a $35 gift certificate good for meals here!). Entry is free. A full menu features barbecued chicken, shrimp, and ribs, along with steaks, prime rib, and seafood. Other areas include the more sedate garden room under a beamed cathedral ceiling and a convivial oak-paneled bar. Atlanta sports teams often party here.

Note: Damon's runs a round-trip shuttle bus to and from all Braves games for just $2.

Prices: Admission is free.

Open: Till 10pm Mon–Thurs, till 1am Fri–Sat, till 9:30pm Sun. **MARTA:** Five Points.

A Jazz Supper Club

Dante's Down The Hatch, 3380 Peachtree Rd. NE, across the street from the Lenox Square Mall. ☎ **266-1600.**

This wonderful jazz supper club is the realm of Dante Stephensen, a bona fide Atlanta character and former Aspen ski bum who makes his home in a posh private railroad car that was designed for the Woolworth family in the 1920s. He mans the decks of this well-rigged schooner, a fantasy 18th-century ship (actually afloat in murky waters) in a colorful seaport village. His aim was not to erect an exact replica but to create the period seagoing setting of everyone's imagination. It's a mix of antiques and nautical kitsch—200-year-old handstitched sails, oak paneling from English banks, pirate and sea captain mannequins, beveled-glass doors, 1892 leaded-glass panels from Lloyd's of London, centuries-old ship's lanterns and bells, Polish ship figureheads. Fish netting forms a canopy over the lower deck. There are many intimate seating areas—a velvet-curtained "bordello," a lighthouse, an English mahogany elevator, and a sail loft among them. Amber streetlamps and candlelight enhance the cozy ambience. The most romantic seating is in semienclosed private booths on the lower deck where the very talented Paul Mitchell Trio plays traditional jazz. Gladys Knight, who lives in Atlanta, occasionally stops in and sings with them, and it's not unusual for visiting musicians to sit in on sets. Earlier in the evening, classical folk guitarists perform on the "wharf." And a solo pianist plays on the ship prior to the show.

Do plan to have dinner during the show. Fondues are featured. An imported cheese fondue is made with Emmentaler, Gruyère, and Swiss cheeses, laced with Kirsch, and served with French and honeynut bread croutons, winesap apples, and fresh vegetables. Or you might opt for a Mandarin fondue of beef, chicken, pork, and shrimp served with four Chinese dipping sauces; Cheese planters and Chinese dumplings are additional specialties. And for dessert, there's delicious chocolate fudge cake served hot. Main courses all including a large and tasty salad, are $11.50 to $18.50. An extensive wine list is reasonably priced. Reservations are suggested.

Prices: $5 cover for seating on jazz ship, no cover on the wharf.

Open: For folk music on the wharf: Mon 6–11:30pm, Tues–Thurs and Sun 6–7:30pm. For jazz on the ship: Tues–Thurs and Sun 7:30–11:30pm, Fri–Sat 7:30pm–12:30am. **MARTA:** Lenox.

A Comedy Club

Punchline Comedy Club, 280 Hildebrand Dr. NE, off Roswell Rd. in the Balconies Shopping Center, Sandy Springs. ☎ **252-5233.**

This popular suburban comedy club, about a 40-minute drive from downtown, features three comedians nightly in each show—two lead-ins and a headliner. The setting is casual. The club has a rustic knotty-pine-paneled interior, its walls plastered with photographs of famous comics. You don't need to dress up. Performers are pros on the national comedy-club circuit—the comedians you see on Leno and

Letterman—except on Tuesday (open-mike night) when the regular show is followed by amateur wannabes (you can be one of them, if you sign up by 7pm). Doors open an hour before showtime. Reasonably priced food—steak and cheese sandwiches, burgers, char-grilled chicken, potato skins, quesadillas—is available, along with drinks. Thursday and early Friday shows are smoke-free. Though you can buy tickets at the club, they often sell out, so it's best to reserve by phone using a major credit card. Seating is first-come, first-served; arrive early.

Prices: Admission Tues–Thurs and Sun is $7, Fri $10, Sat $12.

Open: Tues–Thurs shows are at 8:30pm, Fri–Sat 8 and 10:30pm, Sun 8pm. **Parking:** Free.

Kenny's Alley In Underground Atlanta

Since so many nightclubs offering varying entertainment formats are grouped conveniently at Underground Atlanta, Kenny's Alley clubhopping is very popular. See also Damon's Clubhouse above, another Underground nightspot.

Dante's Down The Hatch, Kenny's Alley. ☎ 577-1800.

This is the original Dante's, the prototype for the Buckhead branch described in detail above. To enter, you literally go down a hatchway similar to any ship's descent to lower decks, except that its walls are lined with photographs of celebrity guests—Bill Cosby, Jimmy Carter, Rod Stewart, Count Basie, and others.

Owner Dante Stephensen earns kudos for highlighting the historic sites within his club. He's the only businessperson in the complex who seems to fully appreciate the historic significance of Underground. A sign informs visitors, for instance, that an exposed wall of the hatchway staircase is from the 1850s Planter Hotel and is the actual site of the hospital depicted in *Gone With the Wind*. An 1810 well on the premises was the water source for Atlanta's first fire department, and a steam engine on view powered the Frank E. Block Candy Company from 1868 to 1888. Like the Buckhead club, this is a fantasy ship moored in crocodile-infested waters (three live crocs swim in the moat). And there's plenty of nautical ambience—oak-plank floors, ship's ropes, steering wheels, and more. A singer and guitar player entertain on the "wharf," while the Brothers Three offer traditional jazz Monday through Saturday and the John Robertson Trio does the same on Sunday. Sometimes well-known artists such as Phyllis Hyman and Chuck Mangione come in and jam with the band. Fondue dinners are featured (see details in Buckhead listing).

Prices: For folk music on the wharf, there's a $1 cover charge; for jazz on the ship, cover is $5.

Open: For folk music on the wharf: Sun–Thurs 2–11:30pm, Fri 2pm–12:30am, Sat 1pm–12:30am. For jazz on the ship deck: Mon –Thurs 7:30–11:30pm, Fri–Sat 7:30pm–12:30am, Sun 7:30–11pm. A jazz pianist entertains on the ship deck Fri–Sat 6:30–7:30pm. **MARTA:** Five Points.

Teddy's Live, Kenny's Alley. ☎ **653-9999.**

This immense club—with bars at either end, gold records lining the walls, and the requisite high-tech lighting system over the dance floor—offers live music (local and national artists) Thursday through Sunday nights. Recent performers have included Physical Therapy, Danny Lernman, Theresa Hightower, Noel Pointer, Top Secret, George Clinton, and Michael Henderson. And sometimes major record companies showcase new artists here. Tuesday and Wednesday a DJ plays a mix of jazz, blues, pop, R&B, and hip-hop (Wednesday ladies enjoy free admission, roses, and champagne). Monday is comedy night featuring four to eight comedians (it's open mike, with a professional emcee), followed by dance music. You must be 21 to get in. A full menu offers prime rib, steaks, and seafood, in addition to lighter fare—burgers, sandwiches, chicken tenders, and salads. Every Sunday Teddy's hosts a gospel buffet brunch from 11:30am to 4pm.

Prices: Fri–Sat cover $8, Sun–Thurs $5.

Open: Mon–Thurs till 1am, Fri–Sat till 4am, Sun till 2am.
MARTA: Five Points.

Fat Tuesday, Kenny's Alley. ☎ **523-7404.**

This New Orleans–concept club has a bar similar to a Mardi Gras float, but with an Atlanta twist—it's adorned with busts of Rhett and Scarlett. Special machines behind the bar mix over 20 flavors of frozen daiquiris—margarita, peach colada (that's mixed with peaches, rum, ice cream, and coconut cream), white Russian, and more—and you can sample an ounce of any flavor on the house. Light fare (po' boy sandwiches, salads, gumbo) is also available. Rock and top-40 tapes are played at an earsplitting level. IDs are checked at the door: You have to be 21.

Prices: Admission is free. Drinks are $4.50–$5.25.

Open: Sun–Thurs till 1am, Fri–Sat till 2am. **MARTA:** Five Points.

Fanny Moon's Beer Hall, Kenny's Alley. ☎ **521-2026.**

In this large club—with southern state flags lining the walls, lacy New Orleans–style wrought-iron railings, and lingerie hung on clotheslines and pipes overhead and draped over a moosehead's antlers—everyone sings along to Fanny Moon's Big Butt Dixieland band. Sometimes the band plays fifties rock tunes as well, and the music stops when major sporting events are aired on a 10-foot-square screen. Fanny Moon's is a casual place, on the pubby side, with checkered cloths on the tables. The menu offers New Orleans specialties (gumbo, jambalaya), nachos, and barbecued ribs, chicken, pork, or shrimp.

Prices: No cover, average drink $3.75.

Open: Mon–Thurs till 1am, Fri–Sat till 2am. **MARTA:** Five Points.

3 More Entertainment

Dinner Theater

Agatha's Mystery Dinner Theatre, 693 Peachtree St., at 3rd St.
☎ **875-1610.**

Thespians manqué and Poirot aficionados: Here's a unique night on the town made to order for you. Agatha's presents comic mystery dramas, with everyone in the audience taking a small role in the play. The action takes place in the dining room during a five-course meal, including a buffet of hot hors d'oeuvres, soup, salad, a choice of five main courses, dessert, wine, and coffee.

When you sit down, you'll be given your lines or instructions. Many roles require finding and collaborating with other members of your performance group. The night I was here, I had to locate other "monkeys" in the room, compose a song with them, and perform it. Don't be nervous about it. Everyone's an amateur, and it's impossible to mess up. In most roles, you're part of a large group. Is it corny? You bet. But it's also an unbelievable amount of fun. Two talented professional actors—who are also the script writers—keep things moving along smoothly, and sometimes they're upstaged by would-be Barrymores in the audience. New shows come on every 12 weeks. Use your little gray cells; all evidence points to the advisability of an evening at Agatha's.

Prices: $38.25–$43.75 per person for the show and a five-course dinner, including wine, tax, and tip. Major credit cards accepted.

Open: Shows Tues–Sat at 7:30pm, Sun at 7pm. **Reservations:** Essential. **MARTA:** North Avenue. **Parking:** There's a paid garage three doors south of the club.

4 Film & Video

The **Image Film/Video Center,** 75 Bennett St. NW, off Peachtree Road between Collier Road and Colonial Homes Drive, Suite M1 (☎ **352-4225**), offers regular screenings of work by the nation's most important independent media artists. Screenings might include animation programs (such as a showcase of works by Will Vinton of California Raisin fame), a gay and lesbian film festival, politically themed films and videos, or works of southern media artists. A wide gamut is covered, ranging from existentialist works to Dr. Seuss stories. IMAGE also sponsors numerous lectures and workshops related to film and video on subjects such as "An Introduction to Computer Graphics," "Beginning Screenwriting," and "VCR and Camcorder Basics." And, of course, there's the film festival in June (for details, see "Calendar of Events" in Chapter 2). Most films are $5.50, $3.50 for students and seniors.

11

About the Olympics

1	Information Sources	240
2	Obtaining Tickets	240
3	The Events	242
4	Accommodations & Dining	242
5	Transportation	243

Since the announcement in 1990 that Atlanta would host the 1996 Olympic Games (July 19 though August 4), the city has been busy gearing up for the big event. The 72,000-seat Georgia Dome (to be utilized for gymnastics and basketball competitions) was completed in 1992. And in the works are: the 85,000-seat Olympic Stadium (which will host the opening and closing ceremonies and track and field events, and, after the Games, become the new home of the Atlanta Braves), a Tennis Center and Velodrome at Georgia's Stone Mountain Park, an Aquatics Center at Georgia Tech, and Herndon Stadium (for field hockey and basketball prelims). Also underway at Georgia Tech—an Olympics Village to provide housing, dining facilities, and practice facilities for participating athletes and officials, which will later be converted to student housing. Other venues are also under construction or in the process of renovation. Most events will take place at venues within the "Olympic Ring"—an imaginary circle, three miles in diameter, centered in downtown Atlanta near the Georgia World Congress Center—and in Georgia's Stone Mountain Park. Some events will actually be held outside of Atlanta, for example whitewater canoeing (to be held on the Ocoee River in Tennessee at the Georgia border) and yachting competitions (which will take place off the coast of Savannah, 250 miles southeast of Atlanta).

If you're planning to attend the XXVI Olympiad, like Atlanta, you, too, should be gearing up. Though the Atlanta Committee for the Olympic Games (ACOG) has not yet finalized all aspects, the following information should prove helpful.

1 Information Sources

For up-to-the-minute information, the best source is the **Atlanta Committee for the Olympic Games** (☎ 404/224-1996). ACOG additionally operates a public-information gallery/gift shop called **The Olympic Experience** (☎ 658-1996) in Underground Atlanta at the corner of Upper Alabama and Peachtree Streets. It is open Monday to Saturday 10am to 9:30pm, Sunday noon to 6pm.

The **Atlanta Convention & Visitors Bureau** (☎ 404/222-6688) will also be able to answer your questions.

Contact **major hotels and airlines** (using their toll free numbers) to find out what they are offering in the way of Olympic packages.

And a good **travel agent** (there's no fee for this service) should be able to put the whole thing together for you—accommodations, transportation, and, probably, tickets to the games.

2 Obtaining Tickets

A **mail-order program**—heralded by widespread national media coverage—will be initiated in the Spring of 1995. Mail-order brochures will be obtainable nationwide through various sources (most likely in major newspapers and magazines and via participating corporate sponsors, though this has not yet been determined). These mail-order forms will provide an overview of all the events. Consumers will check off their first preferences and alternatives, with a lottery system determining who gets tickets to over-subscribed events (such as opening and closing ceremonies and finals). After the mail-order phase, tickets will be available for purchase by phone. About 900,000 tickets will be set aside for purchase outside the United States.

Tickets will also be available in hotel and airline packages (most notably, Delta). Call major hotels and airlines via their toll-free numbers to find out what they're offering. Also check with travel agencies.

ACOG assures me that no one need panic about acquiring tickets, because Olympic Games simply do not sell out—especially the Atlanta Games which will be the largest in history, offering more tickets than Los Angeles and Barcelona combined! ACOG will be distributing an astounding 11 million tickets to the public! Even if you arrived in town with no tickets in hand—not that I'm suggesting you do—tickets will very likely still be available to many events. ACOG is pioneering a new ticket sales system that will allow you to buy tickets for any event at any venue, and regular updates will be available on site about ticket availability.

Ticket Prices

The International Olympic Committee has already set ticket prices for the 1996 Games, nearly all of them at $75 or less. The most expensive tickets, to opening and closing ceremonies, will be $200 to $600. For other events, ticket prices will range from $6 (for preliminary baseball) to $250, the average seat will cost $39.72, and every sport will have at least one session for which tickets are available at or below $25. Only nine sports—the last session of athletics, and finals for basketball, boxing, diving, artistic gymnastics (including gala), soccer, swimming, tennis, and volleyball—have tickets priced over $75. All ticket prices include transportation costs to and from the venue. Needless to say, there are almost infinite ticket combinations. To give you an estimate of probable expenditures, I've listed some ticket options for a family of four:

Four tickets to:

One event—baseball preliminary	$ 24
Two events—gymnastics podium training and basketball preliminary	$ 80
Three events—diving preliminary, soccer quarterfinal, and athletics final	$360
Three events—gymnastics (artistic) preliminary, tennis quarter final, diving final	$500

TOUGHEST TICKETS   The toughest tickets to come by will be for opening and closing ceremonies and finals in basketball, gymnastics, track and field, boxing, and volleyball. Though you may not get to see the finals, you will definitely have access to earlier rounds.

3 The Events

Olympic events include preliminary, intermediate, and final rounds. All in all, there will be about 560 events. The areas of competition are:

Archery	Judo
Athletics (Track & Field)	Marathon
Badminton	Pentathlon
Baseball	Race Walking
Basketball	Rowing
Boxing	Shooting
Canoeing	Soccer
Cycling	Softball
Diving	Swimming
Equestrian	Table Tennis
Fencing	Tennis
Field Hockey	Volleyball
Football	Water Polo
Gymnastics	Weightlifting
Handball	Wrestling
Hockey	Yachting

4 Accommodations & Dining

HOTELS

Here we encounter some difficulties. The good news is that a new Georgia law designed to prevent hotel price gouging is already in effect, forbidding rate raises above a certain percentage over published 1994 rates. And to ensure the availability of rooms in 1996, ACOG has, to date, more than 270 officially designated properties (representing more than 45,073 rooms) in its **Olympic Games Host Hotel Network,** including lodgings in greater metropolitan Atlanta, Augusta, Athens, Columbus, Macon, and Savannah. These host hotels have committed up to 80 percent of their rooms to Olympic visitors and agreed to a fair rate structure. These committed rooms will be distributed—beginning in the Spring of 1995—through a special accommodations phone number (not yet determined) at ACOG.

Now for the problematical aspects: Many of these committed rooms have already been set aside by ACOG for blocks of corporate clients. Also, participating hotels are alloted four tickets per day, per committed room (one high-demand, three low-demand), which means you may be asked to purchase a package that includes room and tickets. Though this could be a good deal, if you have your heart set on certain events, you'll want to know what these hotel-package tickets include in advance of the mail-order program, so that you have the option of obtaining preferred tickets via the latter. Best bet may be to try making hotel (or private residence, see below) reservations on your own—via hotel toll free numbers or your travel agent—as soon as possible (do it now), and purchasing tickets separately when the mail-order program begins in the Spring of 1995. If you do so, be sure to get written confirmation of your reservation and quoted room rates. If you are unable to get a room in this manner, you can always fall back on the ACOG reservations number.

PRIVATE HOMES AND APARTMENTS

It seems like everyone you meet in Atlanta these days is planning to rent out his or her house or apartment during the Olympics (where will they all go, I wonder?). This can be a very viable accommodations option, as many of these residences will be close to Olympic venues and offer more facilities than a hotel room in the same price range. The ACOG accommodations number (to be announced) will serve as a clearinghouse for home and apartment rentals, and it should be your first source for them, since they will cap prices to eliminate gouging. However, you'll probably see numerous classified ads in newspapers and magazines (check especially *The New York Times* and big-city publications such as *New York* magazine and *Washingtonian*) as the Olympics draws closer. Though most of these will probably be fine, you do, of course, run risks renting a place sight unseen; to protect yourself get as much written documentation regarding costs and facilities as possible. Caveat emptor! If you have friends or family in Atlanta, they'll also be a good source of information. And the Ansley Inn (☎ 404/872-9000) has many beautiful and carefully screened apartments and private homes on its roster.

DINING

Many restaurants will be sold out to corporate clients far in advance. And, since there will be so much restaurant traffic generated by the Olympics, some establishments are planning to ask for reservations backed up by advance payment via credit card in order to prevent no-shows. Check out Chapter 6, "Atlanta Dining," and begin making your restaurant reservations as soon as possible. It's best to have them all in hand before you leave home.

5   Transportation

For the first time in Olympic history, bus and rail transportation to and from Olympic venues will be included in ticket prices, and visitors will be able to board free satellite buses from outer areas. Do plan to use these transportation systems to avoid parking fees, traffic jams, and other hassles.

Index

Aaron, Henry, 7, 11, 12, 181, 202
Accommodations, 59–101
    bed-and-breakfasts, 61, 83–86, 96, 110
    Buckhead, 61, 82–83, 86–97
    for children, 73
    downtown, 61–73
    Druid Hills/Emory University/ Brookhaven, 61, 99–101
    off I-20, 101
    midtown, 73–86
    money-saving tips, 69
    for 1996 Olympics, 242–43
    Stone Mountain, 97–98
Air travel, 33–35, 40, 50
    for disabled travelers, 32
Alliance Theatre, 3, 52, 228–29
Alonzo F. Herndon Home, 189, 201, 202, 211–12
Annual events, festivals and fairs, 17–29
Ansley Park, 52, 61
    tour, 202
Antebellum Plantation, 169–70
Antique & Music Museum, 169
APEX (African-American Panoramic Experience) Museum, 159, 162–64
Art museums
    Antique & Music Museum, 169
    Atlanta College of Art Gallery, 190
    Callanwolde Fine Arts Center, 27, 191
    Hammonds House, 190–91, 202
    High Museum of Art, 11, 13, 18, 26, 52, 174
    High Museum of Art, Folk Art and Photography Galleries, 188
    Michael C. Carlos Museum of Emory University, 182
    Philip Shutze Collection of Decorative Arts, 158
    Woodruff Arts Center, 13, 52, 78, 80, 115, 149, 174, 190, 201, 228, 230, 231
Arts Festival of Atlanta, 25
Atlanta, 44, 58, 125, 147, 217
Atlanta Airport Shuttle Vans, 50
Atlanta Ballet, 225
Atlanta Botanical Garden, 3, 4, 18, 21, 23, 26, 28, 176–77, 193
Atlanta Boy Choir, 231
Atlanta Braves, 7, 11, 12, 13, 105, 173, 202, 203, 240
Atlanta Chamber Players, 231
Atlanta Civic Center, 225

Atlanta College of Art Gallery, 190
Atlanta Committee for the Olympic Games, 240
Atlanta Convention & Visitors Bureau, 16, 50–51, 179, 240
Atlanta Dogwood Festival, 19
Atlanta Falcons, 7, 11, 105, 202, 203
Atlanta Fulton County Stadium, 7, 203–204
Atlanta Fulton Public Library, 57–58, 111
Atlanta Hawks, 13, 173, 203
Atlanta Heritage Row, 180–81
Atlanta History Center, 138, 154, 155–59, 208
Atlanta History Center Downtown, 188
Atlanta Journal-Constitution, 9, 10, 12, 32, 44, 58, 81, 82, 96, 180, 195, 225
Atlanta Museum, 190
Atlanta Now, 16, 50
Atlanta Opera, 229
Atlanta Symphony Orchestra, 3, 52, 228, 230–31
Atlanta University, 5, 9, 10, 157, 189, 201
Auburn Avenue Research Library on African-American Culture and History, 212

Babysitting, 56
Bed and breakfasts, 61, 83–86, 96, 110
Bicycling, 193, 206
Big Shanty Museum (Kennesaw), 7, 184–85
Boat trips, 169
Bobby Dodd Stadium/Grant Field, 204, 227
Bookstores, 218, 221–22
Brookhaven
    accommodations, 61, 99–101
Brunch, 149–50
Buckhead, 19, 52–54
    accommodations, 61, 82–83, 86–97
    house and garden tours, 19
    restaurants, 125–40
    sightseeing, 155
Bus travel
    for disabled travelers, 32
    organized tours, 201
    for senior citizens, 32
    to Atlanta, 35, 41, 50
    within Atlanta, 55

Callanwolde Fine Arts Center, 27, 191
Camping, 98
Canoeing, 205
Cars and driving
    automobile organizations, 41
    rentals, 41, 56
    safety tips, 39–40
    to Atlanta, 35
    within Atlanta, 56
Carter, Jimmy, 2, 7, 75, 78, 92, 122, 170, 172, 222

Chamblee
    restaurants, 147
    shopping, 214
Center for Puppetry Arts, 3, 193, 196
Chastain Park Amphitheatre, 22, 162, 228, 230, 231
Children
    accommodations for, 33, 67, 73
    events for, 27, 28
    restaurants for, 112, 123
    sights and attractions for, 3, 193–200
    travel tips for, 33
Churches and Cathedrals, 17, 24, 202, 210, 212
    Ebenezer Baptist Church, 11, 159, 160, 164, 201, 202, 208, 209
Civil rights movement, 3, 6, 10–11, 12, 159–64, 180, 202
Civil War, 2, 3, 4, 5, 6–9, 10
    burning of Atlanta, 5, 8–9
    exhibitions, 3, 19, 21, 52, 155, 156, 157, 166–67, 170, 180, 184–85, 193, 201
    sites, 155, 185–88, 208
Climate, 16–17
Clothes
    packing for your trip, 29
    shopping for, 215–17, 222–23
CNN Center, 2, 11, 13, 52, 155, 173–74, 201
Coca-Cola, 2, 5, 10, 13, 80, 157, 181–82, 201, 202, 226
Coca-Cola Lakewood Amphitheatre, 3, 225–26
Colony Square complex, 52, 77, 114
Comedy clubs, 235–36
Concert halls, 225–228
Concerts, 20–22, 24, 162, 176, 199, 226–228
Consulates, 42
Creative Loafing, 29, 58, 225
Currency exchange, 38, 42
Cyclorama, 3, 21, 52, 155, 157, 166–67, 193, 201

Decatur, Stephen, 54
Decatur, 17, 27, 54, 27
    accommodations, 101
    restaurants, 146–47
Dekalb Symphony Orchestra, 231
Democratic National Convention, 1988, 2, 7
Dentists, 56
Department stores and malls, 219–21
Dinner theater, 238
Disabled travelers, tips for, 29–32
Doctors, 57
Documents required for entry to U.S., 37
Downtown, 52
    accommodations, 61–73
    restaurants, 103–12

Drugstores, 57
Druid Hills/Emory University/Brookhaven accommodations, 61, 99–101
tour, 202
Du Bois, W. E. B., 5, 10

Ebenezer Baptist Church, 11, 159, 160, 164, 201, 202, 208, 209
Egleston Children's Christmas Parade and Festival of Trees, 28
Embassies, 42
Emergencies, 42, 57
Emory University, 13, 100, 157, 182
accommodations, 61, 99–101
Entertainment and nightlife, 224–38
Eyeglasses, 57

Factory outlet stores, 223
Families, tips for, 33. See also Children
Farmer's markets, 223
Fast Facts, 56–58
for foreign travelers, 41–48
Fernbank Museum of Natural History, 3, 155, 164–166, 172–73, 193
Fernbank Science Center, 198
Festivals. See Annual events, festivals, and fairs
Film and Video, 22, 238
Fishing, 204
Food, shopping for, 54, 151, 223
Foreign visitors, information for, 36–48
Fox Theatre, 3, 52, 82, 175–76, 201, 226–27

Gardens. See Parks and Gardens
Gay men, networks and resources for, 29, 33
events for, 23
Georgia Dome, 8, 12, 28, 52, 202–203, 227
Georgia Institute of Technology, 6, 11, 12
sports teams, 157, 202, 204, 227
Georgia Renaissance Fall Festival, 26
Georgia Renaissance Festival Spring Celebration, 26
Georgia State Capitol, 10, 52, 177–79, 201
Georgia World Congress Center, 7, 17, 18, 28, 52, 203, 240
Golf, 12, 184, 205
Gone with the Wind, 2, 6, 10, 12, 13, 52, 58, 74, 122, 154, 156, 168, 173, 180, 185, 188, 192, 236
Grady, Henry, 9, 12, 180
Grant Park, 3, 10, 21, 52, 155, 166, 193
Great Locomotive Chase, 7, 168, 184–85

Hairdressers, 57
Hammonds House, 190–91, 202

Harris, Joel Chandler, 12, 194–95, 202
Hartsfield International Airport, 7, 10, 33, 50, 56, 154, 181
High Museum of Art, 11, 13, 18, 26, 52, 174
High Museum of Art, Folk Art and Photography Galleries, 188
Historical museums
Alonzo F. Herndon Home, 189, 201, 202, 211–12
Antebellum Plantation, 169–70
APEX (African-American Panoramic Experience) Museum, 159, 162–64
Atlanta History Center, 138, 154, 155–59, 208
Atlanta History Center Downtown, 188
Atlanta Museum, 190
Big Shanty Museum (Kennesaw), 7, 184–85
Cyclorama, 3, 21, 52, 155, 157, 166–67, 193, 201
Margaret Mitchell House, 192
Martin Luther King, Jr., Historic District, 52, 155, 159–64, 201
Rhodes Memorial Hall, 191–92
History, 4–13
books about, 13–14
films about, 14
Hospitals, 57

I-20
accommodations, 101
Information sources. See Tourist information
INFORUM, 11
Inman Park, 20
tour, 202
Insurance, 38

Jackson, Maynard, 7, 11, 159, 167
Jazz, 228
clubs, 235
outdoor concerts, 20, 21–22, 24
Jimmy Carter Library/ Presidential Center, 2, 54, 61, 122, 170–72
Jogging, 193
Johnston, Joseph E., 8, 185
Jones, Robert Tyre "Bobby," 12, 168

Kayaking, 205
Kennesaw Mountain/ National Battlefield Park, 155, 185–88, 208
Kenny's Alley, 3, 236–37
King, Coretta Scott, 17
King, Martin Luther, Jr., 2, 6, 7, 11, 12, 159–62, 164, 178, 180, 201, 208
birth home, 3, 11, 52, 159–60, 193, 201, 202, 208, 209

Lasershow, 20, 24, 27, 169
Lenox Square Mall, 25, 26, 51, 54, 87, 90, 91, 92, 93, 95, 154, 220, 221
Lesbians, networks and resources for, 29, 33
events for, 23
Libraries and archives, 57–58
Atlanta Fulton Public Library, 57–58, 111
Auburn Avenue Research Library on African-American Culture and History, 212
Jimmy Carter Library/ Presidential Center, 2, 54, 61, 122, 170–72
Martin Luther King, Jr., Center for Nonviolent Social Change, 3, 11, 17, 21, 22, 159, 160, 161–62, 193, 201, 208
Little Five Points, 54
restaurants, 140–45
shopping, 216–18
tour, 201

Mail, 43–44
Margaret Mitchell House, 192
MARTA rapid rail, 7, 11, 54–55, 58
Martin Luther King, Jr., Center for Nonviolent Social Change, 3, 11, 17, 21, 22, 159, 160, 161–62, 193, 201, 208
Martin Luther King, Jr., Historic District, 52, 155, 159–64, 201
Martin Luther King Week, 17
Metro Atlanta Attractions Guide, 16, 51
Michael C. Carlos Museum of Emory University, 182
Midtown, 52
accommodations, 73–86
restaurants, 112–24
Mitchell, Margaret, 2, 6, 10, 12, 13, 52, 58, 155, 192
Money, 16, 38–39
Morris Brown College, 157, 202
Museums. See Art museums, historical museums, natural history museums, science and technology museums
Music
classical, 20, 21, 228, 230–31
gospel, 22, 24, 25, 225
jazz, 20, 21–22, 24, 25, 228
museum, 169
outdoor concerts, 20–22, 24, 162, 199, 226
rock, 21, 25, 199, 226, 227, 228

National Association for the Advancement of Colored People (NAACP), 5, 10, 160

National Black Arts Festival, 24
Natural history museums
  Fernbank Museum of Natural History, 3, 155, 164–66, 172–73, 193, 198
Neighborhoods, 52–54

Oakland Cemetery, 26, 52, 167–68, 184, 193, 208
Old Courthouse (Decatur), 17
  events at, 19, 20, 21, 23, 25
Olympics, 1996 Summer, 2, 8, 12, 35, 52, 61, 156, 192, 203, 239–43
  accommodations, 242–43
  events, 242
  dining, 243
  information sources, 240
  tickets, 240–42
  transportation, 243
Olympic Village, 12, 240
Omni Coliseum, 17, 25, 26, 52, 70, 71, 203, 227
Opera, 229

Parks and Gardens
  Ansley Park, 52, 61
  Atlanta Botanical Garden, 3, 4, 18, 21, 23, 26, 28, 176–77, 193
  Grant Park, 3, 10, 21, 52, 155, 166, 193
  Piedmont Park, 3, 5, 10, 19, 23, 24, 25, 52, 61, 192–93, 206
  Stone Mountain Park, 3, 4, 12, 19, 20, 21, 23, 24, 25, 26, 27, 97, 98, 155, 162, 168–70, 193, 201, 205, 208, 240
Paschal's Motor Lodge, 202
Peachtree Center, 3, 11, 51, 52, 65, 66, 67, 68, 201, 221
Peach Bowl Game, 28, 203
Performance halls (listing), 3, 225–28
Philip Shutze Collection of Decorative Arts, 158
Phipps Plaza, 26, 54, 87, 90, 91, 95, 220–21, 222
Piedmont Park, 3, 5, 10, 19, 23, 24, 25, 52, 61, 192–93, 206
Planning and preparing for your trip, 15–35
Portman, John, 6, 11, 13, 64, 66, 67, 221

Restaurants, 102–52
  for afternoon tea, 150–51, 162
  for brunch, 149–50
  Buckhead, 125–40
  Chamblee, 147
  for children, 112, 123
  Decatur, 146–47
  dim sum, 151–52
  downtown, 103–12
  fast food, 148
  for Japanese breakfasts, 150

late night/24–hours, 151
local favorites, 148
midtown, 112–24
money-saving tips, 110
picnic fare, 151
Sweet Auburn, 145–46
tapas, 152
Virginia-Highland/ Little Five Points, 140–45
Rhodes Memorial Hall, 191–92
River Rafting, 205
Road Atlanta, 204, 227
Roller Skating, 206
Running, 193

Safety, 39–40
St. Patrick's Day Parade, 18
Science and technology museums
  Fernbank Science Center, 198
  SciTrek Museum, 2, 52, 197–98
SciTrek Museum, 2, 52, 197–98
Segregation, 6, 10–11, 12, 52, 168
Senior citizen travelers, tips for, 32
Seven Stages Performing Arts Center, 229
Sherman, William Tecumseh, 5, 6, 7–9, 10, 167, 185
Shopping, 213–222
  antiques, 17–18, 214
  clothes, 215–17, 222–23
  books, 218, 221–
Sightseeing
  in Buckhead, 154
  bus tours, 201
  for disabled travelers, 30
  itineraries, 154–55
  Sweet Auburn, 201, 202, 207–12
  walking tours, 201–202
Single travelers, tips for, 32
Six Flags Over Georgia, 3, 155, 199–200
Southeastern Flower Show, 18
Southern Christian Leadership Conference, 11
Southern Star Amphitheatre, 199
Sports
  recreational, 205–206
  spectator, 202–204
Sports bars, 234
Stone Mountain, 157, 168–69
  accommodations, 97–98
Stone Mountain Park, 3, 4, 12, 19, 20, 21, 23, 24, 25, 26, 27, 97, 98, 155, 162, 168–70, 193, 201, 205, 208, 240
Stone Mountain Scenic Railroad, 169
Stone Mountain Village
  events at, 19, 23, 24
  shopping 218–19
Student travelers, tips for, 33
Super Bowl, XXVIII, 2, 8, 52, 203
Swan House, 3, 91, 156–58, 201

Sweet Auburn, 11, 20, 52, 159, 162
  restaurants, 145–46
  sightseeing, 207–12
  tours, 201, 202
Swimming, 193, 206

Taste of Atlanta, A, 22–23
Taxes, 44
Taxis, 50, 55, 58
Tea, afternoon, 150–51, 162
Telephone numbers
  for disabled travelers, 29
  emergency, 57
  transit information, 58
  weather information, 58
Telephones, 44–46
Temperatures, average monthly, 17
Tennis, 193, 206
Theaters, 225–28. See also specific theaters
  for disabled travelers, 29
Tipping, 45
Tourist information, 16, 50–51
  for foreign visitors, 40, 44
Tours, organized, 201–202
  by bus, 201
  for disabled travelers, 30
  for senior citizens, 30
  walking, 201–202, 207–212
Trail of Tears, The, 4, 5
Train travel, 35, 40–41, 50
  for disabled travelers, 31–32
  for senior citizens, 32
Transportation
  from the airport, 50
  within Atlanta, 54–56
Travelers Aid Society, 42, 51
Traveler's checks, 38
Traveling
  for disabled travelers, 31–32
  for senior citizens, 32
Turner, Ted, 11, 13, 52, 125, 173

Underground Atlanta, 3, 4, 7, 11, 18, 27, 51, 52, 155, 179–80, 219–220, 236–37
  tours, 201, 202

Variety Playhouse, 227–28
Virginia-Highland, 54
  restaurants, 140–45
  shopping, 214–16

Washington, Booker T., 10
Woodruff Arts Center, 13, 52, 78, 80, 115, 149, 174, 190, 201, 228, 230, 231
Wren's Nest, 193, 194–95
  tour, 202

Yellow River Wildlife Game Ranch, 3, 155,162, 193, 196–97
Zoo Atlanta, 3, 52, 155, 193
Zoos
  Yellow River Wildlife Game Ranch, 3, 155, 162, 193, 196–97
  Zoo Atlanta, 3, 52, 155, 193

Now Save Money On All Your Travels By Joining FROMMER'S™ TRAVEL BOOK CLUB The World's Best Travel Guides At Membership Prices!

Frommer's Travel Book Club is your ticket to successful travel! Open up a world of travel informationand simplify your travel planning when you join ranks with thousands of value-conscious travelers who are members of the *Frommer's Travel Book Club.* Join today and you'll be entitled to all the privileges that come from belonging to the club that offers you travel guides for less to more than 100 destinations worldwide. **Annual membership is only $25.00 (U.S.) or $35.00 (Canada/Foreign).**

The Advantages of Membership:

1. Your choice of **three free** books (any **two** *Frommer's Comprehensive Guides, Frommer's $-A-Day Guides, Frommer's Walking Tours* or *Frommer's Family Guides*—plus **one** *Frommer's City Guide, Frommer's City $-A-Day Guide* or *Frommer's Touring Guide*).
2. Your own subscription to the **TRIPS & TRAVEL** quarterly newsletter.
3. You're entitled to a **30% discount** on your order of any additional books offered by the club.
4. You're offered (at a small additional fee) our **Domestic Trip-Routing Kits.**

Our **Trips & Travel** quarterly newsletter offers practical information on the best buys in travel, the "hottest" vacation spots, the latest travel trends, world-class events and much, much more.

Our **Domestic Trip-Routing Kits** are available for any North American destination. We'll send you a detailed map highlighting the best route to take to your destination—you can re-quest direct or scenic routes.

Here's all you have to do to join:

Send in your membership fee of $25.00 ($35.00 Canada/Foreign) with your name and ad-dress on the form below along with your selections as part of your membership package to the address listed below. Remember to check off your three free books.

If you would like to order additional books, please select the books you would like and send a check for the total amount (please add sales tax in the states noted below), plus $2.00 per book for shipping and handling ($3.00 Canada/Foreign) to the address listed below.

FROMMER'S TRAVEL BOOK CLUB
P.O. Box 473
Mt. Morris, IL 61054-0473.
(815) 734-1104

[ ] **YES!** I want to take advantage of this opportunity to join Frommer's Travel Book Club.

[ ] My check is enclosed. Dollar amount enclosed   *

(all payments in U.S. funds only)

Name _____

Address _____

City _____ State _____ Zip _____

All orders must be prepaid.

To ensure that all orders are processed efficiently, please apply sales tax in the following areas: CA, CT, FL, IL, IN, NJ, NY, PA, TN, WA and CANADA.

*With membership, shipping & handling will be paid by Frommer's Travel Book Club for the three free books you select as part of your membership. Please add $2.00 per book for shipping & handling for any additional books purchased ($3.00 Canada/Foreign).

Allow 4-6 weeks for delivery. Prices of books, membership fee, and publication dates are sub-ject to change without notice. Orders are subject to acceptance and availability.

Please send me the books checked below:

FROMMER'S COMPREHENSIVE GUIDES

(Guides listing facilities from budget to deluxe,
with emphasis on the medium-priced)

	Retail Price	Code		Retail Price	Code
☐ Acapulco/Ixtapa/Taxco, 2nd Edition	$13.95	C157	☐ Jamaica/Barbados, 2nd Edition	$15.00	C149
☐ Alaska '94-'95	$17.00	C131	☐ Japan '94-'95	$19.00	C144
☐ Arizona '95 (Avail. 3/95)	$14.95	C166	☐ Maui, 1st Edition	$13.95	C153
☐ Australia '94-'95	$18.00	C147	☐ Nepal, 2nd Edition	$18.00	C126
☐ Austria, 6th Edition	$16.95	C162	☐ New England '95	$16.95	C165
☐ Bahamas '94-'95	$17.00	C121	☐ New Mexico, 3rd Edition (Avail. 3/95)	$14.95	C167
☐ Belgium/Holland/ Luxembourg '93-'94	$18.00	C106	☐ New York State, 4th Edition	$19.00	C133
☐ Bermuda '94-'95	$15.00	C122	☐ Northwest, 5th Edition	$17.00	C140
☐ Brazil, 3rd Edition	$20.00	C111	☐ Portugal '94-'95	$17.00	C141
☐ California '95	$16.95	C164	☐ Puerto Rico '95-'96	$14.00	C151
☐ Canada '94-'95	$19.00	C145	☐ Puerto Vallarta/ Manzanillo/ Guadalajara '94-'95	$14.00	C028
☐ Caribbean '95	$18.00	C148			
☐ Carolinas/Georgia, 2nd Edition	$17.00	C128	☐ Scandinavia, 16th Edition (Avail. 3/95)	$19.95	C169
☐ Colorado, 2nd Edition	$16.00	C143	☐ Scotland '94-'95	$17.00	C146
☐ Costa Rica '95	$13.95	C161	☐ South Pacific '94-'95	$20.00	C138
☐ Cruises '95-'96	$19.00	C150	☐ Spain, 16th Edition	$16.95	C163
☐ Delaware/Maryland '94-'95	$15.00	C136	☐ Switzerland/ Liechtenstein '94-'95	$19.00	C139
☐ England '95	$17.95	C159	☐ Thailand, 2nd Edition	$17.95	C154
☐ Florida '95	$18.00	C152	☐ U.S.A., 4th Edition	$18.95	C156
☐ France '94-'95	$20.00	C132	☐ Virgin Islands '94-'95	$13.00	C127
☐ Germany '95	$18.95	C158	☐ Virginia '94-'95	$14.00	C142
☐ Ireland, 1st Edition (Avail. 3/95)	$16.95	C168	☐ Yucatan, 2nd Edition	$13.95	C155
☐ Italy '95	$18.95	C160			

FROMMER'S $-A-DAY GUIDES

(Guides to low-cost tourist accommodations and facilities)

	Retail Price	Code		Retail Price	Code
☐ Australia on $45 '95-'96	$18.00	D122	☐ Israel on $45, 15th Edition	$16.95	D130
☐ Costa Rica/Guatemala/ Belize on $35, 3rd Edition	$15.95	D126	☐ Mexico on $45 '95	$16.95	D125
			☐ New York on $70 '94-'95	$16.00	D121
☐ Eastern Europe on $30, 5th Edition	$16.95	D129	☐ New Zealand on $45 '93-'94	$18.00	D103
☐ England on $60 '95	$17.95	D128	☐ South America on $40, 16th Edition	$18.95	D123
☐ Europe on $50 '95	$17.95	D127			
☐ Greece on $45 '93-'94	$19.00	D100	☐ Washington, D.C. on $50 '94-'95	$17.00	D120
☐ Hawaii on $75 '95	$16.95	D124			
☐ Ireland on $45 '94-'95	$17.00	D118			

FROMMER'S CITY $-A-DAY GUIDES

	Retail Price	Code		Retail Price	Code
☐ Berlin on $40 '94-'95	$12.00	D111	☐ Madrid on $50 '94-'95	$13.00	D119
☐ London on $45 '94-'95	$12.00	D114	☐ Paris on $45 '94-'95	$12.00	D117

FROMMER'S FAMILY GUIDES

	Retail Price	Code		Retail Price	Code
☐ California with Kids	$18.00	F100	☐ San Francisco with Kids	$17.00	F104
☐ Los Angeles with Kids	$17.00	F103	☐ Washington, D.C.		
☐ New York City with Kids	$18.00	F101	with Kids	$17.00	F102

FROMMER'S CITY GUIDES

(Pocket-size guides to sightseeing and tourist
accommodations and facilities in all price ranges)

	Retail Price	Code		Retail Price	Code
☐ Amsterdam '93-'94	$13.00	S110	☐ Nashville/Memphis, 1st Edition	$13.00	S141
☐ Athens, 10th Edition (Avail. 3/95)	$12.95	S174	☐ New Orleans '95	$12.95	S148
☐ Atlanta '95	$12.95	S161	☐ New York '95	$12.95	S152
☐ Atlantic City/Cape May, 5th Edition	$13.00	S130	☐ Orlando '95	$13.00	S145
☐ Bangkok, 2nd Edition	$12.95	S147	☐ Paris '95	$12.95	S150
☐ Barcelona '93-'94	$13.00	S115	☐ Philadelphia, 8th Edition	$12.95	S167
☐ Berlin, 3rd Edition	$12.95	S162	☐ Prague '94-'95	$13.00	S143
☐ Boston '95	$12.95	S160	☐ Rome, 10th Edition	$12.95	S168
☐ Budapest, 1st Edition	$13.00	S139	☐ San Diego '95	$12.95	S158
☐ Chicago '95	$12.95	S169	☐ San Francisco '95	$12.95	S155
☐ Denver/Boulder/Colorado Springs, 3rd Edition	$12.95	S154	☐ Santa Fe/Taos/ Albuquerque '95	$12.95	S172
☐ Dublin, 2nd Edition	$12.95	S157	☐ Seattle/Portland '94-'95	$13.00	S137
☐ Hong Kong '94-'95	$13.00	S140	☐ St. Louis/Kansas City, 2nd Edition	$13.00	S127
☐ Honolulu/Oahu '95	$12.95	S151	☐ Sydney, 4th Edition	$12.95	S171
☐ Las Vegas '95	$12.95	S163	☐ Tampa/St. Petersburg, 3rd Edition	$13.00	S146
☐ London '95	$12.95	S156	☐ Tokyo '94-'95	$13.00	S144
☐ Los Angeles '95	$12.95	S164	☐ Toronto '95 (Avail. 3/95)	$12.95	S173
☐ Madrid/Costa del Sol, 2nd Edition	$12.95	S165	☐ Vancouver/Victoria '94-'95	$13.00	S142
☐ Mexico City, 1st Edition	$12.95	S170	☐ Washington, D.C. '95	$12.95	S153
☐ Miami '95-'96	$12.95	S149			
☐ Minneapolis/St. Paul, 4th Edition	$12.95	S159			
☐ Montreal/ Quebec City '95	$11.95	S166			

SPECIAL EDITIONS

	Retail Price	Code		Retail Price	Code
☐ Bed & Breakfast Southwest	$16.00	P100	☐ National Park Guide, 29th Edition	$17.00	P106
☐ Bed & Breakfast Great American Cities	$16.00	P104	☐ Where to Stay U.S.A., 11th Edition	$15.00	P102
☐ Caribbean Hideaways	$16.00	P103			

FROMMER'S WALKING TOURS

(With routes and detailed maps, these companion guides point out the places and pleasures that make a city unique)

	Retail Price	Code		Retail Price	Code
☐ Berlin	$12.00	W100	☐ New York	$12.00	W102
☐ Chicago	$12.00	W107	☐ Paris	$12.00	W103
☐ England's Favorite Cities	$12.00	W108	☐ San Francisco	$12.00	W104
☐ London	$12.00	W101	☐ Washington, D.C.	$12.00	W105
☐ Montreal/Quebec City	$12.00	W106			

FROMMER'S TOURING GUIDES

(Color-illustrated guides that include walking tours, cultural and historic sites, and practical information)

	Retail Price	Code		Retail Price	Code
☐ Amsterdam	$11.00	T001	☐ New York	$11.00	T008
☐ Barcelona	$14.00	T015	☐ Rome	$11.00	T010
☐ Brazil	$11.00	T003	☐ Scotland	$10.00	T011
☐ Hong Kong/Singapore/ Macau	$11.00	T006	☐ Sicily	$15.00	T017
			☐ Tokyo	$15.00	T016
☐ Kenya	$14.00	T018	☐ Turkey	$11.00	T013
☐ London	$13.00	T007	☐ Venice	$ 9.00	T014

Please note: If the availability of a book is several months away, we may have back issues of guides to that particular destination. Call customer service at (815) 734-1104.